ORIENTALISM: EARLY SOURCES

ORIENTALISM: EARLY SOURCES
Edited by Bryan S. Turner

ORIENTALISM: EARLY SOURCES

Volume VII

The Arab Kingdom and Its Fall

J. Wellhausen

London and New York

First published 1927
by the University of Calcutta
Reprinted 2000 by Routledge
11 New Fetter Lane, London EC4P 4EE

Simultaneously published in the USA and Canada
by Routledge
29 West 35th Street, New York, NY 10001

Routledge is an imprint of the Taylor & Francis Group

Printed and bound in Great Britain by
Antony Rowe Ltd, Chippenham, Wiltshire

British Library Cataloguing in Publication Data
A catalogue record for this book is available from the British Library

Library of Congress Cataloguing in Publication Data
A catalogue record for this book has been requested

ISBN 0–415–20898–X (set)
ISBN 0–415–20904–8 (volume VII)

Publisher's note
The publisher has gone to great lengths to ensure the quality of this
reprint but points out that some imperfections in the original book
may be apparent.

THE
ARAB KINGDOM AND ITS FALL

BY

J. WELLHAUSEN

TRANSLATED BY

MARGARET GRAHAM WEIR, M.A.

PUBLISHED BY THE

UNIVERSITY OF CALCUTTA

1927

PRINTED BY BHUPENDRA LAL BANERJI, AT THE CALCUTTA
UNIVERSITY PRESS, SENATE HOUSE, CALCUTTA.

Reg. 46B.—Jan., 27—A.

At the request of the Vice-Chancellor of Calcutta University I agreed to see the translation through the Press, and suggested some minor changes in transliteration to make this important work more serviceable to Indian students especially, and offered to compile an Index. These proposals were accepted; the addition of the Index has been approved by the Translator, and is certain to commend itself to the reader.

A. H. HARLEY.

Calcutta

PREFACE

The old traditions of the times of the Umaiyids are to be found in their most authentic form (because as yet uncontaminated and open to question) in Tabarî, in the most brilliant part of his work, Series II of the Leiden edition, which has now been in print for almost two decades. Above all he has preserved to us, in very considerable fragments, the genuine Abû Mikhnaf, and with him the oldest and best Arab prosewriter we possess. Abû Mikhnaf Lût b. Yahyâ b. Sa'îd b. Mikhnaf belonged to the Azd of Kûfa, and the long pedigree shows that on his father's side he came of a family of high standing. Probably Mikhnaf b. Sulaim, the leader of the Azd at the battle of Siffîn, was his ancestor, and the sons of the latter, Muhammad and Abdurrahmân, his granduncles. We do not know the date of his birth; at the rising of Ibn Ash'ath, A. H. 82, he had already reached man's estate. He was a friend of Muhammad b. Sâ'ib alKalbî (Tab., 2, 1075, 1096), and it is to the latter's son, the well-known Ibn Kalbî, that we are chiefly indebted for the transmission of his writings and traditions : as a rule, Tabarî quotes them from him. He lived to see the fall of the Khalifate of Damascus. His last statements in Tabarî refer to the year 132.

Abû Mikhnaf, quotes, in part, other traditionists, older or contemporary, as his authorities, *e.g.*, 'Âmir ash-Sha'bi, Abu 'lMukhâriq arRâsibî, Mujâlid b. Sa'îd, Muhammad b. Sâ'ib aiKalbî. But for the most part he did not take over the material from predecessors in the same line of study, but collected it himself *ex vivo ore*, by enquiries in the most diverse directions, from all possible people who could have first-hand information or who had been present to see and hear for themselves. The *Isnâd*, the filiation of the guarantors, is with him a reality and not mere literary form. His list of witnesses is always very short and through gradual approximation of events finally shrinks into nothing ; they are constantly changing with the different events and the separate traditions so that a tremendous crowd of otherwise unknown names is brought in. The witnesses cannot see the wood for the trees ; they mention the most trifling things, never leave anything anonymous, place the characters acting and speaking in the foreground, and in the main, keep continually repeating the same thing with slight variations.

Progress is thus rendered exceedingly slow, but
the fulness of detail makes up for this disadvantage. The fresh impression of events and
the first report of them are arresting. The
vivacity of the narrative is increased by its
popular form; it is all dialogue and staging. A
few illustrative examples are to be found in my
treatise upon the Chawarig and the Shia
(Göttingen, 1901, particularly p. 19ff. and
p. 61ff.).

Mommsen once said that to unlearned
persons there is no need of proof that stories
that begin by saying that the narrator had them
from the parties concerned in them, are, as a
rule, not true. Still, we must hope that unlearned people will not make too extensive a
use of their sound common-sense. It would be
a loss to history if Abû Mikhnaf had not
written, and how else was he to proceed than
he did? Original sources did not yield him
much. He used them when they lay to his
hand, but without diligently seeking them out
and systematically using them as a foundation.
Most frequently he quotes songs and verses
to authenticate his narrative. His great
authority lies in his collecting a host of variants
of the same thing from reports of different
origin, so that we can compare them and judge
what is sure or what is uncertain in them. At
the same time he contrives that the side-issues,

as they only appear once, take a secondary place,
and the chief questions, being everywhere repeated, keep constantly cropping up. Traditions that are not parallel he places in a suitable
sequence, so that the result is a progressive
connection. This mosaic work has not been
done without some choice and selection. There
are no contradictions in important points. The
traditions show a general agreement. The
picture has assumed, as a whole, solidity and
unity, not only with respect to the facts, but
in regard to the characters as well. Above the
seemingly chaotic material the plan of the
author and the complete perspective which he
formed for himself, are supremely evident. And
yet he does not cover any considerable period
of time, nor does he link it up pragmatically
and chronologically. He is deficient in sustained
chronology. He mentions only scattered dates,
frequently nothing but the days of the week,
without month or year. He does not string the
events upon a continuous thread, but describes
them singly and independently of each other,
widely apart and with no coherence. In the
Fihrist there are enumerated 22 monographs by
him with their titles.

It is characteristic of Abû Mikhnaf that he
does not start at the beginnings of Islâm, not
indeed until the conquests, and in particular gives
accounts of a period in the midst of which he

stands himself, from the battle of Siffîn onwards.
Also, his interest is limited to the place where
he lived himself, Irâq and its capital Kûfa.
Beyond these limits of time and place his
information is not particularly good. Now, as
Kûfa and Irâq were the seat of the opposition to
the imperial government, the latter affords the
principal theme of his narrative. The themes
which he pursues with particular zest and
exhaustiveness are the risings of the Khârijites
and Shîites under Mustaurid and Shabîb, under
Hujr, Husain, Sulaimân and Mukhtâr, and the
rising of the Irâqites under Ibn Ash'ath. He
hands down the tradition of Kûfa; his sympathies
are on the side of Irâq against Syria, for Alî
against the Umaiyids. Yet in this, there is not
much of a bias noticeable, at least not so much as
positively to falsify facts. Only on occasion does
he seem to hush up what it does not suit him to
state, e.g., that 'Aqîl at Siffîn fought against his
brother Alî.

In the treatise upon the opposition parties of
ancient Islam I have preferred to keep to Abû
Mikhnaf. On the other hand, for the history of
the Arabian Kingdom which forms the subject
of the present book, he does not afford so rich a
store. For this the Kûfa tradition is not the
best source, but the tradition of Medîna, which
is the old main source. In its origin it goes
back further than that of Kûfa, but the only

authorities for it which are of any use to us
are younger than Abû Mikhnaf and do not
flourish until the time when the literary scholar-
ship began to emigrate from Medîna to Baghdâd.
The best-known are Ibn Ishâq, a freedman, Abû
Ma'shar, likewise a freedman, and Wâqidî.
They no longer collect the raw material at first
hand. The traditions have reached them through
a learned medium, and are sifted, edited and
blended together by them. But they do bring
them into a closer connection, and subject them
at the same time to a thorough system of
chronology. Out of the disconnected narratives
of important events is formed a continuous
history. Ibn Ishâq must be considered its
creator. His writings and those of his successors
take the form of annals which is then the vogue.
Chronology presupposes scientific research and
comparison. In these the Medîna scholars were
not found wanting and they produced results
which stand examination remarkably well. Here
and there they may perhaps have followed
records of Christian, especially of Syrian, divines,
e.g., in the dating of earthquakes and other
natural phenomena. We can trace the progress
of the attempt to capture events in the net of
time. In completeness of chronology Ibn Ishâq
is surpassed by his successors (Wâqidî, p. 15 f.).
Abû Ma'shar seems to have had a mind for
nothing but dates, and even with Wâqidî this

interest obtrudes itself. For the relation
between these two see Tabarî, II, 1172, 10 ;
1173, 6.

Medîna was the kernel of the Islamic
community and the Arabian kingdom. The
importance of the town for the general historical
development which started from it gave its
stamp to the tradition which grew up there. It
naturally cherished first the memory of the
proud and sacred time at the beginning when
Islâm was still an unbroken religious and
political unity, and seemed as if it were about
to embrace the whole world within itself. Its
chief theme, to which Ibn Ishâq appears to
have limited himself exclusively, was the *Sîra*
with the *Maghâzî*, *i.e.*, the life of Mahammad,
the foundation of the community through him,
and the foundation of the Kingdom through
him and his Khalîfas in the period of the
conquests. But even when the centre of gravity
of the kingdom had been transferred to
Damascus it did not lose sight of the true centre
of the whole. It did not remove to Damascus
itself, but remained in Medîna, and even under
the Umaiyids this town was not only the seat
of the most prominent Arab society, but also
the spiritual centre of the Islamic culture until
Baghdâd took its place. The course of the
secular history also of the kingdom arrested the
attention of the scholars of Medîna, although

they were not in agreement with the government.
They were far more concerned about Syria than
about Irâq or even about Khurâsân. Certain
official statements, as one might say, are repeated
regularly in Abû Ma'shar and Wâqidî, *e.g.*, when
the rulers came into power and died ; when the
stattholders of the most important provinces
were installed and deposed ; who was commissioned by the Khalîfa each year to lead the Hajj and
the summer campaign against the Romans.
These statements form the framework of the
Medîna annals. The contents are fuller only at
certain crises and turning-points, but generally
they are meagre. The scholarly interest is
directed to dry facts ; we see little of pleasure in
detail, of intimate relations with the subject, of
sympathy with the characters of the drama.
Sympathy with the Umaiyids and Syrians was
not to be found in Medîna ; we need not look for
more than an aloof interest.

Doubtless there was likewise a tradition in
Syria itself, *i.e.*, among the Syrian Arabs, but it
is lost to us. Traces of it are found in Balâdhurî,
perhaps also in the Kalbite 'Awâna, who indeed
lived in Kûfa, but through his tribe was
connected with Syria, and is often quoted in
Tabarî as the reporter of Syrian matters,
generally according to Ibn Kalbî. We are best
acquainted with the spirit of this Syrian tradition from Christian chronicles, particularly the

Continuatio of Isidor of Seville. The Umaiyids there appear in a quite different, and very much more favourable light than that in which we are accustomed to see them. In the case of the Arabs, their enemies had the last word, and their history in consequence suffered severely.

Madâinî takes up a kind of middle position beween Abû Mikhnaf and the historians of Medîna. He is a scholarly historian but gives very detailed accounts, and has a pronounced local interest in Basra and Khurasan. Almost all the accounts concerning Basra and Khurasan in Tabarî are taken from him. He takes up altogether the Abbâsid stand-point and from it describes the fall of the Umaiyids and the rise of the blessed dynasty.

Of the characterisation of these main authorities of Tabarî I say no more. Many other traditionists, not known to us through their own works, give accounts in Tabarî, especially for certain particular parties. But I do not propose here to make a complete survey of the oldest Arab historical writing. It seemed to me necessary merely to give some idea of its origins, for which let this suffice. Wüstenfeld's well-known statement in Vols. 28 and 29 of the *Abhandlungen* of the Göttingen Society will serve to complete my account.

My idea originally was to deal with the time
of the Umaiyids in the same manner and under
the same title (Prolegomena to the oldest history
of Islam) as I dealt with the time of the great
conquests in the 6th Part of my *Skizzen und
Vorarbeiten.* There I succeeded in comparing
the account of Saif b. ' Umar with the rest of
the collected tradition in Tabarî, and proved it
to be a biassed touching-up of the latter. But
Saif stops with the Battle of the Camel, and
from that point historical criticism does not
proceed according to the same unvarying stand-
point. We are no longer guided by a literary
leading-string. We must pronounce judgment
from case to case from actual facts, enter into
the merits of the case, and follow rather an
eclectic or even a harmonising method. The
reporters are, indeed, constantly differing in
credibility, but they only part company now and
then, and not always on the same point.
Discussion then becomes more intricate and
more minute, where it is at all possible and
worth the trouble. But it is not always possible
because the material is not sufficient, and not
always necessary because the guarantors agree
or complement each other. Frequently positive
statement may and must take the place of
inquiry. Compared to the beginning it pre-
ponderates more as the book goes on. The
reproach of inconsistency of style I accept.

Regard for the changing quality of the reports was responsible for my change of procedure. I have indeed been impelled to many inquiries less by the material than by my own predecessors. I felt bound sometimes to give other answers to them than they did.

Göttingen, July, 1902.   WELLHAUSEN.

CONTENTS

ARAB KINGDOM AND ITS FALL

CHAPTER I

INTRODUCTION

1. The political community of Islam grew out of the religious community. Muhammad's conversion and his call to be an apostle took place about the same time. He began with himself ; he was, to begin with, possessed with the certainty of the all-powerful God and of the last judgment, but the conviction that filled his own heart was so great that it forced its way out. He felt bound to show the light and the way to the brethren who were groping in darkness, and thereby save them from error. Straightway he founded a little congregation at Mecca.

This congregation was held closely together by the belief in the One Invisible God, the Creator of the world and the Judge of the soul, and by the moral law arising thence, to serve Him and no other lord, to gain one's own soul and not the world, to seek righteousness and mercy and not earthly possessions. In the oldest chapters of the Qoran monotheism is as emphatically moral as it is in Amos and in the Sermon on the Mount. As in the Gospel, the thought of the Creator immediately awakens the thought of personal justification to Him after death. He claims the soul absolutely for Himself,—to do His will, not merely to submit to it. The original Islam is not fatalism in the usual sense of the word, and its God is not the Absolute, *i.e.* a religious figure-head, but with the Supreme Power morality and righteousness are indissolubly bound up. Sometimes the one, sometimes the other is emphasised according to the feeling of the moment, without any attempt to keep the balance, or any consciousness of inconsistency. Muhammad was neither philosopher nor dogmatist.

Externally the community was bound together by the common observances of religious ceremonies; the oldest name which they had among outsiders, the name *Sâbians*, can have its origin only in these ceremonies. Even in the earliest parts of the Qoran prayers, prostrations and vigils are postulated; they are only not yet so strictly defined and regulated as they are later.

Muhammad began by winning over individuals,—friends, relatives and slaves, but these he regarded only as first-fruits. From the beginning his aim was to draw all Mecca to himself,—his family, the Hâshim and the

Muttalib, and his people, the Quraish. He was
an Arab, and as an Arab his feelings for the
family and the tribe (*i.e.* the people), were such
as we only understand for the narrower household. An order of things aloof from the community and acting independently with sovereign
power, was as yet unknown among the Arabs.
The state was not an institution and not a
territory, but a collective body. There was thus,
in reality, not a state, but only a people ; not an
artificial organisation, but simply a full-grown
organism ; no state officials, but only heads of
clans, families and tribes.[1] The same bond,—
that of blood, held together the people and the
family ; the only difference was their size. The
commonwealth, free from any external constrain-
ing influence, was based upon the idea of a
blood-community and its sanctity. Relationship, or the faith in relationship,—both came
practically to the same thing,—worked as a
religion, and this religion was the spirit which
made the race into one living whole. Along
with this there was also an outward cultus, but
no religion which laid upon them any other
claims, ties or obligations except only those of

[1] Even yet the Beduin are disposed to think of the Daula, *i.e.*
the Turkish Empire, as a tribe, and to rate its strength by the number
of its camels (Doughty 1, 230). Even in the towns the political
unit was not the city but the tribe,—thus, the Quraish in Mecca, the
Thaqîf in Tâif. The Quraishites and Thaqîfites felt that they belonged
together politically even when they lived outside of Mecca or Tâif.

blood. If Muhammad had founded a faith
whose professors did not take cover under the
bond of tribal relationship he would have broken
up the blood-related community there and then,
since it was too closely bound and knit together
to suffer the intrusion of a foreign agent. But
he did not want that, and, besides, he could perhaps scarcely imagine a religious community in
any other setting than that of blood-relationship.
So his mission was not to gain adherents far and
near. He had to begin, of course, with
individuals, but his aim was to gain the whole.
His nation was to become his congregation; he
was not content with an " ecclesiola pressa " in
Mecca.

Failing to win over his own people, the
Quraish, in Mecca, he tried to strike up a
connection with other tribes and towns, for
which he found opportunity in the markets
and fairs in the neighbourhood of Mecca. At
Tâif he approached the elders of the Thaqîf
with regard to the admission of the commonwealth as a whole into Islam. Finally he
gained a footing in Yathrib, *i.e.* Medina. His
emigration thither, the Hijra, was an event
that founded a new era, but the new era
really meant no conscious break with the past.
Muhammaa did not deteriorate by his change
from preacher to ruler. His ideal had long
been to attract not only individuals but the

whole commonwealth. He always considered the prophet as the God-sent leader of His people, and drew no distinction between a political and a religious community. His desire to continue to be in Medina the same as he had been in Mecca, the Prophet and Messenger of God, was not hypocrisy or the acting of a part. Only, in Mecca his efforts were in vain ; in Medina he succeeded ; there he was in the opposition, here he attained his end. That made a great difference, and not an external one only. It is a regular occurrence for the opposition to change when it comes into power, and theory differs vastly from practice since the latter has got to reckon with possibilities. A historical community cannot altogether break with its existing foundations, and might follows laws of its own in order to maintain and extend its power. It is this which explains why the Prophet as ruler became different from the Prophet as pretender, and why the theocracy in practice differed from the theocracy in theory. The political element became more prominent, the religious element less so, but it must always be remembered that, in principle, politics and religion flowed together, though a distinction was made between divine and secular politics, and alongside of them the piety of the heart still kept its place.

2. In Medina the ground was prepared for Muhammad by Judaism and Christianity. There

were many Jews there, and the town stood on
the boundary of that part of Arabia which
was under the Graeco-Roman and Christian-
Armenian influence. The political conditions
were even more favourable for him. In Mecca
peace and order prevailed. The old principle of
a community acted smoothly. The new one that
the Prophet threatened to introduce, was felt to
be a disturbing element and rejected. But blood
did not, by any means, wield this power all over
Arabia. Its effect was not uniform in all the
degrees of relationship, but was stronger in the
narrower circles than in the wider ones ; in the
former it was spontaneous, in the latter more
a matter of duty. Consequently the uniting
element might also become the dissolvent if
the interests of the family became at variance
with the interests of the tribe or people. A
family was particularly unwilling to renounce
the blood-revenge incumbent upon them, even
towards families related to them, of the same
tribe. Then there would arise blood-feuds
between the clans, since there was no authority
in a dispute which could command peace and
punish a breach of it. This was the state of
things that prevailed in Medina. The community
was divided into two hostile camps—the Aus and
the Khazraj. Murder and manslaughter were
the order of the day ; nobody dared venture out
of his quarter without danger ; there reigned a

tumult in which life was impossible. What was wanted was a man to step into the breach and banish anarchy; but he must be neutral and not involved in the domestic rivalry. Then came the Prophet from Mecca, as if God-sent. Blood, as a bond of union, had failed; he put faith in its place. He brought with him a tribe of Believers, the companions of his flight from Mecca, and slowly, advancing steadily step by step, he established the commonwealth of Medina on the basis of religion as an *Ummat Allah*, a congregation of God. Even if he had wished he could not have founded a church, for as yet there was no state in existence there. What had to be done was the elementary work, the establishment of order, and the restoration of peace and right. Since there was no other authority, a religious authority took the lead, got the power into its hands, and secured its position by performing what was expected of it. Muhammad displayed the gift of ability to deal with affairs in the mass. Where he was in doubt he knew the right man to ask, and he was fortunate in finding reliable supporters in some of the emigrants who had come with him from Mecca, and who formed his nearest circle of friends.

In the circumstances stated the power of religion appeared chiefly as a political force. It created a community, and over it an authority which was obeyed. Allah was the personification of the state supremacy. What with us is done in the king's name was done in the name of Allah; the army and the public institutions were called after Allah. The idea of ruling authorities, till then absolutely foreign to the Arabs, was introduced through Allah. In this there was also the idea that no outward or human power, but only a power inwardly acknowledged and standing above mankind, had the right to rule. The theocracy is the negative of the *Mulk*, or earthly kingdom. The privilege of ruling is not a private possession for the enjoyment of the holder of it; the kingdom belongs to God, but His plenipotentiary, who knows and carries out His will, is the Prophet. He is not only the harbinger of truth, but also the only lawful ruler upon earth. Beside him no king has a place, and also no other prophet. This conception of the " monarchic prophet " originates with the later Jews; it is typically portrayed in the contrast between Samuel and Saul, as it appears, for example, in I Samuel : 8 and 11. The Prophet represents the rule of God upon earth; Allah and His Messenger are always bound up in each other, and stand together in the Creed. The theocracy may be defined as the commonwealth, at the head of which stands, not the king and the usurped or inherited power, but the Prophet and the Law of God.

In the idea of God justice, and not holiness, predominated. His rule was the rule of justice, and the theocracy was so far, a " dichaarchy," but by this we are not to understand a rule of impersonal law. There was no law as yet ; Islam was in existence before the Qoran. Nor did the theocracy resemble a republic, notwithstanding the idea that all the subjects of Allah stand in equal relationship to Him. The chief characteristic of the republic, election through the people, was absent altogether. The supreme power rested not with the people but with the Prophet. He alone had a fixed,—even divine—office ; all authorities had their origin in his supreme authority. But he did not appoint actual officials, but only gave certain commissions, after the execution of which the commissioners retired of themselves. His advisers, too, were private individuals with whom he was on terms of friendship, and whom he gathered into the circle of his society.

Of a hierarchy there is no trace. The Muslim theocracy was not marked by an organisation of special sanctity ; in this respect it had no resemblance to the Jewish theocracy after the Exile.[1] There was no order of priests, no difference between clergy and laymen, between

---

[1] The post-exilic hierocracy had foreign supremacy as a presupposition, it had no political autonomy. It therefore differed from the state even if not to the same extent as the Christian Church in its initial stage, since it at least took cover under the nation. The Papal States cannot be compared to it at all, for there the church *was* not the

religious and secular callings. The power of Allah pervaded every function and organ of the state, and the administration of justice and war were just as sacred offices as divine service. The mosque was at one and the same time the forum and the drill-ground ; the congregation was also the army; the leader in prayer (*Imám*) was also the commander.

From the idea of the rule of God there arose no actual form of constitution. The new factor which, through Muhammad, was cast into the chaos, certainly effected a concentration of elements hitherto unknown. It might seem as if the old sacred ties of blood would be overwhelmed by the community of the Faith, but as a matter of fact, they continued unchanged, even though the centre of gravity was transferred from them to the whole. The framework of what had been the organisation up till then,— the tribes, families and clans, was taken over into the new commonwealth; faith in Allah did not provide anything else to put in their place. The Muslims' right to political equality, arising out of the idea of the theocracy, was not established in such a way as to banish party differences. The men of Mecca, the so-called *Muhájira*, kept by themselves ; side by side with them were

state, but it *owned* a state (W. Sickel). The old Israelitish theocracy alone shows a great similarity to the Arabian, though, of course, originally the idea that the lawful theocratic ruler was the Prophet and not the King was not to be found in it.

the indigenous tribes of Arabs of Medina, the
so-called *Ansâr*, and also the tribes of the
Jews of Medina. The settlers remained settlers
and the slaves remained slaves, even when
they accepted Islam.

From the early period after the Hijra, before
the battle of Badr, there is preserved to us a
decree of Muhammad in which appear some of
the chief points of the law of the state at first
current in Medina. It throws light upon how
far the old conditions were, or were not, altered
by the fact that Medina by this time has become
a united *Umma*. *Umma* is not the name for the
old Arab bond of relationship; it merely signifies
"community." Generally it is the religious
community, not only since Islam but even
earlier (Nâbigha, 17, 21). Even in our document
the Umma has something of a religious flavour ;[1]
it is the community of Allah established for
peace and protection. Allah rules over it, and
in His name, Muhammad, who, however, is
never called " prophet." The bond of unity is
the Faith, the Faithful are its supporters. They
have the chief obligations and the chief privileges.
Still it is not only the Faithful who belong
to the Umma, but also all who ally themselves

[1] The leader of the Umma is the Imâm. Etymologically, however,
the two names are not directly connected, perhaps not connected at all.
Umma is derived from the root " Umm " (the mother) ; Imâm, on the
other hand, from a verb-root which means " to precede."

with them and fight along with them, *i. e.*
all the inhabitants of Medina. The Umma
embraces a wide area,—the whole precincts of
Medina are to be a district of inviolable peace.
There are still heathen among the Ansâr, and
they are not excluded, but expressly included.
The Jews are also included, though they have
not so close a connection with the Umma as the
Muhâjira and the Ansâr, and have not exactly
the same rights and obligations. The degree of
communion is not precisely equal,—there still
persists an analogy with the old Arab distinction
between natives and settlers. It is significant
that the Umma includes both heathen and Jews,
and also that it consists in general not of individuals but of alliances. The individual belongs
to the Umma only through the medium of the
clan and the family. The families are enjoined
to remain as they are, and as such to become
members of the Umma. There is no notion of
the possibility of a new principle arising according
to which they might become members of the community. Even the heads of families remain and
are not replaced by, *e.g.*, theocratic officials. As
regards the relation of the Umma with the families and the defining of the mutual duties and
obligations, the families continue, as before, to
be liable for expenses which are not of a purely
private nature, namely, the payment of blood-
money and the ransom of prisoners. As yet

there is no state-treasury. Client-ship, too, is a clan and family affair, no one is allowed to take away another man's client. Even the important privilege of guaranteed protection, the *Ijára*, is not restricted; any individual may take a stranger under his protection, and by so doing puts the whole community under the same obligation. It is only for the Quraish of Mecca, the declared foes of Muhammad, that the Ijâra has no protecting power.

To the Umma the family is obliged to yield the right of civil feud, *i. e.* feud with the other families of Medina, for the first aim of the Umma is to prevent internal fighting. When disputes arise they must be brought to judgment. " If you are in dispute about anything whatsoever, it must be brought before God and Muhammad." But if the internal peace is broken by violence and mischief, then not only the injured person or his tribe, but the whole community, including the relatives of the criminal himself, are obliged to go in united strength against him, and to deliver him up to the avenger so that he may make the latter just amends. The revenge for bloodshed can then no longer resolve itself into a family feud. It is robbed of the dangerous element that is a menace to the general peace and softened down into the " Talio." Indeed the Talio existed before Islam, though it was not often exercised, because it was too like the parts and too dependent upon them to have any coercive power whatever over them. It was in Medina that the Talio was first strictly applied, because here God stood above blood, and, in theory at least, possessed a real sovereignty. As yet it does not amount to a proper punishment. Its execution is still in the hands of the injured party, and it rests with him to exact his right of revenge, or renounce it and accept recompense in money. It marks, however, the transition from revenge to punishment. The duty of prosecution being taken from the individual and given to the whole marks a very important step, making revenge a duty of the state, and thus turning it into punishment. It suffices to prevent internal feud. Inside the territory of Medina a public peace, general and absolute, holds sway. There are not so many alliances for protection as there are families over which protection does not extend, or at least is not properly effective. There is only one general peace, that of the Umma.

The other aim of the Umma is to unite the families for defence against external foes. The " Faithful " are mutually bound to help each other against "men"; they are avengers of each other, a mass against all outsiders. The duty of revenge on a foe devolves not on a brother for a brother, but on believer for believer. As a matter of fact, war is by this means deprived of the idea of a blood-feud, with which it before coincided ; it becomes a military affair. As war with an outside people is common to the Faithful, so also is peace common. No one can, on his own account, conclude a peace which does not serve for all.

Nevertheless, the right of the tribe or family to carry on feud against outsiders is not altogether abolished. This is open to the same criticism as the corresponding inconsistency that even the Ijâra, which assures for a stranger the right to a home in Medina, is not yet withdrawn from the individual, although it is the duty of the whole, and so it must have been a privilege of the Umma and of its leader, the Imâm.[1] This line of demarcation between the whole and its parts is not yet quite defined. The Umma has not yet reached its full growth. But the Faithful were the soul of it, with the Prophet at their head ; they were the leaven, the spiritually stronger and aspiring element which instigated the movement and the propaganda. In proportion as the Faith spread, the Umma increased in strength.

The Quraish, from whom Muhammad and his followers had fled from Mecca, appear as the

---

[1] Similar inconsistencies have arisen until recently even with us. Dr. Schnelle granted to the outlawed Hoffmann von Fallersleben the right of a home at his manor of Buchholz in Mecklenburg, to which he was entitled at the time of the German Confederation. Plainly such a state of things had its advantages.

declared enemies of the Umma in the above-
mentioned arrangement of the community of
Medina. Out of petty feuds there arose an
obstinate war, and this war did a great deal to
increase the internal strength of the Umma.
The first considerable encounter, at Badr (Anno
Hijrae 2), resulted in an unexpected success for
Muhammad. This splendid victory was taken
as a divine sanction to the Faith, made a deep
impression, and had a very great moral effect.
In addition, it helped tremendously to extend
the influence of Muhammad, to break down the
opposition against him, to make Islam paramount in the Umma, and to amalgamate or to
break with the foreign constituent parts which
until then had been tolerated. Islam now no
longer remained tolerant, but acted like a
reign of terror within Medina. This change is
marked by the rise of the *Munáfiqún*, the doubt-
ers and hypocrites. The heathen dared not any
longer remain heathen within the Umma; circumstances compelled them to embrace the
Faith, but they did so with mixed feelings, and
made no secret of their malicious joy whenever
fortune seemed to go against the Prophet. The
Jews were still worse. After the battle of Badr,
Wâqidî states, the position of things changed,
much to their disadvantage. Muhammad took
exception to them, and represented that they
had broken their agreement. Under flimsy

pretexts he drove out, and in tne course of a few years annihilated, the whole of the communities of Jews in the oases of Medina, who were there forming alliances similar to those of the Arab tribes. He handed over their valuable plantations of palms to the Muhâjira, who till then possessed no land or territory, but were delivered as Inquilines to the hospitality of the Ansâr, or supported themselves by trading or robbery. He thus made them independent of the Ansâr, and they became settlers and proprietors in Medina. In this way he strengthened his own power as well, for the Muhâjira were, so to speak, his body-guard, and the still smouldering discord between the two tribes of the Ansâr,—the Aus and the Khazraj—gave them a decided importance.

After their defeat at Badr, the Quraish gathered to make a campaign of revenge against Muhammad, under the leadership of Abû Sufyân, and actually gained a victory over him at Mount Uhud near Medina. They did not however make full use of it, but were content with the honour of it, and marched back home. So the counter-stroke did not do the Prophet much harm ; he was prepared for it and soon repaired the damage. A second attack of the Quraish on Medina, in which they had the assistance of the heathen and Jews, came to naught. Smaller tribes of the neighbourhood became allies of

3

the struggling commonwealth, politically at first, but afterwards in religion also. Islam fought on and passed gradually from the defensive to the offensive. Arabia looked on in suspense at the great feud between heathendom and Allah which was being fought out between Mecca and Medina.

During this external struggle with Arabian heathendom there came about in a remarkable way a thorough Arabisation of Islam itself. Muhammad started from the conviction that his religion was exactly the same in substance as the Judaic and Christian, and so expected that the Jews in Medina would receive him with open arms, but he was bitterly disappointed in them. They did not recognise him as a prophet nor his revelation as identical with theirs, although at first, out of policy, they entered into the Umma which he had founded. Since they did not consider Judaism identical with Islam, but rather opposed to it, he, on his part, pitted Islam against Judaism and even against Christianity. He so fixed the pass-words and counter-signs of his religion, which to us appear of little account, but which are really very important, that they no longer expressed common points between it and the sister religions, but emphasised the differences. Instead of Sabbath or Sunday he fixed Friday as the chief day of public worship; he substituted the call

of *Adhân* for the trumpets and bells; he
abolished the Fast of *'Āshūrâ*, the great day of
atonement; and for Lent he fixed the month of
Ramadân. Whilst he more firmly established
Islam by carefully abolishing the Jewish and
Christian forms, he brought it, at the same time,
nearer to Arabism. He always regarded himself as the prophet sent specially to the Arabs,—
the prophet who received and communicated in
the Arabic tongue the revelation which was con-
tained also in the Thora and in the Gospel.
Apparently he never had a natural sympathy for
the Ka'ba at Mecca and renounced the God of
the Ka'ba, but now circumstances impelled him
to take a much more decisive step. He changed
the *Qibla* and commanded that at prayer the
face should be turned not towards Jerusalem, but
towards Mecca. Mecca was declared to be the
Holy Place instead of Jerusalem,—the true seat of
Allah upon earth. The pilgrimage to the Ka'ba
and even the kissing of the Holy Stone were
sanctioned; a centre of heathen worship and a
popular heathen festival were introduced into
Islam. As usual, history was called in to justify
this appropriation. It was said that the Holy
Place and the Cultus of Mecca were originally
monotheistic and founded by Abraham, and
had only in later times degenerated and become
heathen. Abraham, the Father of the Faith,
was filched from the Jews and made the founder

of a pre-Islamic Islam of the Arabs, with
Mecca as its seat, and so Islam was definitely
sundered from Judaism and changed into a
national Arab religion.

In this way Mecca was already spiritually
incorporated with Islam before the conquest
which followed, in the year 8 of the Flight. It
took the form of a capitulation arranged with
Abû Sufyân. The apprehension that the town
would, through Islam, lose its religious power
of attraction for the Arabs,—the power by
which it lived, was allayed beforehand. Indeed
it rather gained by the fact that it was the only
one of the holy places of the old heathen
worship which retained its sanctuary and the
festival in its neighbourhood, while all the other
holy places were abolished. The war with
Muhammad had caused heavy losses to the
Quraishites. He now tried his best to make
them realise how much they would benefit by
friendship with him, by making presents to
their chiefs and giving them abundant tokens
of his good-will. These methods of convincing
them of Islam he called "the winning of
hearts." He was moved also by a deep sympathy with his native town, and went so far in
the endeavour to be reconciled with it that the
Ansâr were afraid he would make it the headquarters of his rule and forsake Yathrib. But
this fear was groundless; Yathrib remained the

Medina, *i.e.* the government town. Muhammad did not remove to Mecca, but the ambitious Quraishites, who wanted to keep close to him and to the government, emigrated to Medina, Abû Sufyân and the Umaiya at their head. But this was no advantage to the Ansâr; the Muhâjira, not only from Mecca, but from all Arabia continued to gather strength in their town, for Medina offered a great attraction to active spirits who wanted to make their fortunes, and the Prophet received them without question as a welcome addition to his power, even though they might not have a very clean record.

The Arab tribes had so far let things take their course. After the capture of Mecca and the overthrow of the Hawâzin which followed soon after, one after the other yielded to the conqueror and came over to Islam. This was not done by individual action, but the chiefs acted for the people. The representatives and elders capitulated to Muhammad and tried to get the most favourable terms they could for their folk as well as for themselves. If a tribe was internally divided by a dispute about the chieftainship, the one party tried to get the upper hand of the other by means of Islam. Such a favourable opportunity for Muhammad occurred very frequently, and so the transition was a political action, the act of joining the commonwealth of Medina. Only the forms and tokens of Islam were accepted, especially prayer, with the call to prayer and the poor-tax. The missionaries did not come into the country till after the transition was completed, when they instituted the worship of God and taught the elements of religion and law. Outward profession was all that was required; the faith, in point of fact, was "fides implicita."

The incorporation of the whole of Arabia into Islam was sealed by the *Barā'a* of the year 9 and the *Hijjat-al-Wadā'* of the year 10. The worship in Mecca and the ceremonies in the neighbourhood were declared to be exclusively Islamic. The heathen dared no longer take part in them. They were supplanted in their own inheritance, a purely heathen one, and not only so, but the whole of Arabia was claimed for Islam. All Arabs who still remained heathen were, *eo ipso*, outlawed, but the " Peace of God " was open to those who came over to the theocracy; internal feud was to occur no more. Islam cancelled the past and the ancient grounds of feud; all demands and debts of blood were to be " trampled under foot." It was a " seisachthy " of quite another sort from that of Solon, being very much more broad and thorough. From the " cell " of Medina the theocracy spread over the whole of Arabia.

The tribes and their aristocracies still remained, but in the legates of Muhammad received, in various ways, a sort of supervision and were altogether united in a state whose centre of government was Medina. The foundation of this state,—which, even if it were not a very solid one, was still a defence against anarchy and general dissolution,—was the cope-stone of the Prophet's work. He did not die a martyr, but at the height of success. It can hardly be cast as a reproach at him that he built up the Kingdom of God upon a given natural foundation, for even if circumstances often compelled or induced him to use unholy means and to hold up Allah as a pretext, still he is not to be regarded as a hypocrite.

4. The Arabian tribes thought that they had sworn allegiance to the Prophet only, the general view being that the oath of allegiance bound one only to the person to whom it was made. After his death they fell away,—not so much from Allah as from Medina. The situation was also dubious within Medina, but the theocracy got over the crisis caused by the change of ruler and recalled Arabia to obedience. The best means of mending the breach seemed to be expansion towards the outside, for this was the direct method of quelling the interior tumult. Through the *Jihâd*, the holy war, the rebellious tribes were drawn over to the interest of Islam

and reconciled with it. The propaganda of the Faith was not much more than the pretext of the war. The challenge to the foes of Allah to be converted was issued only as a matter of form before the commencement of hostilities ; it was not supposed that they would actually yield to it. There was one rule for the Arabs and another for the " outlanders." The Arabs had no choice ; they had to accept Islam, and the tendency spread to tolerate in the territory of the whole peninsula no religion but that of Muhammad.[1] The levelling of Islam and Arabism went so far that no one could be a Muslim without belonging to, or joining, an Arab family. On the other hand the non-Arabs were not compelled to come over ; the present supposition was that they would abide by their old religion. Being non-Arabs, they did not belong to the native citizenship of the theocracy ; they were not meant to enter into it, but only to be put under its sway ; that was the aim of the war.

Thus, out of the national state which Muhammad had founded there arose after his death a kingdom, a rule of the theocracy over the world. The kingdom had two classes of adherents, who differed both in politics and in religion. The masters in it were the Arabs, as Muslims as well as warriors and conquerors. Muhammad's

---

[1] The Taghlib, who were permitted to remain Christians, dwelt in Mesopotamia.

congregation had been completely converted into an army ; prayer and fasting and the other pious exercises took a secondary place after the Jihâd. In this form Islam became clear to the Beduin also. It was the standard which led them to victory and spoil,—or if the worst came to the worst, to Paradise. In the captured provinces the theocracy under the new conditions was organised throughout as an army. Its citizen-list was the army register, the tribes and families forming the regiments and companies. All Arabs were not included in it, but only the active ones, the *Muqâtila, i. e.* the fighters and defenders. In contra-distinction to those who stayed at home, the Muqâtila were also called the Muhâjira, *i.e.* those who went out to the great military centres from which the war was directed and conducted. For Hijra no longer meant Flight, but emigration (with wife and children) to a military and political centre, in order to serve there.[1] Full citizen's rights could only be enjoyed in the army, and in the capital and garrison towns ; the Beduin who remained inactive in their homesteads and with their flocks were not recognised as citizens with full rights,—scarcely even as adherents.[2] The original

[1] This is the meaning of *Higra, e.g.*, in Hamâsa, 792 v. 3; "Thou hast not left home for the sake of Paradise, but for the sake of the bread and dates." *Cf.* Qutâmî 4, 25.

[2] Yahyâ b. Âdam, Kitâb al Kharâj, 5, 18 and 59, 15. *Cf.* my treatise upon the Khawârij (Göttinger Ges. der Wiss. 1901), p. 9.

4

Dâr-al-Hijra or *Dâr-al-Islâm* was Medina, whither at first went the influx of "active" men; later the provincial capitals (*misr*, pl. *musûr*) were added, and thither the Hijra could also be made. In Syria older towns already in existence were chosen, and in other places new military colonies were founded, such as Fustât in Egypt, Qairawân in Roman Africa, and especially Basra and Kûfa in Iraq.

From these points where they made their headquarters the Arabs kept the provinces in obedience; it was absolute martial law. The Emirs, under whose leadership a land was taken, were the first "stattholders," and their successors were, first and foremost, military commanders. But just as the army was at the same time the Umma, so the Emir was at the same time the Imâm, the leader of the service in the mosque, especially on Friday when he preached. He was '*ala*' *lharb walsalât*; warfare and worship both came into his department. Along with this he possessed naturally the executive power, and consequently also the judicial supremacy in which lies the power of commanding peace. At first the Emir dispensed justice in person, later he appointed a *Qâdî* in the capital.[1]

On the whole he handed over the domestic rule and to a certain degree the dispensing of

[1] There was as yet no such official under Umar I. Presumably at that time there were no disputes at all. We first hear of a Qâdî in Kufa at the time of Mu'âwia or Yazîd I.

judgment also, to the circles most nearly concerned, for even in the captured provinces the Arabs kept up their ancient clan-system. But pretty soon a difference crept in. In the Arabian homeland a comparatively small band formed an actual unity which shepherded their flocks and wandered about in common. It reckoned itself, together with other tribes, into groups ascending in importance, but these had actually not much say. This was changed by the great overflow over the bounds of the desert. As a general thing the whole tribe did not journey from home to settle down " *in corpore* " at one and the same spot, but fragments of the tribe were scattered hither and thither, fragments which could not exist of themselves. So, in order to gain the necessary solidarity, they made a closer alliance with fragments of related tribes belonging to the similar higher group. This was all the easier when there was no longer plenty of room for emigrating, as there used to be before, and when they were crowded together in colonies and lived in the closest contact with each other ; for example, Kufa was a pattern-paper of the widely ramified ethnology of the desert. Thus it can be understood that by a kind of integration the larger alliances attained an actual importance which they had never had before, and which they scarcely possessed even later in Arabia proper. The combination of other circumstances furthered this tendency to the formation of groups, which became momentous for the internal history of the Arabian Empire.

As distinguished from the Arabian military nobility the non-Arabs were subjects,[1] i. e. those reduced to submission or dependence. They formed the financial basis of the kingdom. They had to provide for the support of their lords by means of the tribute, the " subjects' tax," which was far more oppressive than the so-called " poor-tax " of the Muslims, and became scandalous. As far as possible, the Arabian Government took even less interest in their internal affairs than in those of the tribes. In the province formerly Roman, the bishops often became the civic heads of the community also ; in the Persian province the Dihqâns remained so. These native chiefs were responsible for the tax in their district ; the government did not trouble itself except to see that the tax came in all right. It was the business of the " Stattholder " to keep the subjects sufficiently in hand so that they paid the tribute. Later on an independent finance official was often appointed along with him, which did not exactly meet with his approval, for then he had only to hold the cow by the horns and make her stand still while another person milked her.

---

[1] I use the word "subjects" in this narrower sense as distinguished from the Arabs, the actual owners of the state.

The old-Arabian right of plunder, in the somewhat modified form sanctioned by Muhammad in the Qoran, formed the basis of the taxation of the subjects and of the regulation of their position in general. When a town or district had surrendered to the Muslims without fighting (*sulhan*), the inhabitants retained life, freedom and property, but had to pay tribute for the mercy and protection granted, in a lump sum, or according to a contract fixed by the capitulation.[1] But if they were overcome by force of arms (*'anwatan*) they came under the law of war, *i. e.* they had forfeited every right; they and all they possessed were the spoil of the conqueror. A fifth was laid aside for God, *i. e.* the state, and even the crown lands and the ground and properties forsaken by their owners fell into the treasury.[2] Everything else, not movable property merely, but also land and people, was to be divided according to law, and not amongst the Muslims generally, but amongst the warriors of that very army which had effected the particular conquest. This, however, could not go on. It was impossible that this tremendous changing of possessions from hand to hand should continue, not to mention the

[1] In some cases they rendered military services on the frontier and then they did not require to pay tribute, for it was considered that the tribute was payment for the freedom from military service and for its being undertaken by the Arabs.

[2] Yahyâ, p. 45.

hardships it entailed upon the lower classes who only tilled the ground and did not own it. The Arabs could not cast lots among themselves for half the world to keep it from becoming desert. Nor did they dare to distribute themselves over the vast territory in order to manage it. If they wanted to keep their ground their only way was to concentrate themselves in a military fashion. " The stability of my congregation," so Muhammad is said to have asserted,[1] " rests upon the hoofs of their horses and the points of their lances, so long as they do not work the land ; whenever they begin to do that they become like the rest of men." And besides they had to think of the future. If everything was divided straight away among the first and actual conquerors the spoil was squandered as fast as it was won. So the land was treated as solid capital and handed over in fief to its former owners, so that they had to pay interest on it ; and this interest only came to the Arab warriors and their heirs,—not the capital, but the revenue.[2] As a matter of fact the towns and districts captured in this way by force of arms were not much worse off than those which had surrendered themselves, and the name of

---

[1] Yahyâ, p. 59.

[2] This is precisely the same as the tax in Genesis 47, which the Egyptian peasants have to pay to Pharaoh, as a token that their land really belongs to Pharaoh and that they are his bondsmen.

the tribute was the same in both cases,[1] only in the case of the latter the tribute was legally fixed and could not be arbitrarily altered.[2]

Thus arose the difference between *Ghanîma* and *Fai* in the period after Muhammad. The Ghanîma was the spoil brought into the camp in the shape of portable property and also prisoners, which was divided, now as ever, among the warriors. The Fai, on the other hand, was the spoil as represented by estates and the dwellers thereon which was not divided, but was left to the former possessors on consideration of tribute, so that the real owners, (according to the law of war), only received the rents of it.[3] But the state collected the rents through its officials, and did not pay the full amount every year to the rightful Muqâtila or their heirs. They were paid only a fixed pension, while the remainder went into the public exchequer.§ The organisation of the

---

[1] Yahyâ, p. 11 : all the land in the Sawâd, which is watered by canals, is Kharâj and. *Cf.* also pp. 13, 33, 35 ff.

[2] In many cases also the others later on fabricated treaties of capitulation, which was not a difficult matter considering the poor knowledge of diplomacy and the historical obscurity which soon enveloped the stormy times of the conquests.

[3] " Fai " is borrowed from the Qoran (59, 6, 7), but the difference between " Ghanîma " and " Fai " is not made there, but is illegal. The word actually means "return " (Yahyâ, 33 ; B. Hishâm 880, 7), but is used not merely for the interest but for the capital which yields it. The Muslim jurists naturally retain the distinction between " Ghanîma " and " Fai " as an original decree and do not acknowledge that it only evolved itself by usage, contrary to the Qoran.

conquests thus limited itself pretty much to a military occupation for the exploiting of the subjects. There was little change from the previous state of things. The ruling power changed, but the position of the *misera contribuens plebs* remained much as it had been before. The administration of the Arabs was confined to finance, its government office was a counting-house. They retained the Greek and Persian clerks, the only technical officials they had. They also kept, in the main, the old names and kinds of taxes, and did not make much change either in regard to their rate and collection. If the two men of Medina who are said to have measured and laid out Iraq had but half their wits they made a very niggardly use of what they had. In many cases the Khalîfa sanctioned only the provisional measures of his generals, whose actions were regulated by the local conditions.

Most of the conquests were made in the time of the Khalîfa Umar, and he is considered their organiser. As we have seen, he was certainly not the creator of any new system, but it is due to him that the Arabian right of spoil was set aside, and the state intervened between army and subjects. To a certain extent he protected the subjects, and through their capacity for taxation strengthened the state against the army.

5. The development of political law did not keep abreast with the development of political power. No practical science of government was to be found in the old-Arab tradition, and none either in the idea of the theocracy. This want was felt as soon as the momentous question arose as to whom was due the leadership of the theocracy.

As long as Muhammad lived this question did not arise. The Prophet was the representative of God, the true theocratic ruler; the theocracy was exactly suited to him. But the supposition that with his death the hour of the last judgment would immediately arrive, was not realised. The world was not destroyed, and he died without seeing to it that his flock was not left shepherdless. He certainly left behind the Qoran, and in addition the *Sunna, i. e.* the path he had trodden, the road he had pointed out by his practice, but neither from Qoran nor Sunna could it be discovered who was to be his successor. Still less was it to be understood from the Qoran and Sunna that a successor was superfluous; a personal leader of the divine worship and of the government seemed indispensable. There existed neither a regular method of election nor a right of inheritance to the Prophet. § The death of Muhammad seemed to do away with the theocracy, though there were pious folk who would not believe that possible. The Arab tribes defected, and there was a threatened schism in Medina itself. Since no provision of any kind had been made for the succession, a prompt seizure of authority was the only thing possible. Under Muhammad his oldest Meccan followers and friends, few in number, had stood closest to the chief power ; they were, so to speak, the first-fruits of the Faith, the nobility of the theocracy, a nobility of real Islamic origin and character. They had really no official place, but simply formed the council of the Prophet and had a very great influence over him, and now, when deprived of his protection, they did not let the power slip through their fingers, but firmly grasped the reins of government when they fell from his hands. The chief of these, in point of intellect, was Umar b. Khattâb, who may be regarded as the founder of the second theocracy, the theocracy without a prophet. He was tall, quick in movement, loud of speech and strong in fight, and is always represented with the whip in his hand. He did not glide about and whisper like the hypocrites, but was sincerely God-fearing and never indiscreet. He first supported Abû Bakr, Muhammad's most trusted friend, and it was not till after the latter's death, which took place soon after, that he took over the ruling power in name, Abû Bakr transferred

it to him in his last will and testament,[1] but that
was only a confirmation of what was already an
accepted thing. Abû Bakr was quite aware
that they had no legal title to the ruling power
but had usurped it. All they could do was
afterwards to legitimise their originally illegitimate power by wielding it according to the
idea of the theocracy. Since Allah no longer
reigned through his living plenipotentiary,
they secured His reign by the fact of their
taking as their rule of conduct His Word,—the
Qoran, and the example of His Messenger,—
the Sunna. They wished to be considered
only as temporary representatives of the One
and Only authorised Ruler of the theocracy, the
Prophet, and showed this by the official name
which they assumed, Khalîfa, *i.e.* "vicar." Abû
Bakr called himself the Vicar of the Messenger of
God, and Umar the Vicar of the Vicar of the
Messenger of God, until this seemed too
ceremonious and "Khalîfa," with the omission
of the genitive, became an independent title.
They also bore the additional title—Emir of the
Believers.

The influence of the oldest and most
eminent Companions of the Prophet, from whom

[1] The will of the dying man is an old idea with the Arabs. In
war the Emir had the right and the duty to appoint, in the event of his
death, a lieutenant, and often also a lieutenant of that lieutenant, and
so on. The Muslims, however, thought of themselves as a host. *Cf.*
Die Contin. Isidori Hispana, ed. Mommsen, par. 98.

the first Khalîfas were drawn, was shared in by
their tribal-connections, the Quraish, and not
only those who had emigrated to Medina in the
year of the Flight, or at least before the taking
of Mecca, but also those who had embraced
Islam only when compelled to do so after its
conquest. Blood asserted its power by the
side of the Faith. Notwithstanding the fact
that they had resisted Islam as long as they
could, the whole Quraish felt that they were the
people with the right to rule in the theocracy,
because Muhammad was sprung from their
stock, and they found their claims supported by
him and his Companions. Even the Arabs, as a
general thing, considered it quite in order that
the ruling power should remain, if not within a
single family, still within the one tribe or stock,
to be regarded as its common possession, though
only one individual wielded it. Only the Ansâr
strove hard against the precedence of Quraish
in Islam. At first they had received them as
fugitives kindly, and granted them quarter,
maintenance and protection. Neither had they
at first objected to Muhammad's preferring
his Meccan followers in many ways, or to
themselves having the heaviest of the warfare
and the others (Quraish) the lion's share of the
spoil, *e.g.* at the division of the properties of
the expelled Jews. But in time the feeling
grew amongst them that the spirits whom they

had summoned were becoming too much for them, and they made attempts to show that they would be masters in their own house and not be content with the guests' leavings. On frequent occasions their indignation broke out. It was excited especially by a former very influential leader of the tribe Khazraj, who thought himself slighted by the Prophet. At once the jealousy of the other tribe, the Aus, was aroused against this man. The old dangerous schism had not yet disappeared, and the third party who stood outside the quarrel benefited by it. Under these circumstances it was easy for Mohammad to keep the good-will of the Ansâr, but they were also indebted to him for having saved them from self-destruction, and when they came to think of it they recognised that they could not do without him either. They were much troubled by the thought that he might forsake their town, and after the capture of Mecca go and settle there. So things went on as they had begun ; the Quraish continued to gain a firmer footing in Medina, reinforced by numerous emigrants from other tribes, who were likewise called Muhâjira. The Ansâr still possessed a bare majority and fell more and more into the background. On the death of the Prophet they once more made a strong effort to assert their right to the ruling power in their town, or at least to their autonomy.

They forgot that Medina for long had been
no more *their* town but the Prophet's, and
he had made it something totally different,—the
centre of Arabia and of Islam. They were
taken by surprise by the prompt action of
Umar and the other Companions, then divided
by their own old dissensions, and finally put into
the minority by the steady stream of Beduins
of the neighbourhood who sided with the
Muhâjira against them.

Fortunately just at that time the great rising
of the Arabian tribes against Medina took place,
and in face of the common external danger the
internal quarrel disappeared. In accordance
with their traditions the Ansâr were again foremost in fight against the foes ; they had also the
chief hand in the conquests—particularly in
that of Syria. They formed the backbone of the
Islamic forces, but they had no say in appointing
the leaders. Moreover they still remained in a
certain opposition to the rulers, but their opposition rose and fell along with the general
opposition of pious theocrats against the
existing power. Medina as the seat of
the opposition, of Islamic tradition and
of the suppressed Islamic aristocracy, makes
its appearance later, always as a whole; it is
quite erroneous to think only of the Ansâr in
that connection. Even in the great rising which
ended in the Harra, they were united with the

Muhâjira against the Umaiya ; they followed
Quraishite pretenders and did not fight for their
own hand as a separate party.[1] Except, perhaps, by the Khawârij, the leadership of the
Quraish was recognised, if somewhat reluctantly,
by all sides. They took up a neutral position
with regard to the rivalry of the tribes, who, one
after another, yielded the ruling power to the
Quraish in preference to themselves, however
much they were at times exasperated by these
born share-holders in the state.

The Quraish, indeed, were not now very
closely united. Originally they were only the
followers of the Prophet and of his old Companions ; it was only through them, being of the
same tribe and blood-relationship, they had risen
into importance in Islam. But now there
sprang up amongst them a dangerous combination of the real Islamic aristocracy of Companions.

This happened after the death of the Khalîfa
Umar, when the question of a successor again
arose. Umar did not leave a will in favour of
Alî, who claimed as cousin and son-in-law of the

---

[1] There is an idea that the Ansâr had formed the nucleus of the
later opposition party of the Yemenites. I can find no reasons for this.
The Yemenites in Syria were the Kalb, in Kufa the Hamdân, Madhij
and Kinda, in Basra and Khurâsân the Azd Umân,—the latter the
least important. The Ansâr had no connection with any of these.
Neither had they much real concern with the Shîa, though they
adhered to Alî as long as he lived. That the Alids considered Medina
their native place and were held in respect there, is another question.

Prophet, and considered himself already slighted. Umar preferred to leave to open election the appointment of a Khalîfa in his stead. But the *Shûrá*, the electing body, did not, by any means, consist of the whole of the Muslims. The provinces were not consulted ; Medina alone was the " Polis," and in Medina the Ansâr in general were of little account, as also were the Quraish as a whole. The Shûrâ actually only consisted of the six still surviving oldest Companions of the Prophet, and they were sure to agree, like a board of cardinals, in appointing one of themselves. The rest of the people of Medina had only the right or the duty to do homage to the one chosen. The rendering of homage was bound to follow upon an election, and it had to be done in Medina.

The six, on their part, passed over Alî. They were not willing to recognise that he had a prior claim, and they chose to appoint the already aged Uthmân b. Affân of the house of Umaiya. He was the most unassuming and least important, and just for that reason he commended himself to them, for they wanted a log for their king and had no wish for another Umar. But the result disappointed them, for the weakness of Uthmân did not benefit them but his own house, to whose influence he yielded either willing or carelessly. The Umaiya, like the kin of the Prophet, belonged to the family of

Abd Manâf, and were richer, and more important
and powerful than the Hâshim and Muttalib.
After Badr they had taken the place of the
Makhzûm, whose power was broken by that
battle,[1] and through their wise leader, Abû
Sufyân, gained the hegemony in Mecca and
were the chief figures in the long struggle of
the Quraish against Medina and Muhammad.
Though beaten in this struggle they did not on
that account lose their influential position, but
maintained it in the new commonwealth which
they were obliged to join. Muhammad made
the entrance to it easy for them, and was at
pains to show them that they suffered no disgrace in joining it. When Mecca lost its political importance they emigrated to Medina and
soon took the helm of affairs there, and by
adapting themselves to the times and regulating
their faith according to circumstances, they
gained prominence through the very events
which had threatened their destruction. Already under Abû Bakr and Umar, Yazîd, the
son of Abû Sufyân, and after his death his brother Muâwia, became very prominent in the provinces, if not in Medina. With Uthmân the
Umaiyids actually attained to the Khalifate, for
his government was the government of his
house. He appointed his cousin Marwân his

---

[1] For the rivalry of the Makhzûm and Abd Manâf, cf. B. Hishâm
203 f. ; 429.

chancellor in Medina and left the rule to him, and he filled up all the stattholderships with his relatives. By so doing he incurred the displeasure of his peers, the other members of the Shûrâ. There were five of them,—Alî, Ibn Auf, Talha, Zubair and Ibn Abî Waqqâs. The latter had no political ambition, and Ibn Auf died before Uthmân himself, but these two were replaced by Âyesha, the young widow of the Prophet, who had an equal place with them in the high council of Islam and commanded great respect. The eminent Companions found themselves threatened in the position they had held till then by the coming of a dynasty; this was the reason of their enmity to the Umaiya. Were they, the genuine theocratic nobility which had its roots in Islam, to suffer themselves to be supplanted by an old heathen noble family which had headed the Quraish in the struggle against Islam? They first tried to divert the Khalîfa from his clique, as they called it, and when they did not manage that they turned against the Khalîfa himself. In Medina they did all they could to undermine his authority, and encouraged the discontent of the Arabs in the provinces.

6. Things were in a ferment, at any rate in the provinces, *i. e.* in the towns in which the Arabs dwelt. Times had changed through the cessation of the great wars of conquest. Peace

had followed upon turmoil, sobriety upon debauch. The Arab defenders were no longer kept going by service in the field,—they had leisure to reflect. So long as the Ghanîma, the actual spoil, had kept flowing in to them through the constant campaigns, they had suffered the government to claim the Fai,—the persons and immovable estates of the conquered, as they did not then know what to do with them. But now they perceived that in the storm and stress of the times they had unwittingly allowed themselves to be done out of the more valuable share of the spoil. If they had now received payment of, at least, the full income of the Fai, *i. e.* the yearly amount of the subject-tax, they would not have minded, but, as we have seen, that was not the case. The subject-tax, together with the rest of the state revenues, swelled the treasury; the government only gave the Arab warriors pensions from it. It held the purse-strings, the contents of which really belonged to the army. It became independent of the army by the conquests which the army had made, and which were, by right, army spoil, since it did not divide up land and people but annexed their taxation to itself. And the army became dependent upon it through the pensions which it had the power to bestow or withdraw to whatever amount and extent it pleased. The government used to be supported by the army, now the army was supported by the

government. No wonder that the Muqâtila
thought themselves cheated by this villainous
state, whose backbone was the treasury by which
it exalted itself over them and held the whip
hand. They asserted that money collected as
tribute belonged to them and not to the state,—
that it was Mâl al Muslimîn and not Mâl Allâh
(Tab. 1, 2858 f.). They held to their claim that
the revenues of the Fai ought to be divided ;
when they got the chance they plundered the
provincial treasuries and could not endure that
their surplus should be credited to the state
treasury.   Their jealousy of the state was
naturally directed against its functionaries who
had the disposal of its power and its moneys.
They felt it an injustice that the latter should,
as it were, turn them out of their manger.[1]

As a matter of fact it was a protest against
Umar's system. For Umar it had been who had
wrested the Fai from the hand of the army and
passed it over to the state, in defiance of the
Qoran, though in accordance with a fiscal tendency to a great extent already followed by
Muhammad.[2]   That the discontent arose and

---

[1]   The secular name for " rule," " superiority," " state" is Sultân,
the religious name, Allâh. Sultân is of Aramaic origin, and means
exactly ἐξουσία; κυριότης, not κύριος.

[2]   Muhammad had already claimed for the state the property
which he had won without a struggle. Even in the confiscation of
the old Ahmâ (singular Himâ), and in the marking out of the new
Ahmâ as pastures for the camels and horses in the state-depôt,

spread not under Umar, but under Uthmân, can
be explained not only by the change in the times,
but also by the difference in the personality of
the ruler. Uthmân rightly said that things
were said against him which no one would have
dared to say against Umar. He lacked the
imperious authority of his predecessor ; consequently the despotism and self-seeking of the
stattholders and officials showed up more under
him than under Umar, of whom they were afraid,
and this looked all the worse since he was in the
habit of appointing them from among his own
relatives. The kingdom seemed to have altogether become the domain of a few privileged persons who were permitted to fatten upon the
provinces.

The eminent Companions of the Prophet met
in Medina with the provincials. They had the
great majority of the capital, especially the
Ansâr, with Alî, Talha and Zubair at their head,
to support them in the hatred against Uthmân's
clique,—hatred which in their case arose from a
very different motive. It was a simple matter
for them to give to their rivalry with the latter
the necessary religious emphasis, to claim to be
the true representatives of the old genuine
theocracy and the champions of Qoran and Sunna,

Muhammad had anticipated Umar, and had thus set an example for
the confiscation of domains. *Cf*. Reste arabischen Heidenthums (1897),
p. 107 f.

and to use the general discontent to their own
advantage. Audacious and undutiful as their
behaviour was towards Uthmân, they did not
want to declare war against him openly with the
aid of the men of Medina. They preferred to
send into the fray the provinces, which, in a way,
possessed the military and financial power of the
kingdom, while in Medina was concentrated only
the moral authority of Islam. In the year 34
(A. D. 654-5), they wrote to the provincials :—
" If you wish to begin the holy war, the place for
it is now with us in Medina." This first found
a response in Kufa, the headquarters of the
opposition of the Muqâtila against the government. At the end of the year 34 (June, 655),
when the stattholders during the Hajj were as
usual together in Mecca with the Khalîfa, the
rebellion broke out there, led by Mâlik al-Ashtar,
a prominent inhabitant of the Yemen and a
devoted friend of Alî. A thousand men of Kufa
took up their stand before their town and barred
the entrance to their stattholder Saîd when he
came home from Mecca. However, Uthmân
deposed Saîd without further ado, gave the insurgents a stattholder after their own hearts, and
thus silenced them for the time being.

In place of the men of Kufa, the Egyptians
now set out for Medina. In Egypt, instead of
the conqueror Amr b. Âs, Uthmân had appointed
his cousin Ibn Abî Sarh, although the latter was

outlawed by Muhammad. Amr, a very dangerous man, was consequently his foe, helped to
rouse up feeling against him in Medina, and
probably did not refrain from doing the same in
Egypt. Other revolutionaries there were Muhammad b. Abî Hudhaifa, a foster-son of the
Khalîfa, and Muhammad b. Abî Bakr, a jealous
partisan of Alî. In the great naval battle against
the Emperor Constantine on the Lycian coast,
they separated with their ship from the Arabian
fleet, saying that the true holy war was being
deserted. They made malicious accusations
against Uthmân, reproaching him particularly
with placing his relatives in all the rich posts,
and thus sowed dangerous seed. This was in
A. H. 34. In the following year, 500 Arabs from
Egypt obeyed the summons to the war sanctioned by God against the internal foe. They
appeared before Medina about the tenth month of
the year 35 (April, 656), laid certain demands
before the Khalîfa, and threatened violence if he
should refuse them. The men of Medina, with
few exceptions, took their side and backed them
up. As Uthmân, the ruler of what was then
far the most powerful state on earth, had absolutely no external forces at his disposal in his
residence, he condescended to treat with the
rabble. He managed to persuade the Egyptians
to return by promising them a redress of their
grievances, but as soon as they were away, he

again asserted his position, backed by Marwân and the Umaiyid kin. The next Friday he held a pulpit harangue in the mosque, in which he asserted that the Egyptians had perceived their mistake and had therefore withdrawn. Then the men of Medina, of whom the worshippers consisted, burst into a storm of wrath against him, and, not content with reproaches only, they stoned the old man so that he fell down fainting and had to be carried to his house. This was his last public appearance in the mosque. The men of Medina now appeared in groups before. the Dâr of Uthmân,[1] which was close to the mosque, paying no heed to requests to disperse. After a few days the Egyptians also came suddenly upon the scene, bringing with them a Uriah-letter of the Khalîfa, which they placed before him. He denied having composed it and declared he knew no-thing whatever about it. " Such a thing as that can happen against your will ?" said they, " then you are not Regent !"   But he absolutely refused to take the hint to abdicate, declaring " I will not put off the robe with which God invested me." From that time he was actually besieged; his servants and clients and a few relatives defending him in the Dâr. The men of Medina let the Egyptians alone; if they had

---

[1] Dâr is an enclosed collection of houses or rooms (the Arabic language does not distinguish between the two) with only one door.

wished it would not have been a difficult matter
to be a match for the few hundred men. They
had begun the rising against the Khalîfa and only
left the completion of it to the outside mutineers, and even in this they actually lent their
aid, especially some of the Ansâr. The eminent
Companions, Alî, Talha and Zubair, who were
chiefly to blame for the outbreak of the fire,
made no effort to extinguish it. Their attitude
to the Khalîfa was rather one of regret that they
could not help him because they were not free
agents, but they were only trying to keep up
appearances. In reality they did nothing to
stem the course of events, in the hope that
things would work out to their advantage in the
end.

The decisive change for the worse, the first
bloodshed, was caused by the defenders of the
Dâr. One of them threw a stone at the head of
an old " Companion " who was standing outside
in the crowd, and killed him. Uthmân refused
to deliver up the culprit. Then the besiegers
felt justified and in duty bound to cast aside all
considerations, and began the attack upon the
Dâr; the Egyptian Ibn Udais, of the tribe Balî,
commanded, leaning against the mosque. At
the door the friends of Uthmân fought for him,
and even after it was set on fire they tried to
keep the assaulters at bay. But a few of the
latter had meanwhile penetrated into the Dâr

7

through a neighbouring building, and now
pressed into the very chamber of the Khalîfa,
where he, untroubled by the uproar outside,
was praying with the Qoran before him.
Muhammad b. Abî Bakr, the son of his friend
and predecessor, was the first to lay violent
hands upon him; Kinâna b. Bishr al Tujîbi dealt
the fatal blow, and a few others wreaked their
rage upon the corpse. After this scene there
was no more meaning in fighting, and the
surviving defenders were able to get into safety
without much difficulty. The day was Friday,
the 18th Dhulhijja, 35 (17th June, 656). The
burial of the murdered Khalîfa was delayed for a
considerable time, until, at the urgent request of
his widow, the Kalbite Nâila, a few faithful
ones ventured to accomplish it. The unwashed
body, stretched upon a door, against which the
head kept beating with the uneven steps of the
bearers, was hastily carried out in the gloom of
night, followed by stones and curses. It had to
be laid in the Jewish churchyard; the Ansâr
would not even give it interment in the usual
place; it was no better than the burial of an
animal in a knacker's yard.

7. The murder of Uthmân was more epoch-
making than almost any other event of Islamic
history. From that time the question to whom
the leadership of the theocracy belonged was
fought out with the sword. The Janus-gate of

civil war was opened and never again closed.[1]
The unity of Muhammad's congregation, represented by the Imâm at the head, could be, at
the most, outwardly maintained by force ; in
reality the Jamâa broke up, and split into
factions which always tried to break down each
other's policies, and to take up arms for *their*
Imâm against the Imâm actually in power. It
was a painful dilemma for the pious.[2] If they
held back they ran against the command strongly emphasised by Islam, to show their colours
and enlist by word and deed for the right, and
if they took a side they were disregarding the
fundamental hypothesis of the theocracy, that
the Believers must not spill their own blood, or
fight amongst themselves, but only against
infidels. The question, " What say you to the
murder of Uthmân ? " distracted their minds.

The fruit of the fatal deed fell into Alî's lap.
After the deaths of Abû Bakr, Umar and Ibn
Auf, the son-in-law of the Prophet was indis-
putably the chief of the Companions, and commanded greater respect than Talha and Zubair.
Already, during the bombardment of the Dâr,
he had acted as Imâm in the public worship and
also appointed the leader of the Hajj, and he
was generally regarded in Medina, especially

---

[1] The murdered Khalîfa is on that account called the " opened
gate."

[2] The Civil War is therefore called the *Fitna*, the " temptation."

among the Ansâr, as the fixed successor of
Uthmân. The Egyptians likewise adhered to
him,—they worked for him and for no one else,
and in the confusion of the moment, turned the
scale. On the very day on which Uthmân was
killed, he received public homage in the mosque
of Medina. After the first excitement, it is
true, a reaction set in ; their mood grew calmer ;
the men of Medina did not hail with acclamation the new Khalîfa who had received the power
out of such impure hands, nor did they strongly
support him. At this point it was almost a
stroke of good fortune for him that the two
other " triumviri," Talha and Zubair, turned
shamelessly against him, because he thus found
a real cause of quarrel with them. As long as
Uthmân lived they had zealously agitated
against him, apparently in the interest of Alî,
whom they allowed to do as he pleased, but now
they came forward as competitors, and stigma-
tised him as the instigator of the murder which
had turned out to his advantage. They left
Medina and went to Mecca, where Âyesha, the
Mother of the Faithful, was. She had withdrawn into holy seclusion, away from the rising
against Uthmân, in which she likewise had taken
a considerable part, before it reached its climax,
so as to be able to wash her hands in innocence
of it and still retain her position after it was all
over. She could not endure Alî, and on hearing

that homage had been paid to him, she openly declared Uthmân to be a saint and called for vengeance for him upon the new Khalîfa. A number of fugitives, who at heart thought very differently, rallied round her, while Talha and Zubair came and took shelter behind her. The three were the head and front of the movement against Alî in Arabia, but from Mecca they could not carry on hostilities with the far-distant Medina, so they decided to leave Arabia and go to Basra, where they had connections, and they managed to get possession of the town and make it their stronghold. In face of this, Alî did not think it possible to remain in Medina. He followed them into Irâq, and indeed made for Kufa, where the influential Yemenite, Mâlik al Ashtar, prepared the way for him. With the people of Kufa he then attacked the people of Basra, and conquered them near their town in the Battle of the *Camel*, so-called because it raged round the camel of Âyesha (9th Decr., 656). Talha and Zubair fell ; Âyesha's game was lost, and she retired from the stage. The people of Basra made peace with Alî and all Iraq recognised him, and he remained there, choosing Kufa as his residence.

The immediate consequence, therefore, of the murder of Uthmân was that the old Khalifate in the town of the Prophet ceased to exist, and the new one established itself outside Medina.

The sanctity of the Khalifate was gone; the struggle for it depended upon strength, and the strength lay in the provinces. The tribes had mostly emigrated to the towns that were garrisons; Arabia had lost its centre of gravity. The men of Medina themselves put the finishing touch to the situation by calling in the provincials, and letting them do what they pleased in their town, thereby renouncing their hegemony. The eminent Companions, in particular, committed political suicide, for they destroyed the moral authority upon which their security depended; if it came to be a question of force, then others were superior to them. From that time Arabia, devastated by the general Hijra, sank far below the level upon which it had stood before Islam; we hear pitiful complaints about this in old songs.[1] Medina ceased to be the centre of the kingdom, and all attempts to gain back the lost position were in vain. It remained only the site of Islamic tradition, which there developed into a regular study, and was the cave of Adullam of the displaced members of the Islamic aristocracy so favoured by Muhammad, who, from there, occasionally sought to make their claims heard.

---

[1] The Hudhailite Buraiq complains that where once there dwelt a concourse of men he now is left alone, an old man with a few women and children. So also do Abû Khirâsh and others. The Khalîfa Umar found himself compelled to impress upon a young man who applied for admission into the army that filial duty to his parent was a closer obligation than the Hijra,—quite in the spirit of Mark, vii, 10 ff.

It possessed, however, a natural attraction for people who could live where they chose, who had played out their political *rôle* or withdrawn from active life for other reasons. Thus the town of the Faithful became also the town of the rich and prominent Arab society which wanted to be amused, the town of pleasure, music and song, frivolity and dissoluteness.

From Kufa Alî ruled over the whole Arabian kingdom, but not over Syria. This province occupied an isolated position. The Arabs there had mostly come through the Hijra, and had other traditions than those of Kufa and Basra. They had for long been under Graeco-Roman influence, and even before Islam had belonged to a kingdom, that of the Ghassânids, so they were, in some degree, accustomed to order and obedience. They did not rebel against their stattholder, even though he was an Umaiyid. Muâwia b. Abî Sufyân had for 20 years held the stattholdership of Syria to the general satisfaction, and it did not occur to him to vacate it now and to recognise Alî. His position towards Alî was different from that of Zubair and Talha, and more favourable. He was not a pretender and made no claim to the Khalifate. He took his stand upon the province which he governed, did not see that his office was rendered vacant by the murder of Uthmân, but retained it in opposition to the revolution. He was able to

inscribe upon his standard faithfulness and obedience to the legitimate rule, as opposed to
mutiny, which was nevertheless mutiny, even
though it was raised by the Faithful in the
name of Islam. It was in his favour that he, as
cousin of the murdered Khalîfa, had, before other
relatives, the right and duty of avenging him,
because he alone had the means at his command,
for in Syria he possessed a regular standing
army.

Soon after the Battle of the Camel, Alî and
the men of Iraq marched against the Syrians,
and came upon their army at the Euphrates
boundary. The fierce battle at Siffîn turned
finally in his favour, but when the Syrians were
in danger of being cut to pieces, they stuck
Qorans upon their lance-points. The men of
Iraq understood what was meant by this,—" You
are spilling the blood of Muslims, who follow,
like yourselves, the standard of the Word of
God," and it made an impression upon them.
Their championship of the right in the theocracy
had driven them into the struggle against
Uthmân, then against Âyesha and the people
of Basra, and now against Muâwia and the
Syrians. The Jamâa, the unity of Muhammad's
congregation, was thus going to pieces. Was
this right? At a moment of deep emotion
this antinomy was sharply borne in upon them
and they were bewildered. The Faithful who

were foremost in the fight and acted as an example to the others, first laid down their weapons before the Qoran, and the rest followed their lead. They also compelled Alî to stop the fighting and to have the question of the succession to the Khalifate decided, not by the sword, but by the Qoran, *i. e.* by arbitrators who should be guided by reasons taken from the Qoran, and when he objected they threatened him with the fate of Uthmân. But when the return march from Siffîn to Kufa was begun, it began to dawn upon the whole of Alî's army that they had been done out of the victory by a miserable artifice, and those who had been the first to fall into the trap and lead the others with them now regretted it most bitterly. They blamed themselves grievously for having allowed their conscience to be confused and for having, for one instant, wavered in their conviction of the divine justice of the revolution against Uthmân, but they also reproached Alî for consenting to the decision by arbitration, thus virtually making the goodness of the cause for which they were fighting a matter of question. They demanded that he should immediately cancel the act to which they themselves had forced him against his will, and break the treaty just concluded with the Syrians. When he could not comply, and dance to whatever tune they piped, they

8

renounced him and occupied a separate camp at Harûra, near Kufa. They therefore got the name of Harûrites, but more commonly Khawârij (seceders or rebels).

This time they did not draw the crowd with them. The men of Iraq, amongst the foremost of whom are always to be understood the men of Kufa, held fast, as a whole, to Alî. But his relations to them were different from those of Muâwia to the Syrians, and not so kindly. Muâwia was not risen from the ranks, but held the authority of a superior over them ; he did not owe his position to his inferiors, but was independent of them,—when he ordered they obeyed. They were also, of course, con- vinced that he had right on his side in fighting against the murder of Uthmân, but in any circumstances they would have made his cause their own. They had long known and respected him, and besides, from earlier times, they had been used to a certain military atmosphere. On the other hand, men could not forget that Alî owed his power to a revolution, and he had neither the time nor the means to make up for this detraction by exceptional personal qualities. The men of Iraq did not forget that it was they who had advanced him ; they were too undisciplined, or perhaps too devout, to follow their Khalîfa where he led them. They certainly regretted when it was too late that they had lost him the game at Siffin, but they did not make good their error by now strongly assisting him against the Syrians, after the decision by arbitration had passed as a jest and hostilities were renewed. He could not rouse them to a fresh campaign, for they rendered him no obligatory service urgently, as he required it, but allowed Muâwia to conquer Egypt, and to harass Iraq by flying squadrons which made inroads as far as Kufa. When they at last gathered together and were ready for a *sortie*, Alî was killed, and his son and successor, Hasan, felt unequal to the position and sold his claims to Muâwia. The latter was now able to make a formal entry into Kufa, and the men of Iraq had to pay him homage. This ended the civil war.

8. The Umaiyids had won the Khalifate, but it was only in Syria (with Mesopotamia and Egypt) that they had a firm seat. Everywhere else they encountered opposition both secret and open. They could only maintain their position by force, and were almost always occupied in preventing or stamping out a revolution, the centre-point of these revolutions being, as before, Iraq, especially the town of Kufa.

In the contest with the Syrians the men of Iraq were overcome, at least they had lost the game. Consequently the Khalifate, and with it the chief treasury, migrated from Kufa to

Damascus. This they felt bitterly when it was too late. They had been possessors of the kingdom, and now they had sunk to a mere province. The revenue of the land they had conquered was lost to them, and they had to be content with the crumbs of pensions which fell from their masters' tables. They were held in check by means of the dole which they could not do without, and which might at will be curtailed or withdrawn. No wonder they thought the rule of the Syrians a heavy yoke, and were ready to shake it off whenever they found a favourable opportunity. The strongest rising against the Umaiyids originated in Iraq and was made, not by one particular faction, but by the whole of the Arabs of that place, who were at one in their rancour over the loss of their former autocracy, and in hatred of those who had inherited it. Specially powerful officials were always required to keep the difficult province peaceful and obedient, but finally it could only be managed by the suppression of the native military and the introduction of Syrian garrisons, by the establishment of an actual military government, which had its headquarters no longer in the old capital of the country, but in a newly erected fortified town.

The cause of the province became also the cause of Islam. God and the right took the field against force; the opposition united with the Faith. It is the duty of the Muslim to further the good by word and deed, and to prohibit the sinful; he must not only do the will of Allah himself, but also do his best to make it paramount in the community. Quietism is not tolerated; the Faith makes the individual take a share in public life by making him personally responsible for the whole. Its testing-ground is politics,—that is the very idea of the theocracy.[1] In itself the religion had now the power to act as a support to the existing order of things, and to teach men that their duty was to obey their superiors and to do nothing which would cause schism in the community, but in point of fact it used its power chiefly to regulate the opposition. The idea of the theocracy was in critical opposition to the form of the community as it had come to be. It refused to allow that history possesses a legitimising power, that the state follows its own *raison d'être*, the maintaining and increasing of its power, and that the existing government is hardly to be distinguished from it. It was a lasting reproach against the Umaiyids that they had been, root and branch, the most dangerous foes of the Prophet, had only, under compulsion, embraced Islam at the

---

[1] Thanks to the disastrous results, an evangelical tendency asserted itself in Islam, as it were, which kept its distance from politics as a Fitna (temptation) and distrusted its religious motives. Highborn representatives of this tendency were Saîd b. al-Musaiyab in Medina, and Hasan al-Basri.

eleventh hour, and then had contrived to divert to themselves the fruits of its government, first by the weakness of Uthmân, and then by the clever manipulation of the results of his murder. Their origin disqualified them for the leadership of Muhammad's congregation ; it was a disgrace to the theocracy that they should appear as its chief representatives ; they were, and remained, usurpers. Their strength was in their standing army, in Syria, but their might could never become right. The hatred against the Umaiyids was increased by the old grievances against the " Sultân," which were now become grievances against them as its present possessors. It was always the same points which were insisted upon,—that the officials abused their power, that the moneys of the state went into the pockets of the few while the many received nothing, that adultery, fornication, gambling and drinking had become the chief pleasures and went unpunished.[1] The leaders of the chorus of the Faithful were the Fuqahâ and the Qurrâ, the authorities upon religious law and the repeaters of the Qoran. They opposed the Umaiyids just

---

[1]   Zulm, Isti'thâr (in the Fai), Ta'tîl al-Hudûd. It was also re-quired that the officials be held responsible and should give satisfaction (Qawad) for the injustice which they had committed in office to those who had suffered from it. The Khalîfas did not concede this. Their demand of an account of stewardship from the retiring stattholders was limited to the extortion from them of as much money as possible.

in the same way as the Judaean Scribes and
Pharisees opposed the Hasmonaeans. The law
which they opposed to the ruling power was
likewise an absolutely positive law, written and
traditional; it was to be found in the Qoran and
the Sunna. They interpreted it from the Qoran
and manipulated it into the Sunna, which was
still in an extremely fluid state, getting the
political questions of later times decided by the
Prophet in their sense, often, indeed, in a somewhat contradictory fashion.

The most thorough-going representatives of
the theocratic opposition, the most pious of the
pious, were the Khawârij. With them the
divine right became a thoroughly revolutionary
principle. They prided themselves upon the
initial act of the revolution, the murder of
Uthmân; unlike those who were ashamed of the
deed after it was done, they made an open
acknowledgment of it their shibboleth. With the
rest of the men of Iraq, they first maintained
the revolution against Muâwia, who did not
recognise it, but they continued it also against
Alî when he made terms in the affairs of God,
and thus separated from his adherents. Although
they had helped to assert his claim they were
still not willing to be his party in the sense that
the Syrians were the party of Muâwia. The *Dîn*
(the religion) was to them neither Dîn Muâwia
nor Dîn Alî, but Dîn Allâh only, and whoever

sacrificed to the regent, on any point whatever, his own religious and political conviction, whoever placed obedience to him before obedience to God, made him an idol ; and idolaters were idolaters, and not Muslims.   The Khawârij considered that they alone were Muslims, and even claimed the name for themselves alone. Thus they shamelessly spilled the blood of the other Muslims, for it was against them and them only that they waged the holy war. The reproach that they were thus breaking up the Jamâa did not affect them ; they protested against the miserable catholicity which did not separate the wheat from the chaff; they alone, the heretics, formed the true Jamâa.   Islam was concentrated in their camp; thither they emigrated from the false Jamâa, after the example of the Hijra of the Prophet.   Although their ideas were quite anti-dynastic, still, as representatives of the unity of the congregation of Believers, even they had their Khalîfa or Imâm, who led the worship and commanded the army.   But they watched his actions, took him to task as soon as they thought he made a false step, and renounced him as an unbeliever if he did not reform.   Over the question of the rightful Imâm, therefore, they quarrelled not only with the other Muslims, but among themselves as well. Differences of opinion on smaller points caused division amongst them.   They laid such stress upon the theocratic principle, and made it out to be so much a matter of belief and conscience, that they practically reduced it to absurdity, while it proved absolutely useless or positively destructive to the stability of the community. All their energy was directed towards an unattainable goal; religion brought them to an active, but absolutely impolitic and desperate polity. They were not unconscious of this themselves. They renounced success; their only wish was to save their souls. They were content to meet death on the battlefield, and with it pardon in the sight of God; they sold their lives for the price of Paradise. In spite of this, perhaps just because of it, they often overcame great armies, and for a time were the terror of the Muslim world, and although they always were only a small sect, still they could not be extirpated. They seemed to spring up again out of the ground, their principles possessed such an unconquerable recruiting-power. The opposition in other places to the existing government, pious as it claimed to be, was still always animated by worldly interests, and so had a different aspect; it was often made use of by ambitious men who were only striving after power. In the confused concert the Khawârij kept steadily to the key given by the tuning-fork of Islam. They strove most openly and decisively for the Kingdom of God, and also most fiercely for a pitiless Utopia.

9

Though likewise sprung from the revolution against Uthmân, the Shîites had very different aims from the Khawârij. They hated the Umaiyids still more bitterly than the Khawârij, not because they rejected a dynasty in the theocracy in general, but because they set up the just and lawful dynasty in opposition to the false one, namely, the house of the Prophet, the head of which after his death was his cousin and son-in-law Alî. The name *Shia* is contracted from Shîat Alî, which means the " party of Alî." The Shîat Alî were first the men of Iraq specially, as distinguished from the Syrians, the Shîat Muâwia. Even after his death Alî remained for the men of Iraq the symbol of their lost autocracy. Their Shîitism was no more than the expression of the feeling of hatred of the subdued province, especially the degraded capital, Kufa, against the Umaiyids. The heads of the tribes and families of Kufa originally shared this feeling with the rest, but their responsible position compelled them to be circumspect. They did not take aught to do with aimless risings, but restrained the crowd when they let themselves be carried away, and in the name of peace and order placed their influence at the service of the government so as not to endanger their own position. In this way they became more and more strangers and foes to the more open and positive Shîites,

whose attachment to the heirs of the Prophet
was not lessened but increased by the failure of
romantic declarations. The Shîa itself was
narrowed and intensified by the opposition to
the leading aristocracy of the tribes, and broke
off from the majority of the Arabs. In these
circumstances a sect rose into prominence in
Kufa which till then had remained out of sight;
it bore the name of the Sabaïtes. These
Sabaïtes changed the character of Islam completely by setting beside and above the impersonal law (in Qoran and Sunna), which for the
others after Muhammad's death was sufficient,
and, for the Khawârij especially, was the only
authority excluding all human service and all
human deification, the personal Prophet, who,
in their opinion, had not died with Muhammad,
but continued to live successively in his heirs.
They started upon the idea of metempsychosis,
and introduced into it the special idea that even
the spirit of God animating the prophets, after
the death of one passed over to another, that,
in particular, the prophetic spirit of Muhammad
had passed to Alî and continued in his family.
Alî was thus in their eyes not merely the
legitimate successor of the Khalîfas before
him; he was not on the same level as Abû
Bakr and Umar, who had pushed in as usurpers
between him and Muhammad, but he was the
incarnation of the divine spirit, the heir of the

prophecy and therefore, after Muhammad's death, the only possible ruler of the theocracy, which must have, as its leader, a living representative of the Godhead.[1]   The Sabaïtes are said to derive their name from a Jew of the Yemen, Ibn Saba. They originated in a few Arabian tribes of Kufa, but they spread abroad, particularly among the numerous Persian freedmen of that place who had received Islam, *i.e.* among non-Arabs. They attained political importance through the famous Thaqifite, Mukhtâr, who made them his body-guard. He even won over to himself the old Shîites, and took the opportunity, when anarchy and schism were again rife, to overthrow the Arabian aristocracy in Kufa and to set up there a government with himself at its head, in which Shîitism was to wipe out the difference between Arabs and Persians, masters and subjects. But his success was short-lived. His Shîa was suppressed, but he had paved the way for its success later on.

9. This religious, or speciously religious, opposition could, however, hardly have been so dangerous to the Umaiyids if it had not been for the rivalry of the Arab tribes, a rivalry which had nothing to do with the theocracy but

[1]   They certainly allowed the name of the Prophet to Muhammad only, but in point of fact they made his heirs equal to him, ascribed to them divine authority and regarded them as infallible (ma'sûm).

had its origin entirely in "Arabism," and indeed through the Imperium to which the Arabs had attained by the conquests, had risen to a far greater height than it had done in pre-Islamic heathendom. The stattholders excited it still more. They had only at their immediate disposal a small *Shurta*, or *gendarme ie*; for the rest their troops consisted of the Muqâtila of the province, *i.e.* the militia, the defending force of the tribes. By clever manipulation they were able to play off the tribes against each other and maintain their position over them. But this was only successful in the case of a few, and only in the beginning of the Umaiyid period. It mostly happened that the stattholder relied upon one tribe against the others, generally upon his own, which he often brought with him to begin with. Now the tribe which he raised to be his household troops shared with him in the government and the privileges which the disposal of the offices and moneys put into their hands. But with a new stattholder another tribe came into power, with the result that the displaced tribe became the bitter foes of the tribe now in power. So the ethnical distinctions were tainted with politics and disputes over the political spoil. In this respect the province of Khurâsân belonging to Basra was the worst. There, through Ibn Khâzim the Qais reached

great power, and through Muhallab the Azd
Umân. In place of the old quarrel between
Bakr and Tamîm, there broke out first discord
between Qais and Tamîm, then between Azd
and Qais, and finally between Azd-Rabîa and
Qais-Tamîm. In Syria and Mesopotamia the
Qais and the Kalb took different sides in the
dispute about the Khalifate between Ibn Zubair
and the Umaiyids, and thus began a fierce
struggle which caused the hostile relations to
remain after the original political reason for
them had long vanished. The differences
became more dangerous because of the tendency
which already existed to the formation of large
tribal-groups.[1] In Syria as well as in Khurâsân
the Qais played a prominent part in politics.
They were scattered everywhere, and were
strongly represented in the high offices by the
Thaqîf who belonged to them. They held
closely together, and were the first to form
a real clique throughout the whole kingdom,
shamelessly striving to gain the ruling power.
In the same great group as the Qais were
also reckoned the Tamîm, who were most
numerous in Basra and Khurâsân, but they,
to their credit, were distinguished by a
lofty pride in their clan, nor did they strive
so eagerly after posts, nor take so much to do
with high politics. They were not originally

---

[1] *Cf.* above, pp. 27 f.

on good terms with the Qais, but latterly united with them in the great confederacy of Mudar. On the other side, the Azd Umân, in Basra and Khurâsân, were the most venomous foes of the Qais and Tamîm. They joined with the rest of the Yemenites, who in Khurâsân included the Rabîa (Bakr), and lastly the Syrian Qudâa (Kalb) were also drawn into the circle. They passed as Yemenites, but whether they were so is doubtful. In reality they were driven into the arms of the Yemenite party only by enmity towards the Qais.[1] So the dangerous cleavage went on increasing,[2] the Quraish and the Umaiya themselves could not hold their ground above the dualism which was splitting the whole Arab world into two camps.

The non-Arabs pressed into the cleft. They came over to Islam in great numbers, especially the crowds of Iranian prisoners of war in Kufa and Basra, thus gaining their personal freedom,[3] but not full civil and military rights with their

---

[1] *Cf.* Qutâmî (ed. Barth), 29, 56, 93 ff.

[2] The cleavage, however, was not strict ; it might vary with passing motives in the individual. One tribe backed this or that party of its connection so as to prove its adherence to some powerful one or other whose favour was of importance to them. The poets in particular had a weakness for claiming kinship with those in high places.

[3] It was, of course, only a custom and not a duty to set free the prisoners of war if they accepted Islam. The conclusion was never drawn that a Muslim in the sight of God and the law cannot' be the slave of a Muslim ; on the contrary it was understood that slaves followed the religion of their master, especially those born in their master's house,

material advantages; they became Mawâlî, clients of some Arabian family. Only thus, as subordinate adherents of Arab families, were they received into the theocracy; Islam alone was not sufficient, for the theocracy was, in fact, a specifically Arab state, an Imperium of the Arabs over the conquered peoples. This was contrary to the idea of the theocracy, which was not to be an Imperium (*Mulk*), nor even allowed to have one, and especially so when it was a case of Arabs ruling over non-Arab Muslims. Faith in Allah and the acknowledgment of His supreme power utterly excluded national differences. Thus Islam was used as a suitable means of gaining for the Mawâlî their share in the theocracy, so as to snatch the privilege afterwards from the Arabs. The pious Arabs themselves favoured the claims of the Mawâlî; the parties of the opposition, in particular, sought in them allies against the Umaiyids, who actually represented the ruling power of the Arabian nation, and not of Islam. The Khawâ- rij led the way by admitting the Mawâlî with equal rights into their community and army. The Shîites followed suit with much greater effect. As we saw, a Shîite sect in Kufa allied itself with the Mawâlî there, and so at once advanced itself and the Iranians. In Kufa it- self it was certainly soon suppressed again by the Arabs and sank into oblivion, but it later

transplanted itself from Kufa to genuine Iranian
soil, namely, to Khurâsân, and spread there
among the native population that had embraced
Islam. Under the standard of Islam, *i.e.* of
Shîitism, the Khurâsânites first drove the Arabs
out of their own land, and then made a complete
end of the Arabian rule, and set up the Abbâsids
in the place of the Umaiyids.

10. The usual conceptions of Orientalism
are much in need of correction, and in the
history of Islam, at any rate, must be disregarded, so long as the Arabs were the ruling nation.
Politics, and not forsooth the work of civilisa-
tion, here stand in the foreground and completely absorb the interest. Politics do not
mean Fate in the form of an absolute despotism,
but the sacred affairs of all Muslims, in which
they take part, body and soul, even if it be
without understanding of the nature and
limits of a human commonwealth. They
are swayed by universal tendencies, religious, national and social. The amalgamation
of these tendencies and their contest with the
existing order of things, which was seldom
represented by long reigns and men of years,[1]
results in a great confusion, and the review is

---

[1] Most of the Khalîfas and stattholders were young, and did not
live to be old men, except Muâwia and Nasr b. Saiyâr. They generally also ruled only a short time, though the stattholdership changed
hands with even more frequency than the Khalifate.

not rendered easier by the fact that the scene comprises the nations and lands extending from the Indian to the Atlantic Ocean. This introductory chapter seemed necessary as a preparation and guide so that the reader might grasp and retain the thread of the following account, and also to prevent the mistake of supposing that the following researches into the history of the oldest Islam are exhaustive. Their main subject is the Umaiyids, and the struggle of the sway which represents Arabian government with the opposing powers, and its final subjection in face of the revolution which continues from the end of the Khalifate of Medina. There is no room here for a thorough treatment of the parties and provinces each in its particular point of view, although that would be just as important for the proper comprehension of Islam. In a separate chapter I have collected a few notes upon the specially interesting province of Khurâsân. With regard to the Khawârij and the Shîa, and also the wars against the Romans at this period, I refer readers to the lectures printed in the *Nachrichten der philosophisch-historischen Klasse der Göttinger Gesellschaft der Wissenschaften*, 1901.

CHAPTER II.

Alî and the First Civil War.

According to Madâini, on the authority of Abû Mikhnaf (Agh. 15, 71), Nâila, wife of the murdered Khalîfa Uthmân, sent his bloody shirt to Muâwia, with an account of the circumstances of the murder, in which she quoted the prophetic verse, Sura 49, 9. The latest account from Saif which is preserved in Tabarî (1, 3255) says that Nu'mân b. Bashîr brought Uthmân's bloody garment and Nâila's amputated fingers to Damascus. The fingers are added, so Nâila herself does not fit in. According to a further statement of Saif, Muâwia displayed the gory relics in the mosque in order to stir up his Syrians. This exhibition lasted a whole year, because there was just a year between the death of Uthmân and the encounter at Siffin. Madâini, quoting 'Awâna (Tab. 1, 3254 f.; *cf.* Kâmil, 183 f.; Dînawarî, 166 f.) only relates that, in front of Jarîr, who was sent by Alî to demand his allegiance, Muâwia stirred up the vengefulness of the Syrians, and by doing so also created the desired impression. Thus the affair was only a mockery to make Alî afraid of attacking him. According to Wâqidî in Tab. 1, 3252 ff., Muâwia did not incite others

against Alî so much as they did him. In verses
which are still preserved, his cousin Walîd b.
Uqba reproached him with exchanging letters
with Alî and not bestirring himself, as a relative,
to fulfil his duty of revenge. He was by nature
a diplomatist, and was all the less eager for
the struggle with the people of Iraq because
he was threatened at the same time by the
Romans, and also by the Egyptians who were
on Alî's side. He did not aim at the Khalifate;
his first ambition, at least, was only to hold
fast to his province of Syria and get possession
of Egypt, which he dared not leave to his
opponents if he wanted to protect himself in the
rear. Amr b. Âs also urged him to do this, for
he regarded the mutiny against Uthmân as a
means to an end, and did all he could to get back
his former province, and after the old Khalîfa's
death made an honourable but shrewd compact
with Muâwia in order to compass this (3253 f.
cf. Dînaw., 167 ff.). So Muâwia and Amr first
marched against Egypt and succeeded in trick-
ing Alî's stattholder there, Muhammad Ibn Abî
Hudhaifa, and taking him prisoner (3252 f.,
3407 ff.), but they had then to turn back in
order to meet Alî himself. Alî was the aggressor; he was making claims upon the Khalifate
and the rule of the whole kingdom. After
making sure of Iraq and completing his preparations, he left the general camp in Nukhaila,

near Kufa,[1] at the end of the year 36 (Spring,
657 A.D.), and made for the west where a
number of Basraites had made their appearance.
Muâwia and Amr awaited him on the Syrian
border in the plain of Siffîn on the Euphrates,
not far from Raqqa.[2]

The account of the battle of Siffin in Tabarî
is almost exclusively that of Abû Mikhnaf. Alî
with the main body took the usual army route
by the Tigris, and then through Mesopotamia.
Near Qarqîsiâ he was met by his vanguard,
which really ought to have been marching on
the right bank of the Euphrates. After crossing the Euphrates near Raqqa they were met
near the Roman wall by the Syrian vanguard,
which withdrew without engaging. When they
were going to pitch their camp, it turned out
that the Syrians had occupied the approach to
the water, *i.e.* to the Euphrates, and as fair
words were of no avail, the Syrians were driven
back by force, but not cut off from the water
(3259-69). For two months, Dhulhijja, 36 and
Muharram, 37, the armies encamped opposite

---

[1]   To the west or north of Kufa on the road to Syria (1, 3345).
Buwaib was situated there. The battle of Buwaib is also called the
Battle of Nukhaila.

[2]   Between Barbalissus and Caesarium (Theoph., A.M. 6148),
Barbalissus is Balis (Balâdh., 150 f. Assem., B.O., 2, 332). Theophanes,
A.M. 6151, calls the name Sapphin ; in the Syrian inscri tion of Hanash
(Journ. As., 1900, II, 285 ff.) under Sel. 968 it is called Sapphe or
Sepphe in the stat. emph., likewise in the Cosmographer of
Ravenna, where Sephe and Barbalission occur side by side.

each other.   At last on Wednesday, the 8th Safar, 37,[1] a general battle began, which was continued on Thursday morning with greater energy.   The Syrians were better equipped, and had a far more soldierly appearance than the men of Iraq (3322). Before their choice troops the Yemenites of Kufa on Alî's right wing began to waver, notwithstanding the desperate courage of their *readers*. But towards evening Mâlik al-Ashtar rallied them and forced the enemy step by step back to their camp. The battle lasted through the night till morning ; this is the real " Night of Clangour," and not that of Qâdisîa.[2] Muâwia was meditating flight, and victory was on the point of falling to Ashtar, when he had to let it slip out of his grasp and put up his sword at the repeated command of Alî. The Syrians had actually fastened copies of the Qoran upon their lance-points so as to appeal from the decision of arms, which threatened to result unfavourably for them, to the decision of the Word of God. The men of Iraq let themselves be tricked and forced Alî, with threats of personal violence, to stop the battle and treat with Muâwia. On the proposal

---

[1] Wednesday, 26th July, 657 A. D. = 6148 A.M., 968 Sel. *Cf.* the previous note.

[2] Tab., 1, 3027, Kâmil, 753. It must have been Thursday night, but according to Tabarî, 2, 727 the battle of Siffin is on Wednesday night, and likewise in the tradition of Abû Mikhnaf. *Cf.* Anon. Ahlw., 349.3.

of the latter, two trusty men were chosen to decide according to the Qoran to whom the ruling power was due,—Amr from the Syrians, Abû Mûsâ from the Iraqites. The decision was to be pronounced in the month of Ramadân at a place situated between Syria and Iraq.§ Abû Mikhnaf's narrative of the battle of Siffin is very long, after the style of the narratives of the battles of Qâdisîa and Nihâwand. The history of events before the real engagement began occupies a good deal of space, and yet Muharram is empty of events, only the preceding and following months are filled up,—both, indeed, in the same way,—firstly, by a disposition to make overtures of peace, and secondly, after the failure of these overtures, by single combats in which he has the opportunity of introducing the prominent partisans both of Muâwia and Alî. Though the names of the persons concerned vary the second time, this does not alter the similarity of the material, so we might conclude that the prelude in Dhulhijja really coincides with that in Safar, and is not separated from the actual battle by the whole length of Muharram.[1] In this way the time of delay before the battle would be considerably

[1] Dînawarî mentions the single combats only once, and that in the second place, so that they come in as the prelude to the general engagement. Moreover, he has a much more exact knowledge of the whole thing than Abû Mikhnaf, especially of the minutiae. The first Qoran held up by the Syrians was the beautiful copy of Damascus,

shortened. There can be no doubt that on both sides a certain aversion to continuing the decision by the sword had arisen (Dînaw., 192, 5; 195, 9; 201, 15). They were in no hurry to begin. Perhaps also the old traditional scruple against shedding blood in Muharram had to do with it. A verse quoted in Dîn., 182, and Masûdî, 4, 350, alludes to this;—"Only a few days of Muharram remain, and then the dice fall."§ We have no clear picture of the course of the actual battle; it is described with just as great confusion as it was fought. We certainly find over and over again systematic accounts of the distribution, arrangement and leadership of the troops, but they do not agree with each other, and so have hardly any practical value for the real course of the battle. The description is a mass of one-sided traditions dealing with episodes, and the attempt of the editor to make a mosaic unity of it is a failure. There is a lack of inward connection; you cannot see the wood for the trees. Every witness is inclined to regard the station of his own tribe as the centre-point, and to ascribe the chief glory to the heroes of his tribe. It is only the issue that shows plainly that Mâlik-al-Ashtar was the real hero of the day, but as such he

and was fastened to five lances and borne by five men (201, 20). This is exactly as it is in Saif, with whom Dînawarî is in line. Still, the verses which he reports are valuable.

is openly praised only in the verses of the poet Najâshî (Dîn., 198), who himself took part in the battle. "The Syrians pressed forward incessantly; then we called up against them the battering-ram of Iraq, and Ashtar drove them back." But for this he is on a level with many others whose deeds are just as fully celebrated.[1] Besides the tribe-leaders, Alî himself receives special prominence along with his cousin Ibn Abbâs. Great stress is laid upon the fact that the *readers* held their ground when the others fled before the Syrians, and that they went to their death for Alî; they become martyrs for him and furnish the strongest proof of his just claim. As leaders are mentioned Ibn Budail, Hâshim b. Utba and especially the old Ammâr b. Yâsir, of whom the Prophet is reported to have said that he would fall in battle against a godless race (B. Hishâm, 337). Ashtar is put in the shade by this. The later traditionists have a dislike to him, perhaps because, like Saif, they regard him as a revolutionary. Masûdî and Yaqûbî will have nothing to say to him and ascribe all the merit to the supreme command of Alî. Tabarî does the same (3321 f.), but Abû Mikhnaf does not go so far. He describes sympathetically the

[1] Amongst them also some who seem not to have been present at all, as Qais b. Sa'd. *Cf.* below, p. 96. What the pious Abul, Dardâ would have done is invented by Dînawarî, 181.

11

brilliant military appearance of the Yemenite hero (3297) and recognises the effect of his strong personality. He did not stand where Alî placed him, but at the head of his tribe, the Nakha'; his enthusiasm and initiative made him leader both of the Hamdân and the Madhhij, and with them he wrested the victory from the Syrians. Also, he was the only sensible man when the others let themselves be cheated out of the glory of the battle,—a genuine Arab nobleman as opposed to the pious bigots and the lukewarm or cunning politicians.

An account of the Syrian side has not been preserved to us. It would make different reading from that of Abû Mikhnaf, though it would scarcely be more credible, as we see from Theophanes, A.M. 6148: "Muawia's side gained the mastery and took possession of the water; Alî's men deserted because of thirst; still Muâwia did not wish to fight but won the victory easily." Of course Abû Mikhnaf sides with the Iraqites and Alî against the Syrians and Muâwia. Alî has the better cause and the more pious followers. The fact that his own brother Aqîl fought against him is passed over in silence,[1] but there is no concealment of the fact that the Syrians had sons of the Khalifas

---

[1] Bukhârî (ed. Bulaq, 1289), 2. 67 f., 139, 145, 3. 11. Deutsche Morgenl. Ztschr. (DMZ.), 1884, 93.

Abû Bakr and Umar on their side besides 4,000 *readers*, who thus were not solely on the side of Alî, and that they were just as convinced of the justice of their cause as the Iraqites. The latter, indeed, were by no means all firmly convinced of the right of Alî, but kept asking each other for proofs, and held discussions amongst themselves and with their opponents,— discussions which continued long after Siffin and were interminable.[1] They were not eager for the struggle with their brothers in faith and race, and appeared quite willing to put a stop to it. The party-opposition was weak to begin with, and only gained strength later on.

2.   Abû Mikhnaf's report of the succeeding events is as follows. On the return march which was made by the shortest road on the right bank of the Euphrates, the Iraqites thought matters over. They upbraided each other and Alî as well, though he had only stopped the battle under compulsion, and when he marched into Kufa twelve thousand men separated from him and camped in Harûra.

---

[1] There appeared in a dream to the Nakha'ite Alqama his brother who had fallen at Siffin. He said that the slain Iraqites and Syrians had quarrelled in heaven as to which cause was the just one, and God had decided for the Iraqites. Hudhaifa of Madâin referred two men who were doubtful which side to take in the dilemma to the decision of the Prophet that the slayers of Ammâr were the godless side. Verses of Ka'b b. Ju'ail and other poets in Dînaw., 199 ff., 206, testify to the justice of the Syrians' claim.

They are called Khawârij or Harûrites[1] ; their watchword was a protest against the decision by arbitration :—" The decision belongs to God alone ! " Their leaders were Shabath b. Rib'î al Riâhî, Abdullâh b. Kauwâ al Yashkurî and Yazîd b. Qais al Arhabî, the most prominent men of the great tribes Tamîm, Bakr and Hamdân in Kufa. Alî indeed succeeded in winning back these leaders to his side. To one of them he promised and granted the statt-holdership of Ispahan and Rai. The Harûrites now returned to Kufa and joined him, but they expected, and asserted that he had promised them, that he would lead them at once against the Syrians. When he did not do so, but in Ramadân, 37, arranged for the court of arbitra-tion at Duma, they held that he had broken his word, broke away from him again and set up in opposition to him their own Khalifa, the Azdite Abdullâh b. Wahb al Râsibî, to whom they paid homage on the 10th Shauwal, 37 (21st March, 658). Then, one after the other, they left Kufa and gathered in Nahrawân on the other side of the Tigris.[2] Thither also they summoned their confederates from Basra, who

[1] Cf. the Abh. der Göttinger Societät, Band V, No. 2 (190L) upon the religious and political opposition parties in old Islam.

[2] Nahrawân (Ναρβας) is the name of the well-known canal in the district of Jûkhâ belonging to Madâin (Tab., 2, 900), and also the name of a place near it which is more precisely called Nahrawansbridge (Dînaw., 217). For the district of Jûkhâ, see Tab., 3,275 ; 385 ; 406.

joined them to the number of 500 men under Mis'ar b. Fadakî of Tamîm.

After the farce of the arbitration court was over Alî thought himself justified in reopening the hostilities against the Syrians. He gathered his army in the camp of Nukhaila and summoned the Khawârij also to join him. But they did not come; they demanded that he should publicly acknowledge and express regret for his defection,—so they termed his reluctant yielding at Siffin. Alî was now going to march against the Syrians without them, but his army insisted upon an expedition against the Khawârij because the latter, on the way from Basra to Nahrawân, had slaughtered Abdullâh b. Khabbâb b. Aratt, the son of the oldest adherent of the Prophet (B. Hishâm, 234), along with his wife, and Alî had to yield to their urgency. In vain he tried to induce the Khawârij to deliver up the murderers of their own accord. In vain he tried to persuade them that, as a matter of fact, his point of view was the same as theirs, and that he was willing to let the sword decide against the common foe. They replied,—" To-morrow you will again do just as you did at Siffin." They could come to no agreement and prepared for a mortal struggle.

According to Abû Mikhnaf, the battle of Nahrawân took place in A. H. 37,—towards the end of the year indeed, for the Khawârij had

not left Kufa till Shauwal, the third-last month.
Their leaders of Harura had forsaken them ;
Shabath took an eager part in the struggle
against them, and likewise Ash'ath who had
before been reckoned as one of their confederates. In addition, they were not so numerous
as in the camp of Harura, being only 4,000 strong.
Many of these yet slunk back to Kufa, about 100
openly went over to Alî, and 500 horsemen
under Farwa b. Naufal wheeled round towards
Daskara ; the rest were cut down except eight.

With the annihilation of the Khawârij,
however, the men of Kufa were satisfied ; they
no longer wanted war with the Syrians, and Alî
had to yield to their wishes. He had soon to
deal with other rebels whose pretext was likewise the arbitration court, though they used it
very differently from the Khawârij. After the
battle of the Camel Khirrît b. Râshid of the
Nâjia had followed Alî to Kufa with 300 men
and fought for him at Siffin and also at
Nahrawân. But when Alî did not recognise
the decision of the court of arbitration, he
broke away from him and made his way by
Madhâr to Ahwâz. Besides Kufaites and other
Arabs who shared his political views, there
joined him many non-Arabs who objected to
paying the taxes. Overcome at Râmhurmuz
by a Kufaite army under Ma'qil b. Qais
al-Tamîmî, he withdrew to Bahrain, his

native place, and there not only incited the Nâjia, who had withheld the tax since A. H. 37, but also the Abdulqais. He told the people what they wanted to hear. With regard to the Khawârij, he blamed Alî for letting men decide in the affairs of God; otherwise he stuck to his original opinion that Alî ought to have accepted the sentence of the arbitration court. He justified those who refused to pay the taxes by saying that the tax (*Sadaqa*) ought to benefit the poor of its own land and not the treasury. He even won over to himself those Muslims who had fallen back upon Christianity when they saw the deadly strife within the congregation of Muhammad, by showing them that they would have nothing to expect from Alî but execution for their defection. But Ma'qil b. Qais, who had driven him out of Ahwaz, did not let him alone in Bahrain either and a bloody encounter took place. Three times the Nâjia withstood the attack of the superior force, but when Khirrît and 170 men with him had fallen, the rest scattered and all was over.

Such is the account of Abû Mikhnaf in Tabarî, I, 3345-86, 3418-43.[1] According to Yaqûbî and the Kâmil or Dînawarî his account cannot be improved on, but it is open to some objections, especially as regards the chronology.

---

[1] There is a blank in Tabarî's MS. filled in, in the Leiden edition (3364-68), from B. Athîr.

After it has been first stated that the Khawârij had not chosen a Khalifa till a month after the arbitration court, and that then they had betaken themselves to Nahrawân, it is here presupposed that they were already there when Alî got word of the result of the sentence, and straightway gathered in Nukhaila against the Syrians; therefore they must have already left Kufa before the arbitration court. And if Khirrît was still fighting for Alî at Nahrawân, but became incensed at him because of the arbitration court, then actually the battle of Nahrawan took place before the arbitration court.[1] By these alterations in the sequence of events the whole pragmatism in Abû Mikhnaf is now upset. Alî could not think of waging war with the Syrians till after the court of arbitration. If, then, Nahrawân falls earlier, the gathering of the troops in Nukhaila cannot have been concerned with the Syrians but only with the Khawârij. Then it is a matter of no importance that the Kufaites had compelled Alî against his will to lead them against the Khawârij instead of against the Syrians.

In Abû Mikhnaf not merely the relative, but also the absolute dating of Nahrawân is incorrect. He places it in one of the two last

[1] More precisely before the news of the result of the arbitration court reached Kufa. The decision itself may have been simultaneous with Nahrawân, or indeed even earlier. Here the point at issue is only when Alî received information concerning the decision.

months of the year 37. Tabarî has already rightly protested against this (1, 3387-89). We now know the exact date from the Ansâb of Balâdhurî (DMZ., 1884, 393); the battle took place on the 9th Safar, 38 (17th July, 658).

According to this the arbitration court did not rise in Ramadân, 37, and not till the year 38. Wâqidî in Tab., 1, 3407, makes it Sha'bân, 38,—a little late if Muâwia again took up arms against Egypt in Safar, 38 (but not before the arbitration court; cf. Tab., 3450, 16), as Wâqidî (3406 f.) reports. But even if the court was not held till the beginning of 38, then it is surprising that there is a whole year between the agreement at Siffin and its execution. According to Zuhrî, a very old traditionist of Medina, the original time-limit was extended. It was decided that the judges should meet in Duma, or if anything came in the way, in the following year at Adhruh (1, 3341). They did meet at Adhruh (2, 8),[1] and so it was in the year after Siffin, i.e., A.H. 38. Wâqidî (1, 3353 f., 3407) and Abû Ma'shar (2, 198) as well as Zuhrî, mention Adhruh. Abû Mikhnaf leaves the place unfixed in the document of agreement; it was to be one chosen lying midway between Kufa and Damascus (1, 3337). He afterwards

---

[1] The place, situated in ancient Edom, might have been chosen out of consideration for the men of Medina, who by right had also something to say in the matter.

mentions the usual place, Dûma, but in 3354, 10 f. (if the text is in order) he names Dûma and Adhruh asyndetically, side by side.

In this uncertain way are the time and place of one of the most important events of the oldest history of Islam reported. Still more unsatisfactory is our information regarding the substance of this event, the proceedings and the issue of the arbitration court. Abû Mikhnaf gives two versions of it (3354 ff.). The one comes from Sha'bî, and runs thus :—Besides Abû Mûsâ there appeared, for Alî, Shuraih b. Hâni at the arbitration court with 400 men, and Ibn Abbâs as prayer-leader. Muâwia sent Amr with 400 men. As suitors with the nearest claim to the Khalifate appeared the heirs of the Islamic aristocracy, who once had formed the circle and council of Muhammad,—Ibn Umar, Ibn Zubair and others, but not the old Ibn Abî Waqqâs. Amr proved Muâwia's right to rule from the right of revenge according to *Súra* 17, 35, and amplified the argument by promises with which he tried to tempt Abû Mûsâ, whose candidate was Ibn Umar. But Abû Mûsâ was not to be caught. Here Sha'bî's account breaks off ; there is nothing else reported among other *isnáds* but a few of the pretexts brought forward by Amr against Ibn Umar. Then there follows in Abû Mikhnaf another version by Abû Janâb al-Kalbî, which is the only one that reports the

result of the negotiations. Amr and Abû Mûsâ
met in Duma. Abû Mûsâ's method was always
to speak his mind first; he did not want to hear
anything about Muâwia and the son of Amr, and
he proposed to set aside Alî and Muâwia, and to
leave the decision as to who should rule to a
Shûrâ, *i.e.*, not a plebiscite but an electoral
assembly of the aristocracy of Islam, after the
pattern of that which was once summoned by
Umar and agreed upon Uthmân. Amr declared
himself favourable. In spite of the warning
of Ibn Abbâs, Abû Mûsâ as usual took the
first word before the Corona and declared he
had come to an agreement with Amr to set
aside Alî and Muâwia, and to call a Shûrâ. Then
Amr rose and said he also set aside Alî but
adhered to Muâwia as the heir and avenger of
Uthmân. Abû Mûsâ cursed him, and he mocked
Abû Mûsâ; a disorderly scene ensued and Abû
Mûsâ fled from the Syrians to Mecca. Amr
and the Syrians returned to Muâwia to greet
him as Khalifa; Ibn Abbâs went to do the same
to Alî. Alî straightway cursed Muâwia and his
clique in the church service, and Muâwia paid
him back in his own coin.

From this we might get the idea that Abû
Mûsâ had allowed himself to be duped, but Amr
simply breaks his word, an artifice which even
the wisest will succumb to. If there is dupery
in it, it is on Amr's side, and Amr was no

trickster. This story of the arbitration court is incredible, even though taken for granted by Wâqidî (2, 84) as it seems to be.[1] Sha'bî probably had a different version of it, but unfortunately his ending is awanting. We are enabled to make corrections by means of the already quoted narrative of Abû Mikhnaf about Khirrît b. Râshid. Khirrît reproached Alî for not being willing to abide by the dictum of Abû Mûsâ, according to which the choice of a ruler was to be left to a Shûrâ.[2] The reproach implies that the proposal of a Shûrâ was accepted by the Syrians, since, otherwise, it could not have been binding upon Alî. Muâwia did not lose much by it for he was not as yet Khalifa, and was, in fact, not hailed as such till 40 A.H. in Jerusalem, but Alî could not give up the position he had assumed, and could not make his claim dependent upon a Shûrâ. It was easy to foresee that, and Amr made a pretty clever move in concurring with Abû Mûsâ; he did get the better of him at all events so far, since Muâwia was not removable in the same sense as Alî, and the refusal to recognise his right

---

[1] Abû 'Ubaida gives later a somewhat similar account of Basra, in Tabarî 2, 446 f. Cf. 444.

[2] Thus Tab., 3434, 1; 3427, 2. In opposition to this, Khirrît appears (3419, 1) as a thorough Khârijite. This is contradicted by the whole train of events, but is easy to understand from Abû Mikhnaf's representation of the proceedings of the arbitration court.

affected the latter only. After Alî had made
the first mistake, the only way to correct it was
by a breach of his word. The Iraqite tradition
does its best to try to gloss this over as excus-
able, and lays all the blame upon Amr and Abû
Mûsâ, the pernicious *Hakamân* (arbiters), (Tab.,
2, 710; 6, 929, 1).

3. Egypt was conquered by Amr at the
beginning of 38, apparently soon after the
arbitration court. A first attempt had already
been made in 36 A. H., to which I have referred
before, but I return to it at this point of the con-
text in order to clear up many doubtful points.

According to Abû Mikhnaf (Tab., 1, 3234 f.;
3243 ff. ; 3392 ff.) Ibn Abî Sarh, Uthmân's
stattholder who had fled from Egypt, was awaiting on the borders of Palestine the result of the
rising in Medina, when along with the news of
the death of Uthmân he received the tidings
that Alî had set over Egypt Qais b. Sa'd b.
Ubâda, the most prominent man of the Ansâr.
Qais arrived with no army but only seven
followers, bringing with him a letter dated
Safar, 36. Alî's adherents had the mastery in
Egypt, though there were also some there who
took the side of Uthmân,[1] and who had gathered

[1] They were not by any means on Muâwia's side from the beginning. *Uthmânid* does not simply mean *Umaiyid.* In Kufa, too, there
were those of the Uthmânid persuasion who still did not belong to the
Syrian party, but took up a kind of neutral position, something like
Abû Mûsâ. *Cf.* Tab., 2. 659. Maqdisî, 293, 19.

in Kharbitâ in the Delta under the Kinânite
Yazîd b. Hârith. But Qais concluded with
Yazîd a treaty of neutrality, and another with
his tribal confederate Maslama b. Mukhallad
Al-Ansârî, who was likewise on Uthmân's side.
Therefore Muâwia could make no headway in
Egypt much as he desired to do so. He tried to
win over Qais himself by promises of vast
wealth if he would join him, and though unsuccessful in this, he diligently spread the story
that Qais was agreed with him, with the object
of making Alî distrustful of him, which he
contrived to do. In order to test his loyalty,
Alî required Qais to use severity against the
neutral powers in Egypt, and when the latter
raised objections, he deposed him and put
Muhammad b. Abî Bakr in his place; along
with this there were intrigues of his circle
against the Ansârite, whose father Ibn Ubâda
had once disputed the Khalifate with Abû Bakr.
Qais was surprised by the arrival of his successor,
but did not waver in his loyalty; after a short
stay in Medina he went to Alî at Kufa, and
fought along with him at Siffîn (in the beginning of the year 37). Muhammad b. Abî Bakr,
whose commission was dated Ramadân, 36,
challenged the neutrals a month after either to
yield him full obedience or to vacate the district.
For a while they prudently restrained themselves, but after Siffîn they repeatedly repelled

the attacks of the stattholder. Encouraged by
their success, they made a revolt under Muâwia
b. Hudaij as-Sakûnî to avenge the blood of
Uthmân, and became more than a match for
Muhammad. Alî had to make up his mind to
send Mâlik al-Ashtar, the conqueror of Siffîn,
to Egypt. Mâlik was at that time stationed in
Nisibis, on the borders of Mesopotamia, belonging
to Syria. He, too, came without an army, but
he was poisoned at Qulzum. Muâwia, at whose
instigation this took place, triumphantly announced his death in the pulpit at Damascus.
At the entreaties of Alî the deeply mortified
Muhammad remained at his dangerous post.

But this account of Abû Mikhnaf, which is the
basis of the modern versions of Islamic history,
is corrected by more exact accounts. Qais b.
Sa‘d was not the first of Alî's stattholders in
Egypt; he succeeded Muhammad Ibn Abî
Hudhaifa.[1] The latter had remained in Egypt
when the mutineers from there had marched to
Medina against Uthmân, and had driven out Ibn
Abî Sarh and taken possession of the province
for Alî (Tab., 1, 2968). But as early as A. H.
36 Muâwia and Amr managed to entice the
young man out to Arîsh on the borders of
Palestine. They did not penetrate any farther
into Egypt (in spite of 3407, 17), for the followers

---

[1] Wâqidî in Tab., 1, 3252 ff.; 3407; and in Balâdh., 227 f. ; in agreement with these Tab., 1, 3233, without Isnâd.

of Uthmân did not make common cause with them. In Arîsh he was surrounded and taken prisoner, and afterwards murdered. The accounts of the time and manner of the murder are not quite agreed. The Syrian of Nöldeke (DMZ., 1875, 89) says that his nephew Hudhaifa was slain by Muâwia's order in A. 969 Seleuc. (A.H. 38-39).[1] This date is confirmed by Ibn Kalbî in Tabarî, 1, 3408; but he says that Muâwia had meant to let him escape when he had fled from prison (*cf.* Tab., 2, 210; Dînaw., 167, 15), and that against his will a Khath'amite had slain him, when he,—wild asses having drawn his attention to him,—discovered him in a cave of the Haurân. Wâqidî, again (3233, 7; 3407, 15) places the murder in the same year as the imprisonment, A.H. 36, which is probably wrong.

After Ibn Abî Hudhaifa was taken prisoner Qais b. Sa'd succeeded him, so he can hardly have again relinquished his province so soon as Ramadân, 36, and taken part in the battle of Siffîn, as Abû Mikhnaf asserts. According to Zuhrî (3241 f.; 3246; 3391 f.) he was not deposed till after that battle, and even then did not go straight to Alî at Kufa without a grudge, but wanted to stay in Medina. But he was

---

[1] He calls him Hudhaifa although, according to him, his father was not called the father of Hudhaifa ; and the nephew of Muâwia, although he was actually not *his*, but his mother's nephew. (B. Hishâm, 165, 208.)

frightened away from there by Marwân b. Hakam
and other Umaiyids, to the great annoyance
of Muâwia. His immediate successor was Ashtar,
and it was not till the latter was poisoned on his
entry into the province that Muhammad b.
Abî Bakr came. In opposition to this Ibn
Kalbî actually relates that Ashtar (3242) was
only sent to Egypt after the fall of Muhammad
b. Abî Bakr, but that, at any rate, is quite false.

Muâwia and Amr repeated the attack upon
Egypt given up in A. H 36, with greater success
in A. H. 38 against Muhammad b. Abî Bakr.
About this, too, the traditions in Tabarî are contradictory. According to Abû Mikhnaf (3396 ff.),
Muâwia after the arbitration court turned
his eyes again towards Egypt. He made an
alliance with Maslama b. Mukhallad and Muâwia b. Hudaij, who joined him though formerly
they would have nothing to do with him. Amr
came in with 6,000 men, and he and Muâwia
wrote threatening letters to Muhammad b.
Abî Bakr to compel him to vacate the land.
The latter sent the letters to Alî and begged for
support, but got none and was left to his own
resources. At his summons 2,000 men gathered
around him, the best and trustiest among them,
and specially recommended by Alî (3402, 11),
was the Tujîbite Kinâna, the murderer of
Uthmân.[1] The latter, after a fierce struggle,

---

[1] We may compare with this the criticism of this man in Saif.

13

had to yield to the superior force; the others dispersed, and Muhammad b. Abî Bakr fled without any following and took hiding in a ruin. There he was discovered by Ibn Hudaij, dragged forth and killed without resistance. Afterwards he was wrapped in an ass's skin and burnt. From that time his sister Âisha could never eat roasted flesh. *Cf.* Tab., 3, 368.

Wâqidî (3406 f.) has another version. Amr marched out with 4,000 men, amongst them Muâwia b. Hudaij,—who, therefore, was not then in Egypt—and Abu'l A'war. In the battle near the dam [1] Kinâna and Muhammad fled and took refuge with Jabala b. Masrûq. His hiding-place was betrayed; Ibn Hudaij spotted it. He came out and fought till he fell. This was in Safar, 38.

The end of Muhammad is more romantic in Abû Mikhnaf than in Wâqidî; it has a slight resemblance to the fate of the other Muhmamad (b. Abî Hudhaifa), who according to Maqrîzî [2] was killed like an ass, and at his death also, according to Ibn Kalbî, asses play a part. We need not decide between them; we can again see how unreliable is the tradition about this period.

4. Since Siffîn, Alî's position had not improved. In Iraq the opposition of the Khawârij

[1] Musannât. Masûdî, 4, 422 calls the place Kum Sharîk. This is a confusion, *cf.* Yâqût, 4330.

[2] Vloten, Recherches, p. 58 (in the Verhandl. der Amsterdam. Akademie, 1894, Letterkunde 1, 3).

against him was increasing. With few exceptions, such as Abu'l Aswad ad Du'ilî, the Basrians
were luke-warm. The Kufaites certainly stood
by him in spirit, but not with all their strength;
there were amongst them many neutrals or
followers of Uthmân, some of whom went over
to Muâwia. The weakness of his position in the
centre naturally had its effect upon the periphery. As early as the year 37, even before
Khirrît's rebellion, the Arabs in Bahrain had kept
the tax for themselves and many had returned to
Christianity. The Iranian provinces were discontented and lax in their adherence.[1] It is
almost surprising that they did not then contrive
to throw off the foreign yoke and expel the
Arabian garrisons altogether. After Mâlik al
Ashtar's death Alî's two best men were Qais b. Sa'd
and Ziâd b. Abîhi; Ibn Abbâs, to whom he had
entrusted Basra, proved useless and unreliable.

Alî rightly felt his worst loss to be the taking of Egypt by Amr. This left Muâwia's
hands free. He at once made himself secure
from the Romans by purchasing a truce from
Constantine at the price of a yearly tribute. Arab tradition only mentions this inci-
dentally.[2] We learn from Theophanes that it

---

[1] Khurâsân, Balâdh., 408 f. Tab., 1, 3249 f., 3389 f.; Adharbaijân and
Rai, 3254; Fârs, 3245, 3393, 3429, 3449; Ahwâz, 3429.

[2] Balâdh., 159, 1; 160, 8. DMZ., 1875, p. 96. *Cf.* the anecdote in Tab.,
2, 211; Dînaw., 168, which, however, in Masûdî, 5, 224 is told of Abdulmalik.

took place A.M. 6150 (Sel. 969=A.H. 38-39).[1]
But Muâwia did not risk an organised attack
upon Alî; he contented himself with harassing
him here and there. In A.H. 38 he sent Ibn
Hadramî to Basra to rouse the Tamîm to rebellion, but Ziâd b. Abîhi, at that time deputy
prefect for Ibn Abbâs, sought the protection of
the Azd, and they stamped out the fire and
killed Ibn Hadramî, who was abandoned by the
majority of the Tamîm. Such is the account of
Madâinî in Tab., 1, 3414 ff. He also tells in
Tab., 3444 ff., according to 'Awâna, about expeditions undertaken by the Syrians in the year 39
against the Iraqites, viz., those of Nu'mân b.
Bashîr to Ain Tamr, Sufyân b. Auf to Hît and
Anbâr, Abdullâh b. Mas'ada al-Fazârî to Taimâ,
and Dahhâk b. Qais to Qutqutâna.[2] They were
apparently merely roving expeditions, in which
the Syrians made off with the spoil and were
pursued, and once in a while overtaken, by the
Kufaites.

In Agh., 15, 45 f.; Yaqûbî, 2, 231 the well-
known expedition of Busr b. Artât into the Hijâz
and the Yemen is connected with these raids.
Bakkâî, also, in Tab., 1, 3450 (quoting 'Awâna)
places it at the end of the time of Alî, stating

---

[1] I have dealt with the connection of the years of the world with
the Syrian Seleucid years in the Göttinger Nachrichten, 1901, pp. 414 ff.

[2] Cf. Yaqûbî, 2, 228, 6. 229, 3. 230, 9. Agh. 15, 45 f.—Abû Ma'shar
and Wâqidî in Tabarî, 1, 3447 say that even Muâwia himself went out
in A.H. 39, but only went as far as the Tigris and then turned back.

that Jâria b. Qudâma on his march against
Busr heard of the murder of Alî. According
to Wâqidî in Tab., 2, 22 this expedition did not
take place till A.H. 42, after Alî's death.

In Tab., I, 3453, according to Ibn Ishâq,[1]
Bakkâî reports a truce which was agreed upon
between Alî and Muâwia in A.H. 40, after a somewhat lengthy correspondence, but this truce can
only have been of short duration, for at the
beginning of 40 Muâwia assumed in Jerusalem
the title of Khalifa, and made the Syrians pay
homage to him. This was a fresh challenge to
Alî, who answered it by preparing a great campaign against the Syrians, but the undertaking
was prevented by his murder. The homage paid
to Muâwia in Jerusalem is attested through
Nöldeke's Syrian. He places after each other
two independent narratives of the same event.
" In the year 971 Sel. many Arabs gathered in
Jerusalem and made Muâwia king ; he went up
to Golgotha, sat down there and prayed, then
proceeded to Gethsemane, and then went down
to the grave of Saint Mary, where he prayed
again." ...... " In the month of July, 971, the
Emirs and many Arabs gathered and paid
homage to Muâwia. The command went forth
that in all parts of his territory he should be

---

[1] So it is to be read here for *Abû* Ishâq, for in the biography of the
Prophet Bakkâî is the intermediate between Ibn Hishâm and Ibn
Ishâq.

proclaimed king.[1]   He wore no crown, as did
the kings of the world heretofore, but he established his throne in Damascus and would
not go to the residence of Muhammad
(Medina.)"   July, 971 Sel. (660 A.D.) begins on
the 16th Safar, 40 A.H.   According to Masrûqî
also, in Tab., 2, 4 f. (*cf.* 1, 3456) the Syrians did
homage to Muâwia in Jerusalem in A.H. 40 ;
but it is false to say that that did not take place
till after Alî's death.   It is remarkable that
Muâwia waited so long before laying claim to the
Khalifate.   According to the Continuatio Isidori
Byz. Arab., par. 25 (ed. Mommsen) he lived
five years "*civiliter*," *i.e.*, as a "*civis*," namely,
from 36 to 40, and then 20 years more as ruler.

The Syrian also asserts that Alî, before his
death, had meant to march once more against
Muâwia.   The information is put under a wrong
year (969 instead of 971 or 972 Sel.), but is
in itself correct.   Yaqûbî, 2, 235, 15 ; 238, 20,
says the same.   General tradition has it that Alî,
at the time of his death, had at his disposal an
army of 40,000 men which was eager to march
against the Syrians,—who else could have
equipped it, and to what end, if not against
the Syrians ?

The murderous assault upon Alî took place

---

[1] The word not understood by Nöldeke beside φωνάς is κλήσεις,
whence probably is derived the Syrian "qalles " (to acclaim).

on Friday, 15th Ramadân, 40, in the mosque of
Kufa (Kâmil, 553, 9).   He died on the following
Sunday, 24th January, 661.   These dates of
Wâqidî in Tab., 1, 3469 ; 2, 18, are confirmed by
the specified days of the week, and the varying
ones refuted.   The murderer, Ibn Muljam, of
Murâd, or more precisely of Tajûb (Kâmil, 553,
17), was a Khârijite.   The Khawârij proudly call
him, in Tab., 2, 18, " our brother of Murâd."
Verses of his tribal companion, Ibn Maiyâs in
Tab., 1, 3466, testify that he was incited to the
murder by a woman, Qatâm, who made it the
condition of his winning her as his bride that he
should take vengeance upon Alî for Nahrawân.
This rules out the account which can only
artificially be made to harmonise, *viz.*, that he
was one of those Khârijites who had committed
the murder under an oath taken in Mecca to rid
the congregation of Muhammad in one day of
the three tyrants, Alî, Muâwia and Amr.   A
private oath taken thus by three persons is not
even in keeping with the usages of the oldest
Khawârij, as Ibn Athîr has already remarked.[1]
Abu 'l Aswad's insinuation that Muâwia hired
the murderer has never found the slightest
credence even with his foes, though undoubtedly
the murder was to his advantage, for by that

---

[1] It is not to be denied that outrages took place even against
Muâwia and Amr, but the combination is arbitrary, as if the outrages
were committed by agreement *a tempo*.

alone he won the kingdom.   In Tab., 2, 3 Hasan
b. Alî reproaches the Kufaites with having killed
his father, and the Khalifa Mansûr expresses
himself similarly in Tab., 3, 431.   From this it
appears that Ibn Muljam and Qatâm were at
home in Kufa. *Cf.* Tab., 1, 3456 ff. ; 3465 ff. ;
Yaqûbî, 2, 251 f. ; Kâmil, 546 ff. ; 583.

5. Muâwia, on his part, now became the
aggressor (Yaqûbî, 2, 255). He advanced
against Iraq by the usual army route through
Mesopotamia, and pitched his camp near Maskin
on the Tigris boundary of Mosul towards the
Sawâd, but he did not arrive there till some
time after Alî's death.   Meantime turbulent
movements were taking place against Hasan,
Alî's son and successor.   He had no wish for
war although he had at his back 40,000 men
eager to fight, and after six months took the
opportunity of abdicating the sovereignty and
becoming reconciled with Muâwia.   This general
summary is authenticated, but the exact course
of affairs after Alî's murder is related with
confusion and incompleteness.

The following is Zuhrî's version.   Alî had
entrusted Qais b. Sa'd with the leadership of the
army, and promised him as a reward the province
of Adharbaijân, from which Ash'ath was to be
deposed, and Qais zealously carried on the
campaign.   But Hasan wanted to make the
best terms he could with Muâwia.   He deposed

Qais because he opposed him in this, and put Abdullâh Ibn Abbâs in his place (Tab., 2, 1. *Cf.* 1, 3392). He had already made the Kufaites suspicious by his ambiguous behaviour at the paying of homage, and they decided that he was not the man for them. Not long after he had a proof of their feelings towards him by a lance-thrust which he received on an occasion not very closely specified. Thereupon he began negotiations with Muâwia, renounced the rule for a large sum of money, and was sorry afterwards that he had not demanded twice as much (2, 55). Even before him, Ibn Abbâs was also treating with Muâwia and left the army in the lurch. Thereupon the army again chose Qais as their leader, with the commission to carry on the war until the adherents of Alî were guaranteed amnesty and security for their belongings and their life. This he easily gained from Muâwia to whom it meant a good deal to win him over ; but he did not take the money that was offered to himself, and made no dealings for his own hand.

Bakkâî, from 'Awâna,[1] in Tab., 2, 2-4 has a different version. Qais had not the command of the whole army, but only of the vanguard or *shurta* of 12,000 men, which he retained even

---

[1] The beginning of 'Awâna's report is omitted and replaced by another, which is, however, said to agree with that of 'Awâna.

after Alî's death. Hasan himself, with the main
army, advanced to Madâin and sent on Qais
with the vanguard to meet Muâwia (in Maskin).
Suddenly in the camp of Madâin the cry arose,
" Qais has fallen, flee from hence ! " Thereupon Hasan's tent was plundered and he took
refuge in the white castle, from which, in spite
of the protests of his brother, Husain, he opened
communications with Muâwia and got from
him what he demanded,—all the money in the
treasury of Kufa, the year's revenue of Dârâb-
jard, and the promise that his father Alî should
not be reviled from the pulpit in his presence.[1]

Yaqûbî, 2, 254 f. gives still another account.
Hasan sent Ubaidullâh b. Abbâs with 12,000
men against Muâwia, and along with him he
sent, as an adviser, Qais, by whose council he
was to be guided.   Muâwia tried in vain to bribe
Qais, but only succeeded by a bribe of a million
in gaining over Ubaidullâh, who went over to
him with 8,000 men.   Hasan was with the main
army in Madâin, and Muâwia sent Mughîra
and other mediators to him.   These, on leaving
him, spread the story abroad in the camp that
he had declared himself ready for peace, whereupon his own warriors fell upon him and

---

[1] In some places in Tabarî alterations are found in these two
versions.   Thus in 1, 8 f. and 7, 15 : the 40,000 men are not the Shurta
but the whole army.   According to Zuhrî, Qais as well as Ibn Abbâs
has command of the whole.

plundered his tents. He fled on horse-back to
the castle in Sâbât, but was roughly handled by
Jarrâh b. Sinân (alias b. Qabîsa) al Asadî and
wounded by a lance-thrust. Exhausted by loss
of blood, he was brought back to Madâin and
lay there a considerable time seriously ill.
Meanwhile his adherents deserted him, and
Muâwia seized Iraq, and in the end nothing was
left to him but to abdicate. Dînawarî's account
is similar, with a few differences (230 f). He says
the Yemen and Rabîa of Kufa had saved
Hasan in Sâbât out of the hands of the Mudar
of Kufa.

On the whole 'Awâna and Yaqûbî are agreed
against Zuhrî, whose pragmatism is not clear.
A few variations which occur cannot be explained. The lance-thrust, for example, is partly
separate from the plundering of the tent in
time and place, and partly connected with it.
Tendency is responsible for other variations.
In Yaqûbî and Dînawarî also there is the
attempt to palliate Hasan at the expense of the
Kufaites (Dîn., 242, 15); Zuhrî shows him in
the most unfavourable light, but the greatest
difference due to tendency is à propos of the
behaviour of Abdullâh b. Abbâs, the ancestor
of the Abbasid dynasty. Under the Abbasid
sway it was dangerous to speak the truth about
this holy man; the temptation at least was
either to gloss over the part he played or to

leave him out altogether.[1] According to
Zuhrî, the oldest traditionist, who died before
the time of the Abbasids, Abdullâh b. Abbâs
got an inkling of Hasan's intention to make
peace, anticipated him and from Muâwia secured
for himself the moneys which he had seized
upon. He then left the Iraqite army in the
lurch, and betook himself secretly under an
escort to the Syrian camp. 'Awâna says nothing

---

[1] According to Saif (*Skizzen*, 6, 144) the confidant of Alî in Medina
had already been Abdullâh Ibn Abbâs, who always gave him the right
counsel but did not always get it carried out. He then became stattholder of Basra, and as such brought reinforcements to Alî (Tab., 1,
3256, 3370). According to Abû Mikhnaf he distinguished himself at
Siffîn and commanded the left wing of the army of Iraq (3285. 89).
Alî wanted him to be a delegate to the arbitration court (3233), and
in spite of being thwarted in this, sent him to Duma and corresponded
with him only (3354), while he ignored Abû Mûsâ. But according to
Abû Ma'shar (3273, 16) and Yaqûbî (2, 254, 3) he led the Hajj in
A.H. 36 (as in A.H. 35) and so could certainly not take part in the battle
of Siffîn. This leading of the festival does not suit Madâinî, and he
prefers to assert (3448) that according to Abû Ma'shar. Abdullâh never
made the pilgrimage in Alî's life-time. In A.H. 38 he betook himself
from Basra to Alî at Kufa, to console his dear friend by his presence
for the loss of Egypt. Not till he was compelled by disorders in
Fars did he return to Basra, and send Ziâd to Fars. This is Madâinî's
account in Tab., 1, 3414. 30. 43. Abû Mikhnaf's account in Tab., 3412.
49 differs. According to him Abdullâh consoled Alî *in a letter* from
Basra and it was Alî, and not he, who sent Ziâd to Fars. He comes
on the scene again when Muâwia wanted to force the chiefs of the
aristocracy of Medina to do homage to his son, Yazîd. According to
Madâinî (Tab., 2, 175) five men refused to do homage, amongst whom
was Abdullâh Ibn Abbâs. But this heroic opposition to the tyrant
produced no result. He must have felt it bitterly that Muâwia and
Yazîd utterly ignored him. In the same way, too, most of the traditionists on this occasion ignore him.

about this. Instead of the famous Abdullâh,
Yaqûbî makes it Ubaidullâh b. Abbâs, his
younger brother.

Madâinî is already acquainted with the dispute of the traditionists as to whether it is
Abdullâh or Ubaidullâh who went over to
Muâwia under Hasan (Tab., 1, 3456. *Cf.* 3453),
so it is not merely a question of variants of
the copyists.[1] He decides for Ubaidullâh, as
also do Umar b. Shabba (1, 3453 ff.) and Balâdhurî (DMZ., 1884, 392 f.). Now Ubaidullâh
was stattholder of the Yemen when Busr b.
Artât undertook his expedition thither. His
two boys fell into the hands of Busr and were
slaughtered, which caused their mother to lose
her reason. According to Wâqidî this expedition took place in the year 42. At that time
Ubaidullâh was still in the Yemen at war with
Muâwia, and so could not have gone over to him
a year or two before. Wâqidî, in any case,
can certainly not have known of any such
submission. 'Awâna has it that the expedition
took place in the second half of the year 40,
but it is incredible that Ubaidullâh should have
been in such a hurry to make terms with
the murderer of his sons. Besides, it is far
easier to find a motive for Ubaidullâh's being

[1] This is the opinion of de Goeje, DMZ., 1884, 393, who on the basis
of this supposition wishes to read *Ubaidullâh* instead of *Abdullâh* in
Tab., 2, 2; 7; 11. *Cf.* van Vloten, Opkomst der Abbasiden, p. 12, n. 1.

substituted for Abdullâh than for the opposite procedure. The founder of the dynasty under which Madâinî lived and to which he was devoted, must not suffer the disgrace of being said to have been the first to make a compact with the godless Umaiyids; his brother Ubaidullâh, on the other hand, might be sacrificed.

Moreover, even so, Abdullâh is only partially cleared by substituting his brother. The moneys which, according to Zuhrî, he seized and which Muâwia let him have, were moneys out of the state-treasury of Basra,—just as the 5 million granted to Hasan were the contents of the state-treasury of Kufa. This is confirmed by Abû Ubaida in Tab., 1, 3456. He agrees with Zuhrî that after Alî's death Abdullâh went from Basra to Hasan and on that occasion took with him money from the state-treasury. The palliation is certainly extended that it was no more than he could claim for his salary, but it is remarkable that Madâinî, Umar b. Shabba and Balâdhurî do not deny either that Abdullâh made off with the state-treasure of Basra. They only mention that he did so under Alî, soon after the battle of Nahrawân (DMZ., 1884, 392), and that it had no connection with his going over to Muâwia.[1] This makes

---

[1] The "rescue" of the state-moneys was not considered so bad, since it was quite the custom (Tab., 2, 752; 872), but on the other hand the treating with Muâwia was unpardonable.

the treason twofold. Sons of Abbâs with very
similar names twice, in close succession, shame-
fully forsook their post, and on this occasion
helped themselves to large sums of money.
Still it is more probable that it only happened
once; so Zuhrî is still right in saying that
Abdullâh, and not Ubaidullâh, was the confidant
of Hasan, as he was before of Alî, and that he
let himself be bought over by Muâwia even
before Hasan did. Even in Madâinî we find
him with Alî in the year 39, but after the
peace-terms we find him at once in the circle
of Muâwia (Tab., 2, 11).§ The Jamâa under
Muâwia,, *i.e.*, the uniting of the congregation
of Muhammad under one sceptre, took place
in the first half of the year 41, in the summer
of 661 A. D. Accounts vary concerning the
exact date. According to Elias Nisibenus, Hasan
abdicated in favour of Muâwia on Monday,
21 Rabî I, 41, *i.e.*, Monday 26th July, 661.
Wâqidî says in Tab., 2, 9 that Muâwia marched
into Kufa, in Rabî II, 41 (August, 661). An
unknown tradition states (Tab., 2, 9) that the
peace was concluded in Rabî II, but Muâwia
did not enter Kufa till the beginning of Jumâdâ I. Madâinî reports that he made his entrance either on the 25th Rabî I or the 25th
Jumâdâ I (2, 7) but was still in Kufa in
Rajab, since he corresponded from there with
Busr in Basra, and Busr came there in Rajab

and stayed six months (2, 12).   But in Jumâdâ
I, 41, he had already established Mughîra b.
Shu'ba as his stattholder in Kufa (2, 111 ; 114).

CHAPTER III.

THE SUFYÂNIDS AND THE SECOND CIVIL WAR.

During his whole reign Muâwia b. Abî Sufyân carried on the war against the Romans both on sea and land more zealously and continuously than any of his successors, and twice he stretched out his hand against the enemy's capital itself.[1] On the other hand he left the task of establishing his authority in conquered Iraq to his Stattholders in Kufa and Basra. The tradition preserved to us turns most attention to them and relates more of Mughîra and Ziâd than of Muâwia himself, just as it makes Muâwia's *alter ego* Abdulmalik retire into the background in favour of Hajjâj. These three famous Stattholders were, all of them, Thaqifites from Tâif, the high and beautifully situated sister-city of Mecca, which through Islam rose into importance alongside of Mecca and Medina, and as a town occupied a certain privileged position over the tribes, as was already apparent on the occasion of the Ridda in A.H. 11. Unlike the Ansâr, the Thaqîf had a firm and

---

[1] For this *cf.* the *Göttinger Nachrichten*, 1901, pp. 414 ff., where the attempts of the Umaiyids against the Romans are collected

long-standing alliance with the ruling Quraish, especially the Umaiya who had close relations with Tâif and owned property there. They had the reputation of being very clever, [1] a reputation which they preserved, and in the time of the Umaiyids they supplied a superb galaxy of talented men. Mukhtâr and Muhammad b. Qâsim belonged to them, and many other prominent men besides.

Mughîra b. Shu'ba, whom Muâwia set over Kufa in A.H. 41 (Tab., 2, 11f. ; 111 ; 114), had already experienced a turbulent life. Tradition sketches a vivid picture of the much-tempted, unscrupulous man. He was of tall, powerful build ; he lacked one eye and his front teeth ; he had a large head, projecting lips and reddish hair, afterwards dyed black, which stood up in four stiff "horns." [2] On account of a base murder committed upon a sleeping comrade, he was, as a young man, expelled to Medina before the year 8. Even to criminals like this Islam opened a career and blotted out their past. Circumstances having made a new man of him, he retained his old profitable traits,

---

[1] When Muhammad besieged Tâif in A.H. 8 the Fazârite Uyaina joined his army, hoping when the town was taken that he would win a prisoner of war for his wife, so as to have a clever son, for he himself could not transmit any cleverness.

[2] The beginning of the article upon him in the *Kitâb al Aghânî* is missing in the Bulaq edition, but is to be found in a Münich MS., from which I have had it printed in the DMZ., 1896.

and approached the Prophet, who was able to make use of him. In the year 9 he was commissioned to destroy the heathen sanctuary in his native town, on which occasion he also removed the rich contents of the treasury-cellar. He had an exact knowledge of the place, for he belonged to the family who had the office of guardian at the temple. At the Prophet's burial he threw his ring into the grave shortly before it was closed, or at least so he asserted, in order to found upon this the claim that he had been last in contact with the holy man. From that time onwards he continued his shameless pursuit of power, and tried to make it appear that he belonged to the leading aristocracy of Islam. Uninvited, he thrust himself into important affairs of state, as, for instance, into the Shûrâ of Umar and the arbitration-court of Duma, and though turned out he always came calmly back the next time. Bold and God-fearing as he was, he understood excellently well how to flaunt Islam before the great men of Persia. The rôle he preferred as being most congenial to him was that of messenger and mediator, and for this his knowledge of Persian stood him in good stead (Tab., 1, 2560). He first attained the office he sought in Basra. He had come there with the first Stattholder, Utba b. Ghazwân, whose wife came from Tâif, and after his death he succeeded him. He is said to have established the *Dîwân* (tax-court) in Basra, and with it to have set the pattern to all the others. He is said, also, to have slain the Failkân of Izqubâdh [1] and to have conquered Maisân and even Ahwâz. His insatiable inclination for women led to his fall. He was deposed for shameless adultery in A.H. 17, although, by the interposition of Umar, so strict in other matters, the sentence of punishment resolved itself into a comedy. Still, his day was not yet over. He distinguished himself at Nihâwand, and immediately after, in A.H. 21, he came to Kufa as the successor of Ammâr b. Yasîr. It was under his Stattholdership at that time that the Kufaite conquests in Media and Adharbaijân were made. His slave, Abû Lulua, whom he sent to Medina and caused to work there as a mechanic, was the murderer of the Khalifa Umar. Under Uthmân he fell into the back-ground; he belonged neither to the Umaiyids, who now got all the official posts, nor to the intimates of the Prophet who formed the opposition. He took no part in the revolution against Uthmân, but as a result of it he came into prominence again. He is said to have advised Alî to recognise Muâwia as Stattholder of Syria, and when the latter did not follow his advice, he left him and joined Muâwia. In the latter's name he forged

---

[1] Marquart, Eranschahr, p. 41, thinks this the proper pronunciation of *Abarqubâdh* or *Abazqubâdh*.

a commission for himself to lead the Hajj of the year 40. Muâwia knew the value of such a colleague, and soon after the conquest of Iraq bestowed upon him once more his old post in Kufa.

Now, as an aged man, he had, after a somewhat troublous past, reached the haven in which he thought to remain. His endeavour was, as Stattholder, not to give offence either to those above or to those below him. His attitude towards Muâwia was as distant as towards the fluctuations of the Kufaite parties, and he made no secret of it either (Tab., 2, 38). Such at least is Abû Mikhnaf's description of him in his narratives about Mustaurid and Hujr b. Adî, which is certainly a true one.[1] His whole policy was to keep himself in his post, and he succeeded. By stratagem he managed to anticipate occasional impulses of the ruler to depose him (2, 71f.; 173f.; 208f.). He was easily a match for the Khawârij under Mustaurid, as the Kufaites themselves lost no time in relieving him of them, but the Khawârij were not of much importance in Kufa. The overwhelming majority of the Kufaites adhered to Alî as the champion of the political independence of Iraq, and in this sense they were of the same mind as the Shîites. Nor did they make any secret of

[1] Chawârig (*Abhh. der Göttinger Societät, 1901*, V, 2) pp. 19 ff. Shia (in the same Vol.), pp. 56 f.

it, and some were bold enough to utter provok-
ing speeches in public, but Mughîra let them
alone. Instead of combating the beginnings of
the evil he had a certain satisfaction in fore-
seeing their consequences, since it was certain
that he would not live to experience them. His
idea was to save his soul, and to shift on to his
successors the odium of doing what was part of
his office.[1] The Kufaites were naturally quite
pleased with this; they found afterwards that
they never again had such a good Stattholder
(2, 112). He made his way by lying and reaped
the benefits of it till his end. As to the date of
his death accounts vary between the years 49
and 51; *cf.* Tab., 2, 86 f.; 114; Agh., 14, 148.

When Iraq had submitted to him, Muâwia
sent first the commander-in-chief Busr b. Abî
Artât to Basra to quell the rising of Humrân
b. Abân. After restoring peace he went off
with his army and, according to Wâqidî (2, 22),
only then marched into the Hijâz and the
Yemen. The first real Stattholder whom Muâwia
appointed in Basra (at the end of 41) was the
Umaiyid Abdullâh Ibn Âmir, who had held the
office already for several years under Uthmân.
In Basra it was the tribes and not the authorities
who had the power in their hands, and as they

---

[1]   This disposition he shared with many other Stattholders of this
period, Ibn 'Âmir, 2, 67; Walîd b. Utba, 2, 219 : Nu'mân b. Bashîr,
2, 239 : and Babba, 2, 451; 465 f.

were not united and always intent upon never
foregoing any advantage, we can imagine the
consequences. In Kufa the public safety suffered
little under the political and religious party
agitation ; in Basra robbery and murder on the
streets were common. This was the inheritance
left by Ibn Abbâs, but Ibn 'Âmir did not want
to take vigorous measures. Like old Mughîra
he thought he would not sacrifice his soul's
salvation merely to establish the government.
He disliked cutting off any robber's hand :
" How could I look his father or brother in the
face ? " he would say. At last this was too
much for Muâwia and he begged him, in all
friendship, to give up his office, allowing him,
in return, to keep what he had annexed of the
state-moneys, and giving him his daughter to
wife, so that he was at the same time his son-in-law
and his father-in-law.[1] Ibn 'Âmir's successor was
an Azdite, but he was destined only to prepare the
way for Ziâd, who was at that time already selected for the office, and he had to leave again after
four months. This is the account according to
Madâinî in Tabarî, 2,11 ff. ; 15 f. ; 67 f. ; 69 ff.

In Tabarî most of the information about
Ziâd is supplied by Madâinî also. Like Mughîra,
whose *protégé* he was, he belonged to the Thaqifites who had settled in Basra just at the

---

[1] Ibn Âmir was the father-in-law of Muâwia's son Yazîd.

foundation of the town, and in fact to the family Abûbakra, which was there prosperous and highly esteemed, being extensive land-owners (Tab., 2,12).[1] Of humble origin, he was called after his mother Sumaiya because his father was unknown. Islam opened the world to him also. At the age of 14 he became divider of the spoil or account-keeper for the army of Basra, because he was able to write, for in order to count, one had to be able to write. Even then the Khalifa Umar is said to have taken notice of his unusual worth, and under Alî he was a prominent personality in Basra. As the representative of the absent Stattholder he had there to deal with the rising of the Tamîm instigated by Muâwia. The Azd assisted him and he was always grateful to them (2,80). He was next sent by Alî to Fars to keep the doubtful province in order and obedience, a task which he performed brilliantly and without using violence. After Alî's death he established himself in his stronghold at Istakhr, and of all the officials of Alî he defied Muâwia longest. Busr had to threaten him with the murder of his three boys who had been left in Basra if he did not appear. He refused, but the children were snatched from the executioner at the last moment by a counter-order of Muâwia, which Abûbakra, after a wild ride to

---

[1] For the character of this family, cf. the spiteful account of Tab., 2,801, and also B. Hishâm, 874, 17 Scholion.

Kufa and back, managed to gain and to deliver just in time.[1] Mughîra was commissioned to seize the treasures of Ziâd which were deposited in Basra, but, naturally, he could not find them, for one Thaqifite would not peck out the eyes of another. He interposed, however, to induce Ziâd to cease his opposition and give in. This was in the year 42. Muâwia winked at the fact that at the division of the state-moneys of Fars which they effected between them, he was cheated, though he saw through the deceit. It was a deal between brothers who after all had a mutual understanding, and both profited considerably from it.

Muâwia put the finishing touch to the situation by legitimising the son of Sumaiya and recognising him as the son of his own father, Abû Sufyân, so as to bind him in this way absolutely to himself and to his family. It was a great scandal, which Tabarî does not relate, and dates it only as a supposititious event, (2,69f. Cf. 3, 477 f.). The other Umaiyids and Muâwia's own son Yazîd were not much edified by it and for a considerable time stood in strained relations with the bastard, who perhaps was not even that. The well-known and often-quoted satirical verses on his adoption do not originate

---

[1] The story is indeed a legend, but it does not need to be improved upon in A. Müller's account (*Islam*, *1*, 337), that the sons of Ziâd had raised a rebellion in Basra and were arrested for that reason ; they were too young for that.

from the strolling singer Ibn Mufarrigh, though he too was the author of some, but from an Umaiyid, Abdurrahmân, the brother of the succeeding Khalifa, Marwân b. Hakam (2,194).

Muâwia had first assigned Kufa to Ziâd as a place of residence, where he was under the mild supervision of Mughîra, who adopted a fatherly *rôle* towards him, and he frequented the latter's house and paid court to his young wife. Then Muâwia sent for him to Damascus and there, apparently, promoted him to be his brother. When Ziâd returned from there to Kufa, Mughîra was seized with the apprehension that in him (Ziâd) he had been rearing his own successor, but very soon a commission came from Damacus appointing Ziâd Stattholder of Basra and the provinces of the East belonging to it. At the end of Rabî II, or the beginning of Jumâdâ I, of the year 45 he came to Basra and inducted himself with a celebrated pulpit speech in which he started at once upon his programme without beating about the bush. Hence the speech was called "the one without a preface." "Ye are putting relationship before religion," he said; "Ye are excusing and sheltering your criminals, and tearing down the protecting laws sanctified by Islam. Beware of prowling by night; I will kill every one who is found at night in the streets. Beware of the arbitrary summons of relationship; I will cut out the tongue of every one who raises the cry. Whoever pushes anyone into the water, whoever sets fire to another's house, whoever breaks into a house, whoever opens a grave, him will I punish for it. I make every family responsible for those belonging to it. Hatred towards myself I do not punish, but only crime. Many who are terrified at my coming will be glad of my presence, and many who are building their hopes upon it will be undeceived. I rule you with the authority of God and care for your maintenance out of the wealth of God.[1] From you I demand obedience, and ye can demand from me justice. In whatsoever I fall short, three things there are in which I shall not be lacking : at any time I shall be ready to listen to anyone ; I shall pay you your pension at the proper time, and I shall not send you to war too far away or keep you in the field overlong. Do not let yourselves be carried away by your hatred and wrath against me ; it would go ill with you if ye did. Many heads do I see tottering ; let each man see to it that his own remains on his shoulders ! "

By a few examples of relentless severity made at the very beginning, he commanded their respect, and he succeeded in re-establishing a security never known before, not only in Basra itself but also in the Iranian provinces,

---

[1] " God " mean e " State " in the theocracy.

and even in the Arabian desert. Marvellous
tales are told of this. Even the Khawârij in
Basra bowed before him. Except in name part
of them were no better than common robbers
and deserved to be treated as such.[1]

When Mughîra died in A. H. 50 or 51 Ziâd
got his Stattholdership also, and retained his own
post at Basra. In Kufa he had to put in order
the evil inheritance left by Mughîra. The Shîites
there, with Hujr b. Adî of Kinda at their head,
stoned his standing representative, Amr b.
Huraith, as he was conducting the public service
in the mosque. He then hastened from Basra to
interfere. Hujr played into his hands by offering armed resistance along with his adherents
when he was to be arrested, and thereby banning
himself. Ziâd mastered him without much
difficulty, and when the matter became serious
the Kufaites themselves helped the representative
of state authority whom they hated, against
their adherents with whom their sympathies
lay, and even signed the indictment against the
imprisoned ringleader. This document was sent
to the Khalifa at Damascus, and six of them were
executed for sedition under arms since they
refused to renounce Alî. But that was not the
end of the matter. The execution of such
prominent men affected them deeply. The
tribes considered it a disgrace that they had not

[1] Chawarig, pp. 24 f.

managed to snatch their fellows from the authority of the state, and the Shîites regarded Hujr and his companions in suffering as martyrs.[1]

Tradition gives a report of some of Ziâd's measures of administration. He undertook a great rebuilding of the mosque of Kufa (Tab., 1, 2492), on which occasion he removed the gravel from the floor and replaced it by a solid pavement. According to Balâdh., 277, this was done so as to prevent the flinging of gravel from the hand after the performance of the prostrations in the service from becoming a custom, but one should rather imagine that it was done to prevent the critical observations of the pulpit speaker from being interrupted by showers of stones. Another measure was more important, namely the division of the garrison of Kufa into four groups, whereby the most different tribes were united in one group, having at their head not a tribal chief but a chief elected by the government.[2] In the analogous arrangement of the Basraites into five groups the tribal principle, again, is more apparent. We may perhaps trace a political move in the fact that he sent a great number of Kufaite and Basraite families to Khurâsân and settled them there (Tab., 2, 81 ; 156; Balâdh., 410).

---

[1] Shia, pp. 56 ff.
[2] Shia, p. 58, n. 1

He died on Tuesday, 4th Ramadân (23rd
August, 673) aged about 53. As illustrative of his
character there are two anecdotes which have
some value. When, in A.H. 38 or 39, he sought
the protection of the Azd and sounded their
leader as to whether he would be willing to
defend him against an attack of the Tamîm, the
decided answer which he received [1] so delighted
him because of its *naïveté* that he had the
greatest difficulty in restraining the laughter
which at that moment might have been very
dangerous to him. He told old Mughîra's
beautiful young wife, whom he liked very much
and afterwards married, that she might boldly
show herself before him as a harmless relative,
for he was actually Mughîra's father,—since one
of his sons bore the same name as the Stattholder
of Kufa. So he does not seem to have been a
man of gloomy sternness. But in his capacity of
regent he allowed no jesting. Still, he was a
tyrant only according to Arab ideas, which
regard any powerful rule as tyranny, especially
when it uses the sword against mutinous subjects.
As to his manner of dealing with the Shîa in Kufa
we have the detailed and exact account of Abû
Mikhnaf, who was himself of Shîite persuasion.

---

[1] Tab., 1, 3415. From the Leiden text one cannot make out what
is said to be laughable in the deliverance of Sabira b. Shaimân. The
Gentilic names are there distorted. They may be improved from 3418,
1, and B. Duraid, 150 ; 154.

His proceedings against them stopped with the punishment of a few ringleaders who had taken up arms against him. This makes us regard with just suspicion occasional vague accounts of his barbarous persecution of the Shîites in general (Tab., 2,266 ; 624). In Basra especially they had not much to complain of and were pretty comfortable. Their chief, Sharîk b. A'war al Hârithî, held with Ziâd, and later with his son, a position of trust, which shortly before his death he basely abused (2,248). The Khawârij were more dangerous there. They were of different species, some of them honourable, pious people, and some unscrupulous seceders with murderous instincts, but it was not against the feelings of the former, but against the crimes of the latter that Ziâd took action. He only executed a few agitators and malefactors and did not cause wholesale massacres. Abû Bilâl, the most esteemed man among the Khawârij of Basra, approved his conduct, while he execrated those who disgraced the name of the party by indiscriminate bloodshed. Contrary accounts must be regarded as calumniations caused by tendency.

Samura b. Jundab figures as the willing instrument of Ziâd's alleged cruelty in Basra, according to Madâinî and his pupil Umar b. Shabba. He was the captain of the *Shurta*, a kind of body-guard, and Ziâd is said to have greatly reinforced this standing army in order to be able to use it as a basis for his tyranny. But in Kufa he suppressed the rising of the Shîa not by means of the Shurta, but by calling up the tribes themselves. As in Fars, so in Iraq he contrived to be a match for them without extraordinary means. In the evenings, according to old custom, he gathered round him a circle of notables, upon whom an honorary salary was settled, and in easy conversation deliberated with them upon the public concerns. He made the chiefs of the tribes responsible for the good conduct of their tribesmen, while the jealousy of the clans made it possible for him to play them off against each other. Above all he had the state-moneys at his disposal, and the control over the purse which supplied the pensions. He had also a Shurta at his disposal, but not out of proportion in strength to those of his predecessors. Besides, every other Stattholder had command of the same means as he had, only he knew how to use them to better purpose. He possessed all the marks of being a regent by the grace of God; nothing ever miscarried with him. The mosque, the forum of Islam, was the chief scene of his activity and of his success. He told the people what they were thinking and they felt convicted; he announced his measures to them, and they had no doubt that he would keep his word. He had the faculty of ruling with the tongue, and he knew his Arabs. From of old they had ever a fine perception of, and an involuntary respect for, superiority of intellect when it expressed itself by insight into the hearts and affairs of men, and by decisive action. An independent Tamîmite noble, Hâritha b. Badr, paid the most laudatory testimony in verses to the great Wezîr.[1] That the poet Farazdaq had the terror of a foolish youth for him does not detract from him.

In Basra, as in Kufa, the simple task which had to be performed was the establishment of the *Sultân*, *i.e.*, the State, the supremacy of the government. In Basra it was necessary to put an end to the despotism of the tribes and clans, whose first principle, in all cases, was to take the side of their clansmen, and even of their criminals, not merely against other clans but also against the government. Here more than anywhere else the clique-system due to blood-relationship had gained ground, and this in a thickly populated town was bound to have consequences far more insupportable than in the desert. The regulation of justice and the peace of the community through which Muhammad had freed the Arabs from anarchy, were called in question. In Kufa the opposition was more tinged with theocracy; it was directed not against the state-supremacy in itself, but

[1] 78, 10 ; 146, 15. As far as I know the appellation is first found here.

17

against the right of the existing, *i.e.* the Umaiyid, rule. To Ziâd, however, the difference mattered little. Having once made his peace with the reigning house, he recognised no superior other than the one which actually held the power, and on this basis he stood for the public order and well-being and for the citizens' duty of obedience. Even if, according to the prevailing custom, he did not forget himself, and laid up for himself large sums of money, still he did not use his power solely as a means to plunder the provinces entrusted to him for his own private ends. He stood above the parties and clans, had the conscience to feel that he was the official of the state, and was zealous in the performance of the duties thereby incumbent upon him, regardless of the welfare of his soul and of the Qoran, in which each read the policy that suited him. Further his fidelity was acknowledged and requited to his sons, of whom Ubaidullâh b. Ziâd was the most important.

Other Stattholders in Iraq in Muâwia's time were, according to Abû Ma'shar and Wâqidî, the following :—over Kufa, Abdullâh b. Khâlid b. Asîd from A.H. 53 ; Dahhâk b. Qais al Fihrî from A.H. 55 ; Abdurrahmân b. Umm Hakamath Thaqafî A.H. 58 ; and Nu'mân b. Bashîr al-Ansârî from A.H. 59. Over Basra Samura b. Jundab alFazârî, A.H. 53 ; Abdullâh b. Amr b,

Ghailân A.H. 54, and Ubaidullâh b. Ziâd from A.H. 55. Ubaïdullâh took severer measures against the Khawârij in Basra than his father, and even brought upon himself the opposition of the more moderate. It is from his time that we have the martyr stories of the party.[1]

Of the Syrians whom Muâwia governed himself we hear comparatively little. The common interest in the government united them to him, for Syria was the ruling land, a fact which was made evident by its possession of the central exchequer and by the amount of the pensions.[2] But internally also it differed from Iraq. Kufa and Basra had no other traditions but the desert and Islam. Arab armies, confusedly mustered from different tribes, were cast up thither through war and had settled as military colonies. They found themselves suddenly transferred from primitive conditions into culture, and into the centre of a great kingdom, and it is not surprising that they did not all at once change from Beduin into rational citizens of a state. It was into Syria also, in consequence of the Islamic conquest, that many Arabs now emigrated, especially Qaisites into the north of the province. But

[1] Chawarig, pp. 25 ff.
[2] " Muâwia moved the chief state treasury (from Kufa) to Damascus, and raised the pay of the Syrians and lowered that of the Iraqites." Theoph., A. M. 6151, 6152.

in the centre the Kalb and the other Qudâa had the majority, along with some tribes reckoned as belonging to Azd Sarât, which had made their home there for centuries, and had not come only through Islam.[1] The influence of the Graeco-Aramaic culture, the Christian church, and the Roman kingdom under which they had come had not failed to leave traces upon them. A regulated state government and military and political discipline were not new ideas to them; they had an old line of princes, which they had long obeyed, and they transferred their wonted obedience to Muâwia as the rightful successor of their former dynasty; the right of the Sultan did not require to be first beaten into them. They recognised the legitimacy of the existing rule of man and did not test it by the measure of the Koran and the theocracy. They followed their Emir where he led them, because they at heart cared just as little for Islam as he did. In military affairs they showed themselves far superior to all the other Arabs, and all the more so because they were never out of practice, and were systematically trained by the constant wars against the Romans. Muâwia was prudent enough to keep their right side, although in blood he was

---

[1] They boasted that they were not recent incomers into Syria like the Umaiya (Hamâsa, 659, v. 5).

more nearly connected with the Qaisites. The difference of the tribal groups at that time had not yet come to mean a venomous opposition of political parties. He lived in Damascus in the sphere of the Kalb, not far from the residence of their former kings. From amongst them he married a lady of consequence, and intended that her son Yazîd should inherit the kingdom. According to Arab ideas this was a political alliance, and so it proved to be. All the Kalbites felt themselves, as it were, brothers-in-law of the Khalifa and uncles of his successor.[1] There was no question at all of the Arabs in Syria, their relations, being made inferior to the conquerors who had pressed in. Besides, their acceptance of Islam followed very soon and was half spontaneous, even though it only meant a transition to the victorious standard of Arabism. It may be presumed that the alliance into which Muâwia as Stattholder already entered with them had also a reflex effect upon his standing with the non-Arab Syrians who remained Christians. The opposition between masters and subjects seems not to have been so harsh in Syria as it was at first in Iraq. The Muslims there did not live apart in colonies founded especially for them, but together with the

---

[1] Nâila, too, was a Kalbite, and possibly the revenge for Uthmân had the effect of driving the Kalb into the arms of Muâwia.

children of the land in the old towns of
Damascus, Emessa, Qinnesrin, etc. They even
sometimes went shares in the use of a place of
worship, which then became half church and
half mosque. The Christian traditions of
Palestine and Syria (Nâbigha, 1, 24, Ahlw.) were
also held in high esteem by the Muslims; Syria
was for them, too, the Holy Land. Muâwia had
himself proclaimed Khalifa in Jerusalem; afterwards he prayed at Golgotha and at the grave
of St. Mary. Of course one need not draw too
many conclusions from these facts. He showed
how supercilious and superior he stood in relation to dogma when the Jacobites and Maronites
brought their religious dispute to be decided by
him. From the Jacobites, who were worsted
in the dispute, he got a fine of 20,000 dinars
and advised them to be at peace. But he had
no deep relation to Islam either, and as a politician he was tolerant towards his Christian
subjects, and earned their grateful sympathies.
Under his rule they felt at least as well-off as
under the sway of the Romans, as we can see
from the feeling of the traditions originating
from them. Theophanes (A. M. 6170) speaks
of his σπουδή τῶν χριστιανῶν, which he showed
by rebuilding for the Edessaites their church
which had been destroyed by an earthquake.
One of his most influential counsellors, Sarjûn
b. Mansûr, whom he also passed on to his

successors, was a Christian,[1] but it is fictitious
that he actually made a Christian Stattholder in
Emessa.[2] It is a pity that, instead of becoming
Khalifa, he did not confine himself to Syria and
found there a national kingdom which would
have been more firmly established than the
"nationless" universal rule in the East in
which the Arabs perished. He may possibly
have had that idea but have found the execution
of it impossible, for then he would have had to
renounce Islam and come over to the church,
for at that time Islam did not yet tolerate any
separate kingdoms.

Revenge for Uthmân was the title upon
which Muâwia founded his right of inheritance.
In what sense he undertook it is plain from the
fact that to that end he made an alliance with
Amr b. Âs, who had made the most venomous
incitations against Uthmân. Piety was not his
motive, neither did he follow the traditions of
his murdered predecessor. He certainly accepted the general result of the latter's reign, the
rule of the Umaiya, but he did not by any
means, bestow all the rich offices upon the
Umaiyids. He made trials of them, to be sure,

---

[1] Tab., 2.205; 228; 239. Tanbîh (Bibl. Geogr. Arab., VIII) 306f.,
312. In Theophanes, A.M. 6183, Σέργιος ὁ τοῦ Μανσοῦρ ἀνὴρ χριστιανι-
κώτατος is first mentioned under Abdulmalik; cf. Tab., 2,837.

[2] Yaqûbî, 2,265.

but generally was not long in deposing them.
Damascus did not become their headquarters,
but Medina continued to be. This town,
hitherto the centre-point of the kingdom, found
itself forced into the reserve, and likewise the
aristocracy who still continued to live there.
As a general thing, Muâwia left the Stattholdership itself to the Umaiyids, but of what
consequence was Marwân, formerly the all-
powerful imperial chancellor of Uthmân, now
as Emir of Medina! No wonder that he cast
envious looks at his cousin of Damascus who
had so far outstripped him, and that in general
the relations in Medina frowned upon him!
Their sentiments found expression particularly
in the jealousy against Ziâd, as they were afraid
that Muâwia would, through him, strengthen his
house against the whole family and eventually
give him the succession. He, on his part, tried
to rouse up the different branches of the family
in Medina against each other, and so to sap
their strength (Tab., 2, 164). His understanding
with the Quraish, too, left in general something
to be desired. He complained, indeed, that it
was because they had deserted him that he
passed them over. Moreover, he stood in
strained relations with the Makhzûm. They had
long been envious of the Umaiya because by
them they were pushed out of the first place,
which they had taken in Mecca up till the

battle of Badr, and he gave them in addition a
special ground for hatred. Abdurrahmân, son
of the great Makhzûmid, Khâlid b. Walîd, and
himself likewise a deserving and highly-esteemed
man, held at Emessa, in central Syria, such an
independent and important position that he
seemed dangerous to the Khalifa. A Christian
physician poisoned him, it was believed, at the
instigation of Muâwia, and one can imagine
the effect upon the Makhzûm. His relation
to the spiritual nobility of Islam, to the
house of the Prophet, and to the families
of the oldest Companions, as well as to the
Ansâr was naturally one of distrust and
enmity.

His prominent Stattholders in the most
important provinces were not Umaiyids, and
with one exception not even Quraishites. He
kept a watch upon those whom he might need
and placed them in his service. He had the
faculty of winning over and retaining those
whom it was expedient for him to have, and
even of making those whom he distrusted work
for him,—as Amr in Egypt, who felt more like
his ally than his official (Dînaw., 236). His
servants and confidants are frequently enumerated ;[1] they seem to have been mostly *homines novi.*
With them as his συμβουλοι he took counsel as

---

[1] Tab., 1, 3272 ; 3360. 2,139 ; 197 ; 205. Agh., 1, 12.

18

πρωτοσύμβουλος [1]; an example is to be found in
Tab., 2, 136 ff.   They were allowed to presume a
little with him, and in fact did so (2, 144; 185).
Still he did not let the reins slip from his hands,
but he knew how to break them in without
letting them feel the curb. Rude and passionate
scenes never affected him; he bore himself like
an old Arab Saiyid.   God had not granted him
the gift of personal courage, although he unre-
mittingly sent his Syrians into the field against
the Romans, but in all the greater degree
did he possess other qualities of the Saiyid,
the prudent mildness by which he disarmed and
shamed the opposition, slowness to anger, and
the most absolute self-command.   As a pattern
of these qualities he figures in innumerable
stories, along with the Tamîmite Ahnaf, his
contemporary, whom he highly esteemed.   He
was essentially a diplomat and politician, allowing matters to ripen of themselves, and only
now and then assisting their progress, it might
be by the use of a little poison. He made no
denial of his *bourgeois* origin.   He disliked to
have recourse to compulsion, and he did not so

---

[1] Μαυίας καὶ οἱ σύμβουλοι αυτοῦ, Theoph., A.M. 6169; Μαυίας ὁ τῶν
Σαρακηνῶν πρωτοσύμβουλος, A.M. 6171. Later on this designation
was transmitted, after it had long lost its propriety, even to
the Abbasid Khalifas. In A. M. 6165 appears a strange title,
ὁ δεύτερος ἀδελφός. The major-domus of the King of the Nabataei

much conquer Iraq as buy its submission. If
he could reach his goal by means of money, he
spent it lavishly, but he never spent it in vain,
and it amused him to disappoint those who
were counting upon his indiscriminate liberal-
ity, or thought they could cheat him. One of
the oldest traditionists, Sha'bî, heard it told of
him that he was the most amiable companion,
but his secret thoughts could never be distinguished from what he said openly. When listen-
ing to any one he would lean back, cross his
legs and half-shut one eye. In spite of his
corpulence he seemed to the Arabs on public
occasions to command reverence when he had
assumed his black turban and daubed his eyes
with antimony. According to Wâqidî, he died
on Thursday in the middle of Rajab, 60, which
would be Thursday, 18th April, 680. According to Elias Nisibenus, the accession of his
successor took place on Friday, 15th Rajab,
but according to Abû Mikhnaf (2,216) on the
1st Rajab. Abû Ma'shar gives the length of his
reign as 19 years and three months : Wâqidî
adds on 27 days more. He was buried beside
the small gate of Damascus and his grave,
over which there stood a building, was visited

---

was called his brother and certain high officials of the Seleucids were
called their cousins. If there were more than one such brother, then
there might arise a rank-succession.

for centuries. Access to it was given on Mondays and Thursdays.[1]

2. The change of government threatened to cause difficulties, as it always did, but unlike his predecessors, Muâwia tried to settle them in advance. As the only hold he had over the prominent Arabs was the homage which they in person paid to him in person, he wanted, during his life-time, to yoke them with the same obligation towards his son Yazîd, as his successor, but they, naturally without regard to the Syrians, had hoped to shake off this yoke at his death. They pretended he was committing an unheard-of innovation in wishing to introduce a succession from father to son, such as existed with the Sasanids and the Byzantines. According to Arab law the ruling power certainly was passed on as an inheritance within one tribe or clan, but not directly within one house from father to son ; according to Islam it was not a human possession at all to which men could assert their right as heirs, but in spite of that the excitement was out of proportion to the reason alleged for it.[2]   The privilege of the Emir to arrange the succession before his death, held, and even if the son had no right to it, still

---

[1] Masûdî, 5, 14. The poet Kumait fled from the wrath of the Khalifa Hishâm to the grave of Muâwia. (Agh., 15, 115; 117; 121.)

[2] The verses in Masûdî, 5, 71 recall those of Hutaia against Abû Bakr.

he was in no way debarred from it, only, there
apparently had never been a paying of homage
in advance. But they were at the beginnings,
and there was no tradition at all in regard to
this, and no rule of succession.

The common account of Muâwia's procedure which appears in the version of Weil
and A. Müller, runs in B. Athîr as follows,—
the first movement to gain the succession for
Yazîd was made by Mughîra, precisely with
the malicious intention of enticing Muâwia into
a trap. He was commissioned to pave the way
in Kufa, and soon after there appeared in
Damascus deputies from Kufa, whom he
had won over by a small bribe, to urge the paying of homage to Yazîd. But Muâwia was
cautious, and first enquired of Ziâd in Basra.
The latter was persuaded by Ubaid b. Ka'b
an Numairî to make no opposition, but advised
Yazîd, out of regard for public opinion to
moderate a little his *penchant* for heathen
sport,—an advice which was well received and
also followed. But it was not till after Ziâd's
death that Muâwia openly came forward with
his design. First he examined the ground in
Medina, the old capital, which was still regarded
as the proper place for homage-paying, because there dwelt the grandees of Islam, by
whom it was most desirable that it should be
rendered. The men of Medina approved of

his idea of providing for the succession, but when he let it be known to them through Marwân that he had chosen his son as successor, there were disorderly scenes in the mosque. Protests were made, in particular, by the sons of the most prominent Companions, Husain b. Alî, Abdullâh b. Umar, Abdurrahmân b. Abûbakr, and Abdullâh b. Zubair, but Muâwia did not care. He sent for men of consequence from all the provincial capitals to come to Damascus, and delivered an oration before them about the rights of rulers and the duty of subjects in general, and about Yazîd's good qualities in particular. Dahhâk b. Qais alFihrî and other speakers appointed for the purpose applauded him, and drew the conclusion which he refrained from by demanding homage for Yazîd. Ahnaf of Basra alone voiced far-sighted scruples, but their effect was paralysed by gold, and Yazîd received the homage of the deputations. Now only the Hijâz remained. Thither Muâwia went in person with 1,000 horsemen. On reaching Medina he began by giving so great offence to the above-mentioned important objectors, whose homage was specially desirable, that they fled to Mecca. He marched there after them and next tried to win them over by exceptional friendliness. Not till the very end, when he was about to set out on his return home, did he divulge his wishes. He

tried to explain to them that he was not demanding much from them, that Yazîd would be
ruler only in name, and that, under his name, it
would, in fact, be they who would have the
real usufruct of the government. For a long
time they were silent, and at last Ibn
Zubair spoke and in the name of all repu-
diated the suggestion of the Khalifa. Thereupon
he said : "At other times, when I speak in the
pulpit, I permit everyone to say against my
speech what he will; but him who contradicts
me to-day a sword shall silence," and immediately in their hearing he gave the corresponding command to his servants. Then he entered
the mosque of Mecca and declared: "These
four men, without whom no decision about
the succession can be made, have paid homage
to Yazîd; so do ye also pay homage!" Thereupon all did so, and the four keeping silence
from fear, thus acquiesced in the falsehood.
Muâwia made his way back by Medina and
there also received the homage for Yazîd.

This is a clever piece of composition.
Madâinî also relates that Mughîra set on foot
the idea of the homage to Yazîd, and Ziâd, upon
the persuasion of Ubaid b. Ka'b, did not oppose
it. In Tab., 2,173 ff. it is put in the same
year as with B. Athîr. On the other hand there
is nothing in Tabarî about a summoning of
delegates from all the provinces to Muâwia

for the paying of homage to Yazîd ; he mentions (2,196) only one deputation which came from Basra to pay homage, under the leadership of Ubaidullâh b. Ziâd, but does not place it until the year 60, in which Muâwia died. This deputation from Basra is afterwards generalised and antedated. A transition to it is found already in Masûdî.[1] In the old tradition (and also in Masûdî) the fact of greatest interest in which Ibn Athîr's narrative culminates,—namely, the drastic personal interference of Muâwia in the Hijâz, is quite unknown. Only in Tab., 2,175 (Madâinî) it says that after Ziâd's death Muâwia read aloud a document the purport of which was that in case of his death he appointed Yazîd as his successor, and that all agreed to it except five men.[2] The place, presumably Damascus, is not mentioned, and even the time is not precisely stated, for " after Ziâd's death " is only a formula of transition. Further, it says in Tabarî, 2,196 that in the year 60 Muâwia received the homage for Yazîd from the deputies from Basra, and ordered certain measures to be taken after his death against the recalcitrant Quraishites. According to 'Awâna, he charged Dahhâk b. Qais al-Fihrî and Muslim

---

[1] 5, 69. But there the date is not till A.H. 59. For *Ansâr* read *Amsâr*.

[2] Ibn Abbâs is added as the fifth, as he of course could not possibly be left out ; Madâinî is a loyal adherent of the blessed dynasty

b. Uqba alMurrî with the execution of these measures, as Yazîd was absent. We may thus take it that Muâwia had his plan in his mind a considerable time and towards the end of his life tried to carry it through, but in vain as far as concerned the persons whose assent was the most important, because according to Islamic ideas it was they who had the nearest claims to the Khalifate. There is no mention of any more than this. It seems not in keeping with the character of the old man that he should have put himself at the head of 1,000 horsemen in time of peace in order first to hustle the four Quraishites in the Hijâz, then to pamper them, and lastly to force them and yet, after all, to make nothing of it, for those who were chiefly concerned certainly did not take the oath. That he rode into Mecca with an armed force, and there, and not in Medina, had the chief act of homage performed is extremely unlikely, and the dramatic speeches and scenes with which the narrative is adorned do not add to its credibility. The whole thing seems to be a forecast shadow of the events at the beginning of Yazîd's reign, to which we now proceed.

After Yazîd had entered upon the government on the 1st Rajab, 60,—so Abû Mikhnaf relates in Tabarî, 2,216 ff.—he informed the Stattholder of Medina, Walîd b. Utba b. Sufyân, by letter of his father's death, adding upon a leaf no larger than a mouse's ear the command that he was to compel homage from Husain, Ibn Umar and Ibn Zubair,—these three only are named. Walîd took council with Marwân although he was not on very good terms with him, and the latter recommended him to arrest at least Husain and Ibn Zubair at once, before they should hear of the death of Muâwia. But Walîd did not do so immediately, and the two managed to escape to Mecca at the end of Rajab, 60 (beginning of May, 680). Ibn Umar was not considered dangerous; it was said of him that he would only accept the Khalifate if it were presented to him on a salver. Moreover, according to Wâqidî, 2,222 f., he was at that time not in Medina at all, and when he returned he paid homage after he had learnt that everybody else was doing so. Ibn Abbâs did likewise; it was the standpoint of the correct catholicism. Walîd was, of course, soon deposed, and in his stead there came another Umaiyid 'Amr b. Saîd b. Âs, who till then had been in Mecca. According to Wâqidî this happened in Ramadân, 60; in other accounts not till Dhulqada (Tab., 2,226).

Husain let himself be lured out of his retreat in Mecca. He was besieged by the Kufaites begging him to come to them and accept their homage. Their first messages reached him on the 10th Ramadân, and he sent his cousin

Muslim b. Aqîl on in advance to prepare the way for him. The latter found many adherents in Kufa, but finding himself compelled to make a premature attack upon the newly-elected Stattholder Ubaidullâh b. Ziâd, he was left by them in the lurch and came to a lamentable end on the 8th or 9th Dhulhijja. At the same time, on the 8th Dhulhijja, Husain with his followers left Mecca, encouraged by Muslim's first favourable report. He learned, it is true, on the way about the latter's sad death, but either could not or would not turn back, and fell in battle against Kufaite troops at Karbala on the Euphrates on the 10th Muharram, 61 (10th October, 680). The attempt at revolution flickered miserably out, but the martyrdom of Husain had a great ideal significance and a deep after-effect upon the Shîa.[1]

Ibn Zubair proved far more dangerous than Husain. The former was glad to be rid of the rival whom he could not attack. Yazîd was chary of attacking him in earnest because he kept in hiding in the holy city of Mecca where fighting and bloodshed were banned, but the reports of his conduct towards him are inadequate and varying.

Concerning the year 61 (beginning on 1st October, 680) in which Amr b. Saîd was Stattholder of Medina,[2] Abû Mikhnaf in Tab., 2,395 ff.,

[1] Shia, par. 2, pp 61-71.

[2] The accounts of Abû Mikhnaf, whose chronology is not by any means his strong point, cannot have more weight than the fixed dates

relates the following.   Ibn Zubair used the fall
of Husain to over-reach the Kufaites as well as
the government and also, in secret, Yazîd.   His
adherents insisted that he should have homage
paid to him, but he permitted that only in
secret; in public he figured as the fugitive in
the temple.   When Yazîd heard of his doings
he vowed he would throw him into chains, but
on second thoughts sent him a silver chain to
put on.   When the courier passed through
Medina with it, Marwân quoted a verse to show
that to accept the chain was a humiliation.   Ibn
Zubair heard of this and refused the chain.
His importance in Mecca increased; even the
people of Medina wrote to him, and after
Husain's death he was regarded as the next
claimant to the ruling power.

According to a tradition traced back to
Zuhrî in Tab., 2,397 f., the chain which was
composed of silver coins strung together, was
delivered by four messengers, amongst whom
were Ibn 'Idâh and Mas'ada.   Upon their
father's orders, Marwân's sons, Abdulmalik and
Abdulazîz went with them from Medina to
Mecca and recited verses before Ibn Zubair
which were to warn him not to comply. He
understood, and being fore-warned answered
with corresponding verses.

of Wâqidî, 2,223 ff. and Abû Ma'shar, 2,395. Quatremère is right in
differing from Weil (1,325). All the same, Amr b. Saîd may not have
immediately followed Walîd b. Utba (Dînaw., 243, 2, 3).

The two messengers mentioned here appear also in Agh., 1,12, in an account of Wahb b. Jarîr. We may thus conclude that the same event is in question although it is related quite differently, and the silver chain, in particular, is not mentioned at all. Yazîd sent Nu'mân b. Bashîr al-Ansârî to Ibn Zubair with ten other men whose names are given.[1] Nu'mân was to deal liberally with Ibn Zubair separately. Ibn 'Idâh was annoyed at this collusion of the Ansârite and the Muhâjirite,[2] and said to Ibn Zubair that Nu'mân was indeed their leader, but that he had no special commission but only the same one that they all had. Ibn Zubair replied: "What have I to do with thee? I am but a dove of the doves of the sanctuary; wilt thou kill such a dove?" Thereupon the other bent his bow and aimed at a dove, saying to it: "Dove, does Yazîd drink wine? Say 'Yes,' and I will shoot!" And turning to Ibn Zubair he continued: "By God, if you do not pay homage, the horsemen of the Ash'ar will appear, and pay no heed to the holiness of the place; not through them is it desecrated, but through him who uses it as a cover for his sedition." The story with the dove in it has not been

---

[1] In 12, 5 read *alJudhâmî* and *asSakûnî* for *alHizâmî* and *asSalûlî*.

[2] He himself and the others were simple Arabs of Bedouin tribes; Ansâr and Muhâjira, the old inhabitants and the Quraishite emigrants in Medina, are the two classes of the Islamic nobility.

without its effect upon modern historians. It is, however, an anecdote, and the motive is repeated in another form in Tab., 2,430.[1] Even the great number of names mentioned offers no guarantee ; in particular, the name of the leader of the mission seems to be false. Barely a year before, Nu'mân was sent to Mecca by the Khalifa on the same mission as he had to discharge in Medina a year later, but if one must choose, the preference should be given to the tradition of Abû Mikhnaf (2,404) that the Ansârite was sent to Medina to the Ansâr.

The series may be concluded by Wâqidî's version. It comes, in Tabarî, 2,223 ff., under the year 60, but before Husain's death in the beginning of 61. Ibn Zubair had not put in an appearance. After Yazîd had spent his patience in repeated negotiations, he vowed he would not rest till Ibn Zubair stood before him in chains, and when the latter actually obstructed the Emir of Mecca in the leading of the service, he ordered the Stattholder of Medina, Amr b. Saîd, to send an army against him, headed, at his own wish, by a hostile brother of Ibn Zubair, Amr by name. After Amr with his somewhat mixed troop had pushed his way without

---

[1] The Syrian Husain had been having a conference with Ibn Zubair in the sanctuary, and when the doves flew near his horse he took care that it should not trample on one of them. Then said Ibn Zubair, "Thou art unwilling to harm a dove, but art willing enough to slay Muslims."

opposition up to Mecca and had entered it, he spoke to his brother saying he was to appear before the Khalifa with a silver chain round his neck, which he might wear underneath his clothes, that the Khalifa's oath might be fulfilled. Ibn Zubair did not accede, but suddenly caused Amr's bodyguard to be surprised, then seized Amr himself as well and caused him to be cruelly put to death in the prison of ʿĀrim. The ill-fated expedition of Amr is authenticated by Agh., 13,39 f., and by the verses communicated there, and is doubtless historical. But the introduction of the silver chain is not an episode which fits in there ; it is only artificially placed in this connection and rather belongs to the attempts at a peaceable agreement which preceded the violent passages. In this the other traditionists will be right as against Wâqidî.

Towards the end of 61 Amr b. Saîd was deposed from Medina in consequence of an intrigue in the heart of the Umaiyid family. He went to Damascus and justified himself before the Khalifa, and in his place his predecessor Utba b. Walîd returned. According to unanimous tradition he led the Hajj of the year 61 and remained in office during the year 62, for the greater part of the year at least. According to Abû Mikhnaf in Tab., 2,402, Ibn Zubair, by the sending of a letter, contrived that instead of him Uthmân b. Muhammad b. Abî Sufyân was installed, a young man, inexperienced and conceited. According to Tab., 2,405, and apparently also to Abû Mikhnaf (401 f.) he did not enter upon office till after the Hajj of 62, but according to 399,18 that seems to be disputed. In any case the change took place at the end of 62 or the beginning of 63.

The year 63 (which begins 10th September, 682) is, unlike the two preceding years, full of the most important events. As Abû Mikhnaf relates,[1] the new Stattholder sent a deputation from Medina to Yazîd, men of standing from the Ansâr as well as from the Muhâjira. They were influential leaders of public opinion, which in Medina was certainly not decisively in favour of Ibn Zubair, but at any rate was anti-Umaiyid. He hoped that Yazîd would use the convincing power of money to win them over. Yazîd did give them rich presents,[2] but that did not deter them, on their return, from relating the most terrible things of him,—that he amused himself with hunting-hounds,[3] sought out the worst company, drank wine to the accompaniment of music and song : in short, he had no religion. It is a mistake that the deputation consisted

---

[1] In Tab., 2,402f. Wahb b. Jarîr (2,422 f.) has a parallel dated very vaguely, viz., " after Muâwia's death."

[2] Tab., 2, 419 f. differs.

[3] Agh., 20, 106 says "apes."

only of Ansâr and of contemporaries of Muhammad. A. Müller (1,367) speaks of queer old
fellows of the company of the Prophet who
were utter strangers to Yazîd. He forms notions
of his own about them and the Khalifa, who was
naturally quite *au fait* with everything in
Medina, the foremost town of Islam, and like
all Arabs of high position knew personally a
very large number of people. Abû Mikhnaf
tells of one more last attempt made by Yazîd
to conciliate the minds in Medina. He would
not willingly use force against the town because
it was the seat of his own tribe, so he sent
thither the best-qualified apostle of peace,
Nu'mân b. Bashîr, who, however, to his grief,
preached to deaf ears.

The prelude to the revolt of the people of
Medina was, according to Agh., 1, 13 (Madâinî)
a dramatic scene in the mosque. Seized by
a sudden fury, they renounced their obedience
to Yazîd by each taking off his mantle, turban
or shoe,—the customary token of the dissolution
of relations,—and throwing it before him, so that
soon a great heap of them lay on the ground.
Nothing of this is in Tabarî. Abû Mikhnaf
(2,405 ff.) marks the beginning of the rising by
the fact that the people of Medina did homage
to Abdullâh b. Hanzala as their leader, in the
struggle against Yazîd and the Umaiyid rule.
Ibn Hanzala had taken part in the deputation
20

to Damascus; he was an Ansârite, celebrated from his birth as the posthumous son of the martyr of Uhud who was washed by the angels. The next act of the rebels was to attack the Umaiyids in Medina. To the number of 1,000 men they fled to the quarter of Marwân, the oldest and most esteemed head of the family. Marwân sent word of their plight to the Khalifa: "We are being pelted with berries and have no good water to drink. Help! Help!" Although he made light of the lamentation, Yazîd decided to send an army at once. Amr b. Saîd was to lead it, but as he had no wish to spill the blood of the Quraish (of Medina) on the open field he suggested that the command be given to a non-Quraishite, whereupon Yazîd turned to an old and trusty servant of his father, Muslim b. Uqba alMurrî. His opinion was that 1,000 men who could not defend themselves for a while were not worth helping, but was ready to go all the same, since Yazîd explained that he could not leave his relations in difficulties. Troops were now recruited, and for the full pay, with an additional sum of 100 dinars to be paid down at once, 12,000 Syrians were mustered.[1] Meanwhile those besieged in Medina had obtained a free retreat and had set out for Syria, but Marwân's wife had gone to Taîf under

---

[1] They were indeed, as usual, mostly Kalbites; the leader of the Qais, Zufar b. Hârith, fought against them on the side of Ibn Zubair. *Cf.* besides Chawarig, p. 54,

the protection of the one son of Husain who
had been saved at Karbala, and who belonged
to the few Quraishites who had not taken part
in the rising. Muslim, on his march to Medina,
met the fleeing Umaiyids in Wâdilqurâ. He
was furious against them as it was, and was not
sorry now to make short work of their chiefs,
because they, being bound by an oath, would
give him no answer to his questions. Fortunately Abdulmalik, the son of Marwân, managed
to avert his anger ; he was delighted by Abdulmalik's expert counsels and followed them. In
Dhulhijja, 63, he reached Medina and encamped
in the Harra to the N. E. of the town. He gave
the insurgents three days' time for reflection, saying that he wished to be able to withdraw from
them and set out against the hypocrites in Mecca,
for he was unwilling to shed their blood, as they
were the roots (of Islam and the kingdom).
Even after the time of grace had elapsed he
made still another attempt with fair words,
which were answered by abuse. The people of
Medina had protected the exposed north corner
of their town by a rampart and ditch. Their
army consisted of four groups, commanded by
two Quraishites, an Ashja'ite and the Ansârite
Ibn Hanzala, who at the same time had the
supreme command.

From this point onwards Abû Mikhnaf's
report in Tabarî is complemented by traditions of

'Awâna and others, which do not always altogether agree with it. The men of Medina marched against the Syrians on the Harra and pressed on to the station of Muslim himself, who according to one account was seated on horseback ; according to another he was borne in a litter. But finally they were overcome, and a great number of noble Ansârites and Quraishites fell, amongst them Ibn Hanzala with eight sons. The defeat, according to Wahb b. Jarîr (Tab., 2,423) and Samhûdî (*Skizzen*, 4,26) was decided by the treason of the Banû Hâritha, through whose quarter a Syrian division penetrated into the town and attacked the defenders in the rear. Wâqidî gives as the date (2,422) Wednesday, 26th or 27th Dhul-hijja, 63 = Wed., 26th August, 683. The town of the Prophet was for three days given up to the Syrian warriors and they revelled there to their hearts' content. So say Abû Mikhnaf (2,418) and Samhûdî, but 'Awâna differs. According to him on the day after the battle Muslim compelled the prominent people of Medina to do homage in Qubâ, and on this occasion executed some ring-leaders, including, notwithstanding the protest of Marwân, a few Quraishites and also the Ashja'ite Ma'qil b. Sinân.[1] This orderly behaviour on the day

---

[1] Ma'qil was, like him, from Ghatafân, and had a long-standing friendship with him, but he was angered against him. "Thou mettest

after the battle does not agree with the three days' ravaging of the town. It is hardly to be confirmed by the thousand illegitimate children who, according to Samhûdî, were said to be born in consequence. Wahb b. Jarîr (423, 15f.) makes no mention of it either.

After mastering Medina, Muslim proceeded to Mecca, but only got as far as Mushallal, where he died with a calm conscience, convinced that he had done a work well-pleasing to God. He made over his property not to his sons but to his tribe and his wife. The command he left, much against his will, to the Sakûnite Husain b. Numair, because the Khalifa had so ordained it. He impressed upon him never to lend an ear to a Quraishite. 'Awâna's report in Tabarî, 2,424 ff., agrees with Abû Mikhnaf's as far as it, goes. Abû Mikhnaf puts the death of Muslim at the end of Muharram, 64, but according to 'Awâna and Wâqidî, Husain was already encamped before Mecca in Muharram.

The statements of the later writers are in strange contrast with the picture here sketched of Muslim b. Uqba. " Perhaps there was

me in Tiberias when thou camest back from Yazîd, and saidst, ' We have been travelling a whole month and now have come back empty-handed ; when we get home we will renounce this wicked man and do homage to one of the sons of the Muhâjira.' What have Ghatafân and Ashja' to do with the choosing and deposing of Khalifas! I have sworn, if I meet thee in war and have the power, to cut off thy head." The *fima...min* 420, 3 does not deserve a question-mark.

no one who represented the old time and the heathen principle so much as he did. In him there was not even a vestige of Muhammadan faith, nothing of all that was sacred to the Muslims was sacred to him. He held all the more firmly to heathen superstition, believing in the prophetic dreams, in the mysterious words which issued from the Gharqad-bushes, as was seen when he offered his services to Yazîd. He told him that through him alone could Medina be brought to subjection, for he had heard in a dream the voice from a Gharqad-bush say, ' through Muslim.' " Thus Dozy (*Histoire des Musulmans d'Espagne*, 1, 97 f.), and similarly A. Müller, 1,367 : " Muslim b. Uqba was inspired by the same hatred towards Islam, especially against the orthodox, as had made Shamir the destroyer of Husain. Old and ill as he was, the welcome prospect of the long but vainly sought chastisement of these deadly foes of the whole heathen system reinvigorated him for a while. In case he did not live to see the end of the campaign, there was sent with him as his successor, Husain b. Numair, who shortly before had been Ubaidul- lâh's right hand in Kufa,[1] and who felt for the mosque of the Prophet and for the Ka'ba about the same respect as for two empty shells."

---

[1] Here the Syrian Husain b. Numair as Sakûnî is confused with the Kufaite Husain b. Tamîm at Tamîmî, and thereby the account of the former is still more heavily charged.   For Shamir, *cf.* Shia, p. 70.

Because of the Gharqad-bush, which according to Agh., 1,14, he perhaps did not really consult, but only saw in a dream,[1] Muslim b. Uqba has become a heathen incarnate. Inspired by deep hatred of the people of Medina, he in spite of age and sickness, eagerly sought and seized the opportunity to massacre them. The old tradition knows nothing of all this. According to Tabarî, 2,425, he testified on his death-bed that what he laid most value upon was faith in Allâh and His Messenger. He was not eager for the task which Yazîd entrusted him with ; he was not even very willing to undertake it. He had no wish to wreak his vengeance upon the town of the Prophet, but tried to spare it up to the very last moment. It is even doubtful whether he decreed a three-days' pillage after the victory. He compelled it to do homage, but not in an unusually disgraceful manner.[2] He was a faithful servant to his master and subdued the rebels for him. " What has Ghatafân to do with the question as to who is the rightful Khalifa ? " He was glad that for him as a Ghatafanite the question did not exist, and he left political aspirations to the strivers and intriguers who were lurking in both the holy towns. His opinion was that they misused the sanctuary and so cancelled its power of inviolability,

---

[1] Hajjâj is analogous.   Tab., 2, 829, 15.

[2] As Dozy, 1, 107 takes it.   *Cf.* on the other hand Tab., II, 418, 18.

and he acted accordingly with the decision of conviction. As time went on, the more shocking was the sacrilege on his part considered, and thus he became the heathen scarecrow which Dozy and Müller make him out to be.

Dozy, 1,108, spins the thread which he started at the Gharqad-bush still further. "The Syrian Arabs had settled their account with the sons of the fanatic sectaries who had deluged Arabia with the blood of their fathers. The old nobility had annihilated the new. Yazîd, as representative of the old aristocracy of Mecca, had avenged the murder of the Khalifa Uthmân as well as the defeat which his grandfather, Abû Sufyân, had suffered at the hands of the people of Medina under Muhammad's standard. The reaction of the heathen principle against the Muslim was cruel and relentless. The Ansâr never recovered from this blow; their strength was broken for ever. Their almost desolate town was for a time given up to the dogs, and the country to the wild beasts, for most of the inhabitants sought a new home for themselves far afield, and went to the African army. The others were much to be pitied, for the Umaiyids took every opportunity of letting them feel their hatred and their scorn, of mortifying them and making their lives a burden " Müller, 1,368 f., adapts himself to these conceptions, which are altogether distorted and for the most part quite erroneous.

Medina had suffered its worst blow when the old lawful Khalifate ceased with the murder of Uthmân and the new one was transferred to the provinces; the present blow did not bring about any essential changes. Medina did not become desolate, the expelled Umaiyids soon returned, to be again expelled later on. It remained, as before, a gay town, the seat not merely of pious tradition, but also of the most eminent and refined Arab society, and therefore preferred by those who wanted to retire from business and live at ease, the *rendez-vous* of singers, musicians and parasites. All the pertinent articles of the *Kitâb al-Aghâni* give proofs of this. The one about Abû Qatîfa and that about Ash'ab are perhaps specially to be noted, and above all the one about Sukaina, the wanton and witty great-grand-daughter of the Prophet. Besides, the representation is misleading, as if the Ansâr only were severely affected by the consequences of the battle on the Harra. The Ansâr must not be simply identified with the people of Medina. Medina had long ceased to be their town. They dwelt there together with the Muhâjira, who were equal to them in numbers and superior in strength. Amongst the latter the Quraish took first place; since the year 8 they had immigrated in great crowds, and the capital of the kingdom became their real home. They took part in the rising against Yazîd just as

21

well as the Ansâr. The distinction between
Islamic and pre-Islamic nobility which certainly
existed among them was not taken much into
consideration. Yazîd had not a party among
them at all. He was not the representative of
their old aristocracy even although he belonged
to it, and in the Hijâz they turned completely
against him as they had already done against
his father. The eminent Makhzûm, for example,
were thorough-going Zubairites. Even the
Umaiyids of Medina were not on the best of
terms with Yazîd; they did not want to fall
out with the rebels and they coquetted with
Ibn Zubair, and Muslim b. Uqba had reason
enough to be angry with them. Yazîd had only
the Syrians on his side, and from them he raised
an army of a few thousand men, but for an
unusually high pay. Just as he himself was
not filled with a desire for vengeance against
the rebels, but rather sought to win them over
by kindness and showed them great leniency,
so his Syrians were not burning for battle
either. They would have been surprised to
learn that it was their deep hatred " towards
the fanatic sectaries who had flooded Arabia
with the blood of their fathers " which had
provoked them to take up arms. If this was
the reason, the Iraqites who sprang from the
Ahl arRidda would have been far more justified
in hatred of the men of Medina; or was it

indeed the case that the Syrians, perhaps the Kalb, had suffered most ? Dozy rather gives rein to his fancy and rhetoric, and by so doing has also confused the minds of his successors. The plain fact is that the Syrian Arabs, like all the rest, had had to adapt themselves to Islam, which was indeed far less a matter of a religious change than of a political one. Even thus the transition might perhaps have been at first unpleasant to them, but that was soon got over for they derived the greatest advantages from it. Islam allowed them to participate in its government and laid the world at their feet : without Islam they would never have reached the position they now assumed. Thus they could not always continue to feel deeply embittered against those who had helped them to their present prosperity. Least of all can we speak of their deep hatred against the "orthodox," as A. Müller calls the people of Medina. In the teaching of the faith and the law and in the customs of public and private worship they were absolutely at one with the people of Medina, who certainly applied themselves more zealously to religious duties and especially spoke more about them, but in general were far from being dismal old fellows and fanatical sectaries. The modern expression "Orthodox" may lead to a very perverted conception of the relations of the hostile parties.

According to our non-theocratic ideas, the contrast was simply a political one, dealing with
the question,—who had the right to the Khalifate ?   The members of the Islamic nobility, the
sons of the six oldest and most prominent Companions of the Prophet, like Husain and Ibn
Zubair, claimed it for themselves and had also
public opinion and the majority of the Quraish
on their side.   Even the Ansâr, just as at the
mutiny against Uthmân, must have worked
for them, from the point of view that it was a
question of winning back for the old capital
of the kingdom the dominating position which
it had lost.   There are clues which show that
the rising in Medina was instigated by Ibn
Zubair, and Muslim b. Uqba thought it was.
The Sufyânids in Damascus were regarded
as usurpers; only the Syrians, to defend the
primacy of their province, held fast to the
government which had the power, and did not
bother about the question of right.   This question, which for us is purely political, was for
theocratic Islam really part of the religion, and
the claims of the pretenders were supported on
religious grounds.   It was on religious grounds
that Yazîd was declared unworthy of the Khalifate, but in the mouths of the leaders of the
movement these grounds were only pretexts;
their real motive was ambition, and greed of
power.   They wanted to depose Yazîd, not

because he drank wine and amused himself, but because they hoped for his place. The Syrians were so far right in that the question of right only seemed to them a hypocritical glossing-over of the question of might. Also, the reproach of hypocrisy brought by them refers to this and this only, a reproach met by the opposite party by the taunt of profanity.

For the siege of Mecca in A.H. 64, 'Awâna in Tab., 2, 424 ff. is the chief authority. After the battle on the Harra "all Medina" came to Mecca; only a few Quraishites are named (404, 20; 426, 10; 528, 12). Before this the Khawârij of Yamâma, under Najda b. 'Âmir, had already hastened to the help of the Holy House against the attack of the Syrians.[1] Husain b. Numair arrived before the town in Muharram, 64, with the Syrians, and a first battle resulted unfortunately for the defenders. On Sunday, 3rd Rabî I, 64, *i.e.* Sunday, 31st Octr., 683, the Syrians, according to 'Awâna, set fire to the Ka'ba.

This latter account of 'Awâna is incorrect. The Ka'ba certainly did go on fire at that time, and the Holy Stone burst and became black, but it was not the Syrians who caused it. Abû Mikhnaf (528, 17; 529, 4) uses the passive and keeps the matter quiet. According to

[1] Abû Mikhnaf's date in Tab., 401 f., is put too early. *Cf.* Chawarig, 29, Shia, 75. Hamâsa, 319, 22.

Wâqidî (427) one of Ibn Zubair's people had been fetching fire on the point of his lance and the wind wafted it towards the Ka'ba. According to Madâinî (Agh., 3, 84) Ibn Zubair himself was the unhappy man to whom this happened. The verse upon which 'Awâna supports his statement does not mention fire, and according to Hamâsa, 319, refers to another occasion, namely, the siege of Mecca under Hajjâj (Tab., 2, 844 ff. ; 1542, 3) at which the Syrians did really aim at the Ka'ba, but only with stones. 'Awâna thus seems to have made an exchange, with which, indeed, tendency has something to do.

The siege lasted till the tidings of Yazîd's death, which took place on the 14th Rabî I, reached Mecca; according to Wâqidî this was Tuesday, 1st Rabî II, 64, 27 days [1] after the burning of the Ka'ba. On the other hand Abû Mikhnaf (529, 7) says it did not take place till the 15th Rabî II, and according to 'Awâna (429, 18) it even continued 40 days after Yazîd's death. The shortest account is the best. According to 'Awâna, Ibn Zubair received the news first, and the Syrians at first would not believe it until they had it confirmed from another quarter. Husain now negotiated with Ibn Zubair. He was willing to recognise him as Khalifa,

[1] Tab., 427, 8. The day of the week does not agree with the day of the month. For 29 should be read 27, since the burning of the Ka'ba, according to unanimous tradition, had occurred on the 3rd Rabî I.

faute de mieux, if he would annul the bloodshed
in Medina and Mecca and go with him to Syria,
so that the seat of government should remain
there. In the end Ibn Zubair complied with
the first condition, but did not agree to the
second, nor could he without ruining himself.
So the negotiations broke off and Husain
withdrew. His soldiers seemed to be dishearten-
ed because, since Yazîd's death, they had no
longer an Imâm, and no longer knew for
whom they were fighting,—so very personal did
the paying of homage make the conditions of
the political situation. The Umaiyids of Medina
are said to have gone with them to Syria
because they no longer felt secure in the Hijâz,
but 'Awâna himself contradicts this (469, 3),
as well as Wâqidî (467, 10) and Abû Mikhnaf
(481, 10). The Umaiyids did not go of their
own accord, but only when they were driven
out of Medina by Ibn Zubair. The Continuatio
Byz. Ar., *par.* 29, also says so : " Marwan insidiose ab ipso Abdella ab Almedinae finibus cum
omnibus liberis vel (=et) suis propinquis
pellitur. "

    3. According to Abû Ma'shar, Wâqidî and
Elias Nisibenus, Yazîd died at Huwârin (near
Damascus) on Tuesday, the 14th Rabî I, 64, *i.e.*
Tuesday, 11th November, 683.[1] As the wrongful

    [1] Tab., 428, 8 ; 488, 14. The varying accounts 437, 3, and 506, 7
are erroneous, and the year 63 (468, 15, *cf.* 412, 9) is a slip. His

heir of the Khalifate, guilty of the murder
of Husain and the desecration of the holy towns,
his memory is a bitter one to the Muslims, but,
in reality, he was not a despot; he kept the
sword sheathed as long as ever he dared. He
brought to an end the long-drawn-out war
against the Romans. What he may be reproached with is lack of energy and of interest
in public affairs. As a prince, especially, he
was extremely indifferent to them, and so made
the struggle to secure to him the succession a
difficult matter for his father. He took part in
the great campaign against Constantinople [1] in
A. H. 49 only under compulsion. Later on,
indeed, as Khalifa, he seems to have pulled himself together, although he did not give up his
old predilections,—wine, music, the chase and
other sport. In the Continuatio, *par.* 27, it says
of him; "Jucundissimus et cunctis nationibus
regni ejus subditis vir gratissime habitus, qui
nullam unquam, ut omnibus moris est, sibi
regalis fastigii causa gloriam appetivit, sed
communis cum omnibus civiliter vixit." No
other is awarded such eulogy; it comes from
the heart.

"You Banî Umaiya, the last of your rulers
is a corpse in Huwârin, there at rest for ever.

age is given by Zuhrî and Wâqidî at 38 or 39, and by Ibn Kalbî at 35
years. *Cf.* Nöldeke, DMZ., 1901, pp. 683 f.

[1] *Göttinger Nachrichten, 1901*, p. 423. Once he was in the field he
proved brave and capable (Agh., 16, 33).

Fate overtook Yazîd with a beaker by his pillow and a brimming wine-flagon." So sang Ibn Arâda in Khurâsân (Tab., 2, 488). With the death of Yazîd the power of his house seemed to collapse everywhere. Even the Stattholders did not support it; Salm b. Ziâd in Khurâsân and Ubaidullâh b. Ziâd in Basra had homage paid to themselves, though only provisionally. In Syria, indeed, at least in Damascus, the successor designated by Yazîd was recognised,— his very youthful son Muâwia II. On his accession he remitted to " all the provinces of his realm " one-third of the tribute,[1] but he died after a short reign. According to 'Awâna in Tab., 2, 468 and Balâdh., 229, 3, he is said even to have abdicated before his death, but Wâqidî in Tab., 577, 1, says nothing about this. The story is probably connected with the attempt to veil the fact that the older branch of the Umai-yid dynasty, the Sufyânids, was wrongfully supplanted by the younger, the Marwânids. This attempt also explains how in several old records Muâwia II is not included in the list as Khalifa at all, but Marwân follows directly after Yazîd, just as in the Bible Chronicle the reign of Ishbosheth is suppressed and David is placed immediately after Saul.[2]

[1] *Cont. Byz. Ar.*, par. 27. It was customary at an accession to have such a αφεσις.

[2] *Cf.* Nöldeke in the Epimetrum to Mommsen's edition of the Cont. Isidor., and in the DMZ., 1901, pp. 683 ff.

22

Apparently even in Muâwia II's lifetime there began the Syrian disturbances to which we now proceed. They originated with the Qais, who dwelt chiefly in the north of the province and in Mesopotamia on both sides of the Euphrates (Tab., 708. 4), in Qinnesrîn, Qarqîsiâ and Harrân. These alone of all the Syrians are said to have refused homage to Muâwia II. They were enraged at the preference given to the Kalb through Yazîd and his son, both of whom had a Kalbite mother (Hamâsa, 319, 2 ; 4). Yazîd's maternal uncle, Hassân b. Mâlik b. Bahdal al Kalbî, had a powerful place in the kingdom and was the main pillar of Muâwia II, while his brother Saîd was Stattholder of Qinnesrin. To be ruled in their own town by a Kalbite was beyond the endurance of the Qais and they began by expelling him. This took place under the leadership of Zufar b. Hârith alKilâbî (Agh., 17, 111), who had previously fought for Ibn Zubair against Yazîd's army (Ham., 319, 22). Thus he was a Zubairite, and the Qais followed him after Ibn Zubair was recognised also in the neighbouring Iraq, but Ibn Zubair's party was also making progress elsewhere in Syria. Ibn Bahdal alone,— this is the usual contraction for Hassân b. Mâlik b. Bahdal—adhered even after Muâwia II's death to the descendants of his sister. In order to be nearer to Damascus, he moved from Palestine,

which he administered, to the Urdunn. On the
other hand, the Stattholder of Emessa, the well-
known Nu'mân b. Bashîr alAnsârî, recognised
Ibn Zubair, and likewise also Nâtil b. Qais
alJudhâmî, who took possession of Palestine
after Ibn Bahdal had left it. In the imperial
capital Dahhâk b. Qais alFihrî had hilt in hand.
His conduct was wavering and ambiguous, but
as he was in danger of falling between two
stools, he was at last compelled to declare
decisively for the side of Ibn Zubair.

Reports vary concerning the progress of
events up till the bloody decision at Marj Râhit.
According to 'Awâna in Tab., 2, 468 ff. the
Umaiyids who had been expelled from Medina,
and also the Stattholder Ubaidullâh b. Ziâd
who had fled from Basra, had betaken themselves to Damascus, apparently after the death
of Muâwia II. Dahhâk, who ruled there, con-
cealed his real views, for in reality he inclined
to Ibn Zubair, but Ibn Bahdal, the head of the
Kalb and Yemen of the Umaiyid persuasion,
drove the fox from his lair. He sent him a
letter to be read aloud in the mosque, in which
he recalled the merits of the Umaiyids, and gave
warning against the hypocritical Ibn Zubair.
Dahhâk did not make the letter public, but the
messenger, a Kalbite named Nâghida, had, in
case of this, brought with him a second copy,
which he now read aloud himself at the weekly

service. Then followed a scene which is called " the day of Jairûn." [1] The Qais and the Kalb rose against each other in the mosque. The Umaiyids themselves were on different sides; Walîd b. Utba b. Abî Sufyân approved of the contents of the letter; Amr b. Yazîd b. Hakam disapproved. At the close of the service the Kalb beat the latter soundly, but Dahhâk, on the other hand, imprisoned the brawlers who had expressed themselves against Ibn Zubair, but they were immediately liberated by the Kalb ; Walîd b. Utba only had to wait, because he had no tribe, till Khâlid and Abdullâh, two younger brothers of Muâwia II, at last induced the Kalb to set him free also. The next day Dahhâk regretted his action, made excuses to the Umaiyids, and agreed to go together with them to Jâbia and there to treat with Ibn Bahdal concerning the choice of one of them as Khalifa. And yet at the last moment he turned round again, upon the re-monstrances of the Qaisite Thaur b. Ma'n as-Sulamî, and with his followers occupied a camp in Marj Râhit near Damascus. He now openly declared for Ibn Zubair, and the majority of the people of Damascus,—and also

---

[1] The *first* " day of Jairûn " is not the proper term, for what is represented as the *second* (471, 13-19) is only a variant. Jairûn was a large old building where probably the brawl after the service took place. One exit of the chief mosque is called the gate of Jairûn. *Cf.* Hamâsa, 654, v. 4.

of the Yemenites amongst them—followed him.
At his demand the Emirs of Emessa, Qinnesrin
and Palestine who were in favour of Zubair sent
him reinforcements. The Umaiyids betook
themselves to Ibn Bahdal at Jâbia. They were
divided [1]; against the family of the Sufyânids,
which till then was the ruling family, stood
the rest of the very numerous tribe, which, as
a whole, took the side of its old chief, Marwân
b. Hakam. Ibn Bahdal, the agent of the
minor sons of Yazîd, finally let himself be won
over and declared he had cast in his lot with
Marwân, but after him were to follow Khâlid b.
Yazîd, and then Amr b. Saîd, whose family then
also raised claims and had to be paid off.
Marwân now marched to Marj Râhit with the
Kalb of Urdunn, the Sakâsik and Sakûn and
the Ghassân. While the hostile armies stood
facing each other, the Ghassânid Ibn Abî Nims
took possession of the town of Damascus and
assisted Marwân with money and weapons.
The battle at Marj Râhit lasted 20 days; finally the Qais fled with terrible loss. Dahhâk
fell, and with him 80 nobles who wore a robe

---

[1] The Umaiya have a collateral branch, the 'Abalât. They themselves break up into the Anâbis and the A'yâs. The Sufyânids belong
to the Anâbis; most of the other families to the A'yâs. Marwân b.
Hakam and his cousin Uthmân b. Affân are descended from Abu l'Âs;
Amr b. Saîd is descended from al'As. The same names with unimpor-
tant differences recur in Umaiya and Abd Umaiya, al'Âs and Abu
l'Âs. *Cf.* Agh., 1, 8 f. (84, 10); 10, 103 f.; 7, 62; Tab., 1, 2535.

of honour (the *Qatîfa*) and drew a pension of 2,000 dirhems.

Beside this account of 'Awâna stands that of Madâinî, Agh., 17, 111. Madâinî says nothing of the "day of Jairûn" and gives rather a different version about Marwân, but in conclusion is completely in agreement with 'Awâna. When Marwân with the Umaiyids of Medina came to Damascus, he was at first won over by Dahhâk for Ibn Zubair and consented to convey to him in person the homage of the Syrians, but Amr b. Saîd, Ubaidullâh b. Ziâd, and the two Sakûnites, Mâlik b. Hubaira and Husain b. Numair,[1] prevailed upon him to decide to have homage paid to himself. When Dahhâk heard of this, he turned coat, excused himself to the Umaiya and proposed to come into Jâbia together with Ibn Bahdal and in company with him to set about the election of a Khalifa. Ibn Bahdal came with the people of the Urdunn to Jâbia; Dahhâk and the Umaiya, with the people of Damascus, set out on the road thither likewise. At the last moment, however, Dahhâk was besought by the Qaisites: "Thou hast summoned us to do homage to Ibn Zubair, the Khalifa recognised everywhere else, and wilt thou now follow this Kalbite to do homage to his

---

[1] 'Awâna's account in Tab., 2, 474 is somewhat different. *Cf.* also 487.

nephew ?"[1] This had the effect of making him turn round and openly declare for Ibn Zubair, and he encamped in Marj Râhit. Ibn Bahdal and Marwân advanced to Damascus, where the Yemen went over to them, and then continued their march to Marj Râhit. They had 7,000 men, Dahhâk 30,000 ; a battle ensued and Dahhâk and the nobles of Qais fell. Zufar b. Hârith fled to Qarqisia ; and after the battle at the Khâzir he was joined by Umair b. Hubâb as-Sulamî, who till then had remained faithful to Marwân.

Very different, again, is the version of Abû Mikhnaf in Tab., 2,479 ff. Marwân and the Umaiyids who had been expelled from Medina by Ibn Zubair did not go to Damascus, because there Dahhâk was ruling in name of Ibn Zubair, but to Tadmor (Palmyra), the capital and headquarters of the Kalb ; but Marwân was in two minds whether to go in person to Ibn Zubair and beg for favourable terms, when Ubaidullâh b. Ziâd from Basra appeared in Tadmor. The latter called upon Marwân to have homage paid to himself, while Amr b. Saîd urged the same thing and at the same time advised Marwân to marry the widow of Yazîd. So it fell out that Marwân had homage paid to himself in Tadmor, and then with 6,000 men marched

---

[1] This does not quite agree with the premises. The nephew of Ibn Bahdal who is meant is Khâlid b. Yazîd.

against Dahhâk. The latter advanced to meet
him at Marj Râhit, and thither also came
Zufar b. Hârith and other adherents of Ibn
Zubair. In the battle Dahhâk fell and his
army scattered ; Zufar was saved by two youths
who sacrificed themselves for him,[1] and afterwards established himself in Qarqisia. Nâtil b.
Qais fled to Mecca. When Nu'mân b. Bashîr
got the tidings of Marj Râhit he fled by night
with wife and child from Emessa, but was pursued and slain by the Emessaites themselves.
After this success Marwân was recognised all
through Syria.

Wâqidî takes up a sort of intermediate position between Abû Mikhnaf and 'Awâna-Madâinî,
and his scattered accounts in Tabarî may be
collected somewhat as follows. As Muâwia at
his death had not wished to name any successor (577, 1) homage was paid provisionally in
Damascus to Dahhâk, until a definite agreement
of Muhammad's congregation should be arrived
at (468). Dahhâk aimed at getting the rule for
himself, but was forced by the Quraish to do
homage to Ibn Zubair (473 f.), and Marwân
became subordinate to him. On the advice of
Husain b. Numair he was about to betake himself to Ibn Zubair before the latter should
penetrate into Syria (467 f.), when, fortunately,

---

[1] This is testified through his own verses and is doubtless correct.
Cf. Anon. Ahlw. 253 f.

Ubaidullâh b. Ziâd came to Damascus and reinforced the Umaiyids (468). Marwân now went
to Jâbia to ally himself with Ibn Bahdal and
the Yemenites, and there he accepted homage
for himself as the oldest of the Umaiya, for the
Syrians would not do homage to a child, and
then marched with the Yemenites against
Damascus. The Qais were defeated at Marj
Râhit at the end of the year 64, suffering greater
losses than any army ever did before (473, 1).

The chief points on which these versions
differ are the following.—Only in 'Awâna and
no one else does the "day of Jairûn" occur,
the day on which the excitement in Damascus
first broke out. The Hamâsa establishes it
without doubt (656, v. 4). The circumstance is
there given wrongly by the Scholion (actually
under Muâwia I). *Cf.* on the other hand 657,
v. 3. Abû Mikhnaf is the only one who says
the Umaiyids who were driven out of Medina
went to Tadmor and were there met by Ubaidullâh, as opposed to all the others who give
Damascus as the place.[1] Now certainly the
drama of Jairûn at any rate was played in
Damascus, and there were some Umaiyids present, but it does not appear from the description
that the bulk of the Medinan family were there.
Marwân and Amr b. Saîd are not mentioned and
do not appear where one expects them. In

[1] So also *Cont. Byz. Ar.,* par. 29.

23

spite of this Abû Mikhnaf's account has nevertheless been erroneously made the general one.
For with him Tadmor takes the place not merely
of Damascus but of Jâbia also. He makes the
paying of homage to Marwân, which without
doubt took place at Jâbia, happen in Tadmor,
perhaps because Tadmor, and not Jâbia, was the
capital of the Kalb.

In particular, the sudden change of Marwân
is not mentioned by 'Awâna ; only Abû Mikhnaf
and Wâqidî say that he was affected by
the arrival of Ubaidullâh, but these two
deserve the greater credence since in Tab.,
2,459, Madâinî also agrees with them.

According to 'Awâna and Madâinî, Dahhâk
was inclined to the side of Zubair from the
beginning, even if he did not show it openly ;
Abû Mikhnaf says he was simply Ibn Zubair's
Emir over Damascus, but his descendants declared to Wâqidî (473 f.) that this was a falsehood, saying that he had preferred to remain
neutral in order to get to the head of affairs
himself, and only did homage to Ibn Zubair
under external pressure, and we may believe
them. Dahhâk, like Muslim b. Uqba, probably
also maintained under Yazîd the position
which he took up under the old Muâwia, whose
right hand he was. After the throne fell
vacant he became the provisional regent in
Damascus, but he was not able to maintain

his position above the parties, and after long
hesitation he finally joined the side of the Qais
and Ibn Zubair. He was forced from his neutral position especially by his old rival, now an
opponent all the more dangerous, Hassân b.
Mâlik Ibn Bahdal, who had the Kalb behind
him. The latter for a while alone held aloft
the Umaiyid standard, particularly by champion-
ing the rights of the family of Yazîd, who
were related to him by marriage. The Umaiyids of Medina did not join him in this, nor
did they at first put forward any claimant from
their midst, as they believed that they would
have to make their peace with Ibn Zubair upon
any terms, good or bad. It was only through
Ubaidullâh that they changed their mind, and
now when the latter pointed out to Marwân
that he had not merely the choice between
the sons of Yazîd, who were under age, and
Ibn Zubair, but ought to have a try for the
ruling power himself, the only means towards
that end was to come to an understanding
with Ibn Bahdal, for he was the only man
who had command over extensive forces (Tab.,
708, 4). It was for this purpose that the
conference at Jâbia took place, at which
Dahhâk may even have promised to appear,
and it brought them to their goal after lengthy
negotiations. It is certainly historical, even
though Abû Mikhnaf does not mention it, for

without Ibn Bahdal simply nothing could be done. For 40 days he was the leader in prayer at Jâbia, and he was also the real conqueror of Marj Râhit.[1] Theophanes, in

A.M. 6175, says ; "καὶ συναχθέντες οἱ Φοίνικες καὶ οἱ Παλαστίνης ἐπὶ τὴν Δαμασκος ἔρχονται καὶ ἑως τοῦ Γαβιθα πρὸς Ἀσαν ἀμηραν Παλαιστίνης καὶ διδουσι χειρας δεξιὰς τῶ Μαρουαμ καὶ ιστωσιν αυτον αρχηγον."

The later writers, especially Dozy, speak of a radical hostility between the Kalb and the Qais, which is said to have existed since time immemorial and cannot be traced to its source, but in pre-Islamic tradition there is nothing of this to be found. The fact is, the hostility did not exist before the capture of Syria by the Muslims and the immigration thither of the Qais.[2] The genealogical distinction between the Qudâa and the Qais certainly was of old standing, but it was only now that it began to have any rancour. First of all the contrast was intensified by the fact that

---

[1] *Cf.* Ham., 319, 7 ; 'The men are either of the party of Bahdal or of that of Zubair.' But especially *cf.* Ham., 658, v. 2 : 'If it had not been for Jâbia in Jaulân and Ibn Bahdal, Marwân and Abdulmalik would have been of no account.'

[2] Goldziher (*Muh. Studien*, 1, 78) rightly says the rivalry between the Arabs of the north and south first arose in Islam.

the latter were old inhabitants of Syria and
the former had newly immigrated there, and
then more than ever by the fact that by ties
of marriage the Kalb were closely connected
with the ruling house. Consequently the Qais
were filled with envy towards them because
they thought themselves put into the background. It was they who were the originators of the mischief. After Yazîd's death, when
Ibn Zubair came into prominence, they joined his
side, while the Kalb kept loyal to the Umaiya.
Thus the tribal difference was amalgamated with
high politics ; the ethnic groups were substantially, if not altogether, overshadowed by
the political parties which originally were independent of them. At Marj Râhit, according
to old songs on the theme, there fought under
Dahhâk for Ibn Zubair, the Sulaim, the Âmir
(Hawâzin) and the Dhubiân (Ghatafân),—none
but tribes belonging to the group of the Qais.
For Marwân, under Ibn Bahdal, there fought the
Kalb and the Ghassân, the Sakûn and the Saksak, the Tanûkh, the Taiyi and the Qain. This
group whose nucleus was formed by the Kalb,[1]
the chief tribe of Qudâa, was rather more mixed;
it is occasionally designated by the collective

---

[1] The Sakûn (of Kinda) were reckoned as belonging to them (Tab.,
475, 2) ; the Tanûkh and Taiyi also were closely related to them (484,
12) ; the Ghassân (of Azd) were the old ruling tribe of the Syrian
Arabs. In Ham., 71, v. 3, the Kalb are called Taghlib, if the Scholion is
correct.

name of the Yemen, but the subordination of the Qudâa under the Yemen is not old, and the Yemen in Syria had not all joined with the Kalb. The battle of Marj Râhit decided for the Kalb against the Qais, who were twice or thrice as strong, but it did not put an end to the strife between Qais and Kalb, since the Qais had to take vengeance for their many slain. It was only now that the deep and enduring bitterness crept in, which Dozy, quite unhistorically, considers an original phenomenon and traces back to time immemorial. Every time it was calmed down, the blood-hatred broke out again, and kept the hostility active long after the political motives were vanished and forgotten. The battle of Marj Râhit is to blame for it ; there its fatal significance is to be found. It brought victory to the Umaiyids, and at the same time shattered the foundations of their power.

Marwân received homage in Jâbia on Wednesday, 3rd Dhulqa'da, 64 = Wednesday, 22nd June, 684. After the battle of Marj Râhit (at the end of 64) there followed a second homage of a more general and ceremonious character at Damascus in Muharram, 65 = July or August, 684.

Without merit or will of his own, Marwân, by his expulsion from Medina, reached the throne in Damascus. This has justly seemed astonishing to the Continuator Byz. Arab, :—

" Marwan (insidiose ab Almidina pulsus) post modica temporis intervalla aliquantis de exercitu consentientibus deo conivente provehitur ad regnum." The family of the Umaiya kept the power, but the Sufyânids were supplanted by the Marwânids.[1] The marriage of Marwân with Fâkhita, the widow of Yazîd,[2] betokened not so much an alliance as the seizure of an inheritance. By it he injured Khâlid b. Yazîd,[3] now his step-son, and in other ways also wilfully and publicly humiliated him, finally even withdrawing from him the promise of the succession to the government which was made to him at Jâbia, and having homage paid to his own sons Abdulmalik and Abdulazîz, so that the latter should succeed the former.[4] Ibn Bahdal did not oppose the breach of faith, perhaps because Amr b. Saîd also was set aside by it. According to Arab opinion, at any rate, Khâlid, upon the prospective death of the already aged Khalifa, was still too young for the ruling power, which would then have passed to Amr, who thought himself secure, but Fâkhita avenged the false treatment of her son upon her husband, and smothered him in bed. Thus Wâqidî in Tab., 2, 576 f.

---

[1] Cf. above pp. 169 ; 179.

[2] She was not a proud Beduin (A. Müller, 1, 375), but a Quraishite lady.

[3] Cf. the verse BAthîr, 4, 275, and along with it 296, 8.

[4] For time and place, Anon. Ahlw., 151 ; 164 f.

4. According to Tabarî, 577, 17, Marwân died in Ramadân, the actual date, according to 576, 16, being the 1st of the month; according to Elias Nis. on Sunday, 27th Ramadân, 65(=Sunday, 7th May, 685). In Tab., 577 f., his age is given as anything between 61 and 81. Theophanes says he reigned nine months; Tabarî says nine or ten months. In the Contin. Byz. Ar., *par.* 29, it says he died after a year full of struggles. I add these struggles to those of his son and successor Abdulmalik, as they are only the beginning and it is not everywhere easy to draw an exact dividing line.[1]

The great struggle was against Ibn Zubair, at least against the provinces which had recognised him and in which his officials ruled.[2] The situation then was just as it had been after the murder of Uthmân; Syria alone stood opposed to the whole of the rest of the Islamic world, only the ruler of Syria was not quite so sure of this province as Muâwia was then. After Marj Râhit, Palestine and Emessa went over to the winning side without more ado, and Qinnesrin also surrendered, but on the Euphrates the Qais held out defiantly, their leader being Zufar b. Hârith in Qarqisia. In spite of this, Marwân and Abdulmalik appear from the beginning as

---

[1] In Tab., 558, 14; 578, 9; 708, 4, the dividing line is drawn decisively, but wrongly.

[2] For Khurâsân *cf.* Tab., 806; 831 ff., and Chap. 8.

assailants of Ibn Zubair, who indeed was possibly more concerned with internal dispeace, especially in Iraq.[1]

It was in Marwân's time that Egypt was taken, and an attack of Ibn Zubair's younger brother, Mus'ab, on Palestine repulsed [2]; also an attempt to gain Medina was made, but failed.[3] Marwân sent Ubaidullâh b. Ziâd to Mesopotamia in order to be the first to advance over this stepping-stone towards Iraq, which was torn by religious and political factions. He is said to have promised him the Stattholdership over all the land he was to seize, and to have sanctioned a three-days' pillage of Kufa (Tab., 578 ; 642). At the beginning of this campaign, when Ubaid-ullâh was still stationed at the Euphrates bridge of Manbij, there took place the massacre of the Shîites of Kufa under Sulaimân b. Surad at Resaina, through Husain b. Numair, next in command to Ubaidullâh, on Friday, 24th Jumâdâ I, 65 = Friday, 6th January, 685 (Tab., 559, 4.20). Ubaidullâh was then held up for nearly a year by struggles with Zufar and the Qais.[4]

---

[1] *Cf.* for subsequent events Chawarig, pp. 32 ff. ; Shia, pp. 72 ff.

[2] Wâqidî, 467, 10 ; Abû Mishnaf, 481 ; 'Awâna, 576. This was effect-ed by Amr b. Saîd before Marwân had had homage paid to his son, according to Anon. Ahlw., 164, 17.

[3] 'Awâna, 578 f. ; 642; Anon. Ahlw. ; 155, 2; 180, 2. According to BQutaiba, 201, Hajjâj's father was concerned in it.

[4] Tab, 643. Van Gelder (Muchtar. p. 96, 152) declares this to be false, without sufficient grounds.

24

Thereafter he advanced against Mosul on the usual army route into Iraq, just when Mukhtâr had already seized the government of Kufa, whose Stattholder retired from Mosul to Takrît (Tab., 643). He then, after a hard fight, slaughtered the first army sent against him by Mukhtâr on the 10th and 11th Dhulhijja, 66=9th and 10th July, 686 (Tab., 646 ff.), but soon after was defeated by a second army of the Shîites under Ibrâhîm b. al-Ashtar at the battle on the Khâzir [1] at the beginning of 67 ; he himself fell and also Husain b. Numair (Tab., 714, 1). Naturally the Qais now also raised their heads again in Qarqisia, and were reinforced by tribal companions under Umair b. Hubâb, who till then had been serving in the Syrian army, but defected at, or after, the battle on the Khâzir. The work upon which Ubaidullâh had spent almost two years had been in vain, and had to be done all over again. It was fortunate for Abdulmalik that Mus'ab b. Zubair, now his brother's Stattholder in Iraq, was so harassed in his own house by Shîites and Khârijites that he could not think of undertaking any outside offensive.

It was a long time before Abdulmalik again took up the task over which Ubaidullâh had come to grief, namely, the subjection of Iraq,

---

[1] August, 686. De Goeje has drawn my attention to the exact date in the Tanbîh, 312, 17.

where Mus'ab held the command pretty much
independently of his brother. He had plenty
to do at home, for Nâtil b. Qais seems to have
again raised a rebellion;[1] but above all, the
Romans broke the peace and stirred up the
Mardaites in Amanus against the Arabs.[2]
Mus'ab did not fall till A.H. 72, and in A.H. 73
the Civil War was at an end. Of the interval
from A.H. 67, when Ubaidullâh had fallen, till
A.H. 72 the reports are meagre. It is mainly
a matter of fixing the chronology, which is still
a very vexed question. In doing so we must
keep in mind that the turn of the year, according
to the Muslim era, then fell in the summer-time,
and the activities which as a rule ceased in
the winter (Tab., 797, 10), were thus divided
over two years of the Hijra, whilst almost
always only one year is given.

That Abdulmalik in the year 67 did not
interfere with Mus'ab's attack upon Mukhtâr
and did not disturb the Iraqites in their occupation of tearing each other to pieces, is understandable, for, according to Tab., 2,765 and Elias,
there was in the year 68 a great famine in
Syria, on account of which no campaign could
be undertaken. Theophanes also speaks of it
in A.M. 6179 (Sel. 998 ; A.H. 68). But

---

[1]   Yaqûbî 2, 321 ; Masûdî, 5, 225. But perhaps it only provses a
chronological error.

[2]   *Göttinger Nachrichten*, 1901, pp. 428 ff. ·

Madâinî, again, does not agree (Agh. 17, 161, 26), but puts it considerably later.

The time at which Abdulmalik first took the field against Mus'ab was, according to the Arabs and Elias,[1] the summer of 689 A.D. or 69/70 A.H. His camp, the mustering ground of his army and the starting-point of his operations, was Butnân Habîb in the district of Qinnesrîn, in this as well as the following years.[2] The corresponding camp of Mus'ab was Bâjumaira near Takrit.[3] These were boundary stations on the great road from Syria to Iraq. Meso-potamia was an intervening region, but more in the power of Mus'ab than of Abdulmalik, for even the Qais on the Euphrates adhered to Mus'ab. In order that the Romans should leave him in peace, Abdulmalik had agreed to

---

[1] In Theophanes the order of the Arab events in these years is so fearfully confused that we can only make use of his accounts of Ziâd (Ibn Z.) Mukhtâr, Saîd (Ibn S.) and Mus'ab, after divesting them of the chronology.

[2] The account that Abdulmalik was in Butnân with the army as early as A.H. 67 contradicts the preceding account that that year he did not go into the field because of a famine. Butnân is only mentioned here as a peg upon which to hang the anecdote that at that time in the army the name Muddy Butnân arose on account of the rain which fell after the drought. The reason for the appellation must have been chronic rather than acute, as in the case of Dreck-Harburg in the bailiffdom of Lüneburg.

[3] According to Yâqût, 1, 664, Abdulmalik used to spend the winter in Butnân, Mus'ab in Maskin. Maskin has about the same importance from a geographical and military point of view as Bâjumaira. Cf. Balâdh., 149, 8.

make them great concessions,[1] but now he was threatened in the rear by Amr b. Saîd, who rose up in Damascus to establish his claim to the Khalifate, which had been acknowledged at the treaty of Jâbia and then cancelled by a breach of faith. Abdulmalik was compelled to turn round and deal with this danger. He let the sword have full play and slew his enemies (Tab., 805)—Amr, indeed, was slain by his own hand, in a treacherous and horribly cruel manner. Tradition (Tab., 783 f., 796. Anon. Ahlw., 250) places these events partly in the year 69, partly in 70, but we must not therefore make the mistake of thinking they belong together and fall into the same summer. Tradition is also uncertain as to how far Abdulmalik had already got on his march to the north-east. According to Wâqidî in Tab., 783, and according to Elias, he turned back again from Ain Warda, i. e., Resaina ; but according to Wâqidî in Tab., 796, he had not yet proceeded past Butnân Habîb. 'Awâna seems to take the latter view also (Tab., 783 f.) According to him, Abdulmalik was on the march against Zufar b. Hârith in Qarqîsiâ,[2] but had to abandon it because Amr b. Saîd, who had accompanied him as far as Butnân, had decamped

---

[1] *Göttinger Nachrichten*, 1901, p. 428.

[2] In Hamâsa, 658, v. 6, it is mentioned as an attack of the Qais upon Butnân, the repulse of which was due to the Kalb.

secretly by night with some others to Damascus, and had taken possession of the town. Yaqûbî, 2, 321 f. has a similar account.

The next year 70/71, *i.e.* summes of 690, the campaign was repeated. The two great antagonists did not reach each other this time either. Abdulmalik instigated a rising of the Bakr or Rabîa, the so-called Jufriya, in Basra, while Mus'ab kept the field (Tab., 798-803). Two partisans took part, each on his own account, in the feud against Mus'ab and Zufar, not so much from love of Abdulmalik as out of hatred to the latter,—the noble Ubaidullâh b. Hurr al-Ju'fî of Kufa (Tab., 305. 388 ff. 765 ff.) and the fierce Ubaidullâh b. Ziâd b. Zabyân alBakrî of Basra (Tab., 800, 807-10. BAthîr, 4,255, 268, Agh., 11,62),

The result was *nil*. "Abdulmalik marched against Mus'ab, who was encamped in Bâjumaira, as far as Butnân,—at a very respectful distance —and then the winter came on and both turned back home " (Tab., 797). One might be dubious as to whether this were not an erroneous repetition of what already happened in the year 69/70. The rising of the Jufriya which Tabarî mentions under A.H. 71 (*cf.* 813, 11 f.) is said to have already taken place, according to 798, 5 in A. H. 70. Wâqidî, in Tab., 805, seems to place it at the same time as the rising of Amr b. Saîd in Damascus ; in any case he makes the campaign in 70/71 (Tab., 813) not an intermediate one but the last and decisive one.

Thus there would be altogether only two campaigns to be accepted, but that is not sufficient. This is the result, as we shall see, of reckoning backwards, but it is also the result of direct evidences. Mus'ab, in a contemporary verse (Agh., 17, 162 ; Masûdî, 5, 241), is addressed as follows : "Year after year thou art in Bâjumaira ; thou marchest with us into the field and dost nothing." In another verse (Tab., 1038, 4) mention is made of Bâjumairât in the plural, *i.e.*, the plural of the time, not of the place. Madâinî (Agh., 17, 161 f.) speaks expressly of three campaigns in three successive years. According to him Abdulmalik was advised to give himself now a year's rest, after being two years in the field, and in fact to content himself with Syria and leave the accursed Iraq to Mus'ab, but he did not do so, and the third year decided in his favour.

It was the summer of 691, A.H. 71/72. Abdulmalik spent it mostly in the subjection of Mesopotamia. After a lengthy siege Zufar b. Hârith capitulated in Qarqisia, and his son Hudhail had to render forced military service.[1] An exhaustive report of this is found in BAthîr, 4, 275 ff., where there is mention also of an earlier indecisive battle of Abân b. Uqba b.

[1] Anon. Ahlw., 24, 17 ff. BAthîr, 4, 265. In Theophanes, A.M. 6178 the taking of Circesium is put in a wrong connection.

Muait, Stattholder of Emessa, against Qarqisia.
According to it, Zufar was not humbled before
the army of the Kalb and Qudâa, but joined
the Khalifa entirely of his own accord. This is,
of course, a boastful flight of the Qaisites, by
which they sought also to mitigate their own
humiliation. Besides Qarqisia, however, there
was also Resaina to subdue, where Umair b.
Hubâb was maintaining opposition,[1] and after
that Nisibis, where the so-called " cudgel-
bearers,"—a remnant of Mukhtâr's adherents
had till then held out. They surrendered and
were enrolled in the army.[2]

The season was already far advanced when
at last a decisive encounter took place between
Abdulmalik and Mus'ab. The place was the
monastery of the Catholicus, between Maskin,
where Abdulmalik encamped as Muâwia had once
done, and Bâjumaira, the headquarters of Mus'ab
(Tab., 805). The month was the first or second
Jumâdâ, but it is doubtful whether the year
is A.H. 71 or 72 (Anon. Ahlw., 8. Tab., 813).
Wâqidî and Elias say 71, and the others 72,[3] and
the latter date, regarded from the point of view

---

[1] Barhebr., ed. Bedjan, 111 : " Hubab is, of course, Ibn Hubab."
Cf. BAthîr, 4, 254.

[2] Masûdî, 5, 241. Cf. Agh., 5, 155. 8, 33. 11, 47 ; and Shia, p. 80
n.1 ; 84 n. 3.

[3] Thus Madâinî, in Tab, 813 (1466,9) and Agh., 17, 161 ; Ibn
Kalbî from his grandfather and Abû Mikhnaf in Anon., 26, and
Masûdî, 5, 242.

of what has been already said, is proved correct from the fact that Abdulmalik's victory in Iraq was followed by the sending of Ḥajjâj to the Ḥijâz, which without any doubt falls in the year 72/73.[1]

About the course of the battle there are several reports, or more properly compilations of reports, whose relation to each other has given rise to an unusual amount of discussion. Ahlwardt has compared the report of the historical work published by him —a part of Balâdhurî's *Kitâb alAshrâf*—with that of Ibn Athîr (4,263 ff.) and found that the latter has borrowed large portions from the former. Nöldeke has contradicted him, perhaps with the idea that here, as in other cases, we shall get the best result with Tabarî as the source of Ibn Athîr. Brockelmann proved that this is not possible, but after the appearance of the relative series of Tabarî, which Nöldeke was not yet acquainted with.[2] By it, however, the question

---

[1] In support of 71 we can of course refer to the account of Madâinî in Tab., 813, that the battle was on Tuesday, 13th Jumâdâ I or II. Madâinî names also the year 72, but in that year the 13th Jumâdâ I or II did not fall on a Tuesday, but on the other hand the 13th Jumâdâ II of the year 71 was a Tuesday. In spite of this it seems to me impossible and in contradiction to the well-authenticated facts to reduce the three Iraqite campaigns to two, and then to allow two whole years to intervene between the taking of Kufa, which was the result of the battle at the monastery, and the taking of Mecca. I shall return to this point.

[2] *Anon. Ahlw., Vorrede*, pp. xii ff.; *Göttinger Gel. Anz.*, 1883, p. 1102; Brockelmann's *Dissertation über das Verhältnis von Ibn alAthir xu Tabari* (Strassb., 1890), pp. 44 f.

is only partly decided in favour of Ahlwardt.
It is necessary, in fact, to take into consideration a further report, which Ahlwardt, Nöldeke
and Brockelmann have overlooked,—that of
Agh., 17, 161 ff., which in its contents stands
very near to that of the Anonymous Writer, but
yet is not dependent upon it, and is compiled
by Zubair b. Bakkâr. The following is then
obvious,—Ibn Athîr does not follow Tabarî
exclusively, but had just as little knowledge of
the Anonymous Work as of the Article of the
Kitâb alAghânî. In the points which he has in
common with those two, he agrees now more
with the one, and again more with the other,
but always with such formal variations as
exclude a direct borrowing. Sometimes (not
considering of course the part borrowed from
Ṭabarî), he has even an item extra in the
contents over both, for example in the story
of the ground of hostility of Ibn Zabyân
towards Mus'ab. He appears, therefore, to have
used another compilation which indeed went
back mostly to the same sources.[1] The authors
quoted are, in the Anonymous Work and in the
Kitâb alAghânî, partly the same as in Tabarî,
but he still cites Wâqidî and owes to him his

---

[1] A complete proof cannot be given here, since the matter has
only a literary and not a historical interest. To determine the
connection of *Compilations* with each other is always somewhat
perilous.

main report, which with slight interruptions continues from 804, 15 to 808,2.

Historically important differences do not frequently occur. The time before the battle, while the armies lay opposite each other a short distance away in Maskin and Bâjumaira, was employed by Abdulmalik in entering into correspondence with the enemies' camp, just as in a similar situation Muâwia had done before from the same spot. The men of Iraq had no desire for battle, as the verse quoted on page 191 shows. They had never been used to discipline and obedience, and the frightful party-struggles of the last years had not improved them. Political and military loyalty were absolutely unknown to them; they would have liked to change their Emir every day, as a girl her suitors (Agh., 162, 17. BAthîr, 265,23). It was represented to them that they were fighting not merely for Ibn Zubair and his brother, but for the independence of Iraq, and that they must not let the hungry Syrians get into their rich and luxuriant land, but that was of no avail (Tab., 806. BA., 265 f. Anon., 14). His best troops, under Muhallab, had been obliged to forsake Mus'ab in order to protect Basra from the Khawârij.[1] Amongst the men of Basra whom he had with him, there were the more than doubtful Rabîa, whose rising he had had to quell the year before

[1] Tabarî, 806. BA., 265 f. Anon., 14. Chawârig, pp. 36 ff.

(Tab., 807 f. Agh., 162). The greater part of his
army he had brought with him from Kufa,
whence he had started (Tab., 804; 807. BA.,
264 f.). The sympathies of the men of Kufa
were not on his side, and on his own part he
was only summoned of necessity by the noble
party to help them against Mukhtâr; while
many hated him because he had freely spilt the
blood of Mukhtâr's adherents. Thus Abdulmalik had an easy game to play. He applied
his lever to the Kufaites. Contemporary verses
(Anon., 11 f.) which are preserved to us express
apprehension of the perfidy of the men of Kufa,
and the leaders of the army who were worked
upon by him, so far as they are mentioned by
name, were Kufaites only (An., 13, 21-23 ; 27, 14).
The district of Ispahan which he promised to
more than one as a reward for their treachery
(Anon., 13, 32) belonged to Kufa and was administered by Kufaites. Mus'ab could not make
up his mind to deal drastically with the traitors
with whom Abdulmalik was in correspondence,
and in spite of warnings let them remain in
their posts. The man who had warned him and
advised him to put them to death was Ibrâhîm
b. Ashtar, the conqueror in the battle on the
Khâzir. He had delivered the letter which he
got from Abdulmalik to Mus'ab unopened, with
the remark that all the leaders had probably got
their letters as well as he, but had kept them to

themselves. He was the only faithful man of Kufa and at the same time by far the most prominent one, a welcome phenomenon in such an environment, the worthy son of his father, the conqueror of Siffîn. His fall, at the very beginning of the encounter with the enemy at the monastery of the Catholicus, decided the defeat of Mus'ab. 'Attâb b. Warqâ gave way with the cavalry ; the rest of the chiefs or tribe-leaders impudently refused obedience to the field-marshal and did not lead their troops into battle at all. Finally he was left almost alone on the field of battle, which strange situation itself makes the battle famous. One needs no knowledge of tactics and strategy to understand its course. After his son,—a mere boy, for the father was only 36,—had fallen before his eyes he himself, already bleeding from many arrow-wounds, was laid low by the Thaqifite Zâida b. Qudâma of Kufa with the shout,—" This is the vengeance for Mukhtâr ! " Ubaidullâh b. Ziâd b. Zabyân severed the head from the body.

After this not very honourable victory Abdulmalik marched into Kufa, received the homage of the tribes and appointed his officials over the newly subdued provinces.[1] He camped 40 days in Nukhaila, at the same spot as Muâwia had before encamped with the Syrian army.

---

[1] For Khurâsân *cf.*, here and in other cases, Chap. 8.

During this time also he sent Hajjâj b. Yûsuf
to the Hijâz against Ibn Zubair. So says
Haitham b. Adî in the Anonymous Work, 18,1,
with whom Wâqidî agrees. He says in Tab.,
830 and An., 38 that *after* the fall of Mus'ab
Hajjâj was despatched to Mecca with 2,000
Syrians, and this in Jumâdâ, *i.e.*, in the very
month of the battle at the monastery, or a month
later, since the name covers two months. The
year he gives as A.H. 72. He cannot, indeed,
do otherwise because the siege of Mecca, according to him, did not begin till late in the year 72
and lasted well into the year 73. But how then
can he antedate the battle in question in the year
71? From the fragments of him which are
preserved to us this riddle cannot be read. The
close connection of the events in Iraq and in the
Hijâz is indisputable, and therefore so also is
the year 72 as the date of the fall of Mus'ab.

Hajjâj did not advance upon Mecca by the
straight road, according to Wâqidî, but first
went to Tâif, where he arrived in Sha'bân, and
stayed several months.[1] From there he had
frequent skirmishes with the adherents of Ibn
Zubair on the plain of Arafa, in which he almost
always gained the victory. He next asked
permission from the Khalifa to attack the holy
town itself, and at the same time asked for

---

[1] Masûdî, 5, 259. Anon. Ahlw., 139.

reinforcements. By Abdulmalik's orders there
came to his aid Târiq b. Amr, who had occupied
Medina and expelled from it the Stattholder of
Ibn Zubair (Tab., 818. Anon., 34 ff.). According
to Wâqidî in Tab., 844 ff. the siege began on
the 1st Dhulqada, 72, *i.e.*, 25th March, 692.
Stones were cast at the town and the sanctuary.[1]
A terrible storm which came on aroused religious
scruples, but Hajjâj managed to allay them.
Ibn Zubair was more and more forsaken by his
men, and finally they all laid down their arms
and were pardoned by the Syrians, amongst
them even his own sons. But he, now a man
73 years old, was ashamed of this, and after
taking leave of his mother went alone into
the last conflict and was slain (Anon., 38 ff.,
Ham., 319). According to Wâqidî this took
place 6 months and 17 days after the commencement of the siege (Tab., 2, 844, note *f.*), on
Tuesday, 17th. Jumâdâ I, 73, *i.e.*, 18th Sept.,
692. The day of the week does not agree.
According to Tab., 851, 10 and Anon, 57 the
month was not the first Jumâdâ but the second.
Elias gives Monday, 17th Jumâdâ, but in this
case the day of the week does not agree either.

The fall of Mecca was only an epilogue;[2]
the Hijâz had been a lifeless province since the

---

[1] See above, pp. 165-6.
[2] Poetical congratulations upon this are in Hudh., 259, 17 ff.;
pronounce *Wafaddi*.

murder of Uthmân and could not be again made
the centre-point of the political life. Doubtless
this was Ibn Zubair's intention, an intention he
was bound to have from the kind of movement
through which he was brought to the front.[1]
At the same time he put forward the holy
character of his Khalifate by not leaving the
sanctuary in which he had taken refuge, even
when the world was open to him. But the
result was that in the *Fitna* which is called after
him, he himself was quite in the background;
the struggle turned round him nominally, but
he took no part in it and it was decided without
him. Even in Arabia itself he had for years less
influence than the Khârijite Najda (Tab., 737,8.
Chawarig, pp. 29 ff.). Finally he was located in
the building where he kept himself in hiding,
and dragged forth, and so the great Fitna was
ended and the Jamâa again restored.

[1] See above, p. 164.

CHAPTER IV.

THE FIRST MARWÂNIDS.

The storms in Iraq did not cease, however, with the termination of the long warfare against Ibn Zubair; as we shall see, they lasted throughout almost the whole reign of Abdulmalik. In Syria too, the quarrels of the Qais and the Kalb caused further unrest. To be sure, Zufar b. Hârith in Qarqîsiâ had laid down his arms in the year in which Mus'ab fell, but that did not put an end to the tribal feud which outlasted the great war. In order to deal with it in its proper connection we must go back to Marj Râhit (Agh., 11, 61, 31). In this savage battle the Qais suffered most heavily, and according to Arab ideas they were bound to make good their losses from the conquerors; they had their revenge to seek, and it was they who were the aggressors, while the Kalb only retaliated. On the side of the Qais the principal part was taken by the Âmir and Sulaim, along with the Ghanî and the Bâhila,[1] as far as these tribes had settled in Northern Syria and Southern Mesopotamia, on both sides of the

---

[1] B Athîr, 4, 256, 10, 15 ; 258, 18 ; 259, 17 ; 260, 24. In 256, 10 read *A'ṣur* as at 256, 15.

26

Euphrates. On the side of the Kalb were the
rest of the Qudâa,[1] but only the Kalb seem to
have gone into action. The sources of the single
and sometimes widely separated "days" in
which the tedious feud ran its course are contemporary songs and tales connected with them,
which are preserved to us in Ibn Athîr and
the *Kitâb-al-Aghânî*, in the *Hamâsa* and in
Madâinî. The accounts are mostly quite reliable
though partly without connection and chronology, but there are threads to be grasped which
enable us to arrange them in tolerable order.

The feud, according to Agh., 20, 120 ff., was
begun by Zufar b. Hârith al-Kilâbî in Qarqisia,
the leader of the 'Âmir, making a sudden attack
upon a settlement of the Kalbites in Musaiyakh
and killing 20 of their men. The Kalb, headed
by Humaid b. Huraith b. Bahdal,[2] retaliated by
slaughtering 60 Numairites who lived amongst
them in Tadmor. Thereupon Zufar is said to
have murdered 500 or even 1,000 Kalbites on
the day of Iklîl, and after this feat to have got
off scatheless into safety at Qarqisia, Humaid
being unable to reach him. In another place
(122, 17 ff.), however, the attack of Iklîl is
ascribed not to Zufar but to Umair b. Hubâb,
the leader of the Sulaim, who certainly from

---

[1] In one of Zufar's verses in BAthîr, 256, 18 the Qudâa are already
called Yemenites.
[2] With whom the Scholion to Hamâsa confuses him, 658, v. 2.

that time appears as the real avenger of the Qais against the Kalb. Zufar was withdrawn from the blood-feud in the desert by the great struggle between Syria and the Iraq for the Khalifate, being first exposed to the attacks of Abdulmalik, which he withstood, as we have seen, for several years, as warden of the marches for Mus'ab, on whom he depended.

The entrance of Umair affords a chronological starting point, for in the battle on the Khâzir he was in the Syrian army and not till then did he join Zufar, *i.e.*, not before the year 67. Quite a number of "days" are given on which he wreaked vengeance, named after different places of the Samâwa. At Kaâba, Humaid on his swift steed had a narrow escape from him, and the Kalb, who dwelt within the area of his raids, at last left this district and emigrated for a while to Palestine into the Ghor.

Then Umair also went back over the Euphrates and settled with his Sulaimites on the Khaboras. It was through this that the Christian Taghlib, whose settlements there extended as far as the Tigris and beyond it, came into contact with the Qais, and they approached Zufar with the request that he should command the Sulaim to vacate the Khaboras, as they had taken the liberty to encroach and had caused friction. Zufar did not see his way to this, and so a feud arose between the Taghlib and the

Sulaim. Zufar did what he could to allay it, as he did not want to drive the Taghlib into the arms of the Syrians, but Umair, that author of misfortune, did the very opposite. He got round Mus'ab, represented to him that the Taghlib, being Christians, were under suspicion of sympathy with the Syrians, and managed to get permission to act against them in the name of the government of Ibn Zubair and to give free course to his hostility. At Mâkis or Mâki-sîn he committed great slaughter amongst them. With this the report of Agh., 20,120 ff., breaks off, but the continuation is found in BAthîr, 4,255 ff. and Agh., 11,51 f.; 61 f. We learn that Zufar also was dragged into the struggle altogether against his will. Many surprise attacks and encounters followed, the scenes of them, also mentioned in the songs of Akhtal,[1] being on the Khâbor and the Balîkh, on the Tharthâr and in the region of the Tigris The Taghlib mostly got the worst of it, but near Hashâk on the river Tharthâr, which flows into the Tigris from the south, not far from Takrît, they certainly were the victors, slew Umair in A.H. 70 and sent his head to Abdulmalik at Damascus. But then Zufar, finding himself compelled to take up the revenge for Umair, dealt the Taghlib a severe blow near the town of Kuhail on the

---

[1] I was not then able to take into consideration *Qutâmî, ed. Barth.*

Tigris and executed 200 prisoners who had fallen
into his hands. The great events of the years
71 and 72, the scene of which was Mesopotamia,
then put an end to the bloody minor war and
saved the Taghlib.

The feud between the Kalb and the Qais,
however, afterwards broke out again at another
place, *cf.* Hamâsa, 260 ff.; Madâinî,[1] 14, 85 ; Agh.,
17, 113ff.; Yâqût, 1, 739. Humaid b. Huraith
b. Bahdal, the former leader of the Kalb in the
war with Umair,[2] seized the opportunity to
make the Fazâra in Arabia proper,—their headquarters lay to the east of Medina,—atone for
the offences, on the Euphrates, of the Sulaim and
'Âmir, whom he could not harm. These Fazâra
had hitherto taken no part in the feud at all,
but they also belonged to the great group of the
Qais, and some of them, members of its old
princely house who had taken up their domicile
in Kufa, had at any rate lent Zufar and Umair
their assistance (BAthîr, 4, 258, 19 f.). Humaid
got Khâlid, son of the Khalifa Yazîd, whose
grandmother was a Kalbite, to prepare for him
a patent in the name of Abdulmalik, commis-
sioning him to collect the cattle-tax from certain
tribes. As plenipotentiary of the government

---

[1] The translation in Freytag leaves much to be desired.

[2] Ibn Habîb in Madâinî wrongly names his father Huraith instead
of him ; on the other hand see Ham., 260, v. 2; Agh., 17, p. 113 at the
bottom, and 114, 28.

he then marched through the desert with a gigantic following of the Kalbite clans Abdwudd and 'Ulaim, and let the Fazâra, who were his real objective, feel his power. On trifling pretexts he perpetrated dreadful acts of violence against them; several were wounded and killed, particularly at a place called 'Âh. Those concerned now carried their complaint to Abdulmalik, who thought he did enough in giving them recompense in money for the blood that had been shed. They took the money, but with it purchased weapons and horses and equipped themselves for a campaign of vengeance. They then surprised a camp of the Kalb near the Wells of Banât Qain in the Samâwa, and killed 19 men of the Abdwudd and 50 of the Ulaim. Abdulmalik was very angry at this and ordered his stattholder Hajjâj to exact compensation from the Fazâra, whereupon the two chief offenders averted the impending disaster from their people by voluntarily giving themselves up, and the Kalbites had to be satisfied with their execution. The attack of Banât Qain is the most celebrated "day" in the whole feud between Qais and Kalb. Hajjâj was already stattholder of Medina when it took place (A H. 73 and 74), and the cause of it, namely, the massacre at 'Âh, cannot be placed much earlier.[1] The

---

[1] Of course it is not absolutely impossible for it to have happened in the period before the restoration of the Jamâa, as Ibn Habîb gives

supposition found in all the versions of the
narrative that the two hostile brothers Bishr
and Abdulazîz, sons of Marwân, were in Damascus on the day of Banât Qain and even afterwards, is therefore erroneous ; the one had long
been stattholder of Kufa, the other stattholder
of Egypt. They might at most have been for
a time on a visit to the court.

The feud between the Sulaim and the Taghlib had yet another sequel when the dispute over
the Khalifate was ended and peace had long
been restored in the realm ; *cf.* Agh., 11, 59 ff. ;
BAthîr, 4, 261 ff. The poet Akhtal stirred it
up again by boasting at the court of Abdulmalik
of the prowess of his clansmen the Taghlib,
to the Sulaimite Jahhâf b. Hukaim, who had
himself under Umair taken part in the fights
against the Taghlib. Jahhâf then did exactly
the same as the Kalbite Humaid had done
before. He contrived to get a patent made out
for himself by which he was appointed tax-
collector in the district of the Mesopotamian
Taghlib and Bakr, in which official capacity he
started for Mesopotamia with a considerable band
of Qaisite cavalry. On the way he disclosed to
them his real intention, namely, to spill as much
Taghlibite blood as possible, and concluded with
the words : "You have the choice between hell,

it in Madâinî. But Dozy, 1, 120, is quite wrong in putting the day
of Banât Qain into Muawia's time.

if you follow me, and disgrace if you dont."
They preferred hell to disgrace and followed
him, surprised the Taghlib in A.H. 73 at Bishr
(or Rahûb) and made fearful havoc among them.
In this attack they also killed a son of Akhtal
and captured him himself, but let him go
because they took him for a menial. After this
Jahhâf fled into the territory of the Romans.
On the intercession of the Qaisites, Abdulmalik
permitted him to return after a considerable
time, but he had to pay atonement-money to
the Taghlib for the bloodshed at Bishr. As
his means were not equal to this, he asked the
man at that time most powerful among the
Qais, namely Hajjâj, to come forward on his
behalf and undertake the payment, which the
latter, after refusing for some time, eventually
did. In the end Jahhâf became pious, undertook, by way of a penitential expedition, along
with his accomplices, with rings in their noses,
the pilgrimage to Mecca, and there prayed
desperately for forgiveness.

We see that the Arabs in the Syrian and
Mesopotamian steppe had remained unchanged
under the new conditions. Neither Islam nor
Christianity kept them from making the tribe
and revenge paramount. They preferred hell to
disgrace and only felt remorse when it was too
late. Their conduct was even more cruel than
it had been before in their heathenism and their

old home, and they committed murder in a more
wholesale and ruthless manner. They slaughtered
the female prisoners, a custom not usual in Arabia
proper but attested to in Syria by the prophet
Amos. Even after the struggle over the kingdom was decided and peace restored, the
barbarous conduct still went on before the gates
of the capital, under the Khalifa's very eyes,
and occasionally under pretext of his authority.

A second crater of the tribal-hatred yawned
in the far East. In Basra the old tension
between the Tamîm and the Rabîa was increased
by the immigration of the Azd Umân, which
took place in the latter years of Muâwia and
under Yazîd I. The Rabîa allied themselves
with the Azd, and on the other hand, the Tamîm
joined with the Qais, so that here also two great
groups arose, and the feud broke out in the town
during the interregnum after the death of Yazîd.
The stattholder, Ubaidullâh b. Ziâd had to flee;
Mas'ud b. Amr, the chief of the Azd, intended
to occupy his post, and by a trick seized the
citadel and the mosque with the aid of the Azd
and the Rabîa, but while he was standing in
the pulpit in the mosque the Tamîm rushed in,
tore him down and slew him. Blood-revenge
for the slain head of the tribe was now imminent,
but the wise leader of the Tamîm, old Ahnaf,
managed to restore peace upon the payment of
a large sum of compensation-money. Still the

27

hatred between the parties remained, and it
broke out in Khurâsân, then a Basrian colony,
whither the tribal relations passed on from
Basra. There the feuds were always blazing
out anew, first between the Tamîm and the
Rabîa, and then, after the Azd, through Muhallab,
had also appeared on the scene, in Khurâsân,
between the Mudar (Tamîm and Qais) and the
Yemen (Azd and Rabîa). The dualism of the
eastern groups at last united with that of the
western, mainly through the fault of the Qais,
who were equally represented in west and
east, and stuck together everywhere like pitch
and sulphur. It tried to absorb the other
opposing parties and to polarise the entire
Arabian world.

This tendency also weakened the ruling
circles, and it was difficult to keep clear of it.
What was a stattholder to do when the Qais
claimed him as their own ! If he rejected them
he robbed himself of their support and fell
between two stools. Even the princes at
Abdulmalik's court took sides, sometimes even
passionately, according as they had leanings
through their mother to the one side or the
other.

Now indeed the political idea of Islam, the
unity and solidarity of Muhammad's congregation, made a counter-movement. Its born
representatives were the Quraish, who stood, by

right, above the tribes and outside of the rivalry.
To be sure, the ruling Quraish, the Umaiya,
had had to throw themselves into the arms of
the Kalb in Syria, in order to maintain their
sway against the Qais, who were on the side of
Zubair, but for all that the ties of blood bound
them to the Qais,[1] and so it became easier for
them to take up a middle position. Abdulmalik,
recognising his advantage, endeavoured to keep
himself above the parties, and after the Qais
had given up their opposition to him he treated
them kindly and tried to conciliate them.
Zufar b. Hârith and his sons Hudhail and
Kauthar after him were amongst the most
eminent and notable people at the court of
Damascus.[2] The Kalb, naturally, were displeased at this, but their reproaches against
Abdulmalik that he was not grateful enough
to them (Hamâsa, 656 ff.) are really a eulogy of
him. The assertion that he went over from
the Kalb to the Qais puts the facts of the case
quite falsely. Even later we find around him
men still influential in the Kalbite group,

[1] "If it were not for the Khalifa, Qudâa would be master and Qais
servant," Tab., 487, 19 f. The Khalifa is reckoned as belonging to the
Qais (475, 18) since he at least belonged, like them, to Mudar and
not to Qudâa or Yemen.

[2] Cf. Tab., 2, 1300, 1360 f, 1455. Anon. Ahlw., 173, 253, Aghânî, 16,
42, 158 f. We see from this how powerful the position of these Qaisite
princes continued to be even under the Umaiyids, but they did not
abuse it.

e.g., Ibn Bahdal himself and Rauh b. Zinbâ. Abdulmalik acted as he was bound to act, being Khalifa and a politician. The Umaiyids relied upon the Syrians; with their help they had subdued the whole Muslim kingdom, and with their help they held it. It was all over with their rule over the kingdom if the foundation of it no longer held together,—namely if there was a split in Syria. At that time Khurâsân was yet in the background and the schism in that distant region so far affected the centre but little. But it was different with Syria. The feeling that they had to hold with the dynasty in order to keep their own position could not be disregarded even by the Syrian Arabs themselves. It worked against the tribal dualism ; the other provinces were subdued ; their land was the ruling one ; even the material interest in the possession of the Khalifate and the government lent them a feeling of political solidarity, which chiefly expressed itself when they, as an imperial army, had to fight against the internal and external foes of the monarchy—for which abundant opportunity was given them.

2. In order to strengthen the political supremacy of Syria still more, an attempt was made to transfer the centre of the cult thither also. A motive for this was found in the fact that the chief holy place of Mecca had been occupied by Ibn Zubair for nearly a decade and

was therefore hardly accessible to the Syrians,
if they remained faithful to their dynasty, and
Abdulmalik used this as a pretext to forbid
absolutely the undertaking of the pilgrimage
to Mecca by his subjects and to insist upon their
making a pilgrimage to Jerusalem instead. So at
least Eutychius reports.[1] There is no doubt
that Abdulmalik tried hard to invest Jerusalem
with greater splendour as a Muslim place of
worship, for the tradition that he was the
founder of its Dome of the Rock is certified by
the inscription still preserved in the oldest part
of the building. To be sure, the Abbâsid Mamûn
is now named there as the builder, but de Voguë
observed that this name has been falsified.[2]
The old date has escaped alteration, and the
original purport of the words may therefore be
accepted with certainty as follows : "The
servant of God, Abdulmalik, the Emir of the
Faithful, built this Qubba in the year 72." In
Jerusalem Syria possessed the only spot on earth
which could compete with Mecca (Tab., 1666, 3).
It was the Holy of Holies, not only of the Jews
and Christians, but originally of the Muslims
also. Muhammad only established Mecca in

---

[1] *Annales*, ed. Pecoks, 2, 365. Eutychius relates the same thing
of Marwân (2, 362), and a similar thing of Walîd I (2, 373).

[2] *Temple de Jerusalem*, 1864, p., 35 f. *Cf.* also Gildemeister in the
Zeitschr. des Deutschen Palästinavereins, 1890, p. 14; the printer's errors
in the numbers are not to be put to the account of the author who was
dead by the time it was printed.

its place later by way of a timely compromise
with the Arabian heathendom. The Khalifa Umar
had honoured it by his visit and thus excited
the envy of the Iraqites. Muâwia had himself
first proclaimed there as Khalifa, and on that
occasion prayed at Golgotha, Gethsemane and
the grave of Mary. Nevertheless Abdulmalik
gave up his idea of putting Jerusalem in the
place of Mecca,—if he ever had it,—as soon as he
was no longer confined to Syria. For the whole
congregation of the Prophet is seemed hope-
lessly unattainable.[1]   But on the other hand he
made another attempt later on to enhance the
attractions of Syria as a place of worship at the
expense of Medina. Before his time, Muâwia,
in A.H. 50, had already made preparations to
remove the pulpit of the Prophet from Medina
and convey it to Syria, but as a general distur-
bance arose and the sun was darkened, he had
let it alone, saying : " I wanted just to see
whether it was not worm-eaten." Abdulmalik
had the same plan in his mind, but his Keeper of
the Seal persuaded him to abandon it. Then his
son, Walîd I, is said to have tried it once more,
but likewise in vain (Tab., 2,923, according to
Wâqidî). The Umaiyids did not need to observe
such regard for Medina as for Mecca. The town

---

[1] Khâlid al Qasrî indeed is said to have declared that if the Khalifa
ordered it he would remove the Ka'ba and rebuild it in Jerusalem
(Agh., 19, 60).

had oftentimes manifested its hostility towards them, and had finally driven the whole of them outside its walls, for which they bore it a grudge. Abdulmalik seems to have even appointed its stattholders sometimes in his wrath : amongst them the Makhzûmite Hishâm b. Ismâîl (appointed A.H. 82) was noted for special villainy.

From the beginning Abdulmalik's relations to Islam were different from those of his predecessors. He was born and bred in it, nay more, he was brought up in the very town of the Prophet, where the tradition which started with the Prophet and continued in the history of the theocracy was zealously cherished and made the subject of a professional guild. In his youth he had himself taken a deep interest in these pious studies and might rank as a Hâfiz of the Qoran. With his accession to the throne a change is said to have come over him (Anon. Ahlw., 164, 167, 190). Certainly, from that time onwards, he subordinated everything to policy, and even exposed the Ka'ba to the danger of destruction. But from policy likewise did he beware of injuring the religious feelings of his subjects in the careless fashion of Yazîd ; he understood them far more intimately than the latter and therefore knew better how to spare them. The pious Rajâ b. Haiwa alKindî, of whom we shall hear more, was already influential

with him.[1] He had a man put to death for
asserting, in defiance of Muhammad, that he
was a prophet (An., 253). According to
Eutychius, 2, 365 he even wanted to incorporate
the Church of St. John in Damascus with the
mosque near which it was situated, but refrained
from doing so out of consideration for the
Christians. We have not sufficient materials to
estimate his further relations with his Christian
subjects, but at any rate Christianity did not
prejudice in his eyes the Taghlib and their poet
Akhtal. The slaughter of the swine in Syria,
mentioned by Theophanes under A.M. 6186 no
doubt was caused by hostility to the Christians,
but did not originate with the Khalifa.

Where Islam coincided with Arabism it was
convenient to the ruler and could easily be
made to serve the ends of the kingdom. After
Abdulmalik had got the better of his rivals, he
again resumed the holy war against the Romans,
which had been at rest for close on 15 years.[2]
Justinian II was defeated near Cilician Sebaste
or Sebastopolis in the year 73 of the Flight,
which year began at the end of May, 692.
Abdulmalik's field-marshal was his brother

---

[1] *Anon.*, 193. He is even said to have been treasurer at the building of the Dome of the Rock in Jerusalem ; *Zeitschr. des Deutschen Pal.
vereins*, 1890, p. 21.

[2] *Göttinger Nachrichten*, 1901, pp. 431 ff. The war began anew in
Africa also (*Yahyâ, pp.* 434 ff.).

Muhammad b. Marwân, stattholder of Mesopotamia and Armenia, who also had charge of the conduct of the war in Asia Minor and Armenia. As in Muâwia's time, a greater and a smallar campaign were undertaken year by year against the Romans, which, if they had no further result, were at least a useful school for the Arabs of Syria and Mesopotamia, whom they kept constantly in military exercise. A measure connected with the re-opening of hostilities against the Romans, which conciliated the religious as well as the national interests, was the transformation of the coinage by Abdulmalik. Balâdhurî accounts for it as follows (240 ; 465ff.) Paper came to the Romans from Egypt, but on the other hand the dinars of gold came to the Arabs from the Romans. Upon the sheets of paper there had formerly been Christian inscriptions and the sign of the Cross, as watermarks, but under Abdulmalik the Qoran verse " Say—He alone is God " was substituted. The Romans threatened to retaliate by stamping upon the dinars sayings abusing the Prophet, so the Arabs then stamped gold themselves. Abdulmalik began it in Damascus in A.H. 74, and Hajjâj's stamping of silver began in Kufa at the end of A.H. 75. Up till then Greek gold and Persian silver were in circulation, and a few Himyarite silver coins, (with the Attic owl upon them). Wâqidî, indeed, in Tab., 2,939, says Abdulmalik

28

did not begin to stamp the silver drachms and golden dinars till A.H. 76, but if Theophanes' statement were correct that Justinian II's rejection of the Damascene golden coins caused the re-opening of the war between the Muslims and Romans, then Balâdhurî's dating would need to be put forward rather than back. The new coins were struck in the name of Allâh and bore, as superscription, sayings from the Qoran proclaiming his absolute power and the omnipotence of his Messenger.[1] The Arabs certainly stamped gold and silver also before Abdulmalik's time, but according to Roman and Persian types. It seems, moreover, that Muâwia tried to do what Abdulmalik succeeded in doing, for according to Nöldeke's Syrian, Muâwia struck gold and silver money, but it was not accepted because there was no cross upon it. Even Abdulmalik's gold coins were at first regarded with suspicion, especially in Medina (Bal., 466f.) because they only weighed the same as the old worn dinars.[2]

---

[1] The pious reproached Hajjâj with putting his own name on the legends after the name of God.

[2] Cf. again BAthîr, 4, 337f. That it was found impossible to introduce a real uniformity of coinage and measures into the Islamic kingdom is shown by an utterance ascribed to the Prophet in Yahyâ b. Âdam, Kitâb alKharâj, p. 52: "Iraq obstinately sticks to its dirham and qafîz, Syria to its dinar and modius, and Egypt to its dinar and ardab; ye are returning to your old divisions and lack of unity, to the old particularism."

A corresponding attempt to become more independent of foreign influence was the introduction of the Arabic language in the ministry, *i.e.* in the exchequer, for the stability of the government administration was essentially confined to finance. So far the official business of accounts in Damascus was done in Greek, in Kufa in Persian. According to Baládhurî, 300f. (Fihrist, 242) the change to Arabic seems to have begun at Kufa. Zâdanfarrûkh b. Piri[1] or his son Mardânshâh was the last Persian clerk. His assistant, Sâlih b. Abdurrahmân, offered to Hajjâj to do the reckoning in Arabic and managed it, too, though the expression of the fractions gave him trouble, for apparently figures were not used in Kufa. The reason why the government office became " arabianised " in Damascus also is curiously given by Baládhurî, p. 193. Because of an offence committed by a Greek clerk Abdulmalik resolved to make everything connected wth the office Arabian. Sulaimân b. Saîd, who got the commission, completed it in a year's time and received as a reward the ground-tax of Urdunn for one year, amounting to 180,000 dinars. The Greek and Persian system was, of course, retained and only the language changed, and doubtless the existing Greek and Persian officials who were acquainted

---

[1] *Tab.*, 2, 1034. *Anon. Ahlw.*, 343. 352.

with   Arabic,   also   remained.   Sâlih b.
Abdurrahmân, who initiated the change in Kufa,
was himself an Iranian from Sajistân (Balâdh.,
393, 15), but it was necessary to know Greek
and Persian in order to be able to turn them
into Arabic.   In   Damascus,   even   under
Abdulmalik,   the   Greek   Sergius   kept the
influential position which he had had under
Muâwia and Yazîd (Tab., 837, 11). Theophanes,
who ascribes the replacing of the Greek government official language by the Arabic first to
Walîd I,[1] (A. M. 6199), says the Greek numerals
had to be retained by the Arabs and their
notaries were still Christians,—and indeed the
Christian privy-councillors in the time of the
Abbasids, in which the chronicler writes, were
more influential, more powerful and more detested
than ever.   Besides, the Arabs generally were
regarded as useless for the management of taxes
(Tab., 458. 1470), for other reasons besides a
mere lack of technical knowledge.

One   has   the   impression that Abdulmalik
put the government on a somewhat different
footing in other respects as well.   It evidently
became more technical and hierarchical, though
not to anything like the same extent as the
Abbasid government did later on.   Certain high

---

[1] In A. M. 87 Walid introduced the Arabic pulpit-language into
Egypt, not, however, in place of the Greek, but instead of the Coptic
(Maqrîzî, Khitat, 1, 98).

offices are first mentioned under him, though of
course it does not necessarily follow that they
were not in existence before, but this much is
certain, that for him, the title πρωτοσύμβουλος is
no longer fitting,—the title which is characteristic
of the first Khalifas. With his officials he assumed a strict and almost rough manner, even
with the highly. deserving Hajjâj, whom he
treated very differently from the way in which
Muâwia treated his Ziâd. Even with the eminent men whom he, according to old custom,
gathered into his society and council, he did not
establish such a free intercourse with himself
as had Muâwia, whose spiritual superiority was
able to carry it off. The much-lauded amiabili-
ty of the Sufyânid regents, which in their
case, as with the old-Arab Saiyid, was more a
virtue than an innate good quality, was a
characteristic neither of him nor of his successors, for he proved to be a strict master (Anon.,
178).

When his Khalifate came into question he
let every consideration go to the winds. His
cousin, Amr b. Saîd, who attempted to claim
it, he cut off practically by his own hand, while
the death of his brother Abdulazîz, who opposed
the succession of his sons, spared him the
necessity of putting him out of the way. For
the rest, he gave his Umaiyid relations a larger
share in the enjoyment of power than his

predecessors had allowed them. To begin with, practically all the stattholderships were in their hands. In Egypt and Africa Abdulazîz ruled, possibly in virtue of a testamentary arrangement of old Marwân, who had caused homage to be paid to him as the successor after Abdulmalik.[1] Muhammad b. Marwân received Mesopotamia and Armenia, an important charge on account of the wars with the Romans. Kufa and afterwards Basra also were entrusted to Bishr b. Marwân, still a mere youth, and before that another Umaiyid had administered Basra, namely, Khâlid, the grandson of Asîd. At the court the Umaiyids, since they had emigrated with Marwân from Medina to Damascus, presented a far larger contingent of representatives than before ; even Khâlid, the son of the Khalifa Yazîd, played a part there. Abdulmalik sought to console him for his unjust exclusion from the succession by bringing him near to himself and giving him his daughter in marriage. He himself married a daughter of Yazîd, Âtika by name, who became his favourite wife and was allowed to order him about a good deal.

---

[1]   Marwan antequam moreretur...Aegyptum vel (=et) ulterioris Aethiopiae partes, Tripoleos Africae et usque ad Gaditana freta adjacentes provincias Habellaziz filio dereliquit,—so it runs in the *Cont. B. A.*, par. 29. The demand that the tax of Egypt should be delivered up to him was an insult offered to Abdulazîz by Abdulmalik (Anon., 239). Abdulazîz was born of another mother (*ib.*, 261).

Numerous anecdotes about this, the most celebrated Khalifa of the Umaiyid dynasty, are served up in the Anonymous Work of Ahlwardt. They enhance our personal knowledge of him and also supply all sorts of interesting material, *e.g.* about the places where Abdulmalik resided in turn according to the season of the year, about his wives and family, his regular daily business and his care for the education of his sons, his preferences and his weaknesses, his defects,—*e.g.* his offensive breath, and his nicknames. He grew old early and died at Damascus aged 60, on Thursday, 14th Shauwâl, 86 (9th October, 705).[1]

Abdulmalik is called the "father of the kings" because four of his sons succeeded to the rule after him, and only two of the later Umaiyid Khalifas were not directly descended from him. His brother, Abdulazîz of Egypt, had been designated to be his successor, and homage rendered to him accordingly. Abdulmalik did all he could to induce him to renounce his claim so as to be able to divert the kingdom to his own heirs, but in vain ; the latter would neither

---

[1] Following Abû Ma'shar in Tab., 2, 1172 (Cf. *Anon.*, 264), Wâqidî names Thursday in the middle of Shauwâl as the day of his death ; according to Wüstenfeld the Thursday fell on the 14th. of the month, and in Elias Nisibenus there is the same date. His age is given by Madâinî in Tab., 1173 and by the Anonymous Author as 62 or 63 years ; by Abû Ma'shar in Tab. as 60, and by Wâqidî upon other authorities as only 58 (Tab., 1153. Anon., 165, and the same also in the proper reading, Anon., 152). The number 60 lies at the root of the statement in Tab., 467.

be frightened nor cajoled. Fortunately, however, he died before the Khalifa (Tab., 1165. *Cf.*
1171), and then the latter's eldest son Walîd I
came into the succession. Under him Arabian
arms received a fresh impulse : Tyana was taken
after a long siege, and a great campaign against
Constantinople itself was begun. A second
period of great conquests commenced and
Transoxiania and Spain were subdued. In the
interior peace reigned at last and Walîd enjoyed
the fruits of his father's work. He followed in
his footsteps and held firmly to the much-detest-
ed stattholder of the East, namely Hajjâj,
who in a certain respect directed the government
of the Khalifas whom he served. He attached
great importance to appearing as a lord and
master, and is said to have been the first Khalifa
who made a parade of his majesty (Anon., 243).
Expressions which remind one of " oderint modo
metuant " are put into his mouth (Tab., 1178).
He advanced Islam as the imperial religion, but
he may have had a deeper relation to it as well.
He put an end to the harassing of the Pious at
Medina by the stattholder Hishâm b. Ismâîl,
appointing in his place his cousin Umar b.
Abdulazîz, a man after the heart of the scholars
of the Scripture (Tab., 1182ff.), and he emphatically insisted upon knowledge of the Qoran in
the case of everyone (Tab., 1271), though he, to
his father's sorrow, no longer spoke the old

Arabic in which the holy Book is written (Anon.,
236f. 260). He carried out a plan which his
father had already had in his mind but is said
to have abandoned, namely he took from the
Christians in Damascus the Church of St. John,
enlarged, by means of it, the chief mosque
which was adjoining and restored the latter in a
magnificent style in A. H. 84 (Bal., 125f. Tab.,
1275). He removed the gilded cupola of brass
from a Christian church in Baalbekk and placed
it on the mosque of Jerusalem, over the holy
rock (Eutych., 2, 373), and he also had the
mosque of Medina completely rebuilt (Balâdh ,
67). To be sure, he annoyed the Pious by doing so, and likewise by the fact that at the
speech from the pulpit which he held there in
the year 91, he did not stand, but remained
sitting, as he was accustomed to do at home
(Tab., 1233). He had a *penchant* for buildings of all kinds as well as for the laying-out
and improvement of country estates, and he
infected his immediate circle with it (Tab., 1272).
Hajjâj supplied him with Indian buffaloes for
the marshy region at the bay of Issus. But
he also cared for the helpless and endowed the
lepers, the blind and the lame ; so that they did
not need to beg (Tab., 1271). The Syrians
profited most by him and regarded him as the
best of all their Khalifas (Tab., 1271, 3). It is
difficult to believe that he took the side of the

29

Qais against the Kalb in Syria, for he had no
need to do so, and it is not reported by the old
historians. We cannot conclude from them
that his mother Wallâda was a Qaisite (Anon.,
172, 191f. Ham., 672) and that the Qaisite
Hajjâj was his right hand. The later writers
are inclined to gather all the actors under the
one rubric or the other, and Dozy follows their
lead. Walîd died in the middle of Jumâdâ II,
96, on a Saturday, aged about 40. The 13th
Jumâdâ II (23rd February, 715) was a Saturday.[1]

3.   Iraq, which was the scene of the real
history of Islam in this period also, was during
the Khalifate of Abdulmalik and Walîd for long
years under the Thaqifite Hajjâj b. Yûsuf b.
Hakam, who has been frequently mentioned
already and who had first proved his merit in
Mecca and Medina. Heavy tasks awaited him
when summoned to Iraq. The province was in
a tumult of unrest to its very core, and not
merely so because of the lengthy struggle about
the Khalifate. In Kufa the great rising of the
Shîa allied to the Mawâlî under Mukhtâr was
certainly stamped out, but it left a smouldering
trail in men's minds.[2]   Basra was still not rid

---

[1]   " The middle of the month " did not perhaps in older times
exactly signify the 15th. of the month, as it is usually made out to be.
Elias Nis., however, gives Sunday, 14th Jumâdâ II, 96, as the day of
Walîd's death.

[2]   *Shia*, p. 74ff.

of the Khawârij,[1] who for years had been threatening it before its very gates ; Mus'ab had not been able to overcome them. They crippled him in the struggle with the Syrians, for on their account he had to leave behind his best warriors to protect Basra. When he was conquered by Abdulmalik and fell far away on the Tigris, Muhallab was in the field against the Azâriqa. He summed up the situation and placed himself at the disposal of the victor, who valued him as he deserved. But the Umaiyid princes whom he, as stattholder, sent into Iraq, would only have been fit for a sinecure. Khâlid b. Asîd, who came to Basra, set Muhallab aside, first taking over himself the leadership of the war against the dangerous fanatics and then entrusting it to his brother. The result was severe defeats of the imperial troops, and the Khalifa had to interfere himself in order to restore Muhallab to the position to which he belonged. But it was not of much avail for him to depose Khâlid and hand over Basra also to his brother Bishr at Kufa, for Bishr, a vain youth, did no better than his predecessor, and was jealous of Muhallab because the latter received his *commando* direct from the Khalifa, and not from him. In obedie nce to higher orders, he certainly reinforced hi m with Kufaite troops, but expressly insisted that their leader should refuse subordina-

---

[1] *Chawarig*, p. 32ff.

tion to Muhallab, and it was no fault of his
if the latter would not be induced to agree to
this but shook his head at the foolish boy.
Fortunately he died in A. H. 74[1] and Abdulmalik
then, to the joy of Muhallab, sent Hajjâj into
Iraq, where he arrived at the beginning of the
year 75.[2] Such, in essentials, is the account of
Abû Mikhnaf in Tabarî, 821 ff.; 855 ff.

Hajjâj began his career in Kufa with an
introductory speech which is no less famous
than that of his countryman and predecessor in
office, Ziâd, in Basra. The report of it in Tab.,
863 ff. comes from Umar b. Shabba (according
to Abû Ghassân and Madâinî), and with it are to
be compared the accounts in Anon. Ahlw., 266
ff., and in *Kâmil*, 665f. An unknown and obscure young man stepped into the pulpit and for
a long time seemed to find no words to say.
One of the audience picked up a handful of
gravel[3] to throw at him, but it slipped quietly
out of his hand whenever the apparently helpless speaker opened his mouth. The first duty
of the new stattholder was to restore the discipline of the garrisons of Kufa and Basra, who
had taken the death of Bishr as a signal to leave
Muhallab's camp in Râmhurmuz without per-

---

[1] Acc. to Wâqidî in Tab., 852, 8 ; 854, 1 as early as A.H. 73, but
this is impossible.

[2] But not only in Ramadân, as Tab., 872 has it. Cf. 944, 9 ; 876,
3. Anon Ahlw., 270, 1.

[3] So Ziâd seems not to have cleared away all the stones.

mission. It did not suit them to be so long in the
field, far away from their wives and children,
when they were accustomed to a luxurious life at
home (Tab., 865, 12ff.). Hajjâj announced at once
to the Kufaites from the pulpit,—"Whoever
of those deserters from the standard still shows
his face after three days in the town, his life
and property shall be forfeited," and as he could
emphasise the threat it was effective. In the
same way as he had entered Kufa he next
entered Basra, and with the same success.
Those whose duty it was thronged over the
Tigris bridge to get back to Ramhurmuz, and
he himself accompanied them as far as the
general camp of Rustaqabâd, where, in Sha'bân,
75, he had to quell a rebellion which had broken
out because of a reduction in the pay, which
according to Anon. Ahlw., 280ff. was far more
dangerous than appears from the brief notice
given it in Tab., 879. And now the war against
the Azâriqa could be carried on with ample
means, though, as a matter of fact, fully two
years more passed before they were quite annihilated.[1]

The Azâriqa in the East were not yet subdued when there arose in the beginning of 76
other Khawârij in the west of Iraq, who were
distinguished by the fact that they mostly
belonged to *one* tribe, the proud Banû Shaibân

[1] *Chawarij*, pp. 39ff.

of Bakr, who not long before had emigrated
from their former settlements on the right bank
of the Euphrates, in the desert of Kufa and
Basra, to Northern Mesopotamia.[1] Their most
famous and most dangerous leader was Shabîb
b. Yazîd, who with his swift cavalry was at
once everywhere and nowhere. In the year 76
he crossed from Mesopotamia into Iraq, routed
several columns sent against him by Hajjâj,
and actually reached the gate of the capital.
His favourite beat was the classic ground of the
old Khawârij, the territory of Jûkhâ on the
Nahrawân and the range of mountains to the
north of it. After a longish sojourn in the
highlands of Âdharbaijân, during which many
flocked to join him, he advanced in the second
half of the year 77 towards the south with a
considerable force, to attempt a decisive attack
upon Kufa. A general levy was made against
him, but he put to disgraceful flight the whole
Kufaite army. Hajjâj's own resources were
exhausted, and he found himself compelled to
ask the Khalifa for Syrian troops, which arrived
just in the nick of time and repulsed Shabîb,
who then retired to Jûkhâ but soon again with-

---

[1] The family of Shabîb lived not far from Mosul, but it had
emigrated thither (via Kufa,-Tab., 977) from the water of Lasâf in the
Kufan desert (Hamâsa, 15). One section of the kinsfolk had remained
living there, and still frequently received visits from the elders of
Shabîb (Tab., 915. 978). Possibly the breaking-up of the Shaibânites
was not exactly voluntary, but caused by Muâwia.

drew from there into the far-distant Karmân, the stronghold of the Azâriqa. Making a *sortie* again from there he encountered on the Dujail in Ahwâz the Syrian army that had been sent against him, and was drowned on his retreat over the river at the end of 77 (spring of 697 A.D.). The Syrians had saved Kufa, but we shall see how dearly their help had to be paid. The very detailed account of Shabîb in Tab., 881-1002 is taken from Abû Mikhnaf.[1]

In the year 78, after the Khârijite menace in the east and west of Iraq was abolished, Hajjâj also obtained the supremacy over Khurâsân and Sajistân (Tab., 1032f. Anon., 310f.). He bestowed the province of Khurâsân upon the subduer of the Azâriqa, the Azdite Muhallab, who had already won his spurs there (Bal., 432). Muhallab remained there till his death (the end of 82) and bequeathed his authority to his family and his tribe.

To Sajistân[2] Hajjâj sent Ubaidullâh b. Abî Bakra, a prominent Basrian of the well-known Thaqifite family from which Ziâd b. Abîhi also was descended. In the year 79 the former undertook a campaign against Zunbîl of Kâbul and Zâbul, who was withholding the tribute.[3]

---

[1] *Chawarig*, p. 41 ff.

[2] For the previous history of Sajistân. *Cf.* Balâdh., 392 ff.

[3] *Zunbîl* (a proper name as well as a title) and not *Rutbîl*, is the proper pronunciation (*Cunningham* in the *Verhandl. des 10.*

Zunbîl enticed him far into the country and then cut him off in the rear, and it was only with great losses, especially among the Kufaite contingent, that Ubaidullâh made his way through, bringing his army back in a pitiful plight. He died not long after in A.H. 79 (Anon., 320) or 80 (Tab., 1046). Sajistân had need of a tried warrior as stattholder, and Hajjâj selected for the post a proud Kufaite of the family of the old kings of Kinda, Abdurrahmân b. Muhammad b. Ash'ath, who was in the neighbouring Karmân,[1] and strengthened him with a numerous, fully-paid and splendidly-equipped army of Kufaites and Basrians, the so-called "army of peacocks."

Such was the situation when the rebellion of the army of Iraq broke out against Hajjâj, a rebellion which severely shook the Umaiyid kingdom. Tabarî gives preference to the lively

internat. Oriental-congresses, 1, 244. Justi, *Namenbuch, 385;* Marquart, *Eranshahr,* 37). Cf. *Tab.,* 1652, 18. 3, 194, 3 ; a Yemenite *Zankbîl* appears in 1, 1855, 16. The lord of the Turks is called the *Zunbîl,* Tab., 2, 1132f. 1037, 2. 1042, 12. The subjects, certainly, were Iranians, but the dynasties (and soldiers) Turkish. Cf. *Farazdaq, ed.* Boucher, 206, 10.

[1] According to Abû Ubaida (An., 320f., Tab., 1046) he had there to put down a mutiny under the Bakrite Himiân b. Adî as Sadûsî (*Cf.* An., 342), but according to other accounts (An., 318, 2. 320, 10) he had to fight against Khawârij. Anon., 309 says he had originally gone to Sajistân upon business relating to an inheritance, and there had become entangled with the courtesan Mahânôsh. But the latter, according to An., 334f. lived in Karmân and had got not him, but another well-known Arab so much into her toils that on her account he pawned his saddle and Ibn Ash'ath had to redeem it so that he might ride with him. *Cf. Farazdaq,* 209, 12.

and detailed account of Abû Mikhnaf, who stood
quite near the events as they took place.
The account, likewise very exhaustive, in the
Anonymous Work, Ahlw., 308ff. follows different
guarantors. Abdurrahmân, generally called Ibn
Ash'ath after his grandfather, started upon a
different course from that of his predecessor,
undertaking not a *sortie*, but a regular campaign. He occupied the places he had taken
and established a postal service to ensure
his lines of communication. After subduing
a part of the country he made a pause for a
time, so that his soldiers should first get accustomed to the nature of the mountains, and he
sent word of this to Hajjâj. But the latter,
quick and impatient as usual, addressed him
sharply, and insisted in repeated letters on his
advancing without delay, or else giving up the
command to his brother Ishâq. Ibn Ash'ath
then gathered together the chief people, told
them the contents of the letters, and said in
conclusion, "If you want to advance, then I
shall do so; but if you do not want to, then I
will not either." The men of Iraq hated Hajjâj; the prospect of a hard, weary war in distant
lands was distasteful to them, and any opportunity of returning home was welcome, so Ibn
Ash'ath was sure of their reply. "We will not
obey the enemy of God, who like a Pharaoh
coerces us to the farthest campaigns and keeps

30

us here so that we can never see our wives and
children; the gain is always his; if we are victorious, the conquered land is his; if we perish,
then he is rid of us." They all did homage to
Ibn Ash'ath with the idea that he should drive
out Hajjâj, and the most zealous were the
Yemenites of Kufa, to whom he himself belonged.[1] His brothers, however, were not on
his side (Anon., 326f.).

After peace had been made with Zunbîl and
representative stattholders been settled in Bust
and Zaranj, the chief towns of Sajistân, the army
moved on in A.H. 81, collecting on the way
more soldiers from Kufa and Basra, who were
stationed as garrisons in the provinces. On
reaching Fars they saw the impossibility of
separating Hajjâj from Abdulmalik, so they
renounced the latter also and did homage to
Ibn Ash'ath as a preliminary to the conflict
against the Khalifa and the Syrians. Ibn Ash'ath
had no need to force matters; he was urged
on in spite of himself, and even if he would,
could not have banished the spirits which he
had called up. It was as if an avalanche came
rushing down sweeping every thing before it.

---

[1] Farazdaq allows that the Rabîa and Mudar were also included,
but lays the chief blame upon the Yemenites of Kufa, the Sabaites,
who had before extolled the Jew Mukhtâr (211, 10) and now did the
same with the weaver Ibn Ash'ath (208, 9. 209, 16. 211, 11). The
Yemenites were scoffed at as weavers, just as the Azd were derided
as fishers and boatmen.

Muhallab in Khurâsân did not join in the movement. He is said to have advised Hajjâj not to stem the stream of the Iraqites and not to attack them till they had reached home again, saying that once they were back home with their wives and children, it would be all over with their invincibility.[1] Hajjâj, however, did not follow his advice, but with his Syrian soldiers, strengthened by hurried reinforcements from Abdulmalik, marched against the rebels. On the old battle-field on the Dujail, near Tustar and Rustaqabâd, the first encounter took place, when Ibn Ash'ath crossed the river and was victorious on the evening of the 10th Dhulhijja, 81, i. e., 25th January, 701. The vanquished fled to Basra, pursued by the victors, who marched unchecked into the town, where they were received with open arms. But Hajjâj established himself in the suburb of Zâwia, and a few Thaqifites and Quraishites there joined him. He was determined to perish rather than yield. For a month his Syrians, under the leadership of the Kalbite Sufyân b. Abrad,[2] withstood the attack of the Iraqites who where encamped in Khuraiba (An., 355), and at last inflicted on them a decisive defeat in Muharram, 82 (the beginning of March,

---

[1] Thus Tab., 1059. Acc. to An., 343 the counsel was not given to Hajjâj until a later occasion, by his Persian clerk Zadanfarrûkh or by Abbâd b. Husain.

[2] The conqueror of Shabîb. Cf. An., 338. 342.

701). In consequence of this Ibn Ash'ath marched with the Kufaites [1] away to Kufa, the actual centre-point of the rebellion, whither the Iraqite garrison troops from the provinces were gathering from all sides. As his representative in Basra he left the Quraishite Abdurrahmân Ibn Abbâs alHâshimî, who continued the conflict, but only for a few days, as the bulk of the Basrians accepted pardon from Hajjâj (An., 349, 5) and let him march into the town. At the beginning of Safar, 82 (middle of March, 701) Hajjâj was able to set out on the march to Kufa, Ibn Abbâs alHâshimî hanging on to his flank with those Basrians who would not lay down their arms.

In Kufa an officer from Madâin, Matar b. Nâjia atTamîmî, had anticipated Ibn Ash'ath, turned out the Syrian garrison and seized the citadel He unwillingly yielded to Ibn Ash'ath, only doing homage under compulsion after the Hamdân had stormed the citadel and taken him prisoner. This may have also been a reason why Ibn Ash'ath had found himself obliged to hasten his march from Basra (An., 348; 355), but he had already got the better of his rival before Hajjâj followed him. The latter made his way through the desert on the right bank of the

---

[1] Acc. to An., 349,1 there were only 1,000 men, so the great majority of the Kufaites in his army must have already betaken themselves back to their town—which is highly probable.

Euphrates and encamped in Dair Qurra near
Kufa, where he had easy communication with
Syria, the provision of which was indeed enjoined
only upon Ain Tamr and the Falâlîj. According to Arab custom, the rebel Iraqites marched
out of the town and occupied a strong camp near
Dair Jamâjim,[1] opposite the Syrians, at the
beginning of Rabî I, 82 (middle of April, 701).
They are said to have been 100,000 strong, with
as many servants. For months daily encounters
took place, none of them decisive. Abdulmalik
grew restless; he sent a new Syrian army under
his brother Muhammad and his son Abdullâh,[2]
but at the same time caused terms to be offered
to the Iraqites if they would submit. Their
pension was to be raised to be equal to that
of the Syrians; Hajjâj was to be recalled,
and to Ibn Ash'ath any province he liked was
to be granted for life. But in spite of the
persuasion of their leaders they would have
nothing to do with this, but once more renounced
Abdulmalik, trusting that the Syrians would
shortly run out of provisions. They were
mistaken, however. The Syrians held out
stubbornly, and they themselves gave up the
struggle after it had lasted 100 days. In
the middle of Jumâdâ II, 82 (the end of July,

---

[1] Is this the Monastery of Golgotha ?

[2] He thus denuded the marches in the direction of the Romans
and they took advantage of this; see *Göttinger Nachrichten*, 1901,
p. 433.

701) they vacated the field for no proper reason ;
their enthusiasm had not the staying quality
of their opponents' discipline. One of their
chiefs took to flight from Sufyân b. Abrad, who
was again almost reaching a decision, and this
aroused suspicion of treachery and caused a
general panic. Ibn Ash'ath could not check the
flight : Hajjâj furthered it by the means
already approved at Basra,—by issuing a
proclamation promising pardon to all who
returned to their house and garrison, and by
forbidding the Syrians to pursue them. He thus
gained his end without much bloodshed and
was able to make a victorious entry into Kufa,
where he accepted the homage of those who
had laid down their arms. They had also to
acknowledge that they had renounced Islam by
their rebellion, but there were very few who were
unwilling to purchase their life even at the cost
of such self-abasement.

Many of the Iraqites, however, who were
scattered at Kufa banded together again at
other places. Ibn Ash'ath then betook himself
back to the town of Basra, which the Quraishite Ubaidullâh b. Abdirrahmân alAbdshamsî had
won for him again, but he did not stay long,
but returned to Maskin on the Dujail.[1]   With

---

[1] It is not the very out-of-the-way Maskin between Mosul and
Takrît, as Weil and Müller think, but another in Izqubâd (Tab., 1099
1123. Yâqût, 4, 529. 531).

the numerous troops which joined him on all
sides he once again made a stand against
Hajjâj, who was pursuing him, in Sha'bân, 82
(Sept. or Oct., 701). The struggle was long
and obstinate, and was, according to Tabarî,
1123 f., at last decided by the fact that a Syrian
squadron, led by an old man well-versed in the
lie of the land, surrounded the Iraqites by going
through marshes and attacked them by night.
They fled across the Dujail, losing more by
drowning than by the sword.

Ibn Ash'ath now continued his retreat
towards the East. The Syrians pursuing him
under Umâra b. Tamîm alLakhmî, spotted him
twice, at Sûs and Sabûr, but he luckily shook
them off and by Karmân, where he stayed a
considerable time, got to Sajistân (at the end
of 82 or beginning of 83). His stattholder in
Zaranj shut the gates against him, and the one
in Bust actually took him prisoner in order to
hand him over to Hajjâj. He was then freed
by Zunbîl, who had pledged himself to keep a
place of refuge for him in case of need, and who
took him along with his great following to Kâbul,
and showed him much honour. Meanwhile,
however, another crowd of Iraqites followed
their fugitive leader, gathered together under
the already well-known Quraishite Ubaidullâh Ibn
Abdirrahmân alAbdshamsî and Abdurrahmân
Ibn Abbâs alHâshimî in Sajistân, and called

him back. He came, took the capital Zaranj, and punished his unfaithful stattholder there, but when, against his wish, his troops for fear of the Syrians, who were now at last arriving under Umâra, entered upon Khurasanite territory thinking they would not be attacked there, he took the opportunity to return to Zunbîl and left them in the lurch. They now placed the Hâshimite Ibn Abbâs at their head, took the town of Herât and slew Yazîd b. Muhallab's official there, who at the end of 82 had succeeded his father. Thus the latter was compelled, much against his will, to go against them, and he dispersed them after a short fight, in which several prominent men fell into his hands. Those of them who were his Yemenite tribal relations he let go free ; the rest he sent to Hajjâj, who had taken up his quarters in the town of Wâsit, just then being built (A.H. 83), and Hajjâj held a bloody tribunal upon them. So goes the account of Abû Mikhnaf (Tab., 1101-6), but Madâinî (1106-10) differs somewhat.

The Syrian commander U uâra meanwhile became master of Sajistân, after giving a remnant of Iraqite rebels who had remained there an opportunity to surrender under easy conditions. Only Ibn Ash'ath himself was still dangerous. Hajjâj now tried by threats and promises to persuade Zunbîl to hand over his *protégé*, and at last succeeded by offering

to let him off paying tribute for 7 or 10 years.
For all that he did not get his foe into his
hands alive, but only his head severed from the
body. Ibn Ash'ath is said either to have died
previously or to have committed suicide. This
was in the year 84 or 85 (Tab., 1138).

The chronology of these events is not quite
certain. Some of the days and months, indeed,
have remained firmly fixed in the memory,—for
instance, the battle of Tustar is agreed to have
been on the day of Arafa at the end of the year in
which the rebellion began, and in the next year
the month Muharram is fixed for the battles at
Basra, the months Rabî and Jumâdâ for the
battles at Kufa, and Sha'bân for the battle of
Maskin,[1] but as regards the years tradition varies.
I have followed the chronology according to
which the rebellion broke out in the year 81, and
the battles at Basra, Kufa and Maskin fell into
the year 82, and those in Sajistân and
Khurâsân into the year 83. Another chronology puts the dates a year later, namely 82, 83
and 84,[2] in which case the death of Ibn Ash'ath

[1] On the contrary, it can hardly hold if Wâqidî puts the battle
of Dair Jamâjim into Sha'bân, 82, and the beginning of the rebellion
into the same year (Tab., 1070. 1052). The "Arafa-day " in particular
is fixed for Tustar.

[2] Abû Mikhnaf seems to mix up the different reckonings when he
puts the beginning of the rising and the battle of Tustar into the
year 81, and on the other hand, the battles at Zâwia (Basra) and
accordingly the battles at Kufa, acc. to Tab. 1011, not till the
year, 83.

31

in the year 84 or 85 immediately follows the
subjection of Sajistân by the Syrians. But
that is only an apparent advantage, for there
may quite well have been a longer interval
between the two events. On the other hand, it is
significant that coinciding traditions make Ibn
Ash'ath come to Sajistân as early as A. H. 80,
immediately after which he undertook the
campaign against Zunbîl, and was on this very
campaign when he learned of the affront of
Hajjâj which caused him to rebel. The
rebellion cannot therefore very well have broken
out till the second year after 80. We have
also to take into consideration that the prisoners
of Herat were brought to Wasit when this town
was yet building, as is expressly stated (Tab.,
1119 f.). But in A. H. 83 it was still occupied
by Hajjâj, and in A. H. 84, he at any rate lived
there. Thus, then, the battles in Sajistân and
Khurasan might quite possibly take place in
A.H. 83, but *not* in A. H. 84. Unfortunately we
can get at nothing decisive from the repeated
mention of the days of the week, for they do
not agree with the dates given either in the
years 81 and 82, or in the years 82 and 83.[1]

---

[1]   Acc. to Anon. Ahlw. the battle of Tustar took place on Friday,
the 10th Dhulhijja, 81 (340, 10), and on Thursday, the 23rd Dhulhijja,
81, Hajjâj occupied the camp in Zâwia (342, 10). The days of the week
do not agree with those of the month either for A.H. 81 or A.H. 82,
but do for A.H. 80, which is not mentioned in any tradition, and which
one hardly ventures to consider. Acc. to Abû Mikhnaf in Tab., 1094

Alfred von Kremer has shown the rebellion of Ibn Ash'ath in a new light, by which he has dazzled others, *e. g.*, A. Müller and G. van Vloten (*Recherches sur la domination arabe*, Amsterdam, 1894). He has, to wit, connected it with the attempt of the Mawâlî, *i. e.*, the subjects gone over to Islam in Kufa and Basra, to obtain equal political rights with the ruling nobility, *i. e.*, the Arabs, to be freed from the subject-tax and received on the pension list, which hitherto was a register of the Arab nobility. In order to prevent the decrease of the state revenues, which by extending the exemption from taxes and the payment of pensions to the non-Arab Muslims, was bound to result or even had already resulted, Hajjâj (he says) had again imposed the poll-tax upon the numerous Mawâlî who had embraced Islam, a tax which they, as Muslims, should by right have had to pay no longer, and so the fire was kindled. " Hajjâj ordered that those who had embraced Islam,—the whole of the great class of the new Muslims, must pay the poll-tax

the 100-days' battles at Kufa began on Tuesday, 2nd Rabî I, 83 and ended on Wednesday, 14th Jumâdâ II, 83. Here again the days of the week do not agree with the days of the month either of A.H. 83 or A.H. 82. The nearest is A.H. 81, where there is a difference only of one day. Such a difference seems negligible, and explicable by the variations of the beginning of month or the beginning of the day (in the evening or the morning). But should the correct way be neither 82-83 nor 81-82, but rather 80-81? Theophanes, A. M. 6192, says nothing against it.

just as they did before their conversion, a measure which resulted in a dreadful rebellion of the new converts and their clients.[1] Many people of Basra, in particular, took part in it, old warriors, clients and readers of the Qoran. One account has it that of these rebels 100,000 were included in the register of the yearly dole, and so, to put it in a modern way, belonged to the militia, and they were joined by as many more. Hajjâj routed the rebels[2] and determined once for all to disperse the whole class of clients, so that it could never again gather to form a solid opposition. He sent for them and said,—' Ye are miserable strangers and barbarians and were better to stay in your villages.' Then he gave orders to divide them over the villages and scattered their party most effectively, and in order that none should be able to get away from the village where he was settled, he had the name of the village branded on each one's hand." This is Kremer's account in the " *Culturgeschichte des Orients* " (1875) 1,172 and in the " *Culturgeschichtlichen Streifzügen* " (1873), p. 24. He follows chiefly an account of Jâhiz in his book upon the Mawâlî and the Arabs, which is quoted in the *Iqd* of ' Abdrabbih (ed. Bulaq, 1302 : 2, 93).[3]

[1] What the addition " and their clients " means, I do not know.

[2] Kremer proceeds more summarily than Hajjâj.

[3] " Ibn Ash'ath and Abdullâh b. Jarûd had mutinied against Hajjâj, and his experiences with the Iraqites were not happy. The

There is no doubt that the fall of Mukhtâr
did not once for all put an end to the rebellion
of the recent converts, and that Hajjâj had to
deal with the difficulties which arose from the
acceptance of Islam, touching their political position and their taxation. It is also certain that
the rising of Ibn Ash'ath had its real origin
in Kufa, as had that of Mukhtâr.[1]   But
there is no suggestion in the primary sources
in Tab. and the Anonymous Writer of Ahlw.
that in its tendency it was simply a continuation
of that of Mukhtâr. It did not take its tone
from the Mawâlî, though there were certainly

most dangerous he had found to be the Basrians, their religious
scholars, their warriors and Mawâlî. Because they were the most
numerous and the most powerful he wished to abolish their claim to a
pension and to distribute them so that they should no longer hold close
together and form a community. So he said to the Mawâlî : 'Ye are
barbarians and strangers ; ye belong to your towns and villages.' Thus
he scattered them and broke up their alliance as he wished ; sent them
whither he pleased and had the name of the place where each was sent
to marked upon his hand." According to this, the despatch of the
Mawâlî into their villages was one amongst other measures which
Hajjâj carried out in order to break the power of the overgrown town
of Basra, which earlier experiences had shown him to be dangerous.
One of these experiences was the rebellion of Ibn Ash'ath, and another
was the earlier mutiny of Ibn Jarûd (Anon., 280 ff. B Athîr, 4, 309 ff),
which spread over several years. Nothing further is said. Acc. to
Tab., 1122; 1435 the Mawâlî who were turned out by Hajjâj along
with the *readers*, who were in sympathy with them, undoubtedly stuck
to Ibn Ash'ath. But even there, there is nothing to show that the
rebellion was instigated by them.

[1] This allows Farazdaq mockingly to say that as the Kufaites were
former adherents of Mukhtâr (Sabaites) so now again they were
adherents of that new rebel, Ibn Ash'ath.

many of them in it. Abû Mikhnaf (Tab., 1072)
tells that in the camp of Dair Jamâjim there
were 100,000 Arab defenders (*Muqâtila*) entitled
to pensions, and just as many Mawâlî, but they
appear in the following of their Arab masters.
It was customary for the latter to take their
clients, if they had any, into the field with them,
and make them fight on foot whilst they themselves were mounted,—a similar arrangement
to that existing between knights and servants
in the Middle Ages, so the fact that the Mawâlî
took part in it does not give the struggle its
character. They might well have an interest
of their own in the hostility against the Syrian
rule, which formed the backbone of Arabism,
but still they were only secondary; the rising
did not originate with them but with the " Pea-
cock army " of Iraqites in Sajistân, which the
garrisons of the other provinces joined, and to
which the capitals Kufa and Basra opened their
gates. The most prominent and notable Arabs
took part in it,—heads of clans like Ibn Ash'ath
of Kinda, Jarîr b. b. Saîd b. Qais of Hamdân
(Anon., 340), Abdulmumin b. Shabath b. Rib'î
of Tamîm (Tab., 1056); Bistâm b. Masqala b.
Hubaira of Bakr (Tab., 1088, 1099); Quraishites
like Muhammad b. Sa'd b. Abî Waqqâs (Tab.,
1099), Ubaidullâh b. Abdirrahmân alAbdshamsî,
Abdurrahmân b. Abbâs al Hâshimî; scholars
like the Qâdî ashSha'bî and the historian

Muhammad b. Sâib alKalbî, the friend of Abû Mikhnaf (Tab., 1096). Only the name of one single Maulâ is mentioned, that of the rich Fairûz Husain from Sajistân, who is perhaps identical with the son of Sîbucht (Farazdaq, 206). The Arab aristocracy reared itself against the imperious and arrogant conduct of the representative of the state authority, the plebeian Hajjâj. " God and the pride of Ibn Muhammad (b. Ash'ath) and his descent from a race of kings older than Thamûd, forbid us to use ourselves to the rule of wretches sprung from slaves.[1] How many of the ancestors of Ibn Ash'ath have worn the crown on glorious brows ! The home of honour and of fame lies between Muhammad (b. Ash'ath) and Saîd (b. Qais), between Ashajj and Qais;[2] the Hamdân and the Kinda follow their banner. There is no Qais like unto our Qais, no Saîd like ours." In these verses the poet A'shâ of Hamdân expresses the sentiments of the leading circles (Agh., 5,153). The Arab clans, the regiments of the army, followed their chiefs, and that all the more willingly since the long service in war and garrison in outlying districts were particularly detested by them, and they were always

[1] Thaqifites like Hajjâj.

[2] By *Ashajj* here *Ash'ath* seems to be meant ; *cf.* Anon., 335. Qais is the father of the famous Saîd of Hamdân whose grandson, Jarîr, made common cause with the grandson of Ash'ath,

longing for home. The Yemenites of Kufa, in
particular, were numerously represented and the
Kinda, Hamdân and Madhhij. They were in the
majority in Kufa and reckoned Ibn Ash'ath as
peculiarly their own, but the other clans and
those of Basra were not excluded either. Most
passionately and vehemently did the *readers*
take part, as well as the pious scholars of the
Qoran and men of prayer. They were in the
forefront with speech and action on all such
occasions,[1] for in the theocracy the injustice of
the ruling power and the right of revolt against
it had always to have the sanction of the religion. But actually the rebellion under Ibn
Ash'ath had no religious motives. It was rather
a renewed and desperately powerful attempt of
the Iraqites to shake off the Syrian yoke.
Hajjâj had made it still more intolerable for
them by keeping in the land the Syrian soldiers
whom he had summoned against Shabîb, not so
much as a defence against outside foes as against
internal ones. They were the embodiment of
the foreign rule.[2] The Iraqite militia had to
be content with a scanty pension and maintain
the Syrians for it. They were told off for expeditions and garrisons in districts far remote while

---

[1] Their merits received special prominence. Abû Mikhnaf in Tab.,
1086 ff. speaks as though the fall of the pious Jabala were the most
important event at Dair Jamâjim. *Cf.* Chawârig, pp. 9 ff.

[2] In Africa and Spain also the introduction of the Syrians caused
great tumult.

the latter remained in their quarters with their families. The nature of the struggle, therefore, cannot be misunderstood. It was not a contest of the Mawâlî against the Arabs, but of the Iraqites against the Syrian Arabs (Tab., 1089). It was a contest of the two provinces of the Arab kingdom that had always been rivals, and the Iraqite elements, from whatever source they came, held together in the contest. Also, the Syrian imperial troops felt themselves united in the land of strangers. Of course, by preference, they belonged to Kalb and Qadâa; 'Akk and Ash'ar as *pars pro toto* (Tab., 1102) seems to be an insulting phrase to dub them barbarians. In Tab., 1393 they are called Copts and Nabatæans, *i.e.*, Caffres and Botokudi.

The result was that the military rule of the Syrians in Iraq was still more accentuated. In A. H. 83 Hajjâj built the fortified town of Wâsit, midway between Kufa, Madain, Ahwaz and Basra, and made it the seat of government. Thither he also transferred the bulk of the Syrian soldiers, alleging that he did so in order to prevent their committing improprieties in the citizens' quarters at Kufa and Basra. But the chief reason must have been that he wanted to isolate them from the Iraqites [1] and concentrate

---

[1] For this reason he kept the Syrians at a distance from Khurasan, so that they were not infected by the Iraqites, and sent them to India where there were no Iraqites (Tab., 1257; 1275).

them around himself so as to have them as docile instruments ready to hand. He moved his residence from the midst of the community out into a military headquarters, thereby proving that he felt as if he were in a foe's country. He uprooted the government from the patriarchal soil on which it had grown up and openly planted it upon military force. There was no other way if the sway of the Umaiyids over Iraq was to be preserved.

After the fall of Ibn Ash'ath the whole of the East lay without opposition at the feet of Hajjâj. Only the Muhallabids in Khurasan still reared their heads. They relied on their clan, the Azd Umân, who through them had come to Khurasan and had contrived that there, too, as in Basra the Azd should, with the Rabîa, form the one group (Yemen), and the Tamîm with the Qais the other group (Mudar). The chief of the Muhallabids and the Yemenite group was the ruling stattholder, Yazîd b. Muhallab. He was, to be sure, under Hajjâj, but the latter had, apparently, not the power to set him aside, however sufficient a reason he gave him for doing so. It was only reluctantly that he set about dealing with the adherents of Ibn Ash'ath in Herât, and then again exercised clemency towards the captive ringleaders, at least towards the Yemenites among them. He deferred the order to expel the rebel Qaisites who had settled in

Tirmidh (near Balkh) under Mûsâ b. Abdillâh, considering that as long as they were dangerous Hajjâj would let him alone and not put a Qaisite in his place. He did not obey repeated summonses to Wâsit, but excused himself on the score of urgent business, and it was only by bringing to bear strong pressure upon the Khalifa that Hajjâj at last in the year 85 obtained permission to depose him. He made him prisoner and gradually removed his brother also, but this he only managed to do after Abdulmalik's death (86).

Abdulmalik indeed had shown himself to be lord and master over Hajjâj ; Walîd I, for whose succession he was anxious, gave him a free hand, and even in his own sphere of government gave in to him and consulted his wishes. At his instance he deprived Umar b. Abdilazîz of the post which he had bestowed upon him, because under his rule the Hijâz was becoming the refuge of political criminals, especially of religious seditionists (Tab., 1254). In A.H. 89 or 91 Khâlid b. Jarîr b. Abdillâh alQasrî came to Mecca. In A.H. 93 or 94 Uthmân b. Haiyân alMurrî came to Medina. Both undertook the clearing out of suspects with great zeal. Under Walîd Hajjâj reaped the fruit of the hard work which he had had to do under Abdulmalik. In Iraq peace prevailed. He used it to heal the wounds which a twenty-years' war had inflicted upon the well-being of the country. He was just as great a landlord as Walîd. He devoted his attention to the canal-systems upon which depends the fertility of the marshy land on the lower Tigris and Euphrates,[1] and in the midst of the chief marshy region he founded his town of Wâsit. He tried to stem the depopulation of the alluvial lands which was resulting from the thronging of the inhabitants into the large towns. It is said he also forbade the peasants to slaughter oxen, in order to keep

---

[1] The Persian kings took great pains to drain the marshes and to establish crown lands upon them ; when one of them reclaimed a piece of ground from the bog he named it after himself. Under Qubâdh a great dam near Kaskar burst, overflowed a vast stretch of country, which was left till Anoshravân partly repaired the damage. In the year 7 or 6 of the Hijra there again occurred serious bursting of dams against which all the zeal of Parwêz proved unavailing. In the confusion during the Arab conquest the marshy land (ajam rabbati) extended still more ; the Dihkâns (proprietors and district-surveyors), could of their own power do nothing to stop it. It was only under Muâwia, and then more especially under Walîd I and Hishâm, that things improved. Hajjâj made the two canals of Nîl and Zâbi, and introduced into the marshy land the Indian buffaloes, which he also supplied to Cilicia. It was the fault of his limited resources that he did not do still more. He asked for 3 millions for the restoration of the dams. Walîd thought this excessive, but allowed his brother Maslama to execute the project at his own expense, and the latter made a great profit from it. The surveyor who did the designing under Hajjâj and Hishâm was Hassân anNabatî. There is an untrustworthy story that Hajjâj intentionally did not repair the damage caused by a great flood in his time, in order to punish the Dihkâns, whom he suspected of entertaining sympathies for Ibn Ash'ath ; cf. Tab., 1.960 ff. Balâdh. 292 f. Masûdî, 1,225 f. BKhordâdhbeh, 240 f. Yâqût, 3,174 ff.

them for the plough.[1] He only carried on wars
against external foes and that, indeed, with
great success. Under him Qutaiba b. Muslim
alBâhilî, the successor of the Muhallabids
in Khurasan, conquered Transoxiana, and
Muhammad b. Qâsim athThaqafî took the
Indusland. To Hajjâj is due the credit of
having put these men in the right place, and
his name, feared as it was far into the East,[2]
gave them a powerful backing. He did not
take the field himself, but he was scrupulous in
his care for the needs and equipment of the
troops, down to the smallest detail (Bal., 436).
The money which he spent lavishly upon this
was abundantly recovered by him in the fifth
part of the spoil. The chief expedition into India
cost him, according to Bal. (440), 60 millions,
and yielded a profit of 120 millions. For 20
years he remained at his post, and died, as he
had wished, before Walîd, at the end of Ramadân
(Tab., 1217), or in Shauwâl (1268), 95, *i.e.* June
or July, 714, aged 53 or 54 years. Walîd
granted him the successors proposed by himself
and confirmed the appointments of all his officials.
Later on his family was still esteemed in Kufa.[3]

[1] Balâdh., 290, 375. BKhordâdhbeh, 15,241. Agh., 15,98. Yâqût
3,178.

[2] Cf. Balâdh., 400f., 435; and Reiske, Adnot. 194 to Abulfedâ, 1, 427.
For the Indian *Kurk* which Reiske cannot place, cf. Tab., 3., 359, 370,
and De Goeje, *Bijdrage tot de gesch. der Zigeuners*, p. 5.

[3] Tab., 1699, 5. 1711, 7-10. 1712, 7.

Ziâd b. Abîhi and Hajjâj were the two great viceroys of the Umaiyids in Iraq, on account of whom they were, with reason, envied by the Abbâsids. They did not regard them-selves as possessors of a fat living, but as repre-sentatives of the government,—the Sultan, and by the faithful fulfilment of the duties of their office rewarded the confidence of their lords, who gave them great power which they retained as long as they lived, without troubling about the favour or reproach of public opinion. It is not out of place to compare the two. Ziâd had already reached a high position before Muâwia wooed and won him for his ally ; Hajjâj might be called the creation of Abdulmalik. Ziâd understood how to hold the native clans in check (by playing off the one against the other) and to make them work for himself, and he succeeded in doing so. Umar b. Abdulazîz (*Kâmil*, 595) admired him because he had held Iraq in check without ever summoning the help of the Syrians. Hajjâj could only assert himself by means of the foreign government, supported by Syrian troops, which indeed followed from their relationship, for the tension between Syria and Iraq had meantime become accentuated. In his achievements Hajjâj was in no wise inferior to his predecessor ; even after his death he determined the politics,—it was a question of for or against *him*. His government regulations in matters of coinage, measures and taxes, and in the importance assigned to agriculture were epoch-making.[1] In Iraq, exhausted and demoralised as it was by the constant succession of wars, he had difficulty in maintaining the state-revenues, but all the same he was always in funds (Tab., 1062. Anon., 217). He had the gift of ready speech, rather pluming himself on the elegance of his Arabic style, and disliking to be surpassed in it (Tab., 1132), so that it is not without reason that the traditionists adorn his introductory speech in Kufa with carefully-chosen turns of speech. He never let his courage fail under any circumstances; it took misfortune to bring out his greatness. But he was a little too impetuous, and was quick to get impatient with those who were executing his orders. His iron hand was covered with no velvet glove, nor had he any winning ways of conversation. He was harsh and at times hard, but not cruel; neither was he petty and bigoted. He showed mercy, and freed a notable rebel prisoner because he did not try to excuse himself but told the truth (Tab., 1112). He was bold enough to admire openly the pseudo-prophet and anti-Christ Mukhtâr, whose greatness he recognised. The thunder which pealed when he shot at the Holy Town, apparently announcing the anger of God at the wanton attack, he explained

---

[1] Yahyâ b. Âdam, Kitâb alKharâj, passim, especially p. 99ff.

off-hand as the salute of heaven promising
victory. He was not so prejudiced by superstition and tradition as his contemporaries, but
neither was he godless, and certainly not a
hypocrite. Living and dying, he had a clear
conscience. To the ordinary mind in the Hijâz
and Iraq, it was of course a proof of his wicked-
ness that he fearlessly cleared out the nest in
Mecca, and did not allow the piety of the seditionists to be their justification. Other shameful
deeds laid to his charge are inventions and
fabrications of the hatred of his enemies, which
even after his death did not abate. For example
he is said, according to an anonymous account
in Tab., 1123, to have slaughtered in Basra, after
the battle of Zâwia, 11,000 or even 120,000-
130,000 men. Kremer and Vloten apparently
believe this nonsense, and to suit their theory
they make the victims of his blood-thirstiness
the Mawâlî. The old and genuine tradition,
however, says the opposite. In Basra, as in
Kufa, immediately after the victory, he had a
general pardon proclaimed for those who gave
up the struggle, and did his best to prevent the
licence of the Syrian soldiery in the conquered
towns. Only some of the recalcitrants who did
not accept the pardon and then fell into his
hands, were executed by him, *e.g.* in Wâsit some
Quraishites and other prominent ringleaders
who were delivered over to him by Yazîd b.

Muhallab, but even in this he respected the
rights of the private individual and did not
attempt, for example, to confiscate the property
of a rich Maulâ (Fairûz Huçain) who at the last
moment disposed of it by will.[1]

4. Walîd I was succeeded by his brother
Sulaimân, to whom Abdulmalik had already had
homage paid as the heir to the throne after
Walîd, in Jumâdâ II, 96,—the end of February,
715. He followed in his predecessor's steps so
far as to carry out the latter's project to attempt
a great blow at the Roman capital, with immense
forces, though not with much success.[2] In
another respect, however, he was the direct
opposite of his predecessor ; he was displeased at
the influence which he allowed Hajjâj, and
even as heir to the throne must have opposed
him on this point. In the year 90 Yazîd b.
Muhallab fled from the prison of Hajjâj to
Ramla in Palestine, where Sulaimân held his
court. Sulaimân gave him protection, undertook
the payment of the large sum demanded of him,
and interceded so strongly for him with the
Khalifa that the latter ordered Hajjâj to leave
him alone. For nine months he kept him beside
himself, came completely under his influence,
and let himself be still more prejudiced by him

---

[1] Eulogies upon Hajjâj by Jarîr and Farazdaq are preserved
to us.

[2] *Göttinger Nachrichten*, 1901, p. 439ff.

33

against Hajjâj. But the latter knew what he was about; he was in favour of Walîd's intention to divert the succession to his own son, and thus increased the hatred of Sulaimân towards himself.[1] He had reason to fear the worst from him should he succeed to the government, and his earnest prayer (Tab., 1272) that he should die before Walîd was heard. Sulaimân could no longer harm him, but could only wreak his anger upon his friends and officials. Uthmân b. Haiyân alMurrî in Medina and Khâlid b. Abdillâh alQasrî in Mecca were deposed (Tab. 1282; 1305). Qutaiba b. Muslim, the powerful stattholder of Khurasan, tried to anticipate the fate that threatened him. Relying upon his victorious past, he attempted to carry his troops along with him in a rebellion against the new Khalifa, but in vain. The Tamîm, whom he had offended, turned against him, and he surrendered to them, since the others gave him no aid. The conqueror of the Indus territory, Muhammad b. Qâsim ath-Thaqafî, did not rebel, though his Syrians would have been ready to help him, (Tab., 1275, 3); he was taken to Wasit, imprisoned there for a time, and then executed.

---

[1] The usual assumption is that this was the reason of Sulaimân's hatred towards him, but it seems rather to have been the result of it; for there is no question of that intention of Walid till the end of his reign (Tab., 1274. 1283f), but the strained relations between Sulaimân and Hajjâj were of older standing, and even as early as the year 90 are put forward as the reason of Yazid's flight to Ramla.

The bitterest foe of Hajjâj, Yazîd b. Muhallab, succeeded to his place. This is the great mark of distinction between the reign of Sulaimân and that of Walîd. Dozy regards this change as a consequence of the two Khalifas taking opposite sides in regard to the great clan-parties,—Walîd was all for the Qais, but Sulaimân, on the other hand, was inclined to the Yemenites.[1] "In the reign of Walîd the power of the Qaisites reached its height; when he died their fall took place immediately, and it was a terrible one." Yazîd b. Muhallab certainly sided with the Yemenite party, to whom he as an Azdite belonged, against the Qais. Hajjâj, on the other hand, was only compelled by him, and before that by Ibn Ash'ath, to take up his stand against the Yemen, and so far be on the side of the Qais. Indeed, from the beginning he did not deny his descent from the Thaqîf, who might be reckoned under the head of "Qais", and he chose his *entourage* preferably from this circle of his acquaintance. But that was a matter of course, and it cannot be generalised and made into a principle of Qaisitism. From the fact that the Qais themselves claimed him as theirs, it does not look very much as if he was the leader of a party-faction of Qaisites; for the Arab clans clung to any powerful man with whom they could claim a

---

[1] *Histoire des Mus. d'Espagne*, 1, 211, 125.

connection however distant. The reason why
Abdulmalik gave Hajjâj his position and why
Walîd kept him in it was certainly not his
Qaisite tendency—he was in fact come of an
obscure family—but his personal ability. His
personality, not his tribe, gave him his importance. So Sulaimân then directed his hatred
against his person and his personal influence;
and besides, he might well have been persuaded
that Hajjâj was not the right man to conciliate the Iraqites, but was rather making the
Umaiyid rule hateful to them (Tab., 1337), and
he deposed the stattholders of Hajjâj because
they were his creatures, and not because of
their Qaisite tendencies. Khâlid al Qasrî, on the
other hand, was regarded by the Yemenites as
belonging to them (Agh., 19, 61). Qutaiba
belonged to the Bâhila, a neutral clan. His
chief opponents in Khurasan were not the Yemen
but the Mudar, while in Syria he found sympathy with the Mesopotamian Qais, amongst
whom the Bâhila dwelt (Tab., 1300). Mûsâ b.
Nusair, in Spain, was a Yemenite. It is alleged
that it was on that account that he was ill-used
by Walîd,[1] but Sulaimân treated the son much
worse than Walîd did the father,—an extremely
inconvenient fact for Dozy and his disciples
(A. Müller, 1, 429f.). At any rate, Sulaimân did

---

[1] Cf. Balâdh, 231. Contin. Isid. Hisp. par., 76.

not take up such a frankly Yemenite stand-
point as Yazîd b. Muhallab. There is no evidence of his having taken sides even in Syria
against the Qais and for the Yemen. He regretted having injured the Syrian Qais by his
conduct towards Qutaiba. He had the same
mother as his brother Walîd,—she was a Qaisite
from Abs; and he can hardly have denied his
own blood. The polarisation of the Arab world
by the tribal dualism was then only beginning;
personal hostility between powerful men contributed very substantially to it. One cannot
transfer the issue of the history as a kind of
principle into the prehistoric beginnings.

Since the death of Hajjâj, Zunbîl of Sajistân no longer paid tribute, and openly showed
how much inferior he thought the successors of
Hajjâj to be compared with him (Balâdh., 400f.).
The Iraqites breathed freely again when he,
and soon after Walîd also, died, but they were
soon to discover that a change of *personnel* did
not mean a change of system. Yazîd certainly
ill-treated the adherents of Hajjâj (Tab., 1359)
but in the government did not pursue any
different course from the latter. He likewise
resided in Wasit and kept the Syrians in the
country. He also found that he could not
make any change in the system of taxation by
which Hajjâj had made himself hated by the
Arabs, if the revenue were to remain at the

same amount. In order, however, to shift the
odium on to other shoulders, he asked the Khalifa
to relieve him of the management of the taxes
and transfer it to another. This had a different
result from what he expected, for Sulaimân now
made an old finance-official of Hajjâj, who
till then had served in the treasury, independent, and placed him at the head of the administration of the taxes.[1] He was a Maulâ from
Sajistan, Sâlih b. Abdurrahmân, the same man
who had made Arabic the written language of
the treasury. He had in Wasit at his disposal
400 Syrian soldiers and was quite independent
of Yazîd. He flatly refused to charge upon the
exchequer the extravagant expenses which
Yazîd incurred, by which meanness the latter's
stay in Iraq was made disagreeable. He contrived to get Khurasan also made over to him and
was allowed to make his residence in this old
province of his, where no one could pry upon
his doings.[2] But he did not get what he was
reckoning upon there either,—the luxury-loving
and shapelessly-obese man could ill bear comparison with Qutaiba He tried to supplant

[1] Such is Abû Mikhnaf's report in Tab., 1306ff. How Dozy manages
to read his meaning into it may be gleaned from his own works. (loc. cit.,
1,226). Acc. to Tab., 1268 (BQutaiba, 183) in the interval between
Hajjâj and Yazîd the control of the finances had been made a separate
office from the stattholdership. The distinction must therefore have
been abolished again on the succession of Yazîd and then reintroduced
at his instance. There is nothing against this assumption.

[2] A.H. 97. But he also retained the chief command in Iraq.

him by the subjugation of Jurjân and Tabaristân, but he was only indifferently successful, and by boastfully exaggerating the amount of the spoil which he had taken, he prepared his own doom.

As Khalifa also Sulaimân retained his residence at Ramla in Palestine, and in the country there he was much beloved (Tab., 1831), but he was often in the general camp at Dâbiq, in northern Syria, from which the great war against Constantinople was carried on. He died there after a reign of barely three years in Safar, 99 (Sepr., 717); Elias Nis. makes it Tuesday, the 8th., but according to Abû Mikhnaf (Tab., 1336) it was Friday, the 10th Safar.[1] Whilst under Walîd the themes of conversation in the circles of prominent society were buildings and the culture of country estates, under Sulaimân the subjects of conversation were gluttony and women. Though dissolute himself, he gave orders for proceedings to be taken against the debauchery in Medina. It may have been indeed only through a misunderstanding of the stattholder there that he mutilated the libertines instead of counting them (Agh., 4, 59ff.). But his sensuality did not prevent him from having leanings towards the pious. This is to be seen already in the fact that

---

[1] Acc. to Wüstenfeld, Tuesday was the 9th and Friday the 11th Safar. Similar differences of a day often occur and do not seem to be of importance.

he coquetted with the Iraqite opposition to Hajjâj, which was always made in the name of God and his rule against the dominion of tyrants, and also in the fact that he pampered the Alids (1338, 7), and that in Medina he made an Ansârite Stattholder, and a grandson of Amr b. Hazm at that, who had taken a leading part in the rising against the Khalifa Uthmân. But it is most apparent in the fact that he lent an ear to the court theologian Rajâ. The position given to this man by the Umaiyid Khalifas is a measure of their own position towards Islam. His influence began under Abdulmalik, increased under Walîd, and reached its climax under Sulaimân. Rajâ induced him to hand over the Khalifate to Umar b. Abdilazîz. Of this we have Wâqidî's account in Tab., 1340ff. [1]

After Walîd and Sulaimân, Abdulmalik had designated his son Yazîd to be Khalifa and had pledged the two former to this arrangement. Disregarding this, Sulaimân at once named as his successor his own son Aiyûb. The latter, however, died before him, and before he could make over the succession to his second son Dâûd [2], who was besieging Constantinople, he

---

[1] His uncle was as a child present in Dâbiq and upon the accession of Umar secured a few gold coins (Tab., 1361)

[2] The Biblical names which he gave his sons are perhaps another proof of the piety of this Khalifa. They are otherwise seldom to be met with among the Umaiyids at this period. His own name, Sulaimân, was of course none of his choosing.

was on his deathbed himself (Tab., 1335, 1341).
Then Rajâ applied his lever and persuaded him
to make a will pleasing to God. Passing over
the next heir, he appointed in the will his pious
cousin Umar b. Abdilazîz to be Khalifa, and
Yazîd b. Abdilmalik after him. Rajâ remained
with the dying Khalifa, turned him towards the
Qibla, and closed his eyes. Without saying
that he was dead, he had the Umaiyids called
together into the mosque of Dâbiq, and demanded of them homage for the Khalifa whom Sulaimân would name in his will, without mention-
ing any name,[1] and only after they had done
so did he communicate the death of Sulaimân
and the name of the appointed successor. It
was a surprise, for Umar sprang from a collateral branch that had been supplanted by
Abdulmalik, and now, by a son of Abdulmalik
he was preferred to the numerous princes of the
direct line! Nobody had dreamed of this, himself perhaps least of all, but no serious opposition arose against him. Rajâ apparently took
exactly the measures required. Hishâm b.
Abdilmalik, to be sure, made some objection to
the doing of homage, but became reasonable
when he was threatened with the sword. Abdulazîz, the son of Walîd I, was not present in

---

[1] Acc. to Wâqidî's report the dying Sulaimân had already in person
done the same as Rajâ now repeated in the mosque after his death,—a
clear reduplication.

34

Dâbiq. When he heard of the death of Sulaimân, he thought his time had come, but composed himself when he learned that Umar had become Khalifa.

———

CHAPTER V.

UMAR II AND THE MAWÂLÎ.

1. Umar II was the son of Abdulazîz b. Marwân, who had for long been viceroy of Egypt. He was descended on his mother's side from Umar I, a fact which he laid great stress upon. Born in Medina under Yazîd I (Tab., 1361), he spent there the greater part of his youth, and was brought up upon the tradition of the city of the Prophet. After his father's death (A.H. 84 or 85) Abdulmalik attracted him to Damascus and gave him his daughter in marriage. Walîd I sent him to Medina as stattholder over the Hijâz, with the idea of obliterating the evil memory of his predecessors and conciliating the people of Medina. He came into close relations with the masters of the scripture erudition and science of tradition which flourished there, and took no offence at the fact that they found much to censure in the conduct of the Umaiyid government, especially that of Hajjâj. The consequence was that the revolutionaries of Iraq sought refuge in the Hijâz. This, of course, was not pleasing to

Hajjâj, and at his instance Umar was recalled from Medina. However, he did not fall into disfavour; he was the brother of Walîd's wife and remained in favour with him, while Sulai-mân also held him in high regard.

As we have seen, Islam was making progress in the ruling family. Muâwia, Abdulmalik, Walîd and Sulaimân form, as it were, an ascending scale with Umar II as its culminating point. But his piety differed from that of his predecessors; it permeated his whole life in quite another way from theirs and determined his public actions. Sulaimân was a luxurious profligate, Umar almost an ascetic; to the former the ruling power offered unlimited means of enjoyment; upon the latter it imposed a weight of responsibility. In everything he did judgment loomed before his eyes, and he was always afraid of coming short of the requirements of God.

He was disinclined to wars of conquest, well knowing that they were waged, not for God, but for the sake of spoil, though it is uncertain whether the Muslim army was first recalled from Constantinople by him. Nor could he, on principle, put an end to the *Jihâd* against the emperor, but he gave up the advance outposts and withdrew the garrisons towards the rear. He would also have willingly given up Transoxiana, if Islam had not already had too firm a footing in a few of its towns, but at least he forbade a further extension of the boundaries there.[1] His chief attention was directed to internal policy, and with him there set in a change in it, a change of another sort and of far greater significance than that which distinguished Sulaimân from Walîd.

He appointed new men to the most important official posts, and took to task the offensive Yazîd b. Muhallab for not being able to pay up the fifth-part of the Caspian spoil, the amount of which, in his boasting, he had put at too high a figure. Jarrâh b. Abdillâh al Hakamî was sent to Khurasan, Adî b. Artât al Fazârî to Basra, Abdulhamîd b. Abdirrahmân alQuraishî of the family of Umar I to Kufa, Umar b. Hubaira alFazârî to Mesopotamia, and Amr b. Muslim, a brother of Qutaiba, to India. Jarrâh (Tab., 1354) and Amr were of the school of Hajjâj, Adî and Ibn Hubaira were Qaisites. But Umar did not appoint these men in order to take the opposite side from that of his predecessor, nor out of preference for the Qais and Hajjâj, but because he considered them reliable and upright men (Tab., 1383, 3). To Spain he appointed Samh b. Mâlik al-Khaulânî, a Yemenite, and to Africa Ismâîl b. Abdillâh, because he knew they did not belong to any

---

[1] It was from Spain, of course, that in his reign Narbonne was conquered and fortified.

party and were merciful to the oppressed. But he
was not satisfied with choosing men who appeared to him to be suitable and then letting them
rule as they pleased, provided they only handed
over the necessary money.   He felt himself
responsible in every point.   What lay nearest
his heart was not so much the increase of power
as the establishment of right.   The theologians,
who formed a party independent of the government and hitherto rather hostile to it, attained
to influence with him.   Accordingly, the *Qâdî*,
or judge, appears also to have reached a more
independent and more important place.   In a
letter to the Khurasanite Uqba b. Zur'a, he
names as the pillars of the government, (1) the
Wâlî, or executive governor, (2) the judge,
(3) the administrator of the taxes, and (4) the
Khalifa.   The celebrated Hasan was Qâdî in
Basra during his reign, and Amr ash Sha'bi in
Kufa, and he made the juris-consult Abû Zinâd
secretary to the stattholder Abdulhamîd.

The government of the provinces in the Muslim
kingdom meant their financial administration, and the reform of this was one of the chief
objects of Umar II's activity, but it is not easy
to get a clear account of the measures he took
in the matter of the taxation.   The conceptions
of it advanced by Alfred von Kremer and accepted by August Müller are marred by actual
errors.

According to Kremer and Müller,[1] Umar II was impelled to make reforms in the taxation only with the view to a return to the original idea. They say that his model was the first

---

[1] " His theological bigotry made all political judgment impossible for him, and if it cannot be disputed that some of his decrees materially advanced Islam as such, still nearly everything he did contributed in the main to the complete disorganisation of a state that was by this time secularized. The nation then existnig which was most adapted for politics, the Romans, did not unadvisedly lay down the principle that a kingdom can be maintained only by the same means which founded it. But Umar, in place of the exceedingly realistic principles of government of Muâwia's successors, wanted to bring in ideal points of view which he had adapted from the Qoran and from tradition. And if this undertaking, in itself praise-worthy enough, had only been set about with a moderate knowledge of the real conditions ! But the pious Khalifa was so entangled in the shibboleths of his theological circle that he did not even attempt to use reason in applying the leading ideas of the Qoran to the wicked world. His simple logic only said that it was God's will that things should be thus and thus, and that therefore they could be brought to pass. But God had plainly shown the believers how He wished the Khalifate to be governed when He through His servants Abû Bekr and Umar made subject to Islam first the rebel Arabs, and then the whole of Persia, Syria and Egypt. Thus his ideal was no more than a mechanical copy of the organisation given to the state by the first Umar, but which the unworthy successors had disfigured in its most important features by godless alterations. If we bear in mind how these alterations were compelled, not by any subjective arbitrariness, but by the force of brutal facts, it is obvious that there was neither rhyme nor reason in the old principles when applied to the state of Abdulmalik and Hajjâj. But the pathetically pious confidence of the wonderful man was unenlightened by the least glimmering of any such notion. Thus, not long after his accession, he ordered the abolition of the decree of Hajjâj by which the protected kinsmen accepting Islam must in the interests of the treasury continue to pay the old poll-tax. As by this the advantage was again on the side of the followers of other faiths who had received Islam, the pious prince, who organised

Umar, to whose system he wished to revert and
to remove the distortions which it had had to
suffer from the preceding Umaiyid regents. Then
the preliminary question arises,—What was the

simultaneously in all the provinces a zealous missionary activity, had
the sweet satisfaction of seeing in a short time the bands of believers
in East and West increasing by millions. If these were at first only
simulated conversions, we must not forget that according to Muhammadan law from the beginning the punishment of apostacy was death,
and thus withdrawal was made impossible to those once won over for
the Qoran. In this way, afterwards, the second generation at least
already consisted for the most part of good Muslims, and the
preponderance of the confessors of Allah over those of other beliefs
was therefore actually considerably increased by Umar's edict. But
the treasury suffered badly from it and this disadvantage was increased
out of all proportion by a second decree. This much was at any rate
plain, even to Umar himself, namely, that the restoration of the old
prohibition against ownership of land for the Faithful was not to be
made, at least in the fashion of demanding, say, from everybody the
surrender of the estates acquired in the provinces in the course of over
70 years. For various reasons this was simply technically impossible,
and so at least this extremely dangerous experiment was not at tempt-
ed. But while from the year 100 onwards any further purchase of
ground and estate was forbidden to the Muslims, the Khalifa undertook,
in order to abolish an equalisation of believers and protected kinsmen
which was offensive to his orthodoxy, to put those properties of Muhammadan owners which were illegally seized no longer under the Kharâj
so far imposed upon them, but only under the much lower tithe.
Naturally the result of this was a still further deficiency in the state-
revenues, and it was unpractical in so far as the favour shown to those
who so far had acquired no ground or property, and now were destined
never to get any, assumed straightway the character of a *privilegium
odiosum*. It mattered nothing that to the latter a sort of amends was
simultaneously to be made by a more rigorous enforcement of the system of the yearly salary, for these stipends were, comparatively speaking, far from being large enough, notwithstanding the fact that with
the huge increase of conversions they were a drain upon the government. And in addition to all these measures which deeply affected

nature of the pattern which he wanted to copy?
Two measures in particular that are traced back
to the first Umar come into consideration. He
is said to have permitted the Arabs to acquire
landed property in the conquered provinces, and
to have ordered that on the conversion of
subjects, *i.e.* of the conquered non-Arabs, the
new converts should only be relieved of the
poll-tax, but the ground-tax upon the cultivated
land should remain. As a matter of fact he did
neither the one nor the other.

In the cause of God and justice the whole
land gained by conquest would have fallen to
be divided amongst the Arab warriors, to whom
it belonged by right of spoil. For practical reasons it of course remained undivided and became
either State-land or Muslim territory. To the
treasury or the ruler fell those estates vacated
by the old proprietors and yielded without a
struggle, —those of the dynasty, the nobility,
and mortmain, *e. g.* the post and the fire-temple.
These domains (*Sawâfî*) covered a vast extent,
especially in those provinces which generally

the treasury, there came lastly the order issuing from a humane but
unpractical sense of justice, that all excess moneys which might have
been collected from the subjects by illegal extortions were to be returned to those who had been defrauded. Whether this happened in
individual cases we do not know, but the most faithless official could
not desire a finer opportunity for unpunished plundering of the public
treasuries." Thus A. Müller, *Gesch. des Islams*, I, 439 *ff.*, freely following Kremer, *Culturgesch. des Orients*, I, 174 *ff.*

35

were of most financial consideration,[1] particularly in Iraq (Sawâd). On the other hand, what was won in combat by the Arab warriors was considered the collective possession of the Muslims, and was left in the ownership of the vanquished on payment of tribute. Now, the tribute ought really to have been divided every year as income amongst the legal owners of the capital, but the state laid hands upon it and paid the Muslim warriors only fixed pensions, according to its own pleasure. Thus the distinction between estate-land and tribute-land disappeared, the revenues from both flowing equally into the treasury. This development was consummated in the time of the great conquests, and Umar I either introduced it or made it legitimate through usage. But he did not go so far as actually not to permit in the tribute-land any real private ownership of property. A general

---

[1] " The area of the Sawâd amounts to 10,000 square parasangs, the parasang to 10,000 common, or 9,000 Hâshimid ells. A square parasang comprises 22,500 jarîb, so 10,000 square parasangs are 225 million jarîb. In valuation a deduction of one-third is made from this for hollows, hills, saltfields, marshes, streets, river-courses, boundaries of towns and villages and so on, which comes to 75 millions, so that in fields there are left 150 millions. Of this alternately half lies fallow and half is tilled. But there are to be added (for taxation) the palms, vines, and other trees scattered over the whole (all three thirds) which are not assessed according to the square measure of the fields." Thus Qudâma in *Mâwardî, ed.* Enger, p. 301. That the valuation of the whole area got to be false and excessive has been pointed out by Hermann Wagner, *Gött. Nachrichten,* 1902, pp. 224 ff.

prohibition against the ownership of land by the Arabs in the provinces was never made.[1] Like the Prophet himself, his successors also, not excepting Abûbakr and Umar, had full control over the state-lands and presented parts of them (qatâi') to eminent deserving men, not perhaps as fiefs but as allod, and it was thus that Alî, Talha and Zubair became men of great possessions.[2] Further, all the Arab warriors in the Musûr were owners of estates as a matter of course, and owned not merely their house and farm but also estates in the villages round about. During the reign of Umar I they certainly put war and booty first, but in the more peaceful times that followed this was changed. The love of annexing ground and land had been already awakened in them in heathen times, and it was not suppressed by Muhammad and Islam but encouraged, and doubtless lent its additional influence at the time of the wars of conquest. The old law by which ground not already occupied became the property of him who made it productive, held not only in Arabia but in the provinces also, and was there actively enforced. But the eagerness for land did not stop even at the taxable tracts of land belonging to subdued peasants, for they frequently passed into the

---

[1] *Cf.* Juynboll in the Indian *Gids*, February, 1899.
[2] Yahya b. Âdam, *Kitâb al Kharâj*, pp. 42, 56 ff., 61. 67.

possession of Arab lords by purchase or less
honourable means, nor is it anywhere apparent
that the latter were, to begin with, prohibited
from this by law. Umar I had no motive in
objecting to a procedure which in his time had
scarcely begun, and at any rate had not yet led
to harmful consequences.

Neither did Umar I lay down the law that
the Kharâj upon a tract of land should remain
whether the owner were a Muslim or not, and
that conversion to Islam freed men from the
Jizia only, because this, being a poll-tax, was
adjusted according to their position and was a
personal mark of distinction between the vanquished and the Muslim. Both were originally
equally considered as tribute payable by the
serfs to the citizens of the theocracy—the children of the kingdom (Matth., 17, 25). The latter
had not to pay taxes either on their persons
or on the soil of their fields, but had only to
surrender the tenth-part of the crop, and that
not to men but to God. The thought never
occurred to them that it was only the obligation
of paying tribute on the person that was a
dishonour to the Muslim, and not that on
territory. Neither is there in older terms of
speech any difference whatever made between
Kharâj and Jizia ; both mean the same, namely
the tribute of non-Muslims. There is frequent
mention of the Jizia of the land, but just as

frequent mention of the Kharâj of a person. [1]
Under what title the individual tax-payers had
to raise their quota mattered little to the
Arabs, especially in the case where the tribute
was imposed as a lump sum of fixed amount
upon the community, as a whole—which at
first seems to have been rather the rule than
the exception.

The original practice then was that Islam
freed from all tributary obligation, and that a
Kharâj piece of ground became tax-free when
an Arab Muslim acquired it, [2] or when the non-
Arab owner became a Muslim. But this put a
premium first upon the exploiting of the peasants
on the part of the Arab lords, and next upon the
conversion of the tribute-payers to Islam. In
both cases the difference between their positions
and the nature of their holding was abolished,—
the difference which was the basis of Umar I's
system of finance,—and difficulties and embar-
rassments arose. If the tribute were lessened in
proportion to the amounts dropped through the
conversions to Islam, then the exchequer bore

---

[1] Cf. De Goeje in the Glossary to Tab., and further Balâdh., 65, 7
with 66, 15; 351, 1 with 351, 5. 13. In Khurasan Jizia was always
said and not Kharâj, which is more prevalent elsewhere. (Tab., 1354.
1364 ff, 1507 ff.). In Yahyâ b. Âdam's book of taxes the indiscriminate use is found. It is quite usual there to find it called the " Jizia
of the land."

[2] So with us (Germans) formerly a farm became tax-free when a
noble acquired it, for, as a noble, he was exempt from the tax.

the brunt; but if it was further raised to its old amount by a lump sum, then the burden was increased for the community, which had become less able to pay taxes because of the conversions. Neither was it a good thing when the new converts, as frequently, and perhaps mostly, happened, left land and community to their fate and migrated to the Arabian towns. This took the labour away from the land, so that it was in danger of becoming partly barren. The influx into the towns, however, was unwelcome. In Kufa and Basra,—for in all these circumstances we get our best and almost exclusive information from Iraq,—there were already plenty of new Muslims or Mawâlî, originally freed prisoners of war, mostly of Iranian extraction. They occupied a position half-way between the Arab lords and the non-Arab subjects, and while they certainly paid neither land-tax nor poll-tax, were not entered in the Dîwân of the Muqâtila and received no pension, although in time of war they fought in the train of their former masters, to whom they were morally bound to render all kinds of service. Their position being neither one thing nor another, naturally did not content them; Islam made them alive to their claims, and they sought to obtain full equal rights. Their revolt under Mukhtâr showed the danger they threatened to be to the Arab realm, and indeed the suppression of it cost them many

lives. But the gaps that the sword had made in
their ranks were easily filled up again by the
new Muslims emigrating from the villages and
country towns, who, though they might be of
more peaceable disposition, had nevertheless the
same interest in their standing. A significant
breach in Umar I's system was also caused by
the fact that the army and government towns
very soon lost their specifically Arab character.

This somewhat primitive system of administration of Umar I which confined itself to broad
lines, gave rise to a development unforeseen by
him which threatened its destruction. Under
him the disadvantages were not yet perceptible.
The acquisitive instincts of the Arabs at that
time took, on the average, another direction
from that of aspiring after estates and landed
property, and the tax-paying non-Arabs were not
yet coming over to Islam in such numbers that
the treasury suffered thereby,—a treasury which
then indeed was filled to overflowing by the spoil
which ever kept coming in, and had very much
more modest claims to meet than it had later on.
In the next generation, *i.e.* under the Umaiyids,
this was different. But Hajjâj, according to
tradition, only decided to interfere with the
recognised practice in order to remove the injury
which the exchequer was suffering by it. He
did not release from the Kharâj the Arabs who
had acquired property in the Kharâj-country,

and even re-imposed it upon those who had before been freed from it. In the same way he is said to have treated the new converts with regard to their obligation to pay tribute, when they remained in the village and retained their farm. But he forbade Hijra to them,—*i.e.* emigration into the centres of Islam and of Arab government, and eventually brought them back by force. His was a new procedure and did not square with what had hitherto been looked upon as justice, and it aroused the common outcry of the Arabs and Mawâlî affected by it, as being a slap in the face of Islam ; but he paid no heed to it.

Umar II's sentiments made him adopt another way. His aim was not so very much different from that of Hajjâj, but he tried to reach it only in a way which did not offend against the Islamic idea of justice. Thus he agreed with the old way in this respect, that a Muslim whether of first or second rank, whether Arab or Maula, need pay no tribute, either poll-tax or land-tax. But in order to prevent the decrease of the state revenue, he made the deduction, quite in agreement with the Scripture-scholars of Medina, from history, that the Kharâj-land was first of all the joint property of the Muslims, and secondly must be considered the joint possession of the communities concerned, to whom the Muslims had handed it over for

usufruct on payment of tribute, so that therefore portions of it must not be taken from the
whole to become, by passing into Muslim ownership, tax-free private estates. Consequently
he declared the selling of Kharâj-land to Arabs
and Muslims to be prohibited from the year 100,
without, however, giving the prohibition a
retrospective force. In the case of the conversion to Islam of an owner of land liable to
taxes, he seems to have decreed that his property
should revert to the village community. He
might then remain upon it, say, as a lease-hold-
er,—a lease not being tribute ; but he might
also come into the town (a thing which Hajjâj had been against permitting), and this, in
fact, was the rule. Whether he also became
entitled to a pension through the hijra is a
question not to be easily answered.

While by the recognition of the immunity
of Muslims from the subject-tax it was only
the old usage, which had not yet disappeared,
that was again put in force, the prohibition of
a further alienation of tribute-land was a new
legislative measure which cut deep. It was
certainly based upon the historical origin of the
tribute-land, and was a consequence of the fact
that in time of conquest the soil was not
treated as booty but remained undivided. But
in that time itself this practical consequence
had not yet appeared.

36

Umar II did not succeed. By the method he tried the deterioration of the finances was inevitable. The principle of the inalienability of the tribute-land could not be carried through, and the change of property was no more put a stop to than the change of faith. The later practice reverted to the method of Hajjâj, but with a difference, which, though materially small, had much formal significance. There was, in fact, a distinction drawn between Kharâj and Jizia which had not existed before. The Jizia, according to this, rested on the person and only affected the non-Muslims, being a load removed from their necks when they were converted. The Kharâj, on the contrary, rested on the land and did not degrade the person; it was to, and had to, be paid even by Muslims owning tribute-land. Since the land, at any rate, was the chief object of taxation the poll-tax was really a small sacrifice.[1] Thus cheaply did the exchequer settle the claims of Islam. It was a piece of legal *finesse*, an expedient which was only resorted to of necessity, for to the plain human understanding it was certainly not the land that paid the tax, but the owner of it.

[1] Neither was the poll-tax ever exacted from the new Muslims, the Mawali, in Kufa and Basra. They only felt slighted because they were not received into the Diwan of the Muqâtila and made participators in the pension, and in this respect they aspired to equal rights.

We hear of a tax-reform of the last Umaiyid stattholder of Khurasan, Nasr b. Saiyâr. He hit upon the arrangement of raising the tribute in a fixed amount solely from the land-tax, which was imposed as a lump sum upon the individual taxable districts. All land-proprietors, Muslims or non-Muslims, Arabs or Iranians had to contribute to it in proportion to their property. But the poll-tax was separate from it and contributed only by Zoroastrians, Jews and Christians, not by Muslims, not even by newly-converted ones. That the revenue was falling in consequence of the increasing conversions was foreseen, and did not matter when put against the fact that the land-tax alone was already yielding the necessary assured income for the treasury.[1] This regulation was new, and did not exist before, and it was successful in Khurasan as well as, sooner or later, in other parts of the Islamic realm because it cleverly reconciled the financial interest with the principle of the freedom of the citizens of the theocracy from tribute. No doubt the jurists did yeoman service in this, but what had really been the outcome of a complicated process mediating between opposing claims they afterwards regarded as the matter-of-course law which always had been valid. If this law had

[1] This subject is more fully treated in the intermediate piece of Chap. 8 upon Khurasan, to which attention may be directed.

really been valid from the beginning, then no
difficulties would have arisen.

2. The Muslim jurists have everywhere a
way of tracing back to their beginnings the
things that have come about gradually and
which have been brought about by gradually
arising needs or tendencies, and of sanctioning
them by the precedent (the *Sunna*) of the Prophet and the first Khalifas. Thus they even
trace the form to which the laws of taxation
or administration at last attained after long
fluctuation, back to the first Umar, who only
made the first initial steps. We have to beware
of this historical dogma in order to form a just
judgment of the conduct of Hajjâj and the
second Umar. We should, in the first place,
stick for preference to the proper historians, *i.e.*
the oldest ones, who have more respect for the
facts, rely partly upon documentary evidence,
and report not so much the principles of the
rulers as individual differences, which cannot
be made into generalisations without consideration. We may well bring under this stricture
also the historical evidence of the jurists, among
which there is much to be found that is not in
their line at all, and is independent of their
tendency. My view of the difficult and disputed
matter has been evolved gradually and unarbi-
trarily; I did not make, to start with, a collection of the data from which it proceeds. Those

which are by me I gather together here, and
thus an opportunity is given of adding anything
that has not been mentioned in the previous
resumé.

Concerning Hajjâj, Balâdhurî, 368, informs us
that he reimposed the Kharâj on these portions
of land in Mesene which were relieved from
it through the conversion of the old owners
or by passing into the possession of Arabs.
According to the passage quoted on page 244 from
the *Iqd* of Abdrabbih, Hajjâj also brought the
Mawâlî from the Musûr back into their country
towns and villages. " He said to the Mawâlî,—
' Ye are barbarians and foreigners ; your place is
your towns and villages.' So he sent them
where he wanted and had the name of the
place each one was sent to marked on his hand
by the Ijlite, Khirâsh b. Jâbir. Hence the
verse runs, " Thou art he whose hand the Ijlite
branded, and thy sire fled to Hakam ; " [1] and
other verses say,—" A maiden who does not
know what the driving of camels means " [2] has
been dragged forth by Hajjâj from her shadowy
hiding-place. If Amr had been present, and Ibn
Khabal, her hands would not have been marked
without a hot conflict." When, later on, a
Maula, Nûh b. Darrâj, became Qadi of Basra,
this verse was made upon him, " The last day

---

[1] Hakam b. Aiyûb ath Thaqafî was Hajjâj's representative in Basra.

[2] "Who has never yet gone on a journey."

is surely come, since Nûh has become Qadi !
If Hajjâj were still there, his hand would not
have escaped his (Hajjâj's) mark."[1]   The fact
is also testified to by Tab., 1122, 1425 ; Anon.
Ahlw., 336. Here it says in order to prevent
the falling off of the tribute, Hajjâj wrote to
Basra and other towns that those Mawâlî who
had immigrated there from the country should
go back to their villages.   Then those who were
expelled assembled in Basra, not knowing
whither to go, and called in lamentation upon
the name of the Prophet.   The pious *readers*
were on their side, and so they in turn joined the
readers who deserted to Ibn Ash'ath when the
latter came to Basra.

According to Balâdhurî, 368, Umar II made
invalid the inclusion of the Muslims in the
Kharâj, introduced by Hajjâj, not only in
Mesene, but everywhere.   In a letter mentioned
in Tab., 1366f. to the stattholder of Kufa, he
lays down the principle,—no Kharâj for those
who have embraced Islam.   According to Theophanes, A.M. 6210 he relieved from the tax the
Christians who had received Islam.

The further measure of Umar II forbidding
for the future the sale of Kharâj-land to
Muslims, is testified to by a passage from Ibn

[1] Hasan alBasrî, the Qadi at the time of Umar II, was also a
Maula.

Asâkir's History of Damascus given by Alfred von Kremer in the " *Culturgeschichtliche Streif-züge,*" pp. 60 ff. in the Arabic text, and partly translated by him in the " *Culturgeschichte des Orients,*" 1, 76. It deals with Syria and is important precisely because it shows that matters there proceeded in analogy with those in Iraq, about which we have particular information.

" Umar I and the eminent Companions of the Prophet agreed to leave the vanquished their lands on condition that they tilled them and paid the Kharâj on them to the Muslims. If afterwards one of them embraced Islam, then the Kharâj was removed from his head,[1] but his land and house were divided among the village community so that they paid the Kharâj on them, while what he possessed in money, servants and cattle was left to him. He was then received into the army- and pension-list of the Muslims[2] and became entitled to the same rights and obligations. They (*i.e.* Umar and the Companions) were of opinion that he, as a Muslim, had no claim to his land in preference to the village community,[3] because the land as a whole had passed to the Muslims as a joint

---

[1] Here also the same expression is used for the ground-tax and poll-tax.

[2] It is considered a matter of course that the new Muslims emigrated to one of the Arab army towns. Only the *pagani* held to their old religion.

[3] For قراٰبتّه read قريتّه,

possession. Those who stuck to their Christian religion and stayed in their villages were called kinsmen under the protection of the Muslims (*Dhimma*). Umar and the Companions further held that no Muslim by using coercion might buy a piece of land from these protected persons, because the latter could appeal to the fact that they had abstained from war against them and had not assisted their enemies (namely the Romans).[1] Therefore the Companions and rulers were chary of using compulsion towards them [2] and of seizing their estates. But they also disapproved of the Muslims' purchasing freely offered lands for the reason that the owners had no real proprietary right to them, and also because they wished to reserve the land as a collective possession set aside for the Muslim warriors of the future, as a means of carrying on war against the still unconquered heathen, so that it was not sold or inherited like private property. For they were determined to keep the command in *Sur.*, 2, 189 ; 8, 40.

In spite of this [3] many Muslims had long had private estates in Syria, especially the so-called

---

[1] Kremer's translation is incomprehensible.

[2] For قسمهم read غشمهم.

[3] What follows is only briefly given. In Kremer the text is in several places out of order, but on the whole the sense can be followed.

Qatâi'. These were originally the property of the patricians who took to flight at the capture of Syria, and of those who had fallen in the battles. They were taken in as estates (*Sawâfi*) and the revenues from them at first went into the treasury like the Kharâj, but when Muâwia was stattholder of Syria and found it difficult to make his income meet his outlay, Uthmân assigned to him, at his request, these estates, or at least a great part of them. As Khalifa, Muâwia devoted them as an inalienable fund for the needy of his own family and other indigent Muslims. But the estates which Uthmân, in his time, had not yet given to him, he divided among Quraishites and other Arabs who asked him for them as Qatâi', not in fief, but as free property, which they might sell or bequeath. Then Abdulmalik did the same with what was still left, and he also took in Kharâj-land the owners of which had died out, and divided it among the Muslims as tithe-land, so that the Kharâj declined. Thereupon Abdulmalik and his two next successors did not indeed adopt the method of taking away Kharâj-land by force from the owners and giving it to Muslims, but they did allow them to buy it. The price then came to the state-treasury, and the Kharâj of the village was reduced by the corresponding amount; the actual Muslim owners paid only the tenth.

37

Umar II did otherwise. He did not, indeed, go back upon what had happened up till the year 100, but decreed that there should be no Jizia [1] upon the Kharâj-land which had up till then passed into the hands of the Muslims by purchase, but only the tithe. But for the future he declared such purchases to be invalid, and in this his two successors Yazîd II and Hishâm acquiesced. Because of this the year 100 was called the " term." It was not long, however, till the old way of doing returned and on the lands sold to Muslims there was imposed not the Jizia but only the tithe, but as the Kharâj consequently declined Mansûr interfered. He wanted, actually, to give back to the original owners the estates sold against the law of Umar II, but that presented too great difficulties, so he commanded that the Qatâi' and the tracts of Kharâj-land sold up till A. H. 100 should only pay the tithe, but that those sold since then should pay the Kharâj. In the year 141 he sent officials to Syria to separate the lands and rate them accordingly."

Ibn Asâkir is an author of the sixth century of the Hijra who suffers detraction from the view that had then been long prevalent, namely that the first Umar and the Companions, after Muhammad's death the authoritative regulators of the

[1] Jizia is here also used for land-tax.

conditions newly created by the conquest, fixed from the beginning, in all questions, the standard for the future, and that the disposal of domain-lands and the alienation of tribute-paying land were misusages which were in direct opposition to the standard, and only arose since the time of the defection which followed with Uthmân and the Umaiyids. But so far as his accounts are not influenced by this view, we have no reason to doubt that he got them from old sources. They are too positive to have been invented. We may therefore believe that Umar II started with a reaction against the chipping and partitioning of the state and common property prevalent among his predecessors, by forbidding the selling of Kharâj-land. That he also kept the estates together and did not give away any of them Ibn Asâkir does not actually say, but it may be taken for granted.[1]

---

[1] What Ibn Asâkir says about the disappearance of the landed properties is added to by a remarkable notice which we find in Balâdh., 272 f. and Yahyâ, 45. " Umar b. Khattâb made into crown-lands in the Sawâd the property of those fallen in battle, that of those who had fled, that of the Persian king and his adherents, and that of the post and the marshes. The revenue from these amounted to 7,000,000 dirhems. But at the time of Hajjâj, after the battle of Jamâjim, the people burnt the Diwan (the old document with information concerning titles and estates), and everyone took whatever he could lay hands on." So the estates were in danger not merely from the fact that the Khalifas gave away parts of them. There lurked among the people a general rage against the Latifundia of the state, the rulers and the great men. They attempted to destroy or obscure the historical titles upon which rested the right of possession which was offensive to them.

Now when this Khalifa opposed the taking
of tribute-land from the state by its being *sold*,
he cannot either have been willing that the
same thing should come about through *change
of faith*. He seems to have devised measures
by which the principle that no new convert
should be liable to tribute lost the point which
caused the treasury to suffer, and assumed an
ideal rather than a material significance.[1]   In
Yahyâ b. Âdam, 44 it says that Umar II refused to change the Kharâj into the tithe for
those embracing Islam, and declared instead
that those of them who remained by their
canals[2] should, after conversion, pay the same
as before, but those who came into the town
should forfeit their land to the village community.   That the new Muslim who stayed on
beside his canal should have had to go on
paying the Kharâj certainly does not agree with
what we already know, but the contradiction
disappears when we learn that the payment
was no longer regarded as tribute but as lease-
money.[3]   In the passage quoted the statement

---

[1] It would be difficult to find proofs for the assertion that in consequence of the remission of the tax millions accepted Islam underUmar II.

[2] The Kharâj-land in Iraq means the land watered by the canals.
Tithe-land was to be found only outwith the alluvium.

[3] According to Yahyâ 43, Alî is said to have remarked to a newly-
converted proprietor of Aintamr,—"Thy land falls to the Muslims ; if
thou wilt, get thee into the city and receive pension, else must thou
remain as farmer (qahrumân) on the land and deliver to us a part of the
revenue."

is certainly correct, that the Khalifa considered
the arrangement of the tribute-land and the
state-revenue it yielded as a very great blessing.
Even though he could not undo the diminution
that had already taken place, still he wanted
for the future to keep the assurance of the Fai
intact. And even though he did not, in principle, infringe the Muslims' freedom from tribute,—that of the new Muslims as well as the
old,—still he did not want the old historical
right to be injured by additional alterations, and
lands to become free private possessions which
in reality belonged to the inalienable ownership
of the community.

In the provinces already conquered nearly
a century before, whose system of taxation was
regulated once for all by the act of conquest,
according to the somewhat modified law of
spoil of Islam, Umar II, in essentials, maintained the status founded upon this historical basis
and protected it from threatened infringements,
but it was not so in the lands which were only
annexed in his time, or at least were not yet
thoroughly and completely subdued,—in Transoxiana and India, in Africa and Spain. The
course which he here adopted must be considered absolutely by itself and must not be confused
with the other; it does not come under the
same point of view. Before the hostilities against
a heathen people began there had to go

out to them the summons to receive the Faith
and submit to Allah.   If they obeyed the summons they then entered the theocracy with full
privileges and needed to pay no tribute.   Thus
it was prescribed by Islam, but no one took it
in earnest.   The Jihâd was to bring in money
and spoil—that, and not the spreading abroad of
the Faith, had become the aim.   Umar II hated
this Jihâd, and wanted, on the contrary, a peaceful gathering-in of the nations to Islam, and
in this case demanded no tribute.   There was
no mention of giving up the Fai, because no
Fai existed.

According to Balâdh., 441 he summoned the
kings of the Indus-territory to accept Islam and
promised them complete equality of status; they
were then converted, and took Arab names.
According to Balâdh, 426 many Transoxanian
kings received Islam under him, and then needed to pay no tribute and received a pension.
Tab., 1354 says a complaint was lodged with him
that the Mawâlî in the army of Khurasan, although they fought with the Arabs against the
heathen at a strength of 20,000 men, were still
excluded from the pension and actually had to
pay tribute; for them he procured redress.   At
the same time he gave a general order to remit
the tribute in the case of every one who acknowledged Islam.   Then the hitherto heathen Soghdians flocked into the community of the ruling

religion. According to Balâdh., 422 and Tab.,
1364f., Umar did not however deliver up
again to the Soghdians the capital Samarqand,
although he recognised it was only by a breach
of faith that the Arabs had taken possession of it.
What had happened years before he did not redress.

Even the Berbers were, according to Balâdh.,
231, 225 summoned by Umar II to accept
Islam, and troops of them obeyed the call. He
consequently relieved them from the tribute,
which consisted in the handing over of children.
As regards the girls who had already been delivered up, he decreed that their masters should
either take them in marriage in lawful form,
or give them back to their parents.

Different and very unique is a measure which
was passed in Spain, according to the *Conti*, *Isid.
Hisp.*, par. 186, not indeed by Umar himself,
but doubtless with his approval and by his order,
by the stattholder Samh, whom he had appointed over that land. Zama ulteriorem vel (= et)
citeriorem Iberiam proprio stilo ad vectigalia in-
ferenda describit. Predia et manualia vel
quidquid illud est, quod olim predaviliter indi-
visum retentabat in Spania gens omnis arabica,
sorte sociis dividendo partem ex omni re mobili
et immobili fisco adsociat.[1] Whilst therefore a

---

[1] I have altered Mommsen's punctuation and changed *preda* into
predia according to what follows : *res mobilis* = *manualia* ; *res immobi-
lis* = *predia*.

part of the captured land remained to the old inhabitants on consideration of the tax, there was another part till then reserved, after deduction of the fifth, divided among the army. Of what sort this reserved part was is not plain. It may have consisted of such portions of land as had been confiscated in Iraq and in Syria as "estates."[1]   In Spain Umar II had still to some extent a free hand. His procedure was doubtless determined by the idea of attaching the Arab warriors to Spain by possessions of land. He is said to have taken the example of Umar I as his model. If the latter had given the soldiers in India no landed property then the defence of the land would have been impossible.[2] Of course Umar I had nothing to do with India, and as a general thing he rather set the example of the most extensive fiscalisation of the land-spoil possible, but he must, all the same, play the precedent were it even in a sort of round-about way.   Moreover it deserves to be noticed how little the old tradition bears out the more modern opinion that the Arabs in the provinces were not permitted to own any landed property whatever.

I also add some particulars concerning further financial measures of Umar II, taking firstly those that concerned the Muslims.

[1] Cf. the note on page 291. It was at any rate not the fifth.
[2] Dozy, Recherches (1881), 1, 76.

The oasis of Fadak near Medina had till then been regarded as the property of the reigning ruler, but Umar II made it over as the private property of Muhammad to his family, the Alids. By so doing he abolished the contrary decisions of the first two Khalifas, thus showing that he was not slavishly bound to them. (Balâdh., 30-32.) He also gave back to Talha's family their property in Mecca, which had been taken from them (Tab., 1483f.).

In the Yemen a tax in addition to the tithe had been levied by a brother of Hajjâj who ruled there; Umar II redressed this (Balâdh., 73). In Umân the tithe was consigned to the state-treasury of Basra ; Umar II re-established the custom of its remaining in the land and there being divided among the poor (Balâdh., 77f.). This was not the general custom all over Arabia, but differed here and there according to the more or less favourable conditions under which the clans and districts had first gone over to Islam.[1] The order of Umar II, also, that the *Kharâj* of Khurâsân should remain in the land and be spent there (Tab., 1366) must not be made general; there were special reasons for it.

As regards the pensions of the Muslim warriors in the army-towns and garrisons, the government acted at all times very capriciously.

---

[1] *Skizzen*, 4, 95.

It struck unpopular names out of the list and inserted others instead, and curtailed or increased the amount as it saw fit. This gave a continual ground for complaint, for the revenue of the Fai, from which the pensions came, belonged by right of spoil entirely to the heirs of the conquering army, and they never ceased from their demand that nothing less than the whole should be poured out before them. It is certainly not to be credited that in this matter Umar II,—as forsooth Alî is said to have done before him, complied with their wishes. He took care to abstain from very imprudent steps (Balâdh., 458f.). But he did much to appease the claims made upon the state-treasury. He extended the circle of those entitled to pensions further over the Arabs than it had ever been before. To the whole of the Mawâlî of Khurasan who were in the army and had taken part in the campaigns against the heathen, he granted not merely freedom from taxation but also maintenance (rizq) and pay (atâ); he declared he was ready to contribute from the chief treasury of the state if the Kharâj of Khurasan were not sufficient, but this was not necessary (Tab., 1354). But whether it is correct that he regarded every new convert who immigrated from the country into Kufa or Basra as a Muhâjir, and granted him an equal claim with the heirs

of the Arab conquerors must be very much
doubted. Legally it could hardly have been
justified, and practically it would have had the
very worst consequences. The custom of giving
pensions also to the children and the family
of the Muqâtila had already been restricted
by Muâwia and discontinued altogether by
Abdulmalik, but Umar II re-introduced it
(Balâdh., 458f.; Tab., 1367). He also supported
the Muslim poor, especially the needy pilgrims
to Mecca and certain sick people, by fixed
amounts, not indeed confining his benefactions
to Syria, like Walîd I, but exercising them also
in Iraq and Khurasan, as if he made no distinction whatever between the provinces (Tab., 1337,
1364, 1367, 1854).

As regards his conduct towards people of
other faiths, Theophanes, in A. M. 6210, gives
this account. " When in the same year in
Syria a great earthquake took place,[1] Umar
forbade wine in the towns and compelled the
Christians to go over to Islam. And those who
did so he freed from the tax, but slew the
rest and made many martyrs. And he decreed
that the testimony of a Christian against a
Saracen should not be accepted. He also
wrote a dogmatic letter to the Emperor Leo
in the hope of persuading him to receive Islam."

---

[1] The earthquake was on the 15th Jumâdâ I, 99 = 24th Dec., 717
A.D. Umar had succeeded to the government in Safar (Sepr., 717).

In these statements there is a mixture of truth and falsehood. It is true that Umar II was a zealous Muslim and that the Christians had cause to know it. But he did not force them to conversion on pain of death,[1] for then he would have been infringing the existing law, and that he did not do, being a good Muslim. With regard to the Christians he kept absolutely within the bounds of justice even though it might seem otherwise to them. He protected them in the possession of their old churches, which was assured to them by the terms of their capitulation, and only did not allow them to build new ones (Tab., 1371). The church of St. John in Damascus, illegally wrested from them by Walîd I, he was willing to vacate again for them, if they renounced the Churches before the Gate, i.e. of St. Thomae, which they possessed actually but not by agreement, because the land outside of the wall was forcibly taken and not surrendered by capitulation, and when they did not accede to this he made the one compensate for the other (Tab., 1275; Balâdh., 125).

---

[1] Diehl, *Hist. d'Afrique*, 1896, p. 591, asserts that he ordered the Catholics in Africa either to be converted or to leave the land. He refers to *Monum. Germ. Epist.*, 3,267, but there Pope Gregor only instructs Bonifacius that he 'Afros passim ad ecclesiasticos ordines praetendes nulla ratione suscipiat, quia aliqui eorum Manichaei, aliqui rebaptizati saepius sunt probati.' Is that to suffice us as a proof of an order of Umar, which would have been absolutely contrary to the law of Islam ?

The law which he here exercised was certainly
the formal law of the jurists, but he could not
do otherwise without renouncing Islam. Where
it was merely a question of money he was more
open-hearted. In the course of time, under
some pretext or other, the tribute of the Christians in Aela and Cyprus had been increased,
but he reduced it to the sum originally fixed
(Balâdh., 59 ; 154f.). The Prophet had decreed
that the Najrânians in the Yemen should pay
2,000 pieces of cloth yearly, each of the value
of 40 dirhems, and for this had assured to them
the right of remaining as Christians in their
land and on their estates. Umar I broke the
treaty by a flagrant breach of justice which is
excused in various ways. He compelled the
Christian Najrânians along with their Jewish
adherents to leave Arabia and emigrate to Iraq
or Syria, whilst he bought their properties from
them or gave them others in exchange for them
in their new abodes. Their chief colony was
Najrânîya, near Kufa. They were obliged again
to pay their tax at the old amount; their chief
in Najrânîya was responsible for it and exacted
it also from the kinsmen settled in Syria.
Umar's successor, Uthmân, reduced the amount
by 200 pieces of cloth, and Muâwia by 200
pieces more, as the number of the Najrânians
had decreased by death and by conversion to
Islam. Hajjâj, however, raised it again by 200

pieces, because he is said to have suspected them of sympathy with Ibn Ash'ath. Now when Umar II came into power they complained to him of their wrong, saying that their numbers had decreased and dwindled by the constant campaigns. It appeared, in fact, that they had declined from 40,000 souls to 4,000. As a beginning of redress, he thereupon declared that their tax should not rest in its strict amount upon their landed possessions (which indeed were stolen, or at least diverted from them) but was to be raised according to the number of persons after deducting those who had died and those gone over to Islam. According to this principle he reduced their tax to one-tenth, since their number had declined to one-tenth, taking only 200 pieces of cloth instead of 2,000, or 8,000 dirhems instead of 80,000. In doing this he may also have wished to make good to some extent the injustice of Umar I (Balâdh., 67f.).

In the afore-mentioned letter to Abdulhamîd of Kufa (Tab., 1366f.) Umar II directs the stattholder to treat the non-Muslim subjects also justly and fairly, not to extort the tribute with severity and not to levy it equally upon cultivated and uncultivated land. He prohibits all duties over and above the tribute,—duties which had for ages been multiplying in the territories once Persian: presents at the Naurûz-

festival and the Mihrigân-festival, fees for subordinate officials, wedding-fees, stamps for documents, and the *â'în, i.e.*, literally custom, possibly
in the sense of toll, like the English " custom." [1]
These dues, misused and difficult to control,
did not, as a rule reach the state-exchequer
at any rate, and they were all the more difficult
to abolish. The stattholders were quite willing
that people should wait upon them at New Year
and on other occasions, and not with empty hands
either (Tab., 1635ff.).

Fiscal considerations induced Umar to prohibit the alienation of Kharâj-land. He wished
to prevent it from passing into the possession of
tax-free Muslims and so being absolved from the
tribute, which consequently would decline. But
at the same time he put a check upon the
peasant class by doing this; he protected the
tax-paying owners against the Arab lords' greed
of acquiring land, for the land was of more value
to the latter than to the former because they
did not need to pay any tribute for it. Similarly
in North-western Germany, *e.g.* in Braunschweig
Lüneburg, the princes for financial reasons
were against the peasants' land passing over to
the possession of the nobles, simply because
it then became tax-free, but by doing so they at

---

[1] The Muslim tax-legislation is not cognisant of the idea of duty,
but only with that of the Kharâj and the tithe, but these it contrives
to apply even to the assessment of travelling traders.

the same time unintentionally saved the peasant class. Umar, indeed, was not so successful. The conditions in the East, too, were different. There were few peasants in our sense of the term ; even the non-Arab landowners were mostly masters of an estate or village (Dihkâns) and the Fellâhîn were their bondsmen.

3.   But whatever is uncertain, one thing at any rate is pretty clear, that we simply make ourselves ridiculous if we treat this Khalifa with superior scorn, as Dozy has set the example in doing. He may, have been more strongly in- fluenced by theology, *i.e.* in this case by juris- prudence, than one could wish. His scrupulous- ness may frequently have led him to paralysing doubts.   He is said to have once ended a sermon with the words,—" I make these reproaches against you without, for all that, feeling myself to be in the least better than you are."   He lacked the complete consciousness of his personal authority, by which his great-grand-father of the same name impressed the world, but he cared not only for his own soul, but for the *salus publica*. His piety made him discharge well the duties of the government, and act up- rightly in the difficult tasks which it entailed upon him.

To be sure, his ability generally did not cor- respond to his good will.   As the chief proof of his political incapacity it is put forward that he made disorder in the finances, and we have seen how things stood in that respect. If he imposed no tribute upon the nations and kingdoms which became new converts to Islam, he was only putting a check upon the raids made for booty but not surrendering any state-revenue, for the fish were yet to catch. In the provinces seized long before and taxable according to the law of seizure, in Sawâd, for example, and in Egypt, he maintained the historical right and opposed the decrease of the state-property and the state-income, and tried to anticipate the injurious effect which the remission of tribute for all the Muslims here might have upon the finances. By abolishing the abuse of gifts and presents he certainly affected nobody but the officials who annexed them. The most we can reproach him with is that he exacted rather much from the public exchequer by the subsidies and contributions which he made broadcast from it, or was prepared to make. But for himself he neither used nor hoarded any of the state-moneys, nor did he squander them in expeditions against Constantinople,—very differently from his predecessors. He took care, likewise, that the stattholders did not use their office chiefly as an opportunity of enriching themselves, whereby the falling-off which might perhaps have been the result of his reforms was probably made good twice over. We need not decide whether

39

the assertion that under him the state-money
vanished as if by magic, and the amount of the
taxes suddenly fell (Müller, I, 441), is anything
but the result of an error; it is certainly quite
incorrect. In the troubled times of Abdulmalik
and Hajjâj the finances were in a bad state;
under Umar II they had recovered. Besides,
anyhow, the fiscal interest is not the only one
in a state. Who would venture to disallow that
Umar abolished the child-tribute of the Berbers or lightened the burden of the Najrânians;
that he protected the subjects from the officials,
and regarded the government of the provinces
as more than a mere means of financial exploita-
tion ?

Kremer and Müller are of opinion that he
was simply obsessed by his pious Utopia; interfered with the finances without any practical
necessity; disturbed their natural course and
threw them off the lines laid down for them by
previous development. He had, they say, no
idea of the actual conditions. As a matter of
fact it is the other way; it is his modern critics
who have a false conception of the real conditions of that time. They were in a state of
chaos, and required regulating anew. Umar
was not the first to create the confusion in the
system of taxation; it was there already, and
could not continue. It was no chimerical
problem to which he addressed himself, but a

real and pressing one. Hajjâj had first attacked it seriously, but in a manner which roused
public opinion against himself. Umar tried it
in another way, with a considerate regard for
the sensitiveness founded in Islam, or at least
resting upon it. But both had the same problem
which was continually being set, and must
necessarily be solved. The result was that the
tribute-land passed more and more into the hands
of owners who were exempt from tribute.

Thus also is substantially refuted the reproach that Umar II shook the foundation of
the Umaiyid kingdom. It was tottering before,
and was not very secure to begin with. The
paragraph of Roman wisdom which A. Müller
uses to condemn Umar's turning aside from the
tradition of his predecessors, namely, that every
kingdom is maintained only by the means to
which it owes its rise, can be directed with equal
justice against the Umaiyids themselves.
Their government did not by any means carry
on in a straight line that of the Prophet and his
Companions. Instead of being supported by
Islam, on whose foundation it still claimed to
stand, and which it did not dare to deny, it was
rather uprooted by it. The Umaiyids had to be
constantly on the alert to keep down the opposition which rose up against them in the name of
Allah and the religion. They were further
menaced by the implacable hostility of Iraq

which broke out intermittently in gigantic
revolts against the hated Syrian tyranny ; but
the greatest danger for them was a social movement, directed not against them alone, but
against the Arab government generally.   Umar I
had established the Islamic state, according
to the law of seizure, as a sway of the Arabs
over those they had vanquished.   He had founded it on the distinction between two classes,
separated as much by religion as by nationality,
—the Arab Muslims and the non-Arab followers
of other faiths; the Arab warrior-nobility and
the non-Arab tribute-paying *plebs*.   But there
he had not built on a sure foundation, for the
wall of separation between masters and servants
was broken through by the fact that the latter
accepted Islam more and more, and did away
with the Arab army towns.   The increasing
Islamisation of the conquered, a natural and
inevitable process, made the system of old Umar
questionable, not in his time but in the time of
the Umaiyids who had continued it.   In accordance with the theocratic principles at least,
the political status also had to be fixed by the
religion.   It was Islam and not nationality
which conferred the rights of citizenship in the
theocracy.

The Mawâlî were clamouring at the gates
and demanding equal rights with the Arabs.
They had Islam on their side, and were recruited

by the revolution which based itself upon Islam. Umar II tried to satisfy their claims cheaply; he was probably actuated not so much by statesmanlike motives as by religious ones, but the one did not stand in the way of the other. Islam could not be broken ; it had got to be taken into account. Enmity to it threatened the fall of the kingdom of the Umaiyids. An Umaiyid thus did not act against the interest of his house when he put himself on good terms with Islam and tried to avoid the refusal of its alliance by removing justified grievances and supporting claims which could not be gainsaid. That, in all likelihood, was the programme of Umar II. In Islam he tried to find common ground for the government and the hostile powers working against it. From this stand- point he pursued a policy of agreement and conciliation, and that not towards the Mawâli only. He also tried to abolish the ill-feeling of the provinces and especially to remove from the Iraqites the sense of being under Syrian foreign rule. He treated them all with equal care ; he even thought he could satisfy the Khawârij by entering into their arguments, and had at least this much success, that they left the sword in the sheath as long as he lived. He did not punish political crimes, though severe against others. He was gracious to the Alids, restoring to them their confiscated property,—

as well as to the heirs of Talha—and struck out
of the pulpit prayer the curse upon their
ancestors.[1] But it does not follow, and we
cannot believe, that he, at heart, recognised
as just their claims to the Khalifate.[2] He was a
Muslim of the old school. The old Islam had
at bottom no sympathy with the legitimism of
the Shiites, and it would even have put up with
the Umaiyid dynasty, in spite of its illegal
origin, if it had not been hostile to it from the
start. The Abbâsid Mansûr testified that
Umar II's rule in general was worthy of praise,
but that, for all that, he was an Umaiyid and
held fast to the prior claim of his house (Tab.,
3, 534).

Hamer in exercitibus nihil satis prosperum
nec quicquam adversum peregit, tantae autem
benignitatis et patientiae fuit, ut hactenus
tantus ei honor lausque referatur, etiam ab
externis, quantus ulli umquam viventi, regni
gubernacula praeroganti, adlatus est. So
runs the judgment of the Arab-Byzantine
continuer, Isidor (par. 38) concerning this
Khalifa. His intentions were, at any rate,

---

[1] Agh., 8,153. Yaqûbî, 2,366. Weil's doubts of the facts are unjustified. Even after Umar's death the official execration of Alî was
not again introduced (Tab., 1482f.)

[2] The article of the *Kitâbal Aghânî* on Umar tries to make him
out a secret Shiite, but in the same way the Khawârij are said to have
considered him to be a participator in their persuasion, and they were
diametrically opposed to the Shiites.

good, and perhaps not unwise either. What he would have accomplished it is impossible to say, since he reigned scarcely $2\frac{1}{2}$ years. He died at the age of 39 on Friday, 24th or 25th Rajab, 101 (9th Feb., 720) in Khunâsira, near Damascus. According to Abû Ubaida, he was poisoned by the Umaiyids, because they were afraid he would yield to the Khârijites and exclude as unworthy, from the succession, Yazîd b. Abdilmalik, who had been appointed by Sulaimân to succeed him as Khalifa. But of this account those of the old historians who are reliable know nothing. Indeed they only express their disappointment that the reformer of the world was snatched away before his time, and that the old *régime* returned.

CHAPTER VI.

The Later Marwânids.

1. Yazîd II was the grandson of Yazîd I through his daughter Âtika, whom Abdulmalik had married ; he is often called Yazîd b. Âtika, after his proud mother.[1] He fancied himself of higher degree than the rest of the Marwânids and boasted of his Sufyânid blood. He also possessed some of the spirit of his maternal grandfather after whom he was called, though he had not inherited the latter's mildness and affability.

Immediately after his accession there happened an event which had a marked effect upon his reign and upon the time to come. He was nearly connected with Ḥajjâj, whose niece he married, and during her uncle's life-time she bore him his son Walîd, who was Khalifa later. Her first son, who died early, was named Ḥajjâj. Accordingly he was prejudiced against Sulaimân's favourite Yazîd b. Muhallab,

---

[1] At that time great stress was laid upon descent from a well-born mother. Maslama b. Abdilmalik was descended from a slave, so there was no question of him as successor, though he was very brave and also very highly esteemed in the Umaiyid family.

who, as stattholder in Iraq, had ill-treated the
family of Hajjâj. The latter expected no good
at his hands when he came to power; he escaped
from the debtors' prison in which he was
detained—according to Wâqidî not till after
Umar's death, but according to Abû Mikhnaf,
the chief narrator in Tabarî, before that, on
hearing the news of his serious illness. His goal
was Basra, the home of his family, the Mahâliba,
and of his clan, the Azd Umân. He eluded the
Qaisites who pursued him, and the Kufaites who
all but captured him, and appeared before Basra
with a little band, where in the meantime his
brothers and cousins, as many as could be got
hold of, were seized and made prisoners in the
citadel. The stattholder, Adî b. Artât, advanced
with the Basrian clans before the town in order
to keep him from entering, but when he arrived
they all made way for him ; a cavalry-leader
of the family of Hajjâj, who was about to raise
his hand against him, was quietly thrust aside,
and he was able to enter without opposition and
take possession of his quarters. Obviously the
new Khalifa had not a good reputation to begin
with. Syrian troops do not seem to have been
to the fore in any great numbers either in Basra
or in Wâsit ; Umar II may have withdrawn
them.

The son of Muhallab first began to treat
with the stattholder to persuade him to set free

40

the prisoners in the citadel, and when he did not succeed he employed force. He had on his side the Yemen, *i.e.* the Azd and Rabîa, who were allied in Basra as in Khurasan, and he strengthened their allegiance by handsome presents. The Tamîm and the Qais, who since time immemorial had been rivals of the Yemenites, stuck to the stattholder. But as the latter was stingy with money because he was too scrupulous to venture to help himself from the state-treasury, they were lukewarm, and at the first encounter of the parties they scattered. He fled and was besieged in the citadel. The Muhallabids who were imprisoned there, barricaded themselves so that he could not hurt them, and after a few days, the citadel fell and he was taken captive. He cheerfully submitted to his fate because he was confident that out of fear of the " troops of God in Syria " (*i.e.* the government troops), no one would hurt a hair of his head.

A pardon for Yazîd, wrung from the Khalifa, came too late. He had gone too far. He now openly issued a summons in the name of the Book of God and the Sunna of the Prophet to the holy war against the Syrians, which was, he said, more urgent and necessary than that against Turks and Dailamites. His idea was to yoke Islam to his waggon. But there was a man in Basra who dared to raise his voice loudly

against him,—old Hasan, a friend of Umar II
In these citizens' wars, he said, it was a question
not of God, but of the world and its gain.
They upbraided him as a friend of the Syrians,
a traitor and a hypocrite, saying: " If a neighbour were so much as to pull a reed out of his
hut,[1] he would give him a bloody nose, and yet
he reproaches us for seeking what is best for
ourselves and defending ourselves against
injustice ! " He did not let this affect him any
more than Jeremiah did in a similar situation,
but continued to restrain those who were willing
to listen to him from taking part, and his
influence was particularly felt in the case of the
non-Arab inhabitants of some districts in the
neighbourhood of Basra. But the position he
took up was exceptional in that it separated
religion and politics in the sphere of the theocracy,
and his following was insignificant, otherwise he
would scarcely have been left uncontested.
The average pious folk of Basra, the *readers*
first of all, yielded to the allurement of Yazîd,
and the Mawali to a great extent followed them.
This greatly increased his following, but their
war-like capacity did not correspond to their
numbers, and Islam proved to be a stubborn ally.

The districts belonging to Basra, *viz.* Ahwâz,
Fârs and Karmân, also fell to the rebel, but not
his old favourite province of Khurasan, because

---

[1] The houses of Basra were usually of reeds.

there the Azd were held in check by the Tamîm. He was advised to establish himself in Fârs, where he could most easily maintain his power, but he did not want to leave Iraq to the advancing Syrians, but, if possible, to get to Kufa before them. Towards the end of the year 101 (summer of 720) he set out thither by way of Wâsit, which he took, and the Nîl canal. At the point where this canal emptied into the Euphrates he halted at a place bearing the oft-recurring name of Aqr (Castle) and situated near the ancient Babylon.[1] The stattholder there tried to bar his way to Kufa—having taken up his position on the other bank near Nukhaila, but he could not prevent numerous Kufaites from going over to Yazîd, amongst them heirs of the most celebrated

---

[1] According to the verse, Tanbîh, 332, 1, the battle took place between Bâbel and Aqr. So the Aqr that is meant was situated, like Bâbel, on the east bank of the Euphrates and was not the Aqr of Karbala, which must be looked for to the west of the Hindîya. It is only the description of the way that Maslama took (in Tab., 1395) that offers difficulty :—"He marched by the Euphrates and halted at Anbâr, then threw a bridge over the river ('alaihi) opposite the town of Fârit, and marched on till he came to a halt in front of Yazîd (at Aqr)." As Anbâr lay on the east bank, Maslama must have crossed from there first near Fârit in a westerly direction and then back again in an easterly,—just as Qahtaba did later. There is no mention of a second crossing. But there is mention of a bridge over which the Syrians had come and which they burnt behind them. Nöldeke identifies Aqr (ἀκρα) with Qasr (castra) probably rightly, as the old Nîl discharges between Qasr and Babylon and the fortification lay at the influx of the Nîl between Aqr and Babylon. The topographical statements in Tabarî, 1397 are confused, and BSerapion does not make them any clearer.

names, and not only Yemenites and Rabîites, but Tamîmites as well.

It was not long until Maslama b. Abdilmalik, for long the leader of the campaigns in Asia Minor and Armenia, also appeared on the scene with the Syrian main army. Yazîd let him advance towards him over the Euphrates and pitch his camp without molestation quite near him. Then two leaders of sects who had great influence on the crowd, Samaida and Abû Rûba, protested against his attacking the Syrians, who, after all, were also Muslims, in cold blood and even by night, too, without first having given them, by an appeal to Qoran and Sunna, the chance of repenting.[1] He yielded,

---

[1] The circumstances of the case were probably these :—Abû Mikhnaf does not say that Maslama was forced to cross the Euphrates, —see the preceding note. Samaida was essentially a Khârijite, Abû Rûba a Murjiite. The Murjiites blunted the edge of the older parties and tried to bring about an approach to the Jamâa, to Catholicism. They also refused to acknowledge the Umaiyid rule, but left the question " Alî or Uthmân ? " to God. They believed that even such as followed a false Imâm might still be good Muslims. They protested against the Khawârij alone considering themselves Muslims, and having in general their fixed judgment upon the condition of every man's religion and thus forestalling the judgment of God. " We Muslims, as distinguished from idolaters, all acknowledge the same one God and are united through Islam ; the Khawârij err in the theory they oppose to this, however pious and earnest they may otherwise be. I could not say that a decision in the dispute between Alî and Uthmân was revealed in a verse of the Qoran ; both of them are servants of God, and at the last day God will judge them according to their deeds." This is the gist of a Murjiite's creed, incorrectly translated bv Van Vloten, D.M.Z., 1891, p. 163.

as Alî did long before at Siffîn, but lost every remnant of confidence in his troops and expressed aloud the desperate wish,—would that he only had with him his Azdites of Khurasan instead of that countless horde !

On Friday (Saturday), 14th Safar, 102 (24th August, 720) Maslama opened the attack after burning down the bridge behind him. The Iraqites did not hold their ground, and the Tamîm of Kufa were the very first to take to their heels. It was as if the wolf had broken into the sheep-fold. Yazîd was not surprised. Scorning the advice to retreat with the men he could trust to Wâsit, whither the way was open to him, he sought and found death on the field of battle. With him fell two of his brothers and also the pious Samaida. One or two hundred prisoners were taken, mostly at the storming of the camp. Most of them were afterwards executed, including a few Tamîmites, whose expectation of recognition of their having by their flight made the victory an easy one for the Syrians was vain. On the other hand a son of Yazîd in Wasit had the stattholder, Adî b. Artât, put to the sword, with 30 other Basrians of the opposite party who were in his hands.

The crowd of fugitives scattered in all directions, pursuit only being made after the Muhallabids, who were hunted like game. They first gathered in Basra, and with them also

some prominent Yemenites from Kufa, descendants of Ash'ath and Mâlik al-Ashtar. There
they took ship and landed on the coast of
Karman. Driven thence, they sought a refuge
in the Indian Qandâbîl, but failed to find safety
there either. All the men among them fit for
war, with the exception of two, fell by the sword
of the pursuers, and their severed heads were
sent to Syria and exposed in Halab. Eleven
youths were brought as prisoners to the Khalifa
and executed. The rest of the prisoners, women
and children, were, in defiance of all Islamic
usage, exposed for sale in Basra ; but Jarrâh b.
Abdillâh alHakamî, one of the bravest and
most faithful officials of the Umaiyids, with
a sense of the fitness of things ransomed them.
The family estates were, of course, confiscated.[1]

Iraq was first made over to the conqueror
of Aqr, Maslama b. Abdilmalik, who appointed
new officials in Kufa, Basra and Khurasan. But
he was soon deposed because he did not credit to
Damascus the surplus of the provincial exche-
quers.[2] In his place, as viceroy over Iraq and
the East, came Umar b. Hubaira alFazârî
from Qinnesrin, who had governed Mesopotamia

[1] Cf. the verses of Jarîr in Reiske's Abulfidâ, 1, adn. 207. They
are not in the Egyptian edition of A.H. 1313.

[2] Even Abdulazîz b. Marwân in Egypt had not done so, and did
not need to do it. Maslama may have been appointed with the same
privilege as a reward for his victory.

under Umar II. He was a thorough Qaisite
and ruled accordingly. The Azd and the
Yemen in general, particularly in Khurasan,
were made to suffer under his rule, for they
were slighted and humiliated, and those who
were well-disposed to the Muhallabids, or
suspected of being so, were tortured and ill-
treated. But the Qais triumphed, and in all
the East they could not but feel themselves
masters. Although they might play each other
ill tricks, they nevertheless held faithfully
together against foreign clans. A story, not
very trustworthy otherwise, but very enlighten-
ing in this respect is related in Tab., 1453ff.
The stattholder of Khurasan, Saîd b. Amr
alHarashî, a Qaisite, chastised another Qaisite,
Maʻqil b. Urwa in Herât, who thought he
did not owe him obedience because he was
appointed over Herat not by him, but directly
by Ibn Hubaira. Ibn Hubaira sided against
alHarashî and handed him over to the revenge
of his antagonist, who was to torture him to
death. Now when he put the question to the
company that, according to custom, regularly
assembled at his house in the evening, who was
the most eminent man among the Qais, and got

¹ The poet Farazdaq, though himself not belonging to the Yemen
but to Mudar, nevertheless scoffingly said that the only thing lacking
was that a man of Ashjaʻ should rule over Iraq. Fazâra was the head
and Ashjaʻ the tail of the Qaisite Ghatafân.

the answer that he himself was, he said,—"What! The most eminent is Kauthar b. Zufar b. Hârith, for he has but to have a horn blown, and 20,000 men come and never ask why he summoned them[1]; the greatest benefactor of the Qais I certainly am,—always only anxious to be useful to them, but the bravest of them is that ass whom I have given orders to slay." Then a simple Bedouin replied,—"How can you be the greatest benefactor of the Qais if you slay their bravest man? Immediately after this remark he gave orders to let alHarashî live. Later on the tables were turned. Ibn Hubaira had to flee from Khâlid alQasrî, and his foe alHarashî was sent out to pursue him. When he had overtaken his fugitive on his ship, he asked him,—"What, think you, shall I do to you?" "I think," was the answer, "that as a Qaisite you will surely not hand me over to a Qaisite." "There you are right," said the other, "be off with you!"

The spirit of Hajjâj had a power after his death of which he would hardly have been proud. The opposition of the Qais and the Yemen which was embittered by his enmity to Ibn Ash'ath

---

[1] Zufar b. Hârith, the head of the Qais of Mesopotamia, is everywhere described as a man of great nobility, and far above political aspirations. His sons, Hudhail and Kauthar, inherited the respect accorded to him and were also held in high esteem by the Khalifas. Cf. Tab., 1300. 1360f. Agh., 16, 42, and the poems of Qutâmî now published by Barth.

41

and Ibn Muhallab grew still worse after his
death. The action of the Khalifas in taking
sides brought this about, no matter which side
it was they took. From an opposite stand-point
Yazîd II cut open the same wound as Sulaimân,
after it had but partially healed during the
intervening reign. Being influenced by Hajjâj
he distrusted the Muhallabids and nursed his
hatred against them. The distrust of their
aspirations in the East of the kingdom was
justified, and by their rebellion they themselves
brought about the outburst of his hatred. But
the proscription of the whole of the prominent
and powerful family, a measure hitherto unheard
of in the history of the Umaiyids, came like a
declaration of war against the Yemen in general,
and the corollary was that the government was
degenerating into a Qaisite party-rule. The
Khalifa was to blame for this. He put Ibn
Hubaira into power and let him carry on as he
pleased in his wide sphere. His motive was
certainly revenge only. He was no statesman
and did not size up the far-reaching political
bearing of his mode of action. In Syria he did
not favour the Qais more than the Qudâa. The
Qudâa were the nucleus of the army that was
victorious at 'Aqr. A Kalbite cut down Yazîd
b. Muhallab when he was attacking Maslama,
and it was Kalbites who pursued the fugitive
Muhallabids and wiped them out.

Yazîd II had departed far from his immediate predecessor's policy of conciliation. According to BAthîr, 5,50 he made invalid everything in the latter's management of the kingdom that did not please him. Immediately on his accession he appointed new officials in Medina and Africa, without, however, at once proposing a systematic and general change. But he had the Soghdians, who on the promise of freedom from tribute had come over to Islam, relieved from the tribute. His stattholder, Yazîd b. Abî Muslim, acted similarly towards the Berbers, but they killed him, re-established his predecessor, and duly communicated the matter to the Khalifa,[1] who declared himself in agreement with it. He preferred to let things happen, rather than to order them to be done, being weak and indifferent. It was not from policy or intention that he opposed Umar II. If he ever did get hold of any good antecedents he is said to have taken him for a pattern to himself (Agh., 13, 157). But his was quite a different nature from Umar II's. It was not puritanical seriousness but aristocratic frivolity that was the basis of his disposition; he was more of a cavalier than an administrator. He handed over the provinces to the stattholders,

---

[1] Tab., 2, 1435. Acc. to Balâdh., 231, the stattholder was slain by his Berber bodyguard because he had the word "Guard" branded on their hand.

and devoted his time not to business but to the generous passions. The vagrants put down by his predecessor, came into repute again under him. He paid small regard to the dignity of the firm which he had to represent, and did not take the trouble to make a pretence of doing so. Two women singers, Salâma and Habâba, played a great part at his court. Whoever wanted to get anything out of him had recourse to them. Ibn Hubaira himself is said to have attained his high position by this means (BAthîr, 5, 75f.; Agh., 13, 157). He was so beside himself at the death of Habâba that Maslama begged him at least not to show himself in public in this distraught state. Seven days later he died, people believed of sorrow at the loss of the beloved maiden. There was some romance in him and he had a taste for poetry and music, in which he was different from Sulaimân.

Theophanes relates that Umar II hoped to be able to convert the Emperor Leo to Islam. He says further that Yazîd II got a Jew from Phœnician Laodicea to prophesy that he would remain in power for 40 years if he destroyed the images in the Christian churches of his realm, and that, induced by this, he issued a general edict against the sacred images, but it was not executed because of his death, which happened shortly after, and it did not come to the knowledge of outside circles at all; but that the

Emperor Leo shared in the wicked heterodoxy and was backed up in it by a Christian of the Arab name of Bishr, who had received Islam as a prisoner of war in Syria, and after his liberation had not altogether discarded it. It raises serious doubts against the existence of the diabolical decree of the Khalifa that it is said to have been known only to the very few. The simple statement that a Jew foretold to him a 40 years' reign is also found in Tabarî, but the prophecy was not fulfilled. Yazîd II ruled only 4 years and died on Wednesday, 24th Shaʻbân, 105 (26th January, 724) at Arbad in the East Jordan country. Accounts of his age vary between 33 and 40 years.

2. As heir to the kingdom he had first designated his brother Hishâm, and after him his son Walîd. Talis enim inter Arabes tenetur perpetim norma, ut nonnisi cunctas regum successiones prerogative a principe percipiant nomina, ut eo decidente absque scandala adeant regiminis gubernacula. Thus comments the Spanish Continuator of Isidor. The arrangement of the succession by will is certainly noteworthy.

Hishâm b. Abdilmalik was called after his mother's father, the Makhzûmite Hishâm b. Ismâîl, and favoured his mother's brothers. He received the insignia of government,—the staff and ring—in Rusâfa,[1] a Roman settlement on

---

[1] Acc. to Tab., 1463, 16, however, it was in Hims (Emessa).

the border of the Syrian desert not far from
Raqqa, which he had restored and which, even
as Khalifa, he preferred as a place of residence,
because he thought Damascus unhealthy. He
received homage in the capital. He was not
much like his deceased brother, being prudent
and honourable and before all things a thorough
business man. But he differed just as much
from Umar II, for he had no idealism about
him.

His first act was to break up the insolent
Qaisite *régime* in the East of the kingdom by
deposing Umar b. Hubaira, in whose stead there
came Khâlid b. Abdillâh alQasrî in Shauwâl, 105
(March, 724), and thus Iraq again got a ruler
comparable to some extent to Ziâd and Hajjâj.
His personality attracts our interest more than
that of the Khalifa himself, though we hear more
about his fall and its serious consequences than
about the activity of his rule.

He had begun his career under Hajjâj and
at his instigation had come to Mecca in A.H. 91
to prevent the political criminals of Iraq from
finding a refuge there. This task he accomplished by making the owners of houses responsible for their inhabitants. The Holy Town had
also him to thank for a water-conduit, which
indeed brought him as little gratitude as the
one at Jerusalem in former times brought to
Pilate. He was then deposed by Sulaimân as a

creature of Hajjâj and after that did not hold office again until Hishâm preferred him and entrusted to him the most important office in the kingdom. Like Hajjâj, he resided in Wâsit, and devoted himself to peaceful activities. He seems to have been by nature gentle, although he had no lack of energy.[1] He was not regarded as a warrior, but passed for a coward and was despised because he called out in terror for a glass of water when he received, in the pulpit, word of a Shiite riot in Kufa, in which the whole number concerned consisted of eight Iranians, as it turned out afterwards. He had not indeed much occasion to unsheath the sword. About the end of his term of office a few Shiite and Kharijite risings took place, only one of which spread to any great extent,[2]

[1] Weil, 1, 620, appealing to Tab., asserts that Khâlid cruelly ill-treated his predecessor and finally killed him, but in the Leiden edition there is no mention of this. Acc. to it Ibn Hubaira escaped Khâlid's pursuit and then, in his own native place, Qinnesrin, fell into the Khalifa's hands, and he ordered him to receive 100 lashes, and yet afterwards was much annoyed with Yazîd b. Ibn Hubaira for being unwilling to have him as his daughter's father-in-law. Thus also Khâlid treated certain seditionists mildly and only destroyed them upon a direct command from heaven (Tab., 1628). Indeed he is alleged to have only allowed the poet Kumait to escape so that with Hishâm he should be out of the frying-pan into the fire.

[2] The eight Iranians who are said to have caused Khâlid to call for water were the so-called Wusafâ in Kufa, under Mughîra "the wizard" and Baiân. They may have been connected with the Abbâsid propaganda. Also Wazîr asSakhtiânî (the leather-merchant, cf Yahyâ b. Âdam, 34, 18), who with his band rendered the district of Kufa unsafe, seems to have been an Iranian Maula and to have

but on the whole, under him Iraq enjoyed an
unusually long time of peace and flourished
economically (Tab., 1778, 13ff.). Still he was
not beloved but most bitterly opposed. A mass
of ill-natured gossip is collected against him in
the article upon him in the *Kitáb alAghání*
(19, 52ff.), but even in Tabarí we can find plenty
of it as well.

The Qasr family from which Khâlid sprang
was a branch of the Bajîla. The Bajîla, broken
up during the heathen period by serious internal
disputes, had sunk into insignificance, and had
only been somewhat recuperated through Islam.
Khâlid, therefore, had no family connection at
his back, no esteemed and powerful clan to rely
upon. If this was a disadvantage, it might, on
the other hand, seem an advantage for him in
the prosecution of his office that the Bajîla
belonged neither to the Mudar nor to the
Yemen. His descent did not prescribe to him
a fixed position in the dualism of the clan-
groups. But the Qais were naturally bound to
regard him as their foe since he was sent to
supplant their benefactor, Ibn Hubaira, and to

belonged to the Shiite sect. Sahârî and Bahlûl, again, were Arab
Khawârij. The latter, a son of the famous Shabîb, with 30 Bakrites
from Jabbul on the Tigris made an attack upon Khâlid's estate of
Mubârak. Bahlûl b. Bishr raised a more important rebellion from
Mosul and twice conquered a troop sent out against him, but was then
overcome in the battle of Kuhail. The story of these rebels is told in
Tabarí by Abû Ubaida.

set aside their overlordship. Apparently the rest of the Mudar did not receive him cordially either. A prominent Tamîmite in Basra who was refractory to his stattholder there (a descendant of Abû Mûsâ alAsh'arî), had to pay the penalty with his life. Even though he himself had come with the idea of preserving neutrality, he was nevertheless drawn into the party whirlpool, and the hostility of the Mudar drove him for good or ill to the side of the Yemen. In the tradition he appears from the beginning as a Yemenite incarnate, inspired by hatred and suspicion of the Mudar and the Quraish belonging to them, even of those in highest place, and as a proud Bajilite, he is absurdly reported to have given open expression to these sentiments. This is, of course, a great exaggeration. In this respect he is not at all to be compared to Yazîd b. Muhallab, the recognised leader of the Azd. It was only after his deposition, and further after his death, that the Yemen supported him with acclamation and made him a pretext for rebellion, without his sanction and against his will. He himself was quite explicit in his own mind about his absolute dependence upon the Umaiyids (Tab., 1656) and felt that he was their servant and not their clan or party leader. A proof of his fidelity to the dynasty was afforded by his decisively advising Hishâm not to subvert the will of

42

Yazîd II and exclude the latter's son from the
succession, although he could not but have a
good idea of what he himself had to expect at
the hands of the son of Yazîd. Even after his
fall he preserved his honourable loyalty, which
then shone out with a brilliant lustre.

Along with the hostility of the Qais, Khâlid
also drew upon himself the hostility of Islam.
His mother was, and remained a Christian, and
he built a church for her in Kufa. He permitted the Christians in general to build new
churches,[1] and in the same way showed himself
tolerant to the Jews. He took into his service
as officials of finance and administration many
Zoroastrians. The Kharijite Bahlûl reproached
him with the fact that he destroyed mosques,
built synagogues and churches, allowed Zoroastrians to rule over the Believers, and permitted
Christians or Jews to have Muslim wives.
Shocking things were circulated about him,—
that he was descended from Jews, if not actually from slaves from Hajar; that he had grown
up among dissolute companions in Medina and
had there served the poetic libertine Ibn Abî
Rabîa as "*postillon d'amour*"; that he was a
Zandîq (libertine), an infidel and profligate;
in Mecca he had called the Zamzam spring,

---

[1] In Hîra, however, the Christian town near Kufa, the Christians
at his downfall zealously sided against him. (Tab., 1653.)

which by means of his new aqueduct he could cause to overflow, a brackish, verminous stream, and had uttered similar blasphemies against the Ka‘ba, the Prophet and his house, and even against the Book of God itself. The remark directed against the stupidity of the pious fraternity, that there never was a sensible man who knew the Qoran by heart, he is quite likely to have made. He apparently was aware of his spiritual superiority, and did not always keep a check upon his ready tongue, and thus gave offences which could be used against him.

He also laid himself open to other reproaches. He was noted for his zeal for the culture of the ground, and in this emulated Hishâm. He continued what Hajjâj had begun. The engineer who, under him, conducted the drainage works in the district of Wasit, in the marshes of the lower Tigris, was the same Hassân an-Nabatî who had served the latter. But he worked at it more than was good for himself. By the drying of the marshes he gained a very extensive and productive area; his chief estates are enumerated by name in Tab., 1655, and from the crops he had tremendous revenues. He had no need to consider money and practised an extravagant generosity especially towards his servants and confidants, whom he attached to himself by this means. He liked to appear a *grand seigneur*; but at his repasts he did not satisfy his guests' greediness, which was insufferable to him (Agh., 19, 62).

Naturally the people grumbled at this. They were, in general, annoyed at the making of canals, *i.e.* at the occupation of great stretches of virgin soil by favourites whe had the permission and the means to cultivate it. This business was at that time vigorously pursued, mostly by the princes of the ruling house, and by Hishâm himself in particular. But they could not so easily make a complaint against *him*. They confined themselves to his stattholder who was, at any rate, widely hated. The charge itself—that he exploited the means of his official position for his own private use—they may not have laid against him in so many words, for, after all, that was the fashion, if only in the doing of it private property was respected and the surplus of the taxes sent to Damascus to a sufficient amount. But they *did* reproach him with raising the price of his corn by delaying the sale of it. They also thought that the money which he scattered about so lavishly did not come solely from the yield of his estates, but that he was embezzling large sums from the state-treasury. His Mammon excited envy, and his method of gaining friends by means of it only increased the number of his foes.

In spite of this he remained for nearly 15 years at the head of Iraq, longer than any other stattholder with the single exception of Hajjâj. It must be put to the credit of the Khalifa that he kept him so long, but at last he yielded to the pressure of his foes. Prominent Quraish-ites and Umaiyids to whom Khâlid had given offence made common cause with the Qaisites against him (Tab., 1642, 1655f.). Hassân an-Nabatî, who should have known better, was won over to an intrigue against him. Hishâm certainly did not consider him actually to be a political suspect, but he felt a sort of jealousy of him and possibly regarded him as a competitor in business affairs. He also resented the pride and candour of his disposition and his irreverent remarks about himself which were reported to him. So he determined to depose him and to make his successor a Qaisite, the Thaqifite Yûsuf b. Umar, a relative of Hajjâj, who for many years had governed the province of the Yemen. When a change of this kind was made it often happened that the one to be deposed was taken by surprise by the actual accomplishment of the deposition, and heard nothing about it till his successor appeared to bring him to account ; he was not meant to have time to make his preparations. But the secrecy with which Hishâm acted in this case was extraordinary.

There is a delightful story about it told in Tab., 1640 ff. By his orders Yûsuf b. Umar suddenly appeared in Kufa in Jumâdâ I, 120 (May, 738) with a few followers. The Christians in Hîra and the Thaqîf with other Mudar in Kufa put themselves at his service and no one offered him resistance. Khâlid himself was in Wasit and quietly let himself be seized and imprisoned. His prison was in Kufa; Yûsuf took up his residence not in Wasit but in Hîra. Apparently the little Christian town was better suited for a garrison than the populous neighbouring Muslim town of Kufa; also Hishâm had expressly forbidden Yûsuf to quarter the Syrian soldiers with the Kufaites. Khâlid and his sons remained in prison for 18 months. Not a single Yemenite opened his lips on his behalf, only an Absite, a man of the Qais, expressed his sympathy for him in poetry (Tab., 1816). He was required to give an account of the state-moneys, *i.e.* to confess to the embezzlement of a large sum and undertake payment of it. For this purpose the rack was the means resorted to, but it was only after long pressure that Hishâm permitted it, and then only conditionally. He threatened the torturer himself with death if his victim should succumb to his torture, and sent a body-guard expressly to be present at the application of torture. In Shauwâl, 121 (Sept., 739) he commanded the release of the prisoner, since there was nothing to be got out of him. Khâlid then sought him at Rusâfa, but was not admitted to his presence, and had to confine himself to an intercourse in writing with his most trusted counsellor, the Kalbite alAbrash. In Safar, 122 (January, 740) he went to Damascus where he took up his abode. Yûsuf b. Umar did not desist from following up the prey that had slipped through his fingers and at last prevailed upon the reluctant Khalifa to order Khâlid's son Yazîd to be delivered up to him, but he escaped imprisonment by flight. The prefect of Damascus, Kulthûm b. Iyâd alQasrî, acted in concert with Yûsuf, although he may not have had an understanding with him. He was a cousin of Khâlid and by virtue of his office had to oversee him. He may, in quite good faith and out of zeal for his business, whilst making the campaign in Asia Minor with him in the summer of 122 (740), have suspected him of having something to do with great conflagrations by which at that time several quarters of Damascus were reduced to ashes. Hishâm listened to him, as he did not think him capable of any ill-will towards his relative, and had the whole lot of Khâlid's followers arrested. It was soon

---

[1] The matter is also mentioned by Theophanes, A.M. 6232, and must have caused some excitement.

evident, however, that the latter had nothing to do with the incendiarists, although they were certainly Iraqites. When Khâlid came home he was beside himself, and expatiated in treasonable language, adding that they might convey his remarks boldly to the one against whom they were directed. On another occasion, too, when Hishâm, through Abrash, called him to account because he was alleged to have uttered in a great gathering flatteries of a panegyrist which were absolutely blasphemous, he burst into a great passion and let all respect for the ruler go to the winds. The latter pocketed the affront quietly, only remarking that he was out of his senses and did not know what he was saying. It was only against his will that he was constantly compelled to distasteful measures against the old servant of whose fidelity he himself indeed had no doubt, and afterwards he had constant occasion to repent of them. It is to his honour that he felt ashamed and did not take offence at the open wrath of Khâlid, but acknowledged it to be the testimony of his clear conscience. In the last years of his reign he left him unmolested in Damascus even though the popularity which he won there could hardly be pleasing to him.

If under Khâlid there had been peace in Iraq for long years, it was not long till there was a rising in the capital under his successor,

which opened up serious prospects. The Alid
Zaid b. Alî b. Husain b. Alî had very unwillingly come to Kufa from Medina, the seat of the
family, but then remained there because he had
fallen into the hands of the Shiites who detained
him. They told him that the time was ripe, that
the rule of the Umaiyids over Kufa rested only
upon the few Syrian soldiers who could not face
the 100,000 Kufaite warriors, and he suffered
himself to be fooled, only he was wise enough to
keep changing his quarter constantly. His
stay lasted altogether about 10 months, during
which time he prepared for a rebellion and
made recruits also in Basra and Mosul. In
Kufa 15,000 men had themselves enrolled on
his army-list. In the formula of homage-paying it said that the Book of God and the Sunna
of the Prophet were to be taken as the rule of
conduct, unjust usurpers were to be fought
against, the weak defended, pensions returned
to those robbed of them, the state-revenue (the
Fai) divided equally amongst those entitled to it,
atonement made to those who had been wronged,
those sent off upon distant campaigns recalled
home, and the family of the Prophet defended
against all who opposed it and denied its right.
Yûsuf b. Umar was for a long time in the dark
about the movement, but at last he succeeded
in gathering particulars of Zaid's doings from
two of his fellow-conspirators whom he arrested.

43

Then he also discovered that in consequence of these arrests the latter had hurried on the rebellion and fixed the date of it for Wednesday, 1st Safar, 122 (6th January, 740). At his orders the men of Kufa were now summoned on the preceding Tuesday into the courtyard of the mosque, hemmed in there, and guarded by some Syrians. They appear to have been quite pleased at this protection from their own imprudence. When Zaid, with the 218 men whom he had still managed to gather together in the dead of night and bitter cold on the Wednesday, tried to free them, they would hardly lift a hand themselves and presently he had to withdraw from the mosque because 2,000 Syrians from Hira were advancing against him. On Wednesday he repulsed them and still held out against them on Thursday, but at nightfall his few trusty followers had to withdraw into the town before the Kikanite archers, and he himself was fatally wounded by an arrow. His body fell into the hands of the Syrians; the trunk was nailed to a cross in Kufa, and the head exposed in Damascus and Medina. His son Yahyâ, a mere boy, fled to Khurâsân, and kept in hiding for several years in Balkh, but was then discovered and hunted from place to place till he fell with his followers in battle under Walîd II.

Though this rebellion had such a lamentable

ending, it is nevertheless important because later Shiite rebellions, which brought about the final destruction of the kingdom of Damascus, were connected with it. Soon after the death of Yahyâ, Abû Muslim appeared as his avenger and killed his murderers.

3. We should get a false impression of the Khalifa Hishâm if we were to imagine him as interested solely in the government and internal affairs. He was certainly not a soldier, yet did not in any way shrink from warfare and carried on war energetically with all his means, fitting out powerful armies, and sparing neither money nor human lives. He had always his hands full with military undertakings in all quarters.

Just at the beginning of his reign he energetically resumed the war against the Romans, which had been in abeyance after the attack on Constantinople in A.H. 98-99 (716-717) had exhausted all their strength and had yet led to nothing. He again prevented the fortification of the boundaries (Bal., 165-167) and every summer caused great predatory expeditions to be undertaken,—two or three simultaneously in converging directions. His sons, Muâwia and Sulaimân, both ardent warriors, generally had the command. The first, the ancestor of the Spanish Umaiyids, perished in A.H. 118 or 119 (736 or 737) in the enemy's land through a

fall from his horse while hunting.   His   father's
lament was,—" I bred him up for the Khalifate
and he pursues a fox ! "   But the chief hero of
these fights appears in tradition and story to be
alBattâl ("the fighter ").   They put forth great
efforts and managed to capture citadels and
towns, which to be sure were held in winter with
difficulty.   Nonnulla prospera per duces exercitus
a se missos in Romania terra et pelago gessit.
But the Romans   defended themselves fairly
successfully.   In the year 122 (740) they wiped
out an Arab army at Akroinus in Phrygia, where
alBattâl fell. In the following year they, on their
side, made an attack upon the capital of Melitene,
but withdrew again   when   Hishâm himself
hastened thither from Rusâfa in reply to the call
of   the besieged for aid.   Alongside of the
struggles with the Romans, battles with the Turks
were taking place in the north-east, on this side
of the Caspian Sea, in which, also, fortune was
not always on the side of the Arabs.   In the year
112 (730) they suffered a severe defeat, but
afterwards things took a favourable turn, thanks to
Maslama, and especially Marwân b. Muhammad.

With an impetus almost greater than that
from the East the Muslims were pressing forward simultaneously from the west against
Europe,[1] taking the Christian world between

---

[1] The fullest and best information about this is to be found in
the *Contin. Isid. Hispana*, but unfortunately on account of the barbar-

two fires. A year or two before Hishâm's time
they had made an attack from Spain on the
Franks. The Emir alHurr first crossed the
Pyrenees,—perhaps, indeed, in Sulaimân's time.
Under Umar II Samh took the town of Narbonne, and it remained for long the vantage-
point and refuge of the Arabs. But when he
pressed further forward to Toulouse he was
beaten by the Franks under Eudo in Dhulqa‘da,
102 (May, 721). His successor Anbasa, after
several expeditions which he did not always lead
in person, in A.H. 108 (726) undertook a great
campaign, during which he died. This was
under Hishâm. Then a pause followed. The
Emirs changed frequently and had their hands
full at home. The Berbers, who formed a very
large contingent of the army, felt themselves
put in the background by the Arabs, and injured in their rights as Muslims and warriors,
and the Arabs themselves were torn by factions.
A change was first effected by Hishâm making
Abdurrahmân b. Abdillâh stattholder instead of
the passionate and hated Haitham. Abdurrahmân had first a thorn to remove from his own
flesh. The Berber Munuza defected from the

ous Latin, it is very hard to understand. It is collected and arranged
by Dr. Ludolf Schwenkow in a Göttingen Lecture of 1894, entitled
" Critical Consideration of the Latin Sources of the History of the
Conquest of Spain by the Arabs." It does not detract from the value
of the exceedingly careful work that the editor frequently follows
perverted ideas of things essentially oriental.

Arabs, and asserted his independence on the
Spanish northern boundary by striking a compact with Eudo and marrying his daughter.
After dealing first with him, Abdurrahmân
turned against Eudo, besieged him between the
Garonne and Dordogne and pursued him in
the direction of the Loire. Then he fell in with
Charles Martel, whom Eudo had called to his
aid, in Ramadân, 114 (Oct., 732) between Tours
and Poitiers. After several days' skirmishing
the Arabs made a wild combined attack, but
the Austrasian Franks held out all day, and the
next morning they saw with astonishment that
their foes had vacated the field after their
leader had fallen. Gibbon paints what would
have happened if the Arabs had conquered.
Perhaps then the Qoran would now be expound-
ed in Oxford, and before a circumcised people
the holiness and truth of the religion of
Muhammad would be set forth from the pulpit.
The service of the Franks to Christian Europe
was great, but the Romans have done even
greater work in the East than they.

At Tours the Arabs were not repulsed once
for all. The Khalifa himself zealously continued
the war against the Franks. Abdurrahmân's
successor, Abdulmalik b. Qatan (A. H. 115=
733) was brought to book by him for not attacking them. Accordingly he set out on the march
but did not get far, for the Christians in the

Pyrenees barred his way and drove him back into the plain. Thereupon Hishâm put in his place Uqba b. Hajjâj (A. H. 117), whose name in the Spanish chroniclers is prettily latinised into Aucupa. But soon the latter was occupied for a considerable time with internal affairs, and when he did set out towards Gaul letters met him in Saragossa, calling him to Africa to help to suppress a rebellion of the Berbers which had broken out there. He then turned and crossed the strait at the transductine promontory[1] with the Spanish-Arabian army. After he thought he had finished his work in Africa he returned to Spain, and died in A.H. 122 (740).

Involuntarily the Berbers proved to be valuable allies of the Franks. They were enraged that they, although good Muslims and zealous participants in the Jihâd, were still treated by the Arab officials as tribute-paying vassals after Umar II was no more. To certain Khârijite emissaries from Iraq, of whom the Sufrite Maisara was named as the chief, they afforded favourable soil for the sowing of their seed. According to Saif in Tab., 1, 2815f. they first loyally enough applied to Hishâm and asked him to redress their grievances, but their embassies were not admitted to his presence at all, and as their

---

[1] According to the Spanish *Continuatio* there also took place on this promontory the battle in which Roderick, King of the Goths, fell, apparently in the neighbourhood of Gibraltar.

funds went down they withdrew, after some
waiting, disillusioned, leaving their names in
writing, just as if they had been leaving their
cards. They were now convinced that the
Khârijites were right in asserting that the
tyranny of the officials was practised by command of the Khalifa himself, who by his greed
of gain compelled them to extort money from
the subjects. Consequently they made a
tremendous revolt under Khârijite leadership,
—a revolt extending from Morocco to Qairawân.
The African Emirs proved powerless against it
and even the help of Uqba from Spain was of
little avail. They had to fall back upon the
veterans, the Syrian imperial troops, who, as in
Iraq, had to come here also. Despatched by
Hishâm, they appeared in A.H. 123 (741) [1] in
great numbers on the scene of warfare in
Morocco, under the command of the prefect
of Damascus, Kulthûm b. Iyâd al Qasrî, [2] but

---

[1]   Thus rightly Balâdh., 232. Acc. to Tab., 1716 (Theoph., A.M.
6231) as early as A.H. 122, but in that year, when Khâlid alQasrî joined
in the campaign in Asia Minor, Kulthûm was still prefect of Damascus.
In Theoph, 6231 he is called $\Delta a\mu a\sigma\kappa\eta\nu\acute{o}s$.

[2]   He is usually called alQushairî, thus everywhere in Balâdh.,
and BAthir; and also in Tab., 1716, 1871. But alQasrî, as he is called
in Tab., 1814ff., is the correct form, for he was a cousin of Khâlid.
"Naturally a Qaisite," remarks Müller, 1,449, as if he knew *a priori*,
in spite of his knowledge of Arab tribal psychology and the government principles of Hishâm (1,445f.). Kulthûm, in truth, was as little
a Qaisite as Mâlik alAshtar (1,325). The inter change of قسرى with
قريشي و قشيرى، قيسى often appears; *cf.* Tab., 1456, 7.

even the well-armed Syrians who were practised
in warfare went down before the half-naked
Berber cavalry. In a great battle on the river
Nauam, graphically described by the Spanish
chronicler, Kulthûm fell, and it was only with
a third of the army that his nephew Balj
managed to escape to Ceuta and thence to
Spain. It was the worst defeat that the Arabs
had ever sustained up till then, incomparably
worse than that of Tours. In the name of Islam
the Berbers dealt the heaviest blow at the Arabs
in the west, even though the latter in the following year won a victory which enabled them to
assert their possession of Qairawân.

In the Oxus territories, too, quite at the
other side of the kingdom, which were always
turbulent, matters were more stormy than usual
under Hishâm. The Soghdians, following their
princes, had gone over to Islam under Umar II,
with the concession that as Muslims they
needed to pay no tribute. As it fell out, however, the stattholders did not adhere to this
condition ; they did as they pleased, and as they
were often changed, one did one way, and
another another. Still, with all of them might
overcame right ; if one did allow a remission of
the tribute, it was a specially granted favour
that was soon revoked. Provoked and irritated
by this, the Soghdians threw themselves into the
arms of their old foes, the Turks, and called

44

them into the country. They had also on their
side the sympathy of the pious Muslims, which
did not express itself merely in words. Against
this coalition it became very difficult for the
ruling Arabs to assert themselves. More than
once their armies got into an extremely dangerous position, and were forced to be content
with escaping with great loss. How much
the Khalifa was accustomed to bad tidings
from Khurasan may be seen when he would
not believe it when there once actually came
to him the news of a victory. His favourite
method of improving matters—namely, changing the *personnel* of the command—frequently
miscarried and always had bad secondary effects,
but at last he really made a *coup*. After the
deposition of Khâlid alQasrî, the latter's successor in Iraq, Yûsuf b. Umar, was inspired with
the hope that Khurasan also would be put under
his rule. He would have placed there a
thorough Qaisite, and increased the party-strife
still more, though that was already bitter
enough, but Hishâm intervened, and on his own
initiative nominated the old Nasr b. Saiyâr
alKinânî, an experienced officer and official not
belonging to any powerful clan in Khurasan.
He asserted himself as well as he could, but
held a hopeless post.

Hishâm died in Rusâfa on Wednesday, 6th
Rabî II, 125 (6th Feb., 743). He was not yet

old,—had just reached the fifties—but he had
never been young. His outward appearance
did not recommend him,—he squinted. Though
he could make himself respected, he nevertheless had not the qualities which make an
immediate impression upon men, to win them or
compel them. He was rather narrow-minded
but prudent and circumspect. Personally he
gave no offence to the pious; he was a correct
Muslim of the old type—a friend of the traditionists azZuhrî and Abû Zinâd, and a foe to the
new-fangled Qadarîya, who raised dogmatic
questions and asserted the freedom of the will
(Tab., 1777—cf. 1733). To his Christian subjects
therefore, he was not intolerant; he restored to
them (the Melchites ?) the possession of the see
of Antiochia, from which they had been debarred for 40 years, under the condition, certainly,
that they chose as Patriarch not a learned and
prominent man, but a simple monk, his friend
Stephanus, to which they agreed.[1] He took his
own son Muhammad severely to task for having
had a Christian, by whom he thought himself
insulted, flogged, instead of complaining of him
before the Qadi. As regent he tried his best
to keep above the parties; if he could only have
wrought a change in the hearts of the Arabs

---

[1] Theoph., A.M. 6234. Cf. 6236. The execution of the Roman
prisoners, if they were not ransomed or did not accept Islam (A.M.
6232), was nothing unusual, but an old right of war.

and stattholders! He had a certain shyness
of publicity, and liked to withdraw into the
back-ground to lonely Rusâfa, and made use of
the mediation of his " *alter ego*," the Kalbite
Abrash, on whom he could rely, in his intercourse with the men who sought him out there.
(Tab., 1,2816. 2,1813). For all that, he held
the reins, understood his *rôle*, and gave all his
zeal to his work. His Diwan, *i.e.* his exchequer, was in perfect order, and was the admira-
tion of the Abbâsid Mansûr. He put a stop to
the abuse of granting the military pension to
prominent people as a benefice (" living "); no
one got it—not even an Umaiyid prince,—who
had not either seen service in war himself, or
sent a substitute. His own share he gave to
his Maula Yâqût, who had to take the field in
his stead. In the anecdotes told of him, which
are as numerous as those related of Umar I,
Muâwia and Abdulmalik, he seems, above all,
to have been very frugal and economical.

This quality, justified perhaps in itself by
the very opposite behaviour of his predecessors,
in his case degenerated into a fatal fault. His
aim was to fill his exchequer. Theophanes,
thus describes him :—

ἤρξατο κτίζειν κατὰ χώραν καὶ πόλιν παλάτια καὶ

κατασπορὰς ποιειν καὶ παραδείσους, καὶ ὕδατα

ἐκβάλλειν.

He did this in his own interest, and thereby aroused such discontent that the Abbâsids in their plan of government thought the best way to recommend themselves to their subjects was to promise not to build any castles or construct any canals. The canal is the estate and the castle belongs to it. As a large land-owner he vied with Khâlid and forbade him to sell his corn before him in case the prices should be reduced. Still worse, he regarded the state itself as an estate from which the greatest possible amount of money was to be extracted. His prudence in the end amounted to a distinct fiscalism. His stattholders had to hand over to him the highest possible sums, and he did not trouble himself about the means they took to extort them. He raised the tribute of Cyprus and doubled that of Alexandria, and drove the subjects in Transoxiana, Africa and Spain to despair. Cupiditate praereptus tanta collectio pecuniarum per duces Oriente et Occidente ab ipso missis est facta, quanta nulla umquam tempore in reges qui ante eum fuerant extitit congregata: unde non modicae populorum katervae cernentes in eo improbam manere cupiditatem ab ejus dicione suas dividunt mentes. This is the account of him in the Spanish *Continuatio* with the usual exaggeration in the estimate of the moneys collected. The opinion of Alfred von Kremer and his successors may be that he reverted to the old sound principles of the Umaiyids, after the alleged wreck of the state-economy by Umar II, but in any case the end of his fairly long and toilsome reign was as unhappy as it could well be. He was popular nowhere, and everywhere had heavy misfortunes. He left the broad kingdom in a far more disconsolate state than he had found it, and it was not mere accident that the propaganda of the Abbâsids became active in his time.

4. In the will by which Yazîd II passed on the Khalifate to his brother Hishâm, he had appointed his own son Walîd as Hishâm's successor. Walîd II was like his father but surpassed him physically. The Spanish Continuator designates him "The Beautiful." He was well-built and of unusual bodily strength, as well as full of life and of great mental gifts, which were awakened and directed by his teacher, the philologist Abdussamad. He grew up at his uncle's court, but his youth was not happy. He did whatever he had a mind to, and nothing more. His future was, of course, assured. From his youth he felt that he was the heir to power and was encouraged in this idea by his frivolous companions. Hishâm regretted his lack of seriousness and dignity, frowning upon the fact that he passed his time at the chase and over the wine-cup in dissolute company, thinking more of music and poetry than of the Qoran.

He tried to correct him, but did not set about it the right way and failed in his purpose. Walîd did not see any kindly intention in the conduct of the irascible old man, but took it to mean that he did not want to bestow the succession upon him. He may not have been altogether wrong in so thinking; it was only natural. In any case the behaviour of the incorrigible at last induced the Khalifa to make arrangements for his disinheritance and the diversion of the rule to one of his own sons, Maslama b. Hishâm.

He encountered determined opposition, however, among his brother clansmen and prominent officials, especially as Maslama himself was also a gay fellow. In the first place Walîd could not be persuaded to waive his claim, but it was really the many kinds of mortification which were consequently inflicted upon him both at the hands of Hishâm and the court circle that drove him to defiance and hatred, and at last he could stand the court no longer. After the death of the old and respected Maslama b. Abdilmalik, who had in some degree kept him in check, he left Rusâfa[1] and withdrew to an outlying place in the desert east of Palestine.[2]

---

[1] This appears evident from Agh., 6,103. It is also plain otherwise that it did not happen till the latter years of Hishâm. Maslama died in A.H. 122.

[2] Acc. to alAbraq or alAzraq, beside the water of alAghdaf between the district of the Balqain and the Fazâra (Agh., 6,104;

There he pursued his old course, only more
unrestrainedly than before. He had no lack of
visitors who speculated upon his generosity and
upon his expectations and sponged upon him.
He was awaiting the death of Hishâm and made
no secret of it. He never put any constraint on
his feelings, and expressed them in verses which
he did not keep to himself.

He had a year or two to wait. Then the
event took place which was longed for by more
than himself. Hishâm's reign was too long for
the people ; they drew a breath of relief when
he closed his eyes. Scarcely was he dead when
Walîd's correspondent in Rusâfa, who till then
was kept in prison, received his liberty and the
provisional government. He sealed up everything so thoroughly that there was left not so
much as a vessel for washing or a piece of cloth
for wrapping the corpse in, which by his orders
had been at once removed from the bed in the
death-chamber. Walîd received the news of
these events along with the insignia of office,[1]
and celebrated the occasion after his thirsty
fashion, also composing a poem in which, as a
spice to his enjoyment, he imagined the grief

Tab., 1743), in 'Ammân (Tab., 1795, 11). From Tab., 1754, 11 we might
conclude that the place was situated near Zîzâ, but that is too far
south.

[1] He himself in Agh., 109,1 (in the sixth book) only speaks of the
ring ; further on (109,18) ring, staff and legal document are mentioned ;
the legal document (Tomâr) is doubtless the certificate of death.

of the dead man's daughters. Then he gave
orders to seize the fortune of Hishâm in Rusâfa
and to arrest his relatives and officials, with the
exception, however, of Maslama b Hishâm ; for
the latter, though really his rival and formerly
greatly scoffed at by him under a disguised name,
had always behaved honourably and good-natur-
edly towards him. He betook himself for a
while to Damascus so as to receive the homage
in the capital (Agh. 111, 12). Deputies came
from all the provinces, the stattholders sent their
respects by letter, gave reports of the homage
done to him in their residences and described
what enthusiasm the change in the rule had
called forth. There was nothing but jubilation.
Then the new Khalifa also showed himself grateful. The means which his predecessor had
hoarded up enabled him to satisfy people's
expectations of him. He increased the pension
everywhere by 10 dirhams but in Syria by 20,
and restored it to the citizens of Medina and
Mecca, from whom Hishâm had taken it away
as a punishment for their sympathy with the
Alid Zaid b. Alî. For the Umaiyids who came
to visit him he doubled the guests' present, provided liberally for the maintenance of the sick
and blind in Syria and for their attendance
and nursing, and lavished perfumes and
clothes upon the wives and children of the
people.

45

But upon his foes he had revenge. He certainly did not direct it straight against the
family of his predecessor, because that would
have aroused the Umaiyids; Sulaimân b.
Hishâm only he had scourged and afterwards
imprisoned in 'Ammân. But the Makhzûmites
Ibrâhîm and Muhammad had to pay the penalty
for having sided against him for the son of
Hishâm, who was descended from their sister.
They were first pilloried and exposed to the
public insults at Medina (Saturday, 17th Sha'-
bân, 125, *i.e.* 14th June, 743), where they had
earned bitter hatred, and then they were sent
to Kufa to Yûsuf b. Umar to be tortured to
death by him,—an order which he conscientious-
ly carried out. The Banu Qa'qâ' of Abs had a
similar fate; they had likewise backed up
Hishâm in his intention to disinherit his nephew
in favour of his son (BAthir, 5, 198). They were
deprived of their power in Qinnesrin and Hims
and delivered over to the vengeance of the
Fazârite Yazîd b. Umar b. Hubaira, whose
father 20 years before was scourged by them
by order of Hishâm. The old brotherly feud
between Abs and Fazâra had here a bloody
sequel. As in Hims and Qinnesrin, so also in
Medina and Damascus he deposed the stattholders of Hishâm and appointed new ones.
To Medina he sent a brother of his mother,
Umm Hajjâj, Yûsuf b. Muhammad b. Yûsuf

athThaqafî; in Damascus he placed a man of the same family, directly descended from Hajjâj, Abdulmalik b. Hajjâj b. Yûsuf, and connected with the Qaisites through his mother's relation.

But in the two chief posts, Iraq and Khurasan, he left the officials whom he found there, Yûsuf b. Umar and Nasr b. Saiyâr. He even retained to the last as his confidant Abrash alKalbî who had enjoyed the same position with Hishâm. His opposition to the latter was entirely of a personal nature. In religion even, though he differed very much in person from the latter's type, he was not so very different in principles. Of the two theologian friends of his predecessor he hated the one who had expressed his displeasure at him, and was inclined to the other who had prudently kept silent. He maintained the same hostility as Hishâm towards the heretical Qadarites, and gave his unqualified assent to the banishment of their chiefs to the island of Dahlak (near Massaua), and maintained it strictly. Religion was not to pass from use and wont into reflection. Theophanes might, from some of his accounts, give the impression that he persecuted the Christians, but it does not seem like him. As a matter of fact he does not appear to have had anything to do with the measures taken against the metropolitan Petrus of Damascus and the

finance-official Petrus of Maiuma.   Both of these
incurred their martyrdom by insulting Islam
and the Prophet.   The transference of the
Cyprians to Syria had nothing to do with
religion.

On the whole Walîd II only played with
his power.   He treated the duties of governor
as sport and never occupied himself seriously
and carefully with them.   Even as Khalifa he
kept his residence in the desert in the district
east of the Jordan (Tab., 1795, 11).   The bitter,
misanthropic disposition of his youth never
left him.   Even after the death of Hishâm he
kept at a distance from the circle to which he
really belonged, and cut himself off from that of
his relatives and peers (Agh., 137, 6).   For
public opinion he had no regard whatever, and
never allowed it to affect him.   He had, of
course, a government office at the court, but
horses and hounds, singers male and female,
poets and litterateurs formed, as before, the
intimate circle in which he liked to live.   By
day he scoured the desert, feats of physical
exercise were easy and necessary to him.   He
could, when springing into the saddle, tear out
of the ground a peg to which his foot was fastened.   The nights he passed in carousing.   He
was distinguished by a foolish, frothy sense of
power.   He wished that all women were lioness-
es so that only strong and courageous men

should dare to approach them. But he did not
sink into common wildness. in his case his
intimacy with the maidens was compatible with
an enthusiastic love for a noble lady whom he
had long wooed in vain, and whom he soon lost
again by death. Every occasion stirred him to
little songs in which he crystallised the mood of
the moment with grace, lightness and originality.
His biography might be collected from these
if only they had been preserved to us more
completely, but as he was Khalifa his poetry
could not be collected and published, but only
stolen. He actually sometimes preached in
verse. He could do everything, but everything
was to him only a whim and his whims changed
in the turning of a hand. He would plunge
into a learned theological conversation, and
then again he would have a drinking-bout and
scoff at the holy man. He could not refuse
any one a request, and yet at the same time
could be not only passionate but fierce like a
child. Power was a curse to him.[1]

He got through Hishâm's money sooner than
he thought. His regular revenues were not
sufficient for him; he required extraordinary
ones. Yûsuf b. Umar used this fact to buy

---

[1] *Cf.* the article upon him in Agh., 6, 101 ff., much of which is
unreliable. When they sought to stir him up against the Khalifa,
Khâlid alQasrî said that he did not know whether the rumours about
him were true or not (Tab., 1776f.).

over to himself Nasr b. Saiyâr, who was made independent of him. He offered a large sum if Khurasan were again restored to him and got the bargain made. The Khalifa summoned Nasr with his whole family and enjoined upon him that he must bring with him hunting-falcons and horses, musical instruments, gold and silver vessels. To get what was wanted and many beautiful maidens and richly-accoutred slaves as well. Nasr spared no expense, but it took time, and when at last he set out he got news of Walîd's murder and turned back again.

On the other hand the diabolical Yûsuf after repeated vain endeavours, succeeded in getting Khâlid alQasrî into his power. Walîd should have had reason to be grateful to this man, for under Hishâm he had stepped in on his behalf, and even after Hishâm's death let no entice-ments induce him to break faith with him. But he did not trust him, because he knew more than he dared to say. He put him in prison and tried to extort from him all manner of things which the latter would not betray for fear of getting others into misfortune. When he could not make him yield by force he at last sold him to his deadly foes for many millions. Yûsuf transported him with the utmost cruelty to Kufa and there tortured him to death, but could not break his pride or even contrive to make him cry out or distort his features. He died on the rack in Muharram, 126 (Nov., 743) and was buried in Hira.

Shortly before this (Tab , 1820) Yahyâ b. Zaid b. Alî had been killed. The Khalifa had his head sent to him and exhibited it to a distinguished company bidden specially for the purpose, and increased the bitterness which his conduct called forth in the wide circles of the East by the command to treat the calf of Iraq as once the idol of the Hebrews was treated, namely to burn it and scatter the ashes on the water. But the feeling excited by the slow execution of Khâlid was, as we can understand, at the moment still worse. It might be taken as an insult to the Yemen,—Yûsuf against Khâlid meant Qais against Yemen, and the Khalifa apparently identified himself with Yûsuf and the other Hajjâjids. Verses, both spurious and genuine, had the effect of its being so taken up. For the first time there arose a general political agitation in Iraq and in Syria which bound together the Yemenites in both places. The Syrian Yemenites, particularly the Kalbites, were most strongly seized by it, because Khâlid had spent his last years with them in Damascus and had there won many friends. But the feeling was directed far less against the Qais in general than against the Khalifa specially, and it was stirred up by his personal enemies and used as a means to their own particular end.

The participation in the factious rising which resulted from it was not at all general, and even if it might emanate from the Yemenites it was not a matter of Yemenites exclusively on one side and Qaisites exclusively on the other. The Qaisite Abs sided against the Khalifa because he had enraged them by his behaviour to the Banû Qa'qâ'; on the other side there came to his aid not only Bahrânites from Hims (wrongly called Qaisites by A. Müller), but also Kalbites of the tribe of 'Âmir and the family of Sulaim b. Kaisân. The fire did not break out at once with elemental force, but only reached the furthest circles through the murder of Walîd. Any occasion sufficed to awaken the slumbering danger and to bring the morbid tendency to a head; every dispute inclined to degenerate into the general tribe-feud. Naturally Islam bore its part in this as well. The pious were enraged at the godless Khalifa (Tab., 1837), especially the Qadarites, who had most reason.

As far back as the time when Khâlid alQasrî was still living in Damascus, a plot was made against Walîd. The chief conspirators were his own clansmen, Umaiyid princes, though they were not perhaps the intellectual originators of it (Tab., 1823). They were his counsellors by birth, but he withdrew from their company, their influence and their sway, and threatened to dissipate the inheritance of his fathers, to

which they also had a claim. He also offended
them by appointing as his successors two of his
sons, without intermediary,—an arrangement
of which he had had bitter experience in his
youth—although they were still minors, besides
being children of a slave, and for both reasons,
according to Arab and Islamic ideas, not eligible
to reign.[1] By this proceeding the numerous
(Tab., 1794) sons of Walîd I in particular felt
badly used. Their father was Abdulmalik's
first-born, and even at the death of Sulaimân
they had counted upon the succession (Tab.,
1345), but they had never yet had their turn,
and now they were to be supplanted by the
descendants of Yazîd II. The sons of Hishâm
and also the other Marwânids sided with them;
they were not in favour with their reigning
cousin and were sure that he had any amount
of punishments in store for them. Their
helpers, and it may be their instigators, were
prominent Kalbites [2] in Damascus, discontented
and slighted officers and officials who are said
to have attached themselves already to Khâlid
alQasrî in order to stir him up. Their names
are enumerated in Tab., 1778, but it is Mansûr

---

[1] *Cf.* the two letters of Walîd to Nasr in Tab., 1755-64 of Tuesday,
22nd Rajab, 125 (21st May, 743) and of Thursday, 15th Sha'bân, 125
(13th June, 743) written from Samâl and Nadr. Khâlid alQasrî was
disinclined to pay homage in advance to the two children (Tab., 1776).

[2] Some genuine south-Arabian families were allied with the
Kalb, living in the neighbourhood of Damascus.

46

b. Jumhûr who gets most mention later. Naturally the sons of Khâlid alQasrî were also of the party, and Yazîd b. Khâlid emerged from his hiding-place and played a prominent part. On the other hand the Sufyânids took the side of Walîd II, who belonged to them in so far as he was descended through his grandmother from Yazîd b. Muâwia b. Abî Sufyân. Abû Muhammad (Ziâd b. Abdillâh b. Yazîd b. Muâwia) asSufyânî is most prominent among them, and a Marwânid actually stuck to him and had his confidence, Abbâs b. Walîd b. Abdilmalik.

The most ambitious amongst his brothers, and the son of a captive Soghdian princess, Yazîd b. Walîd b. Abdilmalik had himself put forward as opposition Khalifa. He gained men to his side by squandering quantities of money (Theoph., 6235), and managed to captivate even the pious by his speech and manner (Tab., 1837, 1867). At the appointed time he rode in disguise on an ass to Damascus with a few followers, and from thence got into communication with his partisans, who for the most part lived not in the town itself but in the country round about. With their help he forced his way into the chief mosque, in which there was a great store of arms, on a Friday,[1] the day of the special service, a day specially to be chosen for such a movement.

---

[1] An exact date is not given.

He arrested the officials in the town, and had also the absent stattholder[1] and the Emir of Baalbekk apprehended. Through the opened gates there came to join him 1,500 Kalbites from Mizza, and from other neighbouring districts people of Ghassân, Lakhm, Kinda and so on, especially from the south-Arabian clans. Nowhere did serious opposition arise. Evidently the government in Syria had not any great number of soldiers ready. As early as the forenoon of the following day Yazîd III received the homage of the Damascenes. He was in good spirits and hummed a song, to the astonishment of his pious companions; till then he had had nothing but the Qoran on his lips. But when he now invited volunteers to fight against the lawful Khalifa, few came forward. He had to put the reward he offered at a higher figure before he could muster 2,000 men. The command he made over to his cousin Abdulazîz.

Walîd II's reward to the messenger who brought him the first news of the rising was 100 lashes. The counsel of his loyal friends to flee to Hims or Tadmor or any nearer fortified towns he at first rejected, and it was only at the last moment when the army of Abdulazîz was already on the march that he left Aghdaf and took refuge in the fortified castle of Bakhrâ,

---

[1] He was afraid of the bad air of Damascus and lived in Qatan.

not far away. He had with him 200 men, and several small companies of horsemen hastened to him from near and far, Kalbites from Tadmor (under a nephew of Abrash), Bahrânites from Hims and others. Even Abbâs b. Walîd with his thirty sons set out to his aid, but was caught just in the nick of time by Abdulazîz and forced to join his army.

Messenger after messenger kept announcing to Walîd the ever nearer approach of the foe ; he did not trouble about it till he saw them before him. His meagre troops were encamped in Arab fashion before the citadel. They got from him, since his ready money was exhausted, only a note of hand on the future, and considered the present hopeless. The defection of Abbâs to the opposite side set them a dangerous example, and, besides, the Kalbites of Tadmor were not inclined to fight against the Kalbites of Damascus. Under these conditions it was an easy game for Abdulazîz when he advanced to the attack at sunrise. Walîd, who took part himself in the battle and fought with the greatest bravery, soon found himself forsaken by everyone. He then withdrew again into the citadel, sat down in an inner room and read the Qoran, so as to meet death like Uthmân, and thus he received his death-blow.[1] A piece of his

---

[1] The names of those who rushed in upon him and attacked him are enumerated in Tab., 1830. *Cf* Tab., 1778.

skin as large as a man's hand was delivered to
the heir of Khâlid alQasrî as a voucher of
completed revenge. The head was severed by a
man who bore the nickname "Farthing-Face"
(*Wajh al-Fals* ; Tab., II, 1809,5), and delivered
to Yazîd. The latter had it exposed and carried
around everywhere, and only gave it up to the
brother of the murdered man a month after,
but he, out of cowardice did not dare to bury it,
alleging religious reasons. The day of the
catastrophe was Thursday, 27th Jumâdâ II, 126,
i.e. Thursday, 17th April, 744.[1] If we are to
believe Yazîd III, he was called to rule by the
will of the people, and Walîd was killed in
necessary self-defence, as he answered with the
sword the pacific invitation to leave the settlement of the impending dispute to a *Shûrâ* (an
advisory council), and so was the first to shed
blood (Tab., 1843ff.). When the deed became
known in Hims, the inhabitants destroyed the
palace of Abbâs b. Walîd, whom they regarded
as a traitor, and marched upon Damascus with
the idea that the Sufyânid, Abû Muhammad,
whom they had put at their head, had only to
show himself in front of the town and it would
surrender to him. But it fell out otherwise.

---

[1] In Tab., 1810, 6 (Tanbîh, 324) Thursday is given as the 27th
Jumâdâ, but in 1836, 14, Wednesday. Theophanes, A.M. 6235,
makes it Thursday, 16th April ; Elias Nisibenus says Thursday, 25th
Jumâdâ II.

They were totally defeated by Sulaimân b. Hishâm near Damascus and would have been annihilated had not Yazîd b. Khâlid alQasrî and the Kalbites intervened. Abû Muhammad was forced to enter the Khadrâ, the prison of the capital, where two other Sufyânids and Walîd II's two sons were. In the Palestine provinces also insurrections were suppressed without much trouble, either by force or clemency.

5. At the homage ceremony in Damascus Yazîd III made a significant opening speech, in which he took as his pattern the Holy One of the Umaiyids, Umar II. He pledged himself to erect no buildings, construct no canals, store up no treasure, to spend the moneys which accumulated in a province absolutely upon itself, not to keep those in military service too long in the field so that neither they nor their wives should fall into temptation, not to burden the non-Muslim proprietors so much as to make them leave house and home in despair, and always to listen to the complaint of the weak against the strong. "If I fail to do so, then you may depose me or demand atonement from me; if you know a fitter man than me, then put him at your head and I will be the first to do him homage ; not to man is paid unconditional obedience, but to God only." In this the Khalifa indeed spoke sincerely to the Qadarites, who

in their political principles are said to have been
at one with the Murjiites with whom he was
coquetting at the same time (Tab., 1867, 1874).
He was loudly praised by the pious demagogue
Qais b. Hâni alAbsî, who spoke next, for
such a fine and proper assumption of the duty
of a ruler, and at the same time exhorted to
keep his word now, and, if necessary, let him
self be deposed willingly. He further promised
to pay the soldiers' wages duly at the beginning
of the year and the allowance every month,—
which was thus just as far from being a matter
of course as it is today in Turkey. However,
he again reduced the amount of the pay which
had been raised by his predecessor. From this
he received the nickname "nâqis" (lacking),

ὁ λείψος.

He relied to a marked degree upon the
Yemenites and in particular the Kalbites; not
a Qaisite was to be found in his circle (Tab.,
1837). The Kalbite Mansûr b. Jumhûr was
elected stattholder of Iraq, a foolhardy, ruthless
man, and he departed immediately after the
murder of Walîd into his province. 500 Qaisites who were to have lain in wait for him let
themselves quietly be stripped of their arms by
him though he had only 30, or some say only
7, men with him. Yûsuf b. Umar got no
support from the Syrian government troops in

Hira and Kufa; the domestic garrison was, even at that time, a negligible quantity. His attempt to separate the Qaisites from the Kalbites miscarried; they said to him,—"We belong also to the people of Syria and own allegiance to the same Khalifa as they." After Walîd II's death they had no longer an Imâm and did not know whom to fight for. The little, long-bearded goblin wavered between defiance and despair; one moment he stood on tip-toe and then sank back into himself again. He would have fallen into the hands of Mansûr, who had intentions upon his person, had not the colonel of the Syrians in Hira, the Kalbite Sulaimân b. Sulaim, saved him, by urging him and making it possible for him to flee. He went into hiding in the Balqâ, in the East Jordan district, but did not long remain hidden there. He was dragged out of the women's apartment by a Kalbite and then thrown into the Khadrâ of Damascus, where the little man made himself ridiculous by his silly fears, and by his long beard afforded opportunities for practical jokes at his expense. They had the toad on a string.

Mansûr b. Jumhûr entered Hira and Kufa as early as the beginning of Rajab, 126 (the end of April, 744), took possession of the treasury, paid the overdue wages and set the prisoners free. The towns of Wasit and Basra accepted his officials without opposition, but he did not

long keep the upper hand in Iraq. In Ramadân or Shauwâl, 126 (July, 744) Yazîd put in
his place Abdullâh b. Umar. who he might be
sure would be specially acceptable to the Iraqites as the son of his father, the Khalifa
Umar II.

The province of Sajistân and Sind likewise
recognised the new Khalifa and received a Kalbite as stattholder. Egypt also, according to
Theophanes, submitted to him, but it is incorrect
for the Spanish Continuator to assert: omnes
suae patriae (eum) ocius recognoscunt. Nasr b.
Saiyâr in Khurasan and Marwân b. Muhammad
in Armenia and Mesopotamia did not consider
themselves his officials, and adopted the course
of waiting to see what would happen. They
had not long to wait. Yazîd died on Friday,
12th Dhulhijja, 126 (25th Sepr., 744), 162 days [1]
after his accession. He had appointed as his
successor his brother Ibrâhîm b. Walîd, and
that, indeed, as is specially noteworthy, at the
instance of the Qadarites, who thus exercised
over him more than a mere religious influence.

---

[1]   Thus rightly Elias Nisibenus.

CHAPTER VII.

MARWÀN AND THE THIRD CIVIL WAR.

The deed of violence done upon Walîd II was the signal for the overthrow of the Umaiyid dynasty. The ruling family had committed political suicide. Even in Syria its lawful authority and the sanctity of its Khalifate were no more. Even Syria, the corner-stone of the existing order, was drawn into the whirlpool of revolution; there too the revolutionary piety found a footing and gained ground. The Kalbites themselves, hitherto the most loyal of the loyal and the bodyguard of the government, broke their allegiance and let themselves be led to revolt against the rightful ruler. How the shock in the centre of the kingdom affected the periphery can be imagined. Everywhere the bonds which held in check the centrifugal forces were loosed; manifold varieties of opposition reared themselves everywhere. Changing shapes emerged from the chaos; the elements ran together around any centre at all and then again separated to form other combinations. It was just the time for adventurers and place-hunters; in a flash they rose to tremendous power, and then disappeared into nothingness.

In opposition to the successors of Abdulmalik, and in particular to the sons of Walîd I and
Hishâm, who were guilty of, and had profited
by, the murder of Walîd II, there arose a bastard [1] from a side-branch of the reigning family,
Marwân b. Muhammad b. Marwân, a man then
between 50 and 60 years of age (Tab., 940). He
was in mockery called the "ass" because he
liked the peony, which was called the "ass's
rose." [2] His father Muhammad, Abdulmalik's
brother, had for long years been governor of
Mesopotamia and Armenia and as such had
carried on the hostilities against the Romans.
Then Maslama b. Abdilmalik and others had
taken his place. Marwân made his first appearance in the year 115 and was put over at least
Armenia and Âdharbaijân. It was a post which
required a soldier, and Marwân proved himself
one by energetically protecting the Caucasian
boundary against the Turks, and undertaking
successful raids into their territory. This post,
which he held for 12 years, was for him a military school. The army organisation was then
gradually undergoing a change and developing
more in a technical way. The old militia, the
Muqâtila, proved pretty useless for tedious and

---

[1] Anon. Ahlw., p. 26.

[2] Thus acc. to Syrian chroniclers. A. Müller, 1,453 explains the
surname off-hand as *Elogium* and refers to Iliad, 11, 558. Marwân is
also called alJa'dî, for what reason I cannot say. *Cf.* Tab., 1912.

distant campaigns, and for interests which did
not closely affect them. They were abolished
and replaced by Syrian government troops. It
was of little use trying to achieve military de-
signs under the system of fixed pensions for
every Arab capable of bearing arms. If men
were wanted who would obey orders and go
where they were led, it had to be made worth
their while. Yazîd I paid to everyone who
was ready to march against Medina and Mecca
100 dinars over and above the full year's pension. Yazîd III offered to those who enlisted
to fight against Walîd II, 2,000 dirhams each,
while Walîd II, on his part, offered his defenders 500 dirhams each. The Syrians who in the
year 130 (748) took the field against the South-
Arabian Khawârij got every man 100 dinars,
a war-horse and a beast of burden. Even the
Khârijite Dahhâk won his men by the high pay
which he gave (Tab., 1939). Regular regiments,
as the backbone of the army, more and more
took the place of the tribes, its old frame-work;
instead of the tribe-leaders there appeared as
commanders generals whose business it was
(Qâid), and the regiments were partly named
after them, as the Waddâhîya and the Dhakwânîya after Waddâh and (Muslim) Ibn Dhak-
wân. Alongside of this there came about an
improvement in tactics. Before, they had
fought, according to old Arab custom, and one

hallowed by the example of the Prophet himself, in *Sufûf*, (long lines); in the intervening
space between the opposing lines the single
combats took place, according to the issue of
which it often was decided whether the main
body should advance or flee. Now the old
clumsy *Sufûf* were done away with and replaced by *Karâdîs*, smaller units, which were at
once more compact and more movable. The
institution of these *Karâdîs* is ascribed to Marwân b. Muhammad, and even if it goes further
back in its origin, he at any rate brought it to
completion. The fact that he was regarded as
the originator of it shows how great was his
reputation as a military organiser.

He was besides well versed in political intrigue. He kept up connections on all sides
and had exact information of everything that
was on foot in every place. When Walîd II
succeeded, he tendered his sincere congratulations, at the same time censuring Hishâm,
even though it was he whom he had to thank
for his position. In an earnest letter he condemned the conspiracy against him, while at
the same time making a display of sentiments
quite different (Tab., 1853). In any case the
murder of Walîd was very opportune for him;
he was able to rise up against its perpetrators
as avenger, and under a good pretext wrest the
spoil from them. When tidings of the event

arrived he tendered his allegiance to Yazîd III by setting out from Armenia to Mesopotamia. His son Abdulmalik had already taken possession of this province for him, since the change of ruler obliged the stattholder to leave it. In his rear, however, the Syrian Yemenites under Thâbit b. Nuaim alJudhâmî mutinied. These he had left behind by the Caucasian Gate, as a protection against the Turks, because he did not altogether trust them. They would do homage to no other Khalifa than the one their brothers in Syria did homage to, and demanded to be led back home, and this obliged him to turn back again. They gave way to him and handed over Thâbit, but they got their demand acceded to. Marwân allowed them, together with the Mesopotamian Qaisites, who formed the nucleus of his army, to march as far as Harrân. From there he discharged them. He himself remained in Harrân, thinking it advisable to do homage to Yazîd III, all the more since the latter was ready to give over to him the whole district which formerly in Abdulmalik's time had been governed by his father, —Mesopotamia, Mosul, Armenia and Âdharbaijân.

Yazîd III, however, died just six months after his accession, and against the successor he had appointed, Ibrâhîm b. Walîd, who was only recognised in the southern part of Syria,

Marwân immediately set on foot his original
plot. He advanced into Syria over the Euphrates; the Qaisites of Qinnesrin under Yûsuf
b. Umar b. Hubaira joined him, and the Arabs
of Hims [1] also went over to him. He met no
opposition till he got to near Ain alJarr on a
brook of the Antilibanus, which unites with
the Lita. There, under Sulaimân b. Hishâm,
the son of the Khalifa Hishâm,[2] stood the
army of the southern Syrians. This Sulaimân
b. Hishâm had spent his whole youth in war
against the Romans, and was at his best in the
field at the head of his troops. His bodyguard
were the Dhakwânîya. He now encountered
Marwân for the first time, and often later, but
he was no match for him; he was defeated and
fled back to Damascus. His great army broke
up; the victor exercised moderation, only
executing two Kalbites who had fallen into his
hands, and who had taken part in the murder of
Walîd. To the rest of the prisoners he made
presents and let them go free, but they had
first to do homage to the two sons of Walîd who
lay in the prison of Damascus. Marwân
prudently did not come forward in his own

[1] In Theophanes, A. M. 6235 *Emesa* is, of course, to be read instead
of *Edesa*.

[2] The site is described by Theophanes; he calls the place Garis,
and translates Lita as if it were called " the accursed." In Syriac the
place is called En Gara, *cf.* D.M.Z., 1897, p. 581. Ain alJarr lies on
the road from Baalbekk to Damascus, Tab., 3,48.

name, but as the deputy of the heirs of Walîd II, and this cost the latter their lives, since they were in the power of the enemy. For if they came to rule it was plainly to be foreseen that they would take the most terrible revenge upon the murderers of their father, and not even spare the sons of Abdulmalik. So Sulaimân had them executed as soon as he got back to Damascus. Yazîd b. Khâlid alQasrî carried out the order, and killed also Yûsuf b. Umar in prison, whilst Abû Muhammad asSufyânî managed to escape and get into hiding. Then Sulaimân succeeded, just in time before Marwân arrived, in getting away with as much treasure as he could collect in the hurry. He went with Ibrâhîm to Tadmor, the headquarters of the Kalbites.

Now that the two sons of Walîd were successfully removed, Marwân II had homage paid to himself in Damascus on Monday, 26th Safar, 127, i.e. 7th Decr., 744.[1] The first to do homage to him was Abû Muhammad asSufyânî; he asserted that the sons of Walîd had, at their death, made a disposition in favour of Marwân, and complained bitterly that on his mother's side he was connected with the detestable Kalbites, and therefore forfeited the claim to the Khalifate. According to Theophanes,

---

[1] So rightly Elias Nisibenus, only the Tuesday named by him should be corrected to Monday, acc. to the *Tanbîh* in which, on the other hand, the day of the month is wrongly given.

Marwân, after he had occupied Damascus, put to death many prominent people who were accomplices in the murder of Walîd and his sons, and mutilated others. This is hardly correct. He may, indeed, have punished one or two of the actual murderers of Walîd, when he got hold of them. He also seems to have taken severe action against the religious revolutionaries. He executed that Qais b. Hâni alAbsî who had expressed himself so freely at the paying of homage to Yazîd III, and he persecuted the Qadarites,[1] who had been pampered by his predecessor. But according to the Arab tradition he marched into Damascus for the first time without drawing the sword, and did not appear at all in the guise of an avenger. It was not by his orders that the body of Yazîd was exhumed and, in addition, hanged. He even granted to the Arabs of the four great Syrian provinces [2] that they might choose their Wâlî themselves, and he thus consented to Thâbit b. Nuaim becoming Wâlî of Filistîn, the very man who had led the rising of the Syrian soldiers in the Caucasus against him. His aim was to awaken confidence and soothe people's minds. When he returned to Harrân after his work

---

[1] Acc. to Theoph , 6241 he was a fatalist, being an opponent of the doctrine of free will. The truth was, he followed not dogmatic but political considerations.

[2] Filistîn, Urdunn, Damascus and Hims. Qinnesrîn as Qaisite is included with Mesopotamia and separated from Syria.

was completed, his two chief opponents actually came to him and were received into favour, namely, Sulaimân b. Hishâm and the Khalifa Ibrâhîm.

Marwân's struggle against the sons of Abdulmalik was a struggle against the Kalb and Qudâa. The Qais adhered to him and fought for him. He now took up his residence in the midst of the Qais, in the Mesopotamian Harrân. There his father had lived, there he himself had grown up, and there he felt at home.[1] All his predecessors, so it says in the *Tanbîh*, resided at Damascus, a few indeed preferring to sojourn in the desert. In any case, if they did keep away from Damascus, it was not for political reasons, nor with the view of degrading the town from its position as capital. Marwân, however, seems to have really had this intention. He transferred the seat of government to Harrân, and, Theophanes says, also transferred all the business and the treasure from Damascus thither. This had dangerous results for him. All Syria felt, with Damascus, robbed of the government, with the exception, perhaps, of the northern part. The party differences were more and more absorbed in this feeling; people wished for the earlier times back again. Naturally, too, the sympathy with

---

[1] Theophanes explains his fatalism by his close connection with the Aramaeans of Harrân, who had remained heathen.

the lawful ruling family which had been dethroned, and which had ties and connections everywhere, was not so easily rooted out and transferred to the alien usurper, whose mother was a slave.

It was still the year 127 when Syria revolted against Marwân.[1] The rising appears to have started from Filistîn, for Thâbit b. Nuaim was the moving spirit of it, but it extended on all sides and actually spread over the town of Hims, which till then had stuck to Walîd II and to Marwân. On the 2nd Shauwâl, 127, *i.e.* 7th July, 745,[2] Marwân appeared before Hims. Then the inhabitants' courage failed ; they admitted him and betrayed the thousand Kalbite troopers who had hastened to their aid from Tadmor.[3] Marwân now despatched a strong

---

[1] Wâqidî in Tab., 1742 gives the year 128 : Elias Nisibenus actually the year 129. I follow Theoph. (A. M. 6236) and the chief report in Tab. (1890ff.), the reasons for which I shall give in the course of the following statement. Confusion was easily possible because Hims was twice besieged by Marwân, in A.H. 127 and A.H. 128.

[2] Two days after the Fitr, 127 (Tab., 1893).

[3] Acc. to Theophanes, 6236 he had 120 Kalbites ($X\alpha\lambda\beta\epsilon\nu\omega$) hanged, but acc. to Tab. it was only the bodies of the fallen. Abbâs b. Walîd I lived in Hims. The people of Emessa had destroyed his palace in A.H. 126 because he had gone over to the foes of Walîd II. Later, however, he seems to have gained an influence over them again, and to have brought about a political change of mind amongst them and persuaded them to the revolt against Marwân. For the latter, after the taking of Hims, had him seized and put to death in prison. A negro was made to thrust his head into a bag of lime which was brought to the boil. At this the Christians whom Abbâs,

corps to Damascus to relieve the town which was besieged by the Arabs of the country under Yazîd ¡b. Khâlid alQasrî. The besiegers were scattered, Yazîd slain, the Kalbites' nest, Mizza, burnt down. Then an advance was made against the capital of the Urdunn,—Tiberias. Thâbit b. Nuaim, who besieged it, was repulsed, then defeated once again in Filistîn, and finally taken prisoner.[1] He and his sons were executed, after having their hands and feet cut off, and the mutilated bodies were exposed in Damascus. At last came the turn of the only place still rebellious, Tadmor, the headquarters of the Kalbites. Marwân marched thither himself, but Abrash managed to avert the worst and negotiate a peace. The chiefs of the town waited upon Marwân; some few only who did not trust him fled into the desert.

Marwân had homage paid to his two sons in Damascus, and married them to daughters of Hishâm, assembling the whole house of Umaiya to the wedding. It was an act of statesmanship; he thought he could even now reconcile and ally

a zealous Muslim, had incited against himself, rejoiced. They were at that time still numerous in Hims, and may have taken their share in the surrender of the town to Marwân, who was far removed from the fanaticism of Islam. *Cf.* Theoph., A. M. 6236; his exact accounts are to be preferred to those of the summary in Tab., 3, 43.

[1] Acc. to Wâqidî in Tab., 1942, not till Shauwâl, 128. That Nuaim b. Thâbit is none other than Thâbit b. Nuaim is plain from the gentilic alJudhâmî.

the family with himself. He called up the
Syrians also to the campaign which he had on
hand against Iraq, which had not yet submitted
to him. He raised 10,000 men from them,
equipped them with arms and horses, and
ordered them to join forces with the 20,000
Mesopotamians and Qinnesrites already on the
march down the Euphrates under (Yazîd) Ibn
(Umar b.) Hubaira at the beginning of 128
(autumn, 745). As these 10,000 were passing
Rusâfa, they persuaded Sulaimân b. Hishâm,
who was living there in his father's residence,
to put himself at their head as Khalifa. Although
he had been very mercifully treated by Marwân,
and had good reason to keep faith with him,
still the restless, war-loving man could not
withstand the temptation which came in his
way. He took possession of the town Qinnesrin,
which was destitute of troops. From all sides
the Syrians poured in thither to him, so that in
the end he is said to have had 70,000 men under
his standard. Marwân now left a minor portion
of the troops which were on the way to Kufa
under the command of Ibn Hubaira near
Dûrîn, and led the greater portion in person
back against the rebel who had arisen in his
rear. He attacked Sulaimân in his camp
near Khufâf, not far from Qinnesrin, and utterly
defeated him. To the captured Arabs he showed
no mercy ; they had to suffer death unless they

passed themselves off as slaves, and as such were spared. Tabarî tells of 30,000 prisoners who were slain, but Theophanes only mentions 7,000 who fell altogether. Sulaimân with the remnant of his army made for Hims, but fled thence, on the approach of the enemy, to Tadmor and then on to Kufa. The army remained in Hims under the command of his brother Saîd. This town was now besieged for the second time by Marwân, and this time was only forced to surrender after 4 months and 22 days.[1] Marwân executed a few of his deadliest foes; Saîd b. Hishâm and his sons he threw into prison.[2] When he arrested and imprisoned Abû Muhammad asSufyânî is not mentioned, but the fact in itself is confirmed by Tabarî, 3,43, and is interesting because it shows that even this Umaiyid was carried away by the general current. The walls of Hims were rased to the ground; likewise those of Baalbekk, Damascus, Jerusalem and other prominent Syrian towns;

[1] Thus Elias; cf. Theoph, 6237. Tab., 1912 gives ten months, but there is no room for that ; that may possibly be the duration of the whole campaign of the year 128.

[2] Acc. to Theoph. he put to death all Hishâm's relatives and clients, but that is incorrect, cf. Tab., 3,43 with 2,1912. The slaying of the Saksakî celebrated as champion of the Syrians is in Tab., 2,1912 twice related in different ways by the same narrator. Muâwia alSaksakî and Abû Ilâqa alSaksakî are, where possible, to be distinguished from each other. The latter is also called alQudâî, though the Saksak had only allied themselves with the Qudâa and did not actually belong to them.

but not those of Antiochia, where the population
was mostly Christian.[1] Accordingly, Marwân
seems to have unexpectedly met opposition in
these places even then.[2] In the summer of 128
(746) he had finished with Syria; it lay in
fragments at his feet.

2. Meanwhile in the east of the kingdom
everything had gone topsy-turvy. In Iraq
Yazîd III had, in Ramadân or Shauwâl, 126
(July, 744), made a son of the pious Khalifa
Umar II stattholder, in place of the Kalbite
Mansûr b. Jumhûr, who nevertheless retained an
influential position in Kufa. Hîra was and remained the seat of government and the headquarters of the Syrian soldiers. It was to a certain
extent the fortress of Kufa. Besides, the capital was held in check by the citadel, where the
town-prefect had a Shurta (body of police)
at his disposal. Naturally the Kufaites were
not on friendly terms with the foreign military.
Ibn Umar sought to gain their good-will.
Possibly the continual changing of town-
prefects which he went in for (Tab., 1902) was
intended partly to serve this end, but his chief
method was money. He gave back to the Arab
troops the pension which was withdrawn from
them, because they, in point of fact, performed

---

[1] Theoph., 6?37, 6241.

[2] Thus Wâqidî may not be wrong in making the imprisonment and
punishment of Thâbit b. Nuaim not happen till this time.

no war service and took up arms chiefly to raise rebellions. After the death of Yazîd III, on the accession of Ibrâhîm, he raised the amount still more. The Syrians murmured at it,—" Thou dividest our Fai (booty) amongst these folk, who, forsooth, are our foes." But the Kufaites saw only the weakness of the apparent kindness, and when Yazîd III died, they considered his position so insecure that they tried to instigate a rebellion against him.

At that time there was sojourning among them a man who could be reckoned as belonging to the family of the Prophet, Abdullâh Ibn Muâwia b. Abdillâh b. Ja'far, a great-grandson of Alî's brother Ja'far. He had come with his brothers as suppliants to Ibn Umar, and then remained in Kufa and married into a distinguished family. His descent seemed to warrant his fitness to be a pretender, and he was ready to let himself be put forward as such. The Zaidîya, *i.e.* the Shiites who a few years before had rebelled under Zaid b. Alî against the government of Hishâm, formed his principal adherents. They led him into the citadel and drove the prefect out. There were many Mawâlî among them, but the rest of the Kufaites also did homage to Ibn Muâwia. They then marched with him into Hira against Ibn Umar. The latter was anything but energetic, he simply would let nothing disturb his peace of mind. If the waters would not subside, he then swam with the stream, and found that it was possible to get on that way too ; so while he himself ate and drank he left it to his Syrian soldiers to meet the attack. It was not a serious matter. The Kufaites ran away when it came to fighting, in Muharram, 127 (Oct.-Nov. 744). The Zaidîya alone fought bravely, and continued the struggle for some days more in the citadel and in the streets of Kufa, until security to them and a free retreat to Ibn Muâwia were granted.

The latter now betook himself to Media *via* Madâin. He was not yet played out; instead of diminishing, his adherents increased. Many people from Kufa and other places flocked to him, notably Mawâlî and retainers, *i.e.* Iranians. He first settled in Ispahan, but in A.H. 128 (745-746) went to Istakhr in Fârs. Large tracts of Media, Ahwâz, Fârs and Karmân submitted to him, as he seemed from his descent to be called to the ruling power. Other up-starts who appeared simultaneously in the same region recognised him, so as to get their own claims legitimised by him,—such as Muhârib b. Mûsâ and Sulaimân b. Habîb.[1] Umaiyids and Abbâsids who did not feel secure at home took shelter under his wing in the hope of obtaining

---

[1] Doubtless this is not the Qadi of the same name who held office under Walîd I, Sulaimân and Hishâm in Syria.

from him office or reward. Shiitism, by means of which he had arisen, was afterwards to him nothing but a thing of secondary importance; the most motley company gathered about him, and so arose in the masterless East an ephemeral kingdom of wide extent,—a characteristic sign of the times.

Ibn Umar had happily got rid of Ibn Muâ- wia (Muharram, 127); Marwân II (Safar, 127) he did not recognise. Indeed, after the earlier rule in Syria was overthrown, he continued it in Iraq, but still without setting himself up as Khalifa. His supporters were the Syrian Yemen- ites (Qudâa and Kalb), who of course stuck to him only for lack of a better. They had al- ready for a considerable time, as chief compo- nent of the government troops, formed a sort of colony in Kufa and Hira, but came more into prominence now since their own home was made disagreeable or was closed to them. They were reinforced by emigrants who could not, or would not, make peace with Marwân, by brothers and sons of Khâlid alQasrî, by Kal- bite officers of the stamp of Mansûr b. Jumhûr, and by other chiefs of the subjugated party in Syria, who naturally also brought their people with them. By the "Yemenites" who in Tabarî play a part in the war-currents of this time, are generally to be understood the Syrian Yemenites of Kufa.

Marwân at the outset could do nothing more against Ibn Umar than set up in opposition to him one of the latter's chief men, Nadr b. Saîd alHarashî. This man was a Qaisite, the son of a prominent officer and official of the school of Hajjâj, and he managed to win over to himself the Mudarites in the Syrian army. But the Yemenites, and above all the Kalbites, who were in the majority and to whom also the supreme leader belonged, namely, Asbagh b. Dhuâla, one of the murderers of Walîd II, remained faithful to the old stattholder, and he was able to hold his own in Hira, whilst Ibn Harashî established himself in Dair Hind. Then for four months the two rivals fought battles between Hira and Kufa, which indeed are said to have hardly ever reached the stage of a proper bloody engagement, and then a common danger forced them to come to an agreement.

For now the Khawârij came upon the scene and for a time occupied the foreground. On former occasions they were always very small in numbers, and so had been compelled to limit themselves to petty warfare. They had indeed by this means given much trouble to a stattholder like Hajjâj, though they themselves had not seriously aspired to the government, but had pursued a quite unpolitical policy, with the idea of saving their soul, and not of gaining the

Islamic world, with which, on the contrary, they did not wish to have the slightest thing in common. Now their little bands swelled to powerful masses ; they abandoned their rude exclusiveness and accepted every help that offered. Certainly they still exacted from those who came over to them the confession of their creed, but they did not turn away any allies who were willing to fight on their side. The truth was the goal they were striving towards was no longer Paradise, but the earthly kingdom. They joined in the scrimmage for the ruling power, for which there was a general scramble, with the same methods as the others, and they came very near to winning it. Then, indeed, they would have remained Khârijites no longer.

The movement began in Mesopotamia, Marwân's native province, not indeed among the Qais in the south but among the Rabîa in the north. The Rabîa always held themselves a little aloof from the rest of the Muslim Arabs, especially from their old rivals, the Mudar, who had compelled them to evacuate their former district and to whom they grudged the Prophetic office and the Khalifate. The Shaibân of Bakr, who had settled in the region of Mosul on both sides of the Tigris, since the days of Shabîb were the special champions of Khârijitism. From amongst them, after the murder of Walîd II, Saîd b. Bahdal arose as Khalifa of the

Khawârij. After removing a rival at home he
set out for Kufa, where better prospects attracted
him than in the territory of Marwân. When
he died on the way, another Shaibânite took
his place, Dahhâk b. Qais, from the distinguished tribe Murra, to which Shabîb had also
belonged. The Khawârij of Shahrazûr, Armenia
and Âdharbaijân joined him, and with several
thousand men under his standard he advanced
upon Kufa. The two stattholders there, who
were always quarrelling, united against him
but could not withstand him, and in Rajab, 127
(April, 745) they were so decisively defeated
that they had to quit Kufa. Ibn Harashî
betook himself to Marwân in Syria ; Ibn Umar
made for Wasit,[1] whither part of his Kalbites
had already preceded him. In Sha'bân, 127
(May, 745) Dahhâk b. Qais followed him there
and besieged him. In the struggle against the
Khawârij Mansûr b. Jumhûr distinguished
himself, but all the same he was the first to go

---

[1] Thus acc. to Tab., 1899. Acc. to Abû Ubaida (Tab, 1902) both
fled to Wasit, not only Ibn Umar but Ibn Harashî as well, there
renewed their old quarrel, and were only just reconciled when the
Khawârij appeared. But even acc. to Abû Ubaida Ibn Harashî
neither took part with the Khawârij in the fight nor in the surrender.
So he must then have soon disappeared and gone from Wasit to Syria
(Tab., 1913). On this occasion he might have slain the Khârijite
stattholder of Kufa, as Abû Ubaida in Tab., 1903, 1914 reports. But
acc. to Tab., 1899f., 1938 it was the Taghlibite Abû Atîya who did so
when he broke through with 70 or 80 men from Wasit viâ Kufa to
Syria.

over to them and pass their religious test by
promising to embrace Islam [1] and obey the word
of God. After some delay, at the end of
Shauwâl, 127 (beginning of August, 745) Ibn
Umar also capitulated and did homage to
Dahhâk b. Qais. " See'st thou not that God
bestows the victory on His religion, and that
the Quraish pray behind Bakr b. Wâil ! " A
poet thus expresses his astonishment that the
Umaiyid recognised the Khârijite of Shaibân as
his Imam, for the political transition was at the
same time a religious one. The sudden change
was indeed astonishing, and, what is more, Ibn
Umar did not disdain to stay in Wasit as
Khârijite stattholder, over Kaskar, Mesene,
Ahwâz and Fârs, in which position he fell out
with his neighbour on the east, Ibn Muâwia.

Dahhâk himself turned back to Kufa and
from there governed the western half of his
kingdom. After an absence of probably 20
months,[2] certainly not before the middle of 128
(spring, 746), he was recalled to his Mesopotamian
home, at a time when Marwân had his hands

---

[1] The Khâwarij laid claim to the name *Muslims* for themselves
alone, and called the Catholic Muslims *heathen*.

[2] Thus Tab., 1938. Acc. to Abû Ubaida (Tab., 1914) Dahhâk
withdrew as early as Dhulqa'da, 127 (Aug.-Sepr., 745) to Mesopotamia ;
and likewise in Dhulqa'da, 127, according to him (Tab., 1913), Marwân
was finished with Hims and had a free hand to deal with Dahhâk.
The two datings are connected ; in both the year is wrong ; in the
second the month is probably right.

full in Syria. He came and took possession of the town of Mosul, from which he drove out the government official. All flocked to him, especially as he gave high pay. His army is said to have amounted to 120,000 men. The number, of course, rests upon popular estimate, but even Theophanes says Dahhâk had a tremendous armed force. The Kalbite emigrants and adventurers were with him, and with them may also be reckoned the Umaiyid Sulaimân b. Hishâm, who had saved his regiment, the Dhakwânîya, from the *débacle* of Khufâf, and had hurried to meet the Khawârij with 4,000 men.

Whilst Marwân was reducing Syria he came into danger of losing Mesopotamia, the pillar of his strength. However, he did not give up the siege of Hims with which he was just then occupied, but provisionally commissioned his son Abdullâh, whom he had left behind in the residence at Harrân, to advance against Dahhâk and from Mosul impede him in his further advance. Abdullâh came to Nisibis. There after an unsuccessful encounter he had to halt, and withdrew behind the walls of the town, where he was besieged. An attempt of Dahhâk to take possession of the crossing of the Euphrates near Raqqa by a forward push, miscarried. Meantime Marwân had at last subdued Hims and now advanced in person

via Raqqa against the Khawârij. The armies
met at Kafartûtâ. Dahhâk, who was accustomed
to expose himself recklessly, fell in a skirmish.
His successor, Khaibarî, after an interval renewed
the attack, and forced his way into the enemy
camp, but in so doing was outflanked and beaten
to death with cudgels by the baggage servants
in the camp. This took place towards the end
of the year 128, about September, 746.[1]

But it was not till the following year
(A. M. 6239 in Theophanes, A. H. 129) that
the Khawârij were subdued. They were still
40,000 strong, and chose as their Khalifa the
Yashkurite Shaibân b. Abdilazîz (Abû Dulaf).
Upon Sulaimân's advice the latter led them
back to the eastern bank of the Tigris, opposite
to Mosul, but they kept the town in their power
and had communication with it by a bridge
of boats. Marwân encamped opposite on the
right bank. Thus he spent long months of the
year 129 (746-747) without gaining a decisive
victory. It was only after Iraq was meantime
wrested from their power that the Khawârij
could no longer hold out on the Tigris either.
They did not manage to cut off the army which
now was able to hasten from Kufa to Marwân's

---

[1] Theophanes agrees in essentials with the account of the chief
report in Tab. (Abdulwahhâb). Acc. to him Dahhâk made his rising
in A.H. 127 (A. M. 6236) in Persis, *i e.*, in Iraq; in A.H. 128 he appeared
in Mesopotamia. Marwân first sent his son to encounter him,
but after the taking of Hims he came in person and slew the rebel.

help, and in order not to be between two fires
they evacuated their position near Mosul about
the end of 129 (August, 747) and marched
through the mountains towards the east.

The general of Marwân, who snatched Iraq
from the Khârijites, and so made their position
on the Tigris untenable, was the Qaisite Yazîd
b. Umar Ibn Hubaira from Qinnesrin, whose
father, under Yazîd II, had held the stattholdership of Kufa. In the beginning of 128 he
had set out on the march thither, but had
to remain stationary a considerable time on
the boundary at Qarqîsiâ, and could not attack
till the end of the year or the beginning of
129. After several successful fights with the
Khârijite stattholder Muthannâ b. Imrân,
under whom Mansûr b. Jumhûr fought, he
managed, in Ramadân, 129 (May or June, 747),
to enter Kufa.[1] He then took the town of
Wâsit and made Ibn Umar prisoner. Mansûr
b. Jumhûr fled with his Kalbites to the province of Ibn Muâwia, whither the Khawârij also,
who till then had fought on the Tigris with
Marwân, withdrew. Ibn Muâwia, in himself

---

[1] Thus acc. to Abû Mikhnaf (Tab., 1946) who certainly was not
a scholarly chronologist like Wâqidî, but in this case was bound to
have exact information, because he was then still living, an old man,
in Kufa. Abû Ubaida (Tab., 1914 ff.) gives other dates, but is not to
be trusted. He knows interesting details and narrates them excellently well, but as a historian is not to be compared with Abû
Mikhnaf.

50

very insignificant, was for a short space raised
to a great eminence by the circumstances; he
would certainly never have dreamed beforehand
that such a thing could happen. Shîites, Khârijites, Kalbites, Abbâsids, Umaiyids, were all
united under him. All differences seemed to
be adjusted in the fanatical enmity to Marwân,
but it was not long until the remnants that
necessity had swept together ceased to agree.

Marwân turned back to his residence in
Harrân. He needed to get some rest.[1] The
most important provinces of the kingdom,
Mesopotamia, Iraq, Syria and Egypt were now
subject to him. In Arabia, too, the Khawârij
of Hadramaut, who had conquered San'â, Mecca
and Medina, were annihilated in the year 130
(748). For three years he had been almost
constantly in the field, and had performed marvellous feats in the struggle against a world of
foes. He excelled all his predecessors by his
personal capability for carrying things through.

He left the war in the East against the
Khawârij and Ibn Muâwia to his Iraq stattholder, Ibn Hubaira. The army which the
latter had sent to his help against the Khawârij
when they were still on the Tigris, was

---

[1] Whether this was his idea is indeed doubtful. The Romans
had taken advantage of the Arabian civil war to extend their boundary eastwards. He may now have wanted to go against them.
From Egypt he caused Cyprus to be attacked, but in vain.

commanded by 'Âmir Ibn Dubâra. The latter
was now commissioned to pursue them and pressed
forward into the province of Ibn Muâwia;
there he was joined by another military leader
of Ibn Hubaira, Nubâta b. Hanzala. Ibn
Muâwia was overcome in the battle against Ibn
Dubâra near Marwash Shâdhân in the year 130,
left his kingdom to its fate, and fled from his
foes to Khurasan, where he was put to death by
his friends. The Khârijite leader, Shaibân b.
Abdilazîz al Yashkurî, went to the east coast of
Arabia, and at last fell in battle with the princes
of Umân, the old-established Banû Jalandâ, in
the year 134.[1] Sulaimân b. Hishâm and Mansûr b. Jumhûr betook themselves over the sea
to Sind.[2]

Now, however, when Ibn Hubaira's generals
had scattered this curious coalition and were in
a fair way to subject western Iran completely
to Marwân's sway, new and sinister opponents
appeared before them,—the Khurâsânites under
the black flag of the Abbâsids. In vain had
Nasr b. Saiyâr, the old man who had now been
many years stattholder of the Umaiyids on the

[1] Thus acc. to Tab., 3, 78. *Cf.* 2, 1945. 1949. 1979. Abû
Mikhnaf in Tab., 2, 1948 says Shaibân b. Abdilazîz had already
fallen in A.H. 130 and that in Sajistân. He probably confuses him
with the Harûrite Shaibân b. Salama who at the same time played
a part in Khurasan and actually fell in A.H. 130, not indeed in Sajistân,
but in Sarakhs.

[2] For their end see Agh., 4, 96. Yaqûbî, 2, 430. Tab., 3, 72. 80.

north-eastern boundary, warned them of the danger imminent from that quarter, and urgently begged for help to suppress it. Marwân had too much to do in the centre and was thankful to be able to maintain his position triumphantly there. Then, at the height of his success, the black spectre which he had not heeded suddenly appeared before him in the flesh. The Khurasanites rendered his toilsome labour vain, just as he seemed to have attained his goal. With Abû Muslim there came upon him a mightier than he.

CHAPTER VIII.

THE ARAB TRIBES IN KHURÂSÂN.

The final ruin of the Umaiyids was brought about by a rising of the Shîite Iranians in Khurâsân, but the way was paved for this rising already by the preceding history of the province, particularly by the tribal feud of the Arabs of that quarter, which in its turn had its starting-point in Basra, for Khurasan was a colony of Basra. In order therefore to understand the situation in Khurasan we must hark back to the earlier state or trend of conditions in Basra.

In Kufa at the beginning of the Umaiyid epoch the jealousy of the tribes towards each other certainly led to strained relations but did not get the length of violent outbreaks. There it was the political parties who came to logger-heads with each other. On the other hand in Basra the situation at first appeared very much as it was in pre-Islamic times. Both latently and openly the tribal feud retained its power, only its action was not so much between the single tribes as between the tribal groups. The most notable group consisted of the Tamîm and the Ribâb; the Persian Asâwira had joined them, and the Indian Zutt and Saiâbija also

sought their protection, just because they were
the most powerful.[1]   Since remote times the
Rabîa had been unfriendly to Tamîm. In
Basra the Bakr were joined by the Abdulqais,
who were but sparsely represented in Kufa.
The Yemen were represented by the Azd, while
in Kufa the more prominent and more thoroughly Arab Madhhij, Hamdân and Kinda predominated.[2]

The Azd first became powerful in Basra
by a supplementary immigration which took
place towards the latter part of Muâwia's rule
and under Yazîd I (Tab., 450, Balâdh., 373).
It was not considered right that these new-
comers who had taken no part in the great
conquests in the time of Umar and Uthmân
should now claim the same rights as the old tribes
(Tab., 779).   They at once upset the balance
of power hitherto existing, though it was only
through Muhallab and his sons that they attained to their full eminence.   At the beginning
the Tamîm had the idea of winning them over

---

[1] Balâdh., 372 ff. Kâmil, 82, 16f.

[2] In Basra and Khurâsân, the Akhmâs, namely (1) Bakr, (2)
Abdulqais. (3) Tamîm, (4) Azd and (5) Ahl alÂlia (= Ahl alMadina,
mostly Qaisites, Tab.. 461, 21. 1382) correspond to the Arbâ of Kufa.
In Kufa the Arbâ form actual fourths and in Basra the Akhmâs actual
fifths, but these expressions are also used, the same as our *quarter* or
ward, for other divisions, the denominator of which is not necessarily
four or *five*.   To the large tribes after whom the Akhmâs were called
were joined broken fragments of smaller ones, *e. g.* the Kinda and the
Taiyi were taken in with the Bakr in Basra.

to their side and entering into a league with
them, but refrained from taking the first step
because their wisest and most influential counsellor, Ahnaf, said that whoever made the first
move would play second fiddle in the alliance.
So the Rabîa anticipated them and on their
part made a solemn alliance with Azd (Tab.,
450. 1497). As the Tamîm held close to the
Ahl alÂlia, i.e. the Qais, there now came about
a division into two sides, in which the united
Azd (Yemen) and Rabîa stood opposed to the
Mudar (Tamîm and Qais). It must not be
thought, however, that all the Azd had come to
Basra only in the year 60. There were already
Azdites there before that, and these certainly
belonged, just as much as those in Kufa, to
the western branch which had its home on
Mount Sarât,—to the Daus mostly. But they
were of small consequence until they were
strengthened by the later addition which was
far greater in numbers, and streamed in from
the east-Arabian coast-district of Umân. The
Azd Umân, to distinguish them from the Azd
Sarât, were called the Mâzûn, but disliked the
name as it apparently contains a pun upon their
mixed origin. In Umân there lived many who
were not Arabs. They were also jeered at
because of their old industry, namely fishing,
just as the western Azdites were for their
weaving.

In the year 38 or 39 Muâwia sent Ibn Hadramî to Basra to stir up there, with the help of
the Tamîm, a rising against the rule of Alî, and
he must have succeeded in gaining to his side a
great part of the Tamîm. The deputy stattholder of Basra, young Ziâd b. Abîhi, asked
the Bakr for protection but they could not come
to terms. He then turned to the Azd (Sarât)
and found a secure shelter for himself and the
state-treasure with their chief, Sabira b. Shaimân alHuddânî (of Daus). Alî, however, made
attempts to entice the Basrian Tamîm away
from Ibn Hadramî by means of Tamimites who
were devoted to him. The first emissary whom
he sent was murdered, but the second, Jâria
b. Qudâma, was successful. Ibn Hadramî was
abandoned by the Tamîm, besieged by Jâria in
the Dâr Sunbîl and burnt to death with his followers. Satirical verses by the Azdite 'Arandas
concerning the event are preserved to us and
for long the disgrace stuck to the Tamîm (Madâinî in Tab., 1, 3414ff.).

This is the beginning of the friendship of the
Azd with Ziâd and his family. Ziâd always
remained grateful to them (Tab., 2, 80), and
told his sons also to apply to them if they
should at any time be in need (2,440). In
relation to the rival Tamîm and Bakr they were
originally a neutral element and therefore suited
to be a prop of the government.

The actual outbreak of the tribal feud in Basra did not take place till after the immigration of the Azd Umân and after the death of the Khalifa Yazîd I, through whom the Umaiyid rule came to be everywhere in a tottering condition. The report of it in Tab., 2, 433ff. is very detailed but somewhat strange. It is worth while to undo the knot and separate the single threads, and all the more so since elsewhere we find hardly any statement at all and nowhere a correct one about these events which had such important consequences. Tabarî's chief authority is Abû Ubaida, the great collector of Arab tribe tales. His narrative certainly is not in existence *in toto*, but the gaps can be filled in, and in the essentials Wahb b. Jarîr agrees with him.

Abû Ubaida, 435, 17. 436, 15.[1] Ubaid-ullâh b. Ziâd, the stattholder of Iraq, was at variance with Yazîd I, who considered that the slaying of Husain had brought him no advantage, but only harm. One evening the standing messenger whom he kept at the court at Damascus came riding to Basra with news of the sudden death of the Khalifa. He at once called a general meeting in the mosque, announced the event, reviled the dead man and made clear what were his own deserts from

---

[1] Parallel, Wahb, 433, 12.

Basra. He said that on his first coming there
had been registered in the Dîwân 70,000 regular
soldiers (Arabs) and 90,000 tradesmen (Mawâlî);
now there were 80,000 regulars and 150,000
tradesmen. All suspicious persons—by this he
meant specially the Khawârij—were under lock
and key. "You are the most powerful; the
Syrians are at variance. Therefore choose an
Emir for yourselves, and if the Syrians have
agreed upon a Khalifa, then either join with
them or not as you will, for you can dispense
with the others, but they cannot do without you."
His idea was to put himself forward as *interim*
Emir, since by the death of the Khalifa the duty
of obedience to the government, which was
conceived to be an absolutely personal matter,
did not hold any longer.

The Basrians also chose him and paid homage to him by striking hands, but when they
were outside they cleansed their hands and
wiped off their homage upon the doors and walls,
and scoffingly said that he thought they would
follow him in times of quarrels and uncertainty
the same as they did in times of unity and order,
and very soon he found that no one obeyed him
any longer.[1]

---

[1] He gained popularity at the beginning by making his officers of
finance distribute the state-moneys,—Tab., 439 says 8 millions and
443 says 19 millions—day and night to the tribes and warriors to
whom the revenues of the conquests (Fai) actually belonged, and which

Abû Ubaida, 437, 15. The signal for open rebellion was given by the Tamimite Salama b. Dhuaib. He appeared one day on horseback in the camel-market, in complete armour, carrying a banner, and demanded recognition of Ibn Zubair as Khalifa.[1] Thereupon Ubaidullâh collected the Basrians and pointed out to them that they had really chosen him as Emir of their own accord, but they were now hampering his instruments in the execution of his commands, and were passively conniving at the insurrection being proclaimed. Ahnaf, the chief of the Tamîm, promised to bring in Salama, but his following was already too strong, and Ahnaf did not return.

Abû Ubaida, 439, 10.[2] Ubaidullâh was in evil case. Even the police-troops [3] would not interfere on his orders, but only on the orders of their officers. His brothers said to him,—

the government collected and hoarded up after deducting the pensions. But when they became refractory he stopped this, and upon his flight he took the rest of the treasure with him. Later on the jewels were still in the possession of his family. Abû Ubaida, 439, 10.

[1] Brünnow, on his own account, makes him the emissary of Ibn Zubair, and A. Müller even makes him his confidant. Tradition says nothing of this, and we cannot ignorantly adorn tradition. It was matter of course that the opposition turned to Ibn Zubair. Also, a recruiting officer does not appear on horse-back in the market-place carrying a standard. *Cf.* 452, 15 ; 465, 2.

[2] Parallel, Wahb, 441, 20.

In Tab., 443 they are called the Bukhârians (*cf.* 464, and especi ally Balâdh., 441), elsewhere *khâṣṣatu's Sulṭân*, *i.e.* the private troops of the government as opposed to the militia, or general army.

"It is no Khalifa for whom you fight, and who will support you; we are in danger of losing our property in Basra and our lives to boot." He then determined, in accordance with the advice and example of his father to resort to the protection of the Azd against the mutinous Tamîm. At nightfall he set out with his treasures to Mas‘ûd b. Amr al‘Atakî, the leader of the Azd, whom they all followed.[1] He did not venture by day; even by night he ran the risk of being shot down by the watches who were posted against the Khâwarij; an arrow stuck in his turban. When at last he had got safely to Mas‘ûd, the latter was afraid; he did not want, for his part, to plunge into a feud with the rest of the Basrians. Nevertheless they managed to allay his fears. They said that nothing was required of him but to receive the Emir temporarily, and then speed him to a secure place outwith Basra.[2]

Abû Ubaida, 446, 3.[3] The Basrians now commissioned two trusty men to submit proposals to them for a new Emir. One of the two Quraishites who were nominated was recommended by his relationship to the Prophet and to Muâwia, and appointed. He was called

---

[1] ‘Atîk is the most distinguished family of the Azd Umân, whose [old headquarters were Dabâ. Muhallab also belonged to ‘Atîk.

[2] Variants of Abû Ubaida, 445, 7ff. Acc. to Wahb, 441, 10ff Mas‘ûd was ready immediately.

[3] Wahb, 444, 6 ; 444, 17.

Abdullâh b. Hârith b. Abdilmuttalib, with the nickname "Babba." He entered the citadel on 1st Jumâdâ II, 65 (25th January, 684).

Abû Ubaida, 447, 12. 449, 20. The next occurrence was that a Bakrite boasted in the mosque that a tribesman of his had given a prominent Quraishite a box on the ear and that the latter had borne it quietly. Dabbites (of Tamîm) who were present, and who sided with Quraish as belonging to Mudar, beat him almost to death for this. Thereupon the whole of the Bakr were enraged and prepared to march against the Tamîm, headed by Mâlik b. Misma' in place of Ashyam b. Shaqîq who would not go.[1] In view of the attack on the Tamîm he renewed an old alliance with the Azd, in which Ubaidullâh b. Ziâd strongly supported him with his money.[2] It was regarded as due to the Azd that their chief Mas'ûd b. Amr should have the supreme command. The latter then said to Ubaidullâh, "Come with us and we will take you back to the citadel." But he remained stationary in front of Mas'ûd's house, had his camels saddled and loaded before him and every moment had information brought him of the state of affairs. Mas'ûd went into the mosque

---

[1] The same paralysing dualism of the leaders has been already seen in 1,3414. *Cf.* 2,448. Acc. to 455, 5ff. it was the other way about, Ashyam was leader, and not Mâlik.

[2] One of the two documents was deposited with Salt b. Huraith alHsnafî (Tab., 449, 17. *Cf.* Kâmil, 627, 10).

and entered the pulpit, and Babba was content to let him do so. Mâlik marched about for a while in some of the quarters of the Tamîm—till he heard that Mas'ûd was killed.

Abû Ubaida, 452, 6. The Tamîm announced to Ahnaf, " The Rabîa and the Yemen have penetrated into the mosque." After a while they added, " Now they have pressed into the citadel." He was not disturbed ; only the " wolves of Tamîm " under Salama b. Dhuaib started out along with a few hundred Mawâlî under Mâh Afrîdûn. When worse and worse tidings kept arriving Ahnaf at last considered he might use force and the cry resounded : " The philanderer has made a move at last ! " He bound the standard to Abs b. Talq, since Abbâd b. Husain was not on the spot. The latter came soon after, but turned back again with his 60 horsemen because he would not fight under Abs.

Ishâq b. Suwaid, 454, 6.[1] On the side of the Tamîm there fought most zealously Mâh Afrîdûn with his people, each one of whom shot five arrows at the same time. Before such a rain of

---

[1] Abû Ubaida's account of the encounter is lacking in Tabarî, which only tells us of an ironical speech of Hasan alBasrî (455, 9) : " Mas'ûd preached the Sunna and forbade the Fitna ; does not the Sunna say ' thou shalt withhold thy hand from violence ' ? But it was not long till they dragged him down from the pulpit and slew him." Ishâq b. Suwaid supplies the gap, fitting in essentials (even in the dates), and differing in small points ; *e.g.*, he makes not Mâlik, but Ashyam the leader of the Bakr.

darts the opponents could not keep their ground.
The Tamîm thronged into the mosque, dragged
Mas'ûd from the pulpit and slew him. Ashyam
b. Shaqîq of Bakr escaped. This happened at
the beginning of Shauwâl, 64. Abû Ubaida
gives the same date (455, 16) for the flight of
Ubaidullâh, which, according to him (439, 10),
followed upon the death of Mas'ûd.

Abû Ubaida in the Kâmil, 81.[1] Revenge for
Mas'ûd was undertaken by his brother Ziâd b.
Amr al'Atakî, still a young man. He marched
the next day to the Mirbad (the chief square of
Basra) and there marshalled his army, the Bakr
on the right, the Abdulqais on the left, the Azd
in the middle. Ahnaf arranged the Tamîm ;
opposite the Azd were the Sa'd and the Ribâb
under Abs b. Talq ; opposite the Bakr were
the Hanzala under Hâritha b. Badr ; facing the
Abdulqais stood the Amr b. Tamîm. But it did
not come to an encounter, for Ahnaf caused the
Azd and Rabîa to be addressed in this wise :—
" You are fellow-citizens of Basra, dearer to us
than our Tamimite tribal brothers in Kufa ;
yesterday it was you who began, broke the
domestic peace and kindled the flame,—we only
defended ourselves, but all the same would
be glad now to try every means to find a

---

[1] Neither is this concluding piece of Abû Ubaida preserved in Tab.
He puts in place of it a variant of 'Awâna (461, 18).

settlement." Ziâd offered three peace proposals
to choose from, and then the armies separated.
Next morning Ahnaf decided to accept the proposal that the Tamîm should leave out of consideration their own spilt blood, but on the
other hand should expiate that of the Azd and
Rabîa, and should pay an exceptionally high fine
for Mas'ûd. Until the payment was completed
the Tamîm gave hostages who came forward of
their own accord. Lines from Farazdaq and
Jarîr confirm this. Ahnaf, as on other occasions,
so notably on this one, performed in an unpre-
cedented manner the chief office of the Arab
Saiyid, namely the preservation of peace.[1] Along
with him the wealthy Tamimite Yâs b. Qatâda
gained a great reputation by taking upon himself the chief share of the debt of atonement
(Anon. Ahlw., 187).

In a few points Abû Ubaida is to be corrected by fragments given by other narrators.
The flight of Ubaidullâh did not immediately
follow upon the murder of Mas'ûd, in Shauwâl,
64 (455, 18). It rather appears from the verse
463, 5 that it was Mas'ûd himself who had him
taken to Syria. Wahb b. Jarîr (456) says this
also, and likewise 'Awâna (461), who even makes
Ubaidullâh go to Syria in the middle of Jumâdâ

---

[1] The merit of Ahnaf is really somewhat exaggerated. Acc. to
Madâinî (465, 5. 6) it was two Quraishites who were the mediators
for peace.

II, 64,—90 days after the death of Yazîd. So
he was then not a silent spectator of the bloody
events, but was not there at all.   And it was not
while he was still present that the choice of a
new Emir   was made,—indeed   an agreement
would hardly have lasted so long,—but only as
the result of the treaty of peace of the tribes
after the threatened rupture.   Thus 'Awâna, 463
says : "After the death of Mas'ûd and the settlement of the dispute, the Basrians united and
first of all made Abdulmalik b. Abdillâh b.
'Amir, and then Babba, Emir, until Ibn Zubair
three months after appointed a stattholder for
them."   It is thus also explained why Babba
in Abû Ubaida remains quite passive in face
of the intrusion of the Azd into the mosque and
the citadel,—just because he was not yet there
as Emir.

   'Awâna further says (461) that Ubaidullâh, upon his flight, left Mas'ûd behind in
Basra as his representative. In any case the
rise of Mas'ûd took place *during the interregnum*
after the flight of Ubaidullâh. He wanted to
usurp the vacant post of Emir (456, 16).   He
did not march against the Tamîm, but into the
citadel and the mosque, and ostentatiously took
the place of Emir in the pulpit, and from the
pulpit he was dragged down. The Tamîm had
driven away Ubaidullâh.   The Azd would not
let them have the upper hand, but wanted to
   52

have the say and thus the struggle arose. From
this it is at once plain that Mas'ûd acted on his
own initiative and in his own interest, and was
not brought to the step by the Rabîa. The
tale of the box on the ear is quite a secondary
matter.

From 'Awâna the moral of the whole is
plain,—the attempt of one tribe and its head,
authorised perhaps by the late Emir, to put
itself at the head of the whole, was completely
ship-wrecked upon the opposition of the rival
tribe. Only the Quraish standing outside the
tribal system were eligible as Emirs. But
'Awâna is wrong (461) in asserting that it was
some of the Khawârij, united with the Tamîm
who dragged Mas'ûd from the pulpit and slew
him. According to the others it was Persians
under Mâh Afrîdûn, more strictly the Asâwira
(465) who for long had been allies of the Tamîm.
The Khawârij were the common foe to all the
tribes of Basra and the Tamîm also, and it was
this danger more than anything that induced
them not to follow out the feud and to agree
upon an Emir. And the chosen Emir was
bound to resign soon just for the very reason
that he did not fulfil the end he was chosen for,
and did not seriously attack the Khawârij.
The account of Madâinî is decisive (465).
According to it the Khawârij are smuggled in
by a historical forgery of the Azd. The Azd

did not want to lie under the disgrace of having
had their prince destroyed by the Tamîm and of
having renounced revenge for a money-payment.
The remark of 'Awâna (461, 10) that the Khawârij by whom Mas'ûd was killed dwelt on the
canal of the Asâwira, betrays a bad conscience.

2. Thus the enmity between Azd and Tamîm,
Yemen and Mudar sprang from a circumstance
fixed and datable, as is plain from the story just
related, a story which is important for that very
reason.   The peace pact did not abolish the
variance.   Two years after it was ready to break
out again when Mukhtâr tried to make a rising
in Basra (Tab., 680ff.).   But in the struggles
against the Khawârij, which had a salutary
effect, it changed into emulation ; the Tamîm
would not be inferior to the Azd under
Muhallab.   But if the tribal-feud abated in
Basra itself, it grew all the more dangerous in
Khurâsân, whither the tribe-relations of Basra
were transferred because its conquest was
achieved from there.   The Khurâsân Arabs were
Iraqites, mostly Basrians, and divided, like the
latter, for military purposes into five divisions.
The stattholder was, as a rule, dependent upon
the Iraq stattholder, but was frequently appointed by the Khalifa himself and occasionally
even placed immediately under the latter.

Khurâsân was the storm-quarter of the
kingdom, reacting upon the centre far more

significantly than, say, Africa or Spain.   It was a
province that was never pacified and never had
fixed boundaries.   Here the Arabs were constantly disputing with the Turks and Iranians,
but they employed the intervals to rend each
other.   Exposed as they were, they still behaved
with exactly the same lack of policy as before
in their old home.   They felt free and untram-
melled in the vast and, to a great extent, desert
land, even although they had not come to it
altogether of their own accord.   The external
danger did not unite them, but excited them
and made them savage, and even Islam only
increased the factors of discord and tumult.
Khurâsân became a second Arabia, with this
difference, that it lay in enemy territory, had
vast and complicated connections, and permitted
anarchical tendencies to be more regardlessly
and unrestrainedly expressed.   The narratives
of Madâinî, which Tabarî almost exclusively
follows in regard to affairs of Khurâsân, are in
places reminiscent of the epic narrative of the
past ages of Arabia which are familiar from the
Kitâb al-Aghânî.   He often only gives a loose
tissue of tribal traditions, a collection of " Days "
(1516, 16), the chief interest lying in the heroic
or the rapacious.   The Khurâsân Arabs, and
especially the Tamîm, stuck proudly to their
nationality and in the far East continued the
old tribal life and the old songs and sagas about

their own doings and experiences. But there is a lack of the close and sober realism with which the remains of the genuine old Arabism is stamped.

The conquest of the Iranian East, from Basra, took place under the stattholdership of the Umaiyid Abdullâh b. 'Âmir in the time of the Khalifa Uthmân. It was a series of simultaneous attacks at different points. They were not successful at one attempt and in one year; generally pacts were made by which the Persian Marzbâns retained their old position with some alterations and limitations. Side by side with the greater campaigns under appointed leaders, by whom the first blows were struck, there went on an anonymous petty warfare in which the tribes acted for themselves, so as to establish themselves where they could. In the west, where Abarshar (Naisâbûr) was the chief town, the Qais were predominant, especially in the later period (Tab., 1929). In the east the lands of the Bakrites and the Tamimites were mixed up; both tribes laid claim to some districts by right of first possession, and they were competitors not only in Khurâsân but in Sajistân as well. These two neighbouring provinces belonged together though they were frequently administered separately, and the centre of gravity which at first lay in Sajistân was later on transferred to Khurâsân. The capital of Sajistân was Zarang; that of Khurâsân Marw.

According to old custom, the army-leaders were rewarded with the command of the districts whose conquest they had successfully effected. Ahnaf at that time also played a brilliant part in military affairs, but did not long remain as governor in the conquered territory. As tribal prince of the Tamîm of Basra, he was perhaps too proud for that. The oldest stattholders of Khurâsân (or of parts of the land) of whom we hear were Qais b. Haitham and Abdullâh b. Khâzim, both of Sulaim, a Qaisite tribe. The disorders after the murder of the Khalifa Uthmân found their echo even in the extreme east of the kingdom. The Marzbân Mâhûya of Marw, the betrayer of the last Shâhanshâh, obtained from Alî the right of making the Dihkans pay tribute to him first of all, but in spite of this concession he did not uphold the authority of Alî.[1] How the Arabian rule was re-established we do not gather (cf. Baladh., 409). Under Muâwia, Qais b. Haitham became stattholder again, and then his rival Abdullâh b. Khâzim.[2] When Ziâd b. Abîhi came to Basra in A. H. 45, Khurâsân and Sajistân also fell under his government, so that he had to appoint the officials there. He

---

[1] Simultaneously the Arabian Khabatât, who pretended to be followers of Uthmân (i.e. neutral), took possession of the capital of Sajistân. They were only subdued two years after by Alî's officer, Husain b. Mâlik, after whom the famous Feroz Husain, his Maula, is named.

[2] With Balâdh., 408 cf. Tab., 2, 65f.

divided Khurâsân into four independent districts,
Marw, Abarshahr (Naisâbûr), Marwrûdh (with
Fâriâb and Tâliqân) and Herât (with Bâdhaghîs
Qâdis and Bûshang), but united them in A. H. 47
under Hakam b. Amr al-Ghifârî, who died in
A. H. 50. He was succeeded by Rabî b. Ziâd al-
Hârithî, a tall, ruddy, wide-mouthed man, the
conqueror of Sajistan, who after a battle before
the gates of Zarang, had received the Marzbâns
on the battlefield to make terms of capitulation,
he and his Arabs sitting at their ease upon the
bodies of the fallen. He was a pious Muslim and
grief over the execution of Hujr b. Adî is said to
have broken his heart. At that time there were
25,000 Basrians and 25,000 Kufaites settled in
Khurâsân, probably not of the most peaceable type.
After Ziâd's death (A. H. 53) the East seemed to
become an institution for the maintenance of his
sons. In the latter part of Muâwia's time and
under Yazîd I, Ubaidullâh b. Ziâd was governor
in Khurâsân ; then, after an interval, Abdurrahmân b. Ziâd, and lastly Salm b. Ziâd. In
Sajistân Abbâd b. Ziâd and Yazîd b. Ziâd held
the government. These were all very young men,
and meanwhile the business was attended to by
the old officers and officials well versed in the
ways of the land, like Qais b. Haitham as Sulamî,
Aslam b. Zur'a al-Kilâbî and others, who as a
matter of fact bore each other a grudge and
abused each other whenever they had the power.

With the death of Yazîd the tribal disorders began here also. Zunbîl of Kâbul rose up, slew the stattholder Yazîd b. Ziâd of Sajistân and took his brother Abû Ubaida prisoner. Talba atTalahât, the wealthy Khuzâite, then took Yazîd's place, concluded a peace with Zunbîl and ransomed the imprisoned Abû Ubaida for a large sum. But he soon died and the Tamîm would not submit to the Bakrite whom he left as his successor, but turned him out, whereupon the feud between the Mudar and Rabîa broke out and Zunbîl took advantage of it (BAthîr, 4, 84. Balâdh, 397). This reacted upon Khurâsân. Salm b. Ziâd, the governor there, attempted to keep secret the death of the Khalifa and the misfortune of his brothers (in Sajistân and Basra), and when this did not work any longer he invited the Arabs to pay homage to him as provisional Emir in the *interregnum*. They did so, but soon renounced him and he took to flight, leaving behind as his vice-gerent the Azdite Muhallab, whom he had brought with him from Basra. But the petty Arab chiefs were not content with this. The Bakrite Sulaimân b. Marthad defied him and obtained for himself the government of Marwrûdh, while he had to bestow Herât upon another Bakrite, Aus b. Tha'laba b. Zufar, and when he did manage to depart for Naisâbûr, and there met Abdullâh b. Khâzim asSulamî,

the latter called him to account for dividing up
Khurâsân amongst the Bakr and Mazûn (*i.e.*
Azd Umân) and forced him to grant him a
patent as stattholder of the whole of Khurâsân.
Muhallab retired from Marw as he had no tribe
to support him, for at that time the Azd were
not numerous in Khurâsân. He left as his
representative a Tamimite, who certainly op·
posed Ibn Khâzim in self-defence, but was
worsted in the struggle and died of his wounds
(Tab., 488-90).

The Tamîm in general supported Ibn Khâzim, who after all did not really belong to them
but to Mudar, and was hostile to the Bakr,[1]
and with them he now began the struggle
against the Bakr. He first of all marched from
Marw to Marwrûdh against Sulaimân b. Marthad and killed him; then against the latter's
brother Amr in Tâliqân and slew him as well.
The fugitives went to Herât to Aus b. Tha'laba.
Greatly incensed at the loss of Herât, the
Bakrites in general now flocked to him and
wanted to expel all the Mudar from Khurâsân.
Negotiations to which Ibn Khâzim was forced
by the Tamîm fell through, as he had foreseen:
"Rabîa always rages against God, since he has
raised up the Prophet from Mudar." The
battles before Herât are said to have continued

---

[1] Acc. to Balâdh., 414 he was confirmed by Ibn Zubair.

53

over a year.[1] The Bakr had the support of the
town behind them and in front were protected
by a ditch. They thus defied all the attacks of
Ibn Khâzim, till he touched them on their honour,
calling to them,—"Ye want to have all Khurasan
to yourselves. Perhaps you think this ditch is all
Khurasan?" Moved by this they left their
strong position, were overcome in the open field
and suffered heavy losses. All the prisoners
amongst them who were brought in till sunset
had to pay the extreme penalty. Aus b. Tha‘laba
escaped to Sajistân which was then in the hands
of Zunbîl, but died there of his wounds. This
tribal feud between Bakr and Tamîm in the east
was contemporaneous with that between Kalb
and Qais in the west and took place in the year
64 or 65 (Tab., 490-96); the result of it was a
permanent weakening of the Bakr.

Ibn Khâzim had subdued Herat with the
help of the Tamîm, but all the same he did not
want them now to establish themselves there
as conquerors. He made over the town to his
young son Muhammad, appointed as his assistant Bukair b. Wishâh[2] to be commander of

----

[1] The episode in Tab., 493, 6—494, 17 (by Sulaimân b. Mujâlid,
a contemporary of Abû Mikhnaf, who is often quoted by him), does
not belong to this place, but to a much later period. On the other
hand, the tradition of AbulHasan alKhurâsânî, 494, 18 - 495, 7, fills
in a blank in the main narrative of Madâinî.

[2] He was likewise a Tamimite and a Sa‘dite at that. His being
called athThaqafî in Tab., 495, 7 is an oversight. *Cf.* 860, 10ff. 1022, 1,
1030, 13. 20f. 1047, 18.

the standing government troops, and charged
the latter not to admit the Tamîm. Bukair
offered them a good sum of money to withdraw,
but this attempt to get rid of them had only
the effect of irritating them. They forced an
entrance into the town, bound Muhammad,
abused him and caroused the whole night, and
in the morning killed him. This was the
fashion in which they showed their friendship
to his father. Then they went to Marw, were
reinforced by tribal companions there and made
Harîsh b. Hilâl alQuraiꞌî their supreme leader
in the feud against Ibn Khâzim. For it was a
feud in the old style; battles were not fought,
but single champions, each one of whom was
of more value than a squadron, made sudden
attacks and encountered adventures. Zuhair b.
Dhuaib alAdawî (of Tamîm) slew every one
whom he met on a tawny steed because his
brother Ashꞌath was slain by an unknown rider
on a tawny steed, and consequently the colour
was disliked. This was characteristic of the
events of the war. When it became tedious the
Tamîm dispersed and so lost their strength.
Shammâs b. Dithâr alUtâridî withdrew to Sajistan (Tab., 546. 1026), Harîsh b. Hilâl went to
Marwrûdh and there for a while asserted
himself,[1] but in the end had to retire from

---

[1] In Tab., 598, 3 he says he slept for two years with a stone for
a pillow, and his hand under his head. It does not necessarily follow

Khurasan (Tab., 593-98). Other Tamimites under Zuhair b. Dhuaib betook themselves to the caste of Fartanâ, not far from Marwrudh. There they were besieged by Ibn Khâzim, forced to surrender and executed without mercy (Tab., 696-700). Peace then seems to have reigned in Marw for a space, but a few years after he had to fight against a new Tamimite rising in Abarshahr, headed by Bahîr b. Warqâ as Sarîmî (596, 9). He entrusted Marw to Bukair b. Wishâh, but did not leave his son Mûsâ in the capital for fear of the Tamimites there, but ordered him to cross the Oxus with his valuables and seek refuge in a fortress or with a king. He then advanced against Abarshahr. Whilst fighting there with Bahîr, there reached him, at the end of 72,[1] a letter from Abdulmalik promising to grant to him for a term of 7 years the stattholdership of Khurasan, if he would recognise him as Khalifa. This he merely regarded as an insult, since he wanted to rule independently, and he made the messenger eat the letter. Thereupon the Umaiyid offered the stattholdership to the representative in Marw, Bukair b. Wishâh, who accepted it. Now Ibn

---

(595, 14) from this that he fought two years against Ibn Khâzim ; he may also have included the war against the Bakr, for even in A. II. 66 we find him outside of Khurâsân. *Cf.* Chawarig, p. 34. He fell in A. H. 82 (1066, 15).

[1] A later date, Tab., 834f.

Khâzim could not withstand Bukair and Bahîr together, so he tried to reach his son Mûsâ at Tirmidh, but was overtaken by Bahîr and fell after an obstinate resistance, and as he died spat in the face of Wakî' Ibn adDauraqîya[1] who despatched him. The stattholder Bukair forcibly possessed himself of his severed head and sent it to Abdulmalik, giving out that it was himself who had overcome and slain the tyrant. The real conqueror, Bahîr, he ill-treated and for a time threw into prison (Tab., 831-35).

This was the opportunity for a brothers' feud among the Tamîm themselves, especially among the Sa'd Tamîm who in Khurasan and particularly in Marw preponderated still more than in Basra, and to whom Bukair as well as Bahîr belonged. The Muqâ'is and Butûn took the side of Bahîr, the Aus and Abnâ that of Bukair, but as it became evident at last to the Khurasan Arabs that they must lose the lordship over the land, if it were not rescued from their dispute for superiority and legitimised by a higher authority, they begged Abdulmalik of their own accord, in A. H. 74, for a Quraishite as stattholder, who should stand above the hatred and envy of the tribes. He sent a scion of his house, Umaiya b. Abdillâh b. Khâlid b. Asîd, a genial and liberal-minded man. When

---

[1] So called after his mother, a prisoner of war, who came from Dauraq in Khûzistân.

the latter came to Abarshahr, Bahîr received him and tried to prejudice him against Bukair, but did not succeed. Umaiya confirmed the appointment of all the officials of Bukair, and offered to himself the chief command of the standing government troops, and it was only when the latter refused this post, which included the representation of the stattholder, that he bestowed it upon his opponent (Tab., 859-62).

Bukair was angry at having to give way to the Quraishite, and when the latter was absent upon a campaign he used the opportunity to raise a rebellion in Marw behind his back.[1] The families of the troops which were on service were in his hands, and for that reason Umaiya, who marched back in a hurry, entered upon friendly negotiations with him. He paid his debts and gave him 40 days' space of security to withdraw, if he chose, into any town in Khurasan, but Bukair remained in Marw and continued to stir up strife. Umaiya took no account of the complaints laid against him by Bahîr until they were confirmed from another quarter. He was then arrested and in spite of his denial found guilty, since the witnesses seemed incorruptible. He was executed on a Friday with his own sword, and the executioner must have been Bahîr, since there was no other who could say as he did it,—

---

[1] This could hardly be before A. H. 77, the last year of Umaiya. With Tab., 1023 cf. 1028, 4f. as well as Balâdh., 416.

" One of us two must die, if the Banû Sa'd is
to be at rest " (Tab., 1022-31).

The last act of the feud among the Banû
Sa'd did not come to an end, however, till A. H.
81. Seventeen men of the Abnâ, the family of
Bukair, had conspired against Bahîr, but they
did not act in concert, but each for his own
hand. One of them succeeded in an attempt
upon the life of Sa'sa'a b. Harb. He obtained
from Bahîr's relatives in Sajistân a recommendation to him, wormed himself into his
confidence, and then stabbed him with a dagger
tempered in asses' milk, in public before the
people, as was proper, with the exclamation,—
" This is the revenge for Bukair ! " He was
arrested and cheerfully suffered death. The
Abnâ, who had come to him in prison to kiss
his head, made a great uproar at his execution
since he had only done his duty and exacted
legitimate revenge, but when the blood-money
for the executed man was paid to them, they
allowed themselves to be appeased after it had
long seemed as if the dispute between them and
the Butûn were about to break out anew (Tab.
1047-51).

There was one remnant of the rebellion of
the Qaisite Abdullâh b. Khâzim still unsup-
pressed ; a scion of his rule still held out for
12 years after his fall. His son Mûsâ, " the
beardless," had escaped from Marw in the nick

of time and had crossed the Oxus with a few hundred men. Various attempts to find somewhere a place to settle were of no avail, and at last he established himself in Tirmidh, a little way from Balkh on the other bank of the Oxus, actually in the citadel which stood on a rocky promontory. The Qaisites gathered round him till he had about 1,100 men as his following. With these he made raids in all directions and the neighbours were filled with deadly fear of him and his mounted devils. An expedition which the stattholder Umaiya sent against him failed, while his successor Muhallab and his son Yazîd left him unmolested. By the addition of the scattered remnant of Ibn Ash'ath's army his troops increased to 8,000 men and he began to make more extensive expeditions, in which he was also supported by two Iranian officers, who with their following had come over to him from the Arabian army,—Huraith b. Qutba and his brother Thâbit. They had previously had relations with the native dynasties of the land, especially with the Tarkhûn of Samarqand, and by their help got ready an army to fight along with Mûsâ against the ruling Arabs. But Mûsâ did not want to assist in an attack upon Yazîd in Khurasan, but only to drive out his officials from Transoxiana, and they were thoroughly successful in purging

Transoxiana of all that was left of the Arab sway, but it was Huraith and Thâbit who distinguished themselves most in the business and were in consequence so powerful that Mûsâ was jealous of them. Then followed an incursion of the Turks, with the Haital and Tubbat, into Transoxiana. Mûsâ had once before successfully withstood an attack by them and on this occasion also he powerfully drove them back from Tirmidh, and then himself took the offensive and inflicted a defeat upon them near Kafiân, which scattered them. On this occasion Huraith b. Qutba fell, but that did not distress Mûsâ; he would willingly have been rid of the other brother, Thâbit, as well. A plot to assassinate him was, however, betrayed to Thâbit by a spy and he fled to Khushwarâgh,[1] where many Arabs and Iranians gathered round him and the Tarkhûn of Samarqand came to his aid with a great army. With united forces the two now advanced before Tirmidh and pressed Mûsâ desperately hard, but an Arab Zopyrus contrived to sneak up to Thâbit and murder him. Mûsâ then ventured upon a night attack upon the enemy's camp and made them retire, but not long after Mufaddal, Yazîd's brother and his successor as stattholder of Khurasan, made an alliance with the Tarkhûn

---

[1] To be read thus : cf. Tab., 1594, 9.

of the Soghd and the Sabal of the Khuttal against him. In face of this coalition he could not hold out and he was slain as he attempted to escape. Tirmidh capitulated and the captured warriors were executed. This took place in the year 85.

3. During the time that the strength of the Arabs of Khurasan was being spent in bloody discord, the earlier conquests in Transoxiana[1] were completely lost. The Turks, turning the tables, dared to invade Khurasan, extending their raiding excursions as far as Naisâbûr (Bal., 415), and even after the return of peace and order the old attacks were renewed. The stattholder Umaiya was, after a long interval, the first to march again across the Oxus, but he was no warrior. By his shameful flight from the Kharijite Abû Fudaik he had spoilt his position in Iraq and he did not regain it in Khurasan. After successes to begin with (Bal., 426, 10f.) he at last suffered a decisive defeat, was hard put to it to get himself and his army safely over the Oxus, and drew upon himself the sarcastic line, " Whoever named him ' the little girl' (Umaiya) hit the mark !" The result was that he had to resign in A. H. 78. Hajjâj

---

[1] Expeditions across the Oxus were undertaken before this under Ibn 'Âmir. They were repeated by Ubaidullâh b. Ziâd who brought a band of Bukhârite prisoners with him to Basra ; also by his successor, Saîd b. Uthmân, who was murdered by his Soghdian servants, and by Salm b. Ziâd, whose wife bore him a son in Samarqand.

appointed in his place the Azdite Muhallab, after Khurasan and Sajistan had been put under him in addition to Iraq. The latter had subdued the Khawârij in Karmân in the middle of 78, but did not come in person to Marw till A.H. 79. In Transoxiana he did not follow in the steps of his predecessor. In his last year he besieged the town of Kish, but in vain,[1] and he was glad to accept the inhabitants' pledge of a money payment on consideration of his withdrawal. On the way home he died in Zâghûl, near Marwrûdh, in Dhulhijja, 82 (Jan., 702). He did not add to his renown in war in Khurasan, but in spite of this his coming there was of great importance. He brought with him his tribe, which till then had fought under him against the Khawârij.[2] The Azd also made alliances in Khurasan with the Bakr and Rabîa,[3]

---

[1] Madâinî twice tells of the siege of Kish in the same circumstances, under A. H. 80 and A. H. 82 (Tab., 1040 ff. and 1077 ff.). The chronological difference may be considered adjusted from the fact that the siege is said to have lasted two years (from the middle of 80 till 82).

[2] The poets Thâbit Qutna and Ka'b alAshqarî, both of Azd, came to Khurasan from Fârs and Karmân, the scene of the wars against the Khawârij. To be sure individual Azdites might well have settled there earlier, but it was through Muhallab that the tribe first reached eminence there. In the earlier feud between Tamim and Bakr we do not see any trace of the alliance of the Azd and Bakr.

[3] Concerning the numerical proportion of the divisions (Akhmâs) see Tab., 1291. The Tamîm gave 10,000 men to the army, the Azd 10,000, the Qais (Ahl alÂlia) 9,000, the Bakr 7,000, the Abdulqais

and thus the Mudar (Tamîm and Qais) lost their superiority, so long, at least, as the stattholder at the same time threw the weight of his official position on the other side.

As head of his mixed family and his provisional successor in office, Muhallab named his son Yazîd, who was confirmed by Hajjâj. Yazîd fought in Farghâna and Khwârizm, and also on this side of the Oxus in Badhaghis, but without any success, or at least any that lasted. He was certainly enterprising, in spite of his luxury and corpulence, but ambitious and imperious rather than capable of execution. He felt his dependence upon Hajjâj all the more painfully since he was the head of the Azd and the latter *parvenu* was a Qaisite. He was very unwilling to mete out the fitting punishment to the Iraqite rebels, who, after the defeat of Ibn Ash'ath, fled into his province. Of the ringleaders who fell into his hands he let the Yemenites go and only delivered up the Mudar. Hajjâj was not deceived about his sentiments, and in Rabî II, 85 (April, 704) he deposed him and put in his place Mufaddal b. Muhammad, who was plotting against his half-brother Yazîd. He would in reality have preferred to withdraw the province

4,000. The total in round numbers is 40,000 men capable of bearing arms ; so the total number of the Arabs in Khurasan can hardly have amounted to more than 200,000.

altogether from the rule of the Muhallabids and
the Azd, but he dared not, so long as Mûsâ b.
Ibn Khâzim still held his position in Tirmidh
and Transoxiana—at least people assumed so, and
not without reason.   Muhallab and Yazîd were
convinced that a Qaisite stattholder was not
desirable in opposition to Mûsâ, since Mûsâ
himself was a Qaisite and had the sympathies
of the Qais on his side, so they spared him as a
useful foe, so as not to make themselves superfluous by his removal.   But Mufaddal swerved
from this domestic policy and used severity
against Mûsâ, and thus, in fact, sawed off the
branch he sat on.   For as soon as he had got
the better of Mûsâ he was removed from his
post, after being in possession of it nine months.
Habîb b. Muhallab and Abdulmalik b. Muhallab,
too, were dismissed from their offices and Yazîd
himself put in prison.   As stattholder of Khurasan Qutaiba was now (A.H. 85 or 86) appointed ;
he was a son of Muslim b. Amr of Basra, who
was faithfully devoted to the Umaiyid rule. Thus
the preponderance in Khurasan of the Azd-Rabîa,
who a potiori were called the Yemen, was
broken ; the Arabs at the time of Qutaiba were
called simply the Mudar (Tab., 1185, 5).   He
himself belonged to the scattered and unimport-
ant tribe Bâhila, which stood outside the large
groups and occupied a low place in the ethnic
genealogy,   but   in   the circumstances allied

himself with the Qais.[1] Hajjâj was glad that Qutaiba had not a powerful house at his back and had to rely on the government for support.

Before Qutaiba b. Muslim the districts which lay beyond Khurasan to the north and east had been only partially taken in and subdued only in a very cursory fashion, as we recognise from the story of Mûsâ b. Ibn Khâzim. He was at least the first to set on foot a real conquest. For a better comprehension of his campaigns we may here find space for a few brief geographical and ethnological remarks concerning the Thaghrân, i.e. the two boundaries of Khurasan.

The one was Tukhâristân, the old Bactria. It is, properly speaking, the mountainous country on both sides of the middle Oxus as far as Badakhshân. Tab., 1180, 7 includes also Shûmân and Akhrûn, but usually only the country south of the Oxus is understood under this name. The Arabs reckoned it virtually in the territory of Marwrûdh, their most easterly army town, for their occupation of Balkh (Baktra) had not been of long duration, though Balkh was, nevertheless, the capital of the country. In the zone of Balkh were situated, further east, Khulm, Tâliqân, Fâriâb and other towns. Further south, and higher up the Paropamisus (Ghûr) lay the districts of Jûzjân or Jûzistân and

---

[1] So also in Mesopotamia, cf. Tab., 1300, BAthîr, 4,256 ff., and above, p. 201, n. 1.

Gharshistân or Gharjistân (with Bâmiân commanding the pass). Further west was Bâdhaghîs between the valleys of the Marghâb and
the Harîrûdh; to the south-east were Ghaznîn
and Wâlishtân, which belonged rather to
Kâbulistân and Sajistân.

The other and far more important boundary
of Khurasan was Mâwarânahr, *i.e.*, Transoxiana.
Taken in its broader sense it includes as its
eastern part, Khuttalân, the mountainous region
of the Khuttal (Salzgebirg 1596), stretching
westwards from Badakhshân to the river (Wakh-
shâb[1]).   Then comes Saghâniân, the land of the
Saghân;[2] further west, between Tirmidh on the
Oxus and Samarqand on the Polytimetus are
the towns of Shûmân and Akhrûn, and then
Kish and Nasaf.   The last two are, in Maqdisî,
267, 282 ff., included with Saghâniân, but are
usually regarded as belonging to Sogdiana.
Sogdiana is the land of the Soghd on both sides
of the lower Polytimetus, "the river of the
Soghd," which disappears in the oasis of Bukhârâ, without quite reaching the Oxus.[3]   The old
capital is Samarqand, and by the Soghd are

---

[1] Now Surghâb.   In Wakhsh-âb is preserved the name Oxus,
which is no longer used of the main stream.

[2] The king is called Ṣaghân-khudâh, Tab. 1596. 1600 ff.

[3] Now called Zarafshân.   The name *Polytimetus* is incomprehensible ; *Polytmetus* would be more suitable, since the river is cut
up into mere canals.   The ancient irrigation-system of this country
is equal to any in magnificence and fame.

chiefly understood the inhabitants of the town
and district of Samarqand. To the east of
Sogdiana, on the one side lies the mountainous
Ushrûsana, on the narrow upper course of the
Polytimetus; on the other side, to the north of
the mountains, lie Shâsh and Farghâna on the
Jaxartes at the crossing into the territory of
the Turks. The lower course of the Oxus, from
where it bends towards the north, goes through
deserts till it at last forms the oasis of Khwârizm. The main crossing on this stretch is at
Âmul, on a bridge of boats.

The population, the language and the
industry [1] in this fairly extensive region was
Iranian. In politics there was a great amount
of division, which cannot only have set in since
the fall of the Sasanid kingdom. Under the
aristocracy of the Dihqâns the ruling dynasties
soared above the simple nobility, landed proprietors and bailiffs in the villages. Everywhere in
the isolated districts and larger towns we find
hereditary princes with their own peculiar titles.[2]
The titles are partly Aryan, but non-Aryan titles
are to be found as well. For the much scattered

---

[1] Besides the culture of the ground which was established upon
a rational management of the water, trade (in skins, silk, water
(weapons ?), slaves) was very important on the road to Sina,

[2] Frequently Khudâh ; in Khwârizm, Shâh ; in Balkh, Ispadbadh ;
in Farghâna, Ikhshêd ; in Gharshistân, Shêr. On the other hand,
Ikhrîd and Wîk in Kish, Ashkand in Nasaf, Afshîn in Ushrûsana are
actual proper names.

Iranians had not remained purely Iranian and unsubdued; in Parätacene the Khuttal settled over their heads. Their king is called the Sabal,[1] and they are apparently identical with the old Hephthalites, the Haital. The latter had once been supreme in all Transoxiana, which Maqdisî therefore simply calls "the land of the Haital." At the time with which we are concerned they had, however, fallen back behind the Turks. The Turks had their real seat east of the Jaxartes, but by means of raids which they made from there to very great distances, they had gained a footing in many of the Iranian towns round about, and there founded dynasties and levied tribute from the district. The Turkish title Tarkhûn or Tarkhân is found on the far side as well as on the near side of the Oxus, and denotes a prince who is under the protection of the Khâqân.[2]

In Transoxiana and Tukhâristân the real rulers at that time were the Turks. It was really with them that the Arabs had to fight, at least in the last resort. They drove them back out of Khurasan and put a stop to their raiding expeditions. In Transoxiana and Tukhâristân,

---

[1] If it is not a proper name, cf. Jaish (Hanash) b. Sabal.

[2] Tab. 3,647 : the Khâqân and his Tarkhâns. cf. the *Rûbkhân* of Rûb, the *Tûsik* (Tarsal) of Fâriâb, the *Sahrak* (Sahrab) of Tâliqân, the *Shadh*—all in Tukhâristân. The overlord of the Turks is always called *the* Khâqân, as if there were only one.

in the matter of the lordship over the
Iranian population, they competed successfully
with them, but even they were content with a
superficial subjection. They everywhere left
the local authorities in power and demanded
only one tribute, which bore the distinctive
name of "Fidya," *i.e.* the ransom paid to escape
a declaration of war and pillage. If the tribute
were withheld,—which might easily happen, the
hostilities then began anew, and as a matter of
fact the Arabs were not always sorry to have
once more the opportunity for plundering excursions.

Even through Qutaiba there did not come
about any systematic change, but for all that he
extended the Arab power over the boundaries far
more effectively than had hitherto been the case.
Year after year he undertook expeditions ; every
spring the contingents from Abarshahr, Abîward
and Sarakhs, from Herât and Marwrûdh, came
voluntarily to the campaign. In A.H. 86 he led an
expedition, already set on foot by his predecessor
(after the conquest of Tirmidh), against Akhrûn
and Shûmân. The king agreed to the payment
of tribute. In the following years he turned his
attention to the towns of the oasis of Bukhârâ. In
A.H. 87 and 88 he conquered Baikand, Tumush-
kath and Râmîthana. In Baikand, an industri-
al town with large warehouses,[1] he seized a rich

---

[1] Elias Nis. (under A.H. 87) must mean this town.

supply of weapons and with it fitted out his
Arabs, who till then were poorly armed, possess-
ing altogether only 300 shirts of mail (1180,
15).   In A.H. 89 and 90 he reduced Bukhara
itself, under the pressure of Hajjâj, who had
himself furnished a map of the   district   and
sketched out the plan of campaign.   In A.H. 91
he had his work cut out for him in Tukhâristân
suppressing a widespread rebellion, the moving
spirit of which was the Tarkhan Naizak. He
lured him out of the fortress near Iskêmisht [1]
to which he had betaken himself, and treacherously put him to death with other Tarkhans and
Dihqans. Then he crossed the   Oxus   and
conquered the town of Shuman whose king had
likewise taken part in the Tukharian   rebellion,
continued his march through the Iron Gate,[2]
reduced Kish and Nasaf,[3] and set up a new
government in Bukhara under pretext of necessary executions.   In A.H. 92 he was in Sajistan
and is said to have forced Zunbîl of Kabul to
pay tribute.   In A.H. 93 he invaded Khwarizm
quite unexpectedly, being   invited to do so
privately by the Shah himself, and at first took

---

[1] Istakhrî, 275. The town is situated a little north of Lat. 36,
and slightly east of Long. 69, and on English maps is called Ishkêmish.
Cf. Marquart, Eranshahr (1901), p. 219.

[2] This is the name of a famous narrow pass on an arm of the river
now called Kashka, described in Reclus, 6,502.

[3] By Fâriâb in Tab., 1229, 3 Firiâb is meant ; cf. 1566, 3,

the side of the latter against his younger brother, but later on drove him out and established an Arab *régime* in the land. From Khwarizm he marched to Samarqand, keeping his troops as long as possible in the dark as to their goal. The Tarkhun of that place had purchased peace from him in A.H. 91, but because of this humiliation he was overthrown by his own subjects and driven to suicide, and Ikhshêd Ghûzak had succeeded him. This afforded Qutaiba a welcome opportunity to interfere, and after a long-drawn-out siege a capitulation was made. Ghûzak pledged himself to pay tribute; Qutaiba was to march into Samarqand and hold divine service in a newly-erected mosque and then evacuate the town immediately. But after he was once in he did not evacuate it, but turned it into an Arab garrison town and a point of vantage for his further conquests. From there, in the last three years of his statt-holdership (A.H. 94-96) he penetrated into the upper Zarafshân valley as well as into Shâsh and Farghâna; he is actually said to have got as far as Kashgar and to have come into contact with the Chinese.[1] The accounts of Madâinî in Tabarî and Balâdhurî agree in essentials, except that the latter says nothing about Sajistan and

---

[1] *Cf.* the verses in Tab., 1279f. 1302, 8, and the account of Bal., 426, 18.

Kashgar. They are also repeatedly confirmed by contemporary songs.[1]

As a rule Qutaiba also left the native dynasties in power on payment of tribute, only manifold Arab inspectors or bailiffs were set over them. But a few very important places were still,—if we may express it in a Roman fashion—colonised, *i. e.* selected as seats of Arabism and Islam, even though the former inhabitants were not driven out, and here even retained a certain self-government under the old authorities, who in particular had the allotment and collection of the taxes. Samarqand in particular was intended to become an Arab headquarters. A strong garrison entered with war-gear of every kind, the fire-houses and idols' temples were destroyed; it is alleged that no heathen dared remain over-night in the town. Similar, but apparently not quite so drastic, measures were taken in Khwarizm and in Bukhara. In Bukhara also heathendom was suppressed, for to the statement that there was

---

[1] The most important poets of Khurasan are Thâbit Qutna alAzdî (Agh., 13, 49ff.), Ka'b alAshqarî alAzdî (Agh., 13, 56ff.), Nahâr b. Tausi'a alBakrî (Agh., 14, 115), Ziâd alA'jam Maula of the Abdulqais (Agh., 14, 102ff.), Mughîra b. Habnâ at Tamîmî (Agh., 11, 162ff.). Several others, otherwise unknown, are mentioned in Tab. only. Farazdaq, Kumait and Tirrimâh also occasionally touch upon Khurasan affairs. The poets always take the side of their clans, and their interest and judgment are influenced accordingly, in spite of Nahâr b. Tausi'a in the Kâmil, 538, 15. They are therefore to be used with caution, though they are valuable enough witnesses for the bare facts.

a fire-house there and also a sanctuary, in which peacocks were kept, it should be added that for the future these establishments vanished.[1] These towns were to become for their surroundings what the Arab army-towns Naisabur, Marw, Marwrudh and Herat were for Khurasan, and their colonisation was doubtless a great step beyond anything attempted and carried through in that district before. The permanent result of it was that Bukhara, Samarqand and even Khwarizm became important nurseries of Islam and of Arabian learning.

The enthusiasm of the Arabs over their successes, as it finds expression in numerous songs, was not unjustified. The struggle was not made an easy one for them. They were deficient in numbers and at the beginning badly armed. The long distances, the difficulty of the ground and the climatic conditions put great impediments in their path. They had to take with them stores and warm clothing, and could only carry on the campaign in the better season of the year. The enemy were not contemptible. In most cases great armies, often from long distances, came to the help of those who were besieged. These armies were led by Turks and to a large extent were composed

---

[1] We must bear in mind that the conversion of the Iranian subjects to Islam was in general not demanded, but that they were freely allowed to continue their own cult.

of Turks. In fact the Arabs were fighting
with the Turks for the hegemony in these
regions, and wrested it from them. That was
a feat indeed, and a just title to their lordship
over the Iranians, who had not been able to
defend themselves against the Turks. A great
share of the merit is probably to be ascribed to
the leader, Qutaiba, who far excelled his predecessors, and the great men of Iran had far
more respect for him than for Muhallab and
Yazîd. In war he certainly behaved cruelly
and treacherously ; for the sake of God, *i. e.* for
the benefit of Islam, he did not shrink from
treachery, and pretty often it was his unscru-
pulousness which he had to thank for his successes, but in this he was not very different from
the general run of Arab commanders.

The fall of Qutaiba took place when he was
at the height of his fame and power, and the
event made a great stir in the Islamic world.
Madâinî, in his detailed account of it, has also
borrowed pieces of a narrative of Abû Mikhnaf.
The Khalifa Walîd I died in the middle of Jumâdâ
II, 96, (end of Feb., 715). His successor
Sulaimân hated Hajjâj and his adherents, who
had wanted to exclude him from the succession.
Death removed Hajjâj from his vengeance,
but he was able to wreak it upon Qutaiba,
against whom he was specially incited by Yazîd
b. Muhallab and Abdullâh b. Ahtam. Qutaiba

received the tidings of the change of government when he was in the field with the army
in Farghâna. He knew that deposition and
worse were threatening him and did not mean
to suffer quietly anything that might happen to
him, but it was some time before he made a
decision what to do.[1] The plan to return to
Samarqand, establish himself there and only
keep with him those warriors who offered themselves voluntarily, he rejected, and decided to
carry the whole army with him in the rising
against the Khalifa. In the mosque of
Farghâna he explained to the representatives of
the army who he was and who Sulaimân and
Yazîd were, and invited them to side with
him. They were at the end of that year's
campaign[2] and longing for wife and children,
and did not show much zest for an undertaking
which looked so far in advance and was so
dangerous, so they made no response at all.
Qutaiba had not expected this, and at once lost

[1] He is said to have sent three letters to Sulaimân, but did not
wait for an answer. Sulaimân's messenger was only at Hulwân
when he heard the news of his insurrection. Of the two letters of
Sulaimân mentioned in Weil, 1, 555f., there is no mention in Tab.;
Qutaiba is falsely represented in these as still present in Marw, and
under orders to set out for Farghâna. The Bâhilites who appear here
in Madâinî rather frequently as representatives of a special tradition,
try to whitewash their tribal companion, Qutaiba; e.g. Tab., 1311.

[2] The news of Walîd's death could hardly reach Farghâna before
July, and then some more time passed before Qutaiba came forward
with his scheme.

his equanimity. Still standing in the pulpit, he broke out into abusive reproaches against the different tribes and recalled every shameful thing that was said of them, not sparing a single one, and even when he had descended from the pulpit he would not be appeased by his relatives, but repeated the insults in the most violent manner.

He thus gave offence to one and all of the Arabs in the army, who were accustomed to wipe out such a disgrace by bloodshed. They secretly set on foot negotiations to mutiny against the arch-traitor. The Azd, who hated him from the beginning as the supplanter of the Muhallabids, and were most deeply insulted by him, made an agreement with their allies the Rabîa and offered the leadership to the Bakrite Hudain b. Mundhir, but he was afraid of competing with the powerful Tamîm: "They will, inspite of everything, stick to Qutaiba, if the rising against him emanates from us." Thus the first step was left to the Tamîm. They were angry with Qutaiba because of his behaviour towards the Banû Ahtam, who belonged to them. He had, indeed, years before, during his campaign against Bukhara, left Abdullâh b. Ahtam behind as his substitute in Marw. The latter had seized the opportunity to intrigue with Eajjâj against him, but had fared badly and had been compelled to flee to Syria to Sulaimân, who at that time was still the prospective heir-apparent. Qutaiba had then made his brothers and cousins pay the penalty in his stead, thereby calling down the revenge of the Tamîm upon himself.[1] He had, besides, personally insulted their leader Wakî b. Hassân b. Abî Sûd,[2] by ascribing to his own brother in an official report the honour of gaining a great victory over the Turks, an honour due to the former, and again by taking away from him the command of the Tamîm division and giving it to a Dabbite. Wakî headed the mutiny. The Iranian Haiyân anNabatî[3] supported him, a man who, for obvious reasons, nursed a deep hatred of Qutaiba (Tab., 1253). He was a dangerous man in an influential central position, and through the Iranian servants had connections on all sides with the Arab masters so that he learned and knew everything, and was versed in conspiracy in a fashion quite different from the Arabs. He was particularly important as the leader of the Mawâlî, *i.e.* the Iranians who had embraced Islam, who served in a corps of their own in the Arab army. They were personally devoted to Qutaiba, but Haiyân managed to alienate them

---

[1] Bal., 425f. Agh., 13, 61. Tab., 817, 1309f., 1312.

[2] He must not be confused with the man of the same name, the murderer of Ibn Khâzim, who, to be sure, was also a Tamimite, but of another family.

[3] He was called a Nabataean only on account of his imperfect pronunciation of the Arabic (Tab., 1291).

from him by making it clear to them that the internal dispute of the Arabs was no concern of theirs since it was not waged for Islam.

Qutaiba at first regarded the warnings he received as envious calumnies, but at last it struck him that Wakî was never showing face in his presence, and he summoned him to come before him. When the latter feigned illness, painted his foot red and bound a cord with amulets round his calf, he ordered him to be fetched by force. But when the order was to be carried out, Wakî cut off the magic cord and sprang as he was from his sick-bed into the saddle. He rode off all alone, but in a very short time had enough men about him to be able to attack Qutaiba. The latter was only joined by his brothers, his few tribal cousins from Bâhila, and some other trusty men. The Iranians under Haiyân, upon whom he thought he could rely, went over to the aggressors. Again Qutaiba changed from defiance to despair; he was as if paralysed. His horse reared and would not let him mount. Sitting on a chair in front of the fortress of Farghâna, he awaited in the evening the certain issue of the struggle with resignation. His brothers and helpers fell and even he himself was slaughtered; an Azdite cut off his head. He had been deceived in the expectation that he could carry the army with him. If he had had a tribe or a powerful

family at his back it would perhaps have
fallen out differently (1659, 4ff.), but that was
not the case. The Bâhila were too weak, and
the Qais whom he had held by abandoned him
just as did the Iranians. Even the power of an
over-mastering idea availed him nothing; he
only wanted to make himself and his position
secure. To stand by a man, however capable,
who was only officially connected with them,
against the authority which sanctioned his
position, was a course that the Arabs would not
easily follow, as Ubaidullâh b. Ziâd in Basra
had already experienced. Where they miscal-
culated was in thinking they could carry on the
government in their provinces independently of
the Khalifate. A stattholder, who was not head
of a tribe as well, could do nothing without, and
nothing against, the Khalifa ; personal prowess
was not sufficient. The Iranian princes, indeed,
could not understand the conduct of the Arabs
towards Qutaiba ; they regarded it as suicide,
and they were so far right, for by his fall the
rule of the Arabs over the boundaries which he
had founded was severely shaken.

According to Tabarî, the catastrophe took
place in A.H. 96; B. Qutaiba makes it not till
the beginning of 97. Wakî, recognised by the
tribes as the provisional successor of Qutaiba,
demanded his head, and when the Azdite who
had it, at the instigation of his tribe refused to

hand it over, he pointed to a pole and said, —
"The horse there (*i.e.* the gallows) wants to
have a rider." This was effective, and he then
sent the bloody trophy to the Khalifa, but not
through Tamimites,—they were too much on his
side for that. His inaugural address in the
mosque [1] consisted only of a few drastic pro-
verbs and verses, which, however, served to
express his meaning. In conclusion he said,—
"The Marzbân has raised the price of corn ; to-
morrow in the market the bushel costs 4
dirhams—not more, on penalty of death." By
the Marzbân he appparently indicated Qutaiba
as an alien grandee after the Iranian fashion. [2]
He himself turned out an Arab of the old stamp.
He was strict with Islam, but hated the punishment of flogging, which the Qoran allots to
certain transgressions, and preferred to sentence
a drunkard to death at once. He also executed
an Arab who had robbed the body of one of the
Bahilites who fell with Qutaiba, and expressly
forbade such deeds. His actions were done
en grand seigneur. The Khalifa Sulaimân confirmed his position at first, but 9 or 10 months
after Yazîd b. Muhallab took his place without,
however, having to resign his former province,
Iraq. Unlike Qutaiba, Yazîd had a tribe behind

[1]   But of Marv, not of Farghâna.
[2]   There was, indeed, a proper Marzbân in Marw, who probably
controlled the policing of the market.

him, a fact which was borne in mind. With him the Azd returned to the leadership and the emoluments, the Tamîm were repressed, and Wakî abused. Moreover he also brought with him Syrian government troops, and so introduced them into Khurasan, from which Hajjâj had designedly kept them away (1257) by employing them exclusively in India. As usual he filled up all the posts with his sons and relatives. He was at home in Khurasan, felt freer there than in Iraq and had better opportunities for theft and extortion. He required the money for his expensive necessaries, e.g. for beautiful maidens, and he kept up a great display.

Before this, whenever there had been any mention before Sulaimân of the great deeds of Qutaiba, Yazîd is said to have always objected that Jurjân was still untouched, although it barred the way to Khurasan. Indeed the mountainous country to the south-east of the Caspian Sea obtruded somewhat inconveniently upon the Muslim territory. Yazîd, however, was induced to attack it not so much as a duty which honour demanded, as because of an opportunity which offered. In Jurjân a dispute for the throne was in progress. The prince Feroz had fled from his cousin, the Marzbân, who was in alliance with the Turk Sûl in Dahistân, and came to Yazîd and asked his help. In the spring

of the year 98 [1] the latter set out with an exceptionally large army, the smaller proportion
of which were Khurasanites and the greater
Iraqites and Syrians. Without striking a blow,
he re-instated Feroz in Jurjân, and after he was
received, lured Sûl with his Turks from the
mountains into the marshland where he got him
into his power, and he is said to have slain
14,000 prisoners and gained uncountable spoil.
After the subjection of Dahistân and Baiâsân
he advanced upon the Ispahbadh of Tabaristân,
whose peace proposals he rejected thinking he
would gain more by a forcible conquest. But
he suffered a severe defeat, and at the same time
found himself threatened in the rear by a rising
in Jurjân. Haiyân an Nabatî then made his
appearance as mediator. He represented himself to be a compatriot of the Ispahbadh and
induced him to forego his momentary advantage
in favour of a far-sighted policy, to suspend
the struggle and pledge himself to the payment
of the sum which he had before offered for peace.

---

[1] The year 98 is given. That the campaign was begun in spring,
which fell in the second half of the year, is a matter of course. It
cannot have lasted beyond the autumn, and in autumn there was the
change of Khalifate which resulted in the fall of Yazîd. If this
is so, then the siege of Sûl cannot have lasted six months, and that of
the Marzbân cannot have taken seven. On the other hand it is probably correct that Yazîd marched out three or four months after his
arrival in Khurasan. This then happened in the year 98, the first half
of the year, but he had sent his son Muhallab on in advance.

Relieved from his predicament, Yazîd now turned back to Jurjân where the Marzbân had
again arisen, and after a lengthy siege took
possession of the mountain fastness in which the
latter was defending himself. To fulfil an oath
of vengeance he caused the blood of the executed prisoners to flow into a brook, and ate
bread made from the flour of the mill driven
by this water. Then he triumphantly reported
to Sulaimân his success, which in reality was
anything but brilliant, and in any case quite
ephemeral, and declared the fifth of the spoil,
which was to be handed over to the Khalifa, at
4 or 6 million dirhams, thus preparing for himself the fate he deserved, for when Sulaimân
died in Safar, 99, in the same summer[1] in which
the campaign took place, his successor Umar II
recalled the perverse fellow and cast him into
a debtors' prison, since he was unable to pay
the specified amount of the fifth.

4. In Khurasan the Azd had come into prominence with the Muhallabids, and with them
they fell again into obscurity, retiring into the
background and the opposition. Indeed, the
reaction made by Umar II against the partial-
ity of his predecessor was only that of complete
neutrality towards the tribes, and he showed
himself not unfriendly to the Azd although he

---

[1] Sepr., 717. The change of the year from A.H. 98 to A. H. 99 was
in the middle of August, 717.

put an end to their hegemony by deposing their leader. But with his successor there set in a party reaction against the party-government of Sulaimân, particularly after the suppression of the great rebellion which the Muhallabids had stirred up in Iraq. Yazîd II made vengeance upon the Muhallabids and their following the chief motive of his reign, and the Azdites of Khurasan were also made to feel it although they had not taken part in that rebellion at all. They were expelled from all offices, their chiefs were abused, and the Bahilites were allowed to take revenge for Qutaiba upon them. The Mudar again got the supremacy, with the Tamîm at their head, but for all that the stattholder was never chosen from the Tamîm, though frequently his assistant, the commander of the standing government forces, was. But the stattholders belonged almost always to the Qais, who, since Hajjâj, played the rulers. The Qaisite stattholders, however, were not prevented by their tribal and party community from enmity and ill-will towards each other. The general rule was that the successor abused his predecessor and extorted money from him under the pretext of requiring a statement of accounts, and he behaved similarly to the latter's subordinate officials as well. That was the Arab form of ministerial responsibility. The constant, abrupt, and absolute change of government hindered any continuity.

57

The government was a purely personal thing and was equivalent to robbery, which was to benefit its possessor as speedily as possible or, as it was expressed, to be "devoured." Indeed this was the case not only in Khurasan, but it was there that it went on most shamelessly, and there it was most dangerous, because in this exposed province more than anywhere, a firmly established goverment was necessary. Under these circumstances, the conquests of Qutaiba very soon became insecure and had to be constantly repeated. Certainly the strong buttresses of Arabism and Islam in Sogdiana which the latter had founded, especially Samarqand and Bukhara, were maintained, and the process of Islamisation continued there, but from that very fact there unexpectedly appeared for the rule of the Arabs a new mischief which grew and consumed everything around it.

The stattholder sent to Khurasan by Umar II in place of Yazîd, namely Jarrâh b. Abdillâh alHakamî, was a man of Hajjâj's school. He undertook an expedition against the Khuttal in Parätacene, who so far had scarcely been attacked at all, and sent a report of it to the Khalifa. Among the messengers was the pious Abû Saidâ adDabbî, who although an Arab[1] felt impelled, from religious reasons, to put in

---

[1] He understood no Persian (1507). The fact that he was a Maula does not make him an Iranian.

a good word for the Iranians who had embraced
Islam. He said they were represented in great
numbers in the army and yet received no pension; they were zealous Muslims and yet had
to pay the subject-tax. Umar ordered a change
to be effected here, and when Jarrâh attempted
to stem the rush to Islam which now resulted [1]
by requiring circumcision, he deposed him after
he had put in nearly a year and a half of his term
of office, in Ramadân 100 (April, 719). In his
place he appointed the gentle Abdurrahmân b.
Nuaim alGhâmidî, who was certainly an Azdite,
though he did not belong to the Azd Umân, *i.e.*
to the Azdite party in Khurasan, and chose to
assist him as tax-supervisor a Qaisite, the energetic Abdurrahmân b. Abdillâh alQushairî.
Ibn Nuaim still remained in office for
a while after Umar's death, but in A. H. 102
was replaced by Saîd Khudhaina,[2] an Umaiyid
prince, who, commissioned by the Khalifa
Yazîd II, brought pressure to bear upon the Azd
and treated them as enemies. Towards the
Iranians he behaved with indulgence, at least
in the conduct of war with the Soghdians, who
at that time had risen against the Arabs in the
district of Samarqand, though not in the capital itself, and had formed an alliance with the
Turks, who were again gaining ground. On

---

[1]   Many kings in Transoxiana accepted Islam (Bal., 426).
[2]   Tab., 1357. 1421. 1867. Balâdh., 427. Agh., 13, 52.

account of this very mildness, which the Arabs thought misplaced, he was soon recalled and in his place in A.H. 103 there came the Qaisite Saîd alHarashî.[1] He was severe with the insubordinates, who from fear of him decided to migrate to Farghâna where the Arabs were then no longer in power. These were chiefly the inhabitants of the towns of Qî, Ishtîkhan, Baiârkath, Bunjîkath and Buzmâjan,[2] with their princes headed by Kârzanj of Qî, who, like many other Soghdian dynasts, was really a Turk.[3] The emigrants mostly[4] betook themselves to the town of Khujanda (Khokend) on the Jaxartes, but Saîd marched against them and shut them up in Khujanda. Disappointed in their hope of the support of the Turkish king, they surrendered and promised to pay the tribute again and return to their home. They soon had cause to regret this, for Saîd made a pretext to compass the execution of the prince of Ishtîkhan. As Kârzanj perceived the same fate in store

[1]   Gentilic of Harîsh b. 'Âmir.

[2]   Ishtîkhan and Buzmâjan lay not far from Samarqand, and so by Bunjîkath it is not the town in Ushrûsana that we are to understand, but the town of the same name near Samarqand. Qî also (1422,16. 41,4) lay near Samarqand on a canal of Zarafshan. For Baiârkath cf. the personal name Baiâr, 1446, 10. Kath is the usual ending of town names.

[3]   In the verse 1281, 5, which is there placed too early, Kâzarank is written in mistake for Kârazank; cf. 1446, 10. Acc. to Tab., 1423; 1425, the king of Qî, who is there given the title *Turkkhâqân*, was originally friendly to the Arabs.

[4]   On the other hand see 1441, 7. 1446 ff. *Cf.* 1418, 1.

for himself, he said to the Arab in whose prison
he was,—" It is not becoming that I should meet
death in worn-out breeches; send word to my
nephew Jalanj to let me have some new ones."
This was the sign agreed on that the latter
(who had stayed at home or lived in another
place in Farghana) should come to his aid. Jalanj
came and tried to invade the Muslim camp,
but in vain. Saîd then ordered the whole of the
Soghdian warriors to be slaughtered, the princes
with their following, and though they defended
themselves with clubs, it was of no avail.
The next day a few thousand more peasants
were put to death and only 400 merchants
spared.   Still there remained many Soghdians
in Farghana, since they had not all settled in
Khujanda (16₁3f. 1717).   On the way back
Saîd subdued several more rebel towns, chiefly
by capitulation, but if it seemed to him advan-
tageous he did not abide by the capitulation in
the case of the princes, but executed them as
well.   His superior, the Iraqite stattholder
Umar b. Hubaira alFazârî, used this as an
opportunity to vent his wrath against him,
which in reality was caused by other reasons.
Saîd had, in fact, several times ignored him and
had not carried out his command to extort money
from some Arabs of Muhallabid leanings in
Khurasan, and also had a prefect of Herat,
appointed direct by Ibn Hubaira, shaved and

flogged for defying him. He was therefore deposed, taken in chains from Marw to Kufa, and there tortured to the point of death. It was a domestic feud of the Qaisites who under Yazîd II were absolutely supreme,—for Saîd as well as his opponent, and above all Ibn Hubaira himself were Qaisites,—and an edifying example of how they let all consideration towards each other go down before the desire for office and money, but for all this they stuck together against the non-Qaisites.

Saîd alHarashî was succeeded by Muslim b. Saîd alKilâbî, a pupil of Hajjâj. He collected from wealthy Iranians the sums which Ibn Hubaira would have assigned to certain Arabs; after all, it was all the same to him whence the money came, if only he got it. He continued the struggle against the Soghdians and Turks, and in the spring of the year 105 (724) equipped an expedition against Farghana.[1] But the Azd and Rabîa in Tukhâristân mutinied and refused to serve. Their leader was Amr b. Muslim al-Bâhilî, a brother of Qutaiba.[2] Muslim sent against them his assistant Nasr b. Saiyâr alKinânî

[1] It is not clear whether he conquered Afshîna on this occasion or earlier. This is a town belonging to the district of Samarqand (1462, 9. 63, 1. 1517, 8), but Balâdh. (428, 3) puts instead the proper personal name Afshîn.

[2] The Bahilites changed their position towards the tribal groups always just according to the circumstances, as they did not belong to any of them naturally.

who vanquished them near Bârûqân, the fixed quarters of the Arab garrison of Balkh, which also contributed to widen the breach between Mudar and Yemen. Muslim then set out. When he was in the neighbourhood of Bukhara news came that the Khalifa Hishâm, who had succeeded Yazîd II in Sha'bân, 105 (Jany., 724), had placed over Iraq the Qasrite (of Bajîla) Khâlid b. Abdillâh in place of the Qaisite Ibn Hubaira. Thereupon many of his fighting men deserted; nevertheless he continued his march and advanced beyond Khujanda into the land of the Turks, but there he was surprised and overcome, and with difficulty managed to get back across the Jaxartes [1] to Khujanda, where he was met by tidings of his deposition (A.H. 106, summer or autumn, 724). His successor was Asad b. Abdillâh, brother of the Iraqite statt-holder, a mere youth.

Asad's inclination, like that of his brother, was towards the Yemenites, although by his tribe he did not exactly belong to them, for the Bajîla, like the Bâhila, stood outside the great groups. He had a number of Khurasan Arabs in high positions scourged. The Bakrite

---

[1] In an anticipatory short report in Tab., 1462 (which is really identical with Tab., 1477ff.), the river which here can only be the Jaxartes is made the Oxus. The Arabs often only say "the river" and leave it to the geographical sense of the reader to distinguish which river is meant.

Bakhtarî b. Abî Dirham (of Hârith b. Ubâd) was content to suffer the chastisement because Nasr b. Saiyâr underwent it at the same time, —a man whom he hated because of the affair of Bârûqân.[1] The officials he appointed were some of them Azdites, but the exultation of the Azd over the fact that they had once more emerged from the shadow into the sunlight was not of long duration, for at the instance of the Khalifa Asad was recalled in A.H. 109. The Dihqâns of Khurasan to whom he had been friendly disposed, gave him a convoy to Iraq.[2]

His successor, Ashras b. Abdillâh asSulamî was again a Qaisite. He tried to appease the ever restless Soghd by the method taken by Umar II, at the suggestion, it is said, of his Iranian scribe Umaira. He sought out the man who is said to have before induced that Khalifa to make the Iranians equal to the Arabs if they embraced Islam, Abû Saidâ Sâlih b. Tarîf adDabbî, and charged him to invite the Soghdians to accept Islam, guaranteeing that the subject-tax should be remitted to the

[1] *Cf.* besides Tab., 1530.

[2] Later on he came back again to Khurasan. The two periods during which he held office are identified by Balâdh. and also confused by Madâinî in Tab. from their contents. The removal of the residence to Balkh certainly falls into the period of his second stattholdership, —for afterwards Marw is again the residence without any mention of a removal back there,—and also possibly the scourging of Nasr. There is not much known about the first term of office.

converts. Accompanied by some Arabs of a like mind with himself Abû Saidâ betook himself to Samarqand. The prefect there, Ibn Abî 'Amarrata alKindî, a son of that Shiite of Kufa who had first drawn the sword for Hujr b. Adî, lent him his aid, and his propaganda had a great success. Many new mosques arose and the heathen came over to Islam in great crowds, but the native princes, who were not interfered with by the Arab government, were exceedingly displeased at this. The fact was, they were responsible for the tribute, and could with difficulty produce the fixed amount of the prescribed sums if so many who were hitherto liable for tribute got clear of paying their share. For this reason they complained to Ashras that everyone had either become "Arab" or was about to do so. The Dihqans of Bukhara are mentioned, and in particular Ghûzak, the Ikh-shêd of Samarqand, whom we came across already in Qutaiba's time. Ashras now tried to get rid of the spirits he had called up. He first of all limited the entrance to Islam by demanding circumcision and some religious knowledge, and when that did not suffice he put other officials in place of Ibn Abî 'Amarrata with instructions to levy the tax again to the old extent upon all those whom they must have already declared exempt. Several thousand converts then left Samarqand and moved to

58

a camp some distance from the town, being
incited and accompanied by Abû Saidâ and his
like-minded friends from different Arab tribes
(Tamîm, Azd and Bakr) including Thâbit
Qutna, Abû Fâtima and Bishr b. Jurmûz.
However, partly by force and partly by persuasion, these Arabs were diverted from the cause
which they had taken up, and so the seceders of
Samarqand lost their support and were brought
back to the old state of subjectdom. The taxes
were exacted with severity and the Iranian
nobility treated with contempt.

But this was not the end of the matter. The
revoking of the conciliatory measure resulted
in the utmost wrath and bitterness of the Soghdians throughout the whole land. In order to
free themselves from the Arabs they made an
alliance with the Turks. A descendant of
Yazdejard, the last Sassanid, is said to have been
concerned in this. The centre-point of the
rising was the oasis of Bukhara, whither the
Khâqân arrived with a great army of Turks and
Iranians. In A.H. 110, probably at the end of
the year,[1] i.e. in spring, 729, Ashras set out with
the Arab army from Marw to cope with the
danger, but near Âmul the Turks barred his
way at the crossing of the Oxus, and it was
only after a lengthy sojourn that he managed to

---

[1] Asad did not leave till near the end of 109 (in Ramadân), and
the mission of Abû Saidâ and its results also take up some time.

get as far as Baikand, where he pitched his camp. The Turks then cut off the water from him, 700 of his fighting men died and the rest were too weak to go on. At last, by the sacrifice of some volunteers, notably Hârith b. Suraij, they succeeded in leading back the water again. It was then that Thâbit Qutna fell. The Arabs now continued their march and after a hot contest in which Ghûzak of Samarqand went over to the Turks, reached Bukhara where they encamped and whence they undertook expeditions (e.g. to Khwârizm). Several divisions, however, were scattered. One of these had made for Kamarja (near Baikand), and the Khâqân then turned against it with his whole strength and shut it within Kamarja, but the besieged defended themselves so well that at last he granted them a free egress, only they were not allowed to join the main army in Bukhara, but had to retire to Dabûsia.

The Khâqân now had a free hand against Ashras in Bukhara. The latter could not gain a footing and apparently was hardly able to move any further, so the Khalifa appointed a successor who was to displace him. This was Junaid b. Abdirrahmân alMurrî,[1] who till then had been in India, from which he brought with him 500 Syrians. Immediately after his arrival[2]

---

[1] *AlMuzani* is a slip of the pen which is frequently met with.

[2] In A.H. 111, but hardly before the end of the year, for the road from Bukhara to Syria, from Syria to India and from India to

he hurried to Ashras' aid, and after some difficulties joined him in Bukhara. He succeeded in defeating the Turks near Zarmân, and in relieving Samarqand which they were besieging, and then led the army safely back to Khurasan, —which was, perhaps, the main thing.

At the end of the year 112, in spring, 731,[1] Junaid had despatched the Arab troops upon different expeditions, particularly in Tukharistan, when a cry for help reached him from the Tamimite Saura b. Hurr of Samarqand, who was attacked by the Khâqân and the princes of the Iranians who were his allies. Although he had not a sufficient force at hand he set out at once and advanced over the Oxus as far as Kish. From there two roads led to Samarqand. He avoided the one through the steppe because it was already summer and he was afraid the enemy might set fire to the grass and the bushes, and chose the road through the mountains. But in a ravine not far from Samarqand he was surprised, and if it had not been for Nasr b. Saiyâr and the especial bravery of the Iranian slaves in the Arab army-baggage, who cut themselves clubs and hewed a way with them, he would have

Khurasan was long and tedious. Ashras probably held on in Bukhara in the winter, A.H. 111.

[1] Spring, 112 may be taken either as the beginning or as the end of the year, but from the circumstances the end is more probable here. The dates in what follows vary by a year between 112 and 113; 113 and 114; I think the higher numbers correct.

been annihilated. But he was still in a dangerous plight. In order to extricate himself from
it he summoned Saura to come to his help from
Samarqand. Saura and the Arab garrison
perished in making the attempt, but Junaid
managed to escape and enter Samarqand. The
Khâqân now turned against Bukhara where a son
of Qutaiba was in command, and besieged the
town. Junaid followed by the shortest route,
defeated him near Tawâwîs in the month of
Ramadân, made his entry into Bukhara on
the feast of Mihrigân,[1] and pleased at having
made sure work of Bukhara and Samarqand,
turned back before winter should set in. The
new troops sent him by Hishâm from Basra
and Kufa, which joined him on the way in
Saghâniân, he sent to Samarqand. For the
years 114 and 115 nothing is reported about
him, and at the beginning of 116 (spring, 734),
he was deposed and succeeded by 'Âsim b.
Abdillâh alHilâlî. To be sure this was also a
Qaisite like himself, but his foe, and chosen as

Certainly not A.H. 112, as is given, but not till 113 (Nov., 731).
The feast of Mihrigân (1552, 7 ; cf. 1550, 13f.) must thus have been
celebrated at that time later than about the time of the autumnal
equinox ; also the New Year's festival, acc. to 1846, 16, fell far beyond
the spring equinox. The account in 1635, 18, must, on the other hand,
be false. Under the Abbasids the calendar of festivals was apparently
adjusted. In A.H. 239 the New Year's festival coincided with Palm
Sunday (Tab., 3, 1420), and in A.H. 245 it was put back still further
(Tab., 3, 1448). Cf. also Tab. 3, 2024. 2143f. 2163.

his successor on that very account, in order to torment him, for Hishâm was angry with him because he had married a daughter of the arch-rebel Yazîd b. Muhallab (*cf.* 1633). Luckily, however, Junaid died of dropsy before 'Âsim arrived at Marw and the latter could only torture his relations and officials.

5. The Arab rule in Transoxiana was seriously affected by its unprincipled vacillation between indulgence and force. Umar II tried to fuse the Iranian subjects with the Arabs by means of Islam, by granting equal political rights to the converts to Islam and removing the subject-tax, but under his successors this measure seems to have been immediately revoked. Although not expressly stated, still it follows from this that immediately after his death force must have been used towards the Soghdians to compel them to pay the tribute which they evidently refused as being now Muslims, and that in order to avoid it many of them left the country under their princes and betook themselves to the protection of the Turks. It is to be noted at the same time that though the command of Umar is said to have been binding upon all, the Muslim Iranians in Khurasan nevertheless did not rebel when it was set aside. During long years they had grown accustomed to their political subordination and had become identified with the Arabs

through the common interest in Islam, and indeed could not so much as lift a finger,—which is true also of the towns of Samarqand and Bukhara where the position of the Arabs was too strong. The insurgents were rather the Soghdians outwith the chief towns, who had been but imperfectly subdued and only recently, and merely because of the material advantages had embraced Islam, following their princes' example. There is no doubt that they forthwith defected from Islam, which had not yet struck root amongst them. But the ineffectiveness of Umar's attempt appears far more clearly from the fact that Ashras made it a second time, and thus the whole thing was repeated. Abû Saidâ and those who shared his ideas, who had already inspired Umar, were also the workers of the reform under Ashras. Once again it came to grief for financial reasons, which no doubt had been the deciding element the first time as well. And again it was not the Iranians of Khurasan but those of Sogdiana who rebelled on account of it. Under Ashras the offer of relief from the subject-tax actually does not appear to have been made to the Mawâlî at all, not even to those in Khurasan, but only to the new converts in Sogdiana. But the revolt of the Soghdians in his time was far more widespread and dangerous than the one after the death of Umar II, especially because the Turks

came into the country and assumed the leadership. The Arabs could alone maintain their
position in the chief towns and at some other
strong points; the movement in Samarqand
itself was suppressed without trouble.[1]

A third attempt to procure for the Iranian
Muslims full citizens' rights in the theocracy
emanated not from above but from below, namely
from the Tamimite Hârith b. Suraij from
Dabûsia,[2] whom we have already met with as a
doughty warrior. In earlier times, as a pious
revolutionary, he wouid have been called a
Khârijite, but he was not pledged to the extreme
consequences to which the Khawârij pinned
their faith; he neither had homage paid to
himself as Khalifa nor did he run any other for
the office. He made his appearànce as a
Murjiite, his scribe, Jahm b. Safwân, being the
best-known theologian of this sect, and he also
took part himself in speeches and discussions
concerning their principles. In practice Murjiitism amounted to a policy of collectivism. The
questions of discussion, especially the ever-
lastingly insoluble one regarding the only rightful Imam, were set aside and left to the decision
of God, and therefore stress was laid upon the

---

[1] *Cf.* with this and what follows G. van Vloten, *Recherches sur la
domination arabe*, in the *Verhandlungen der Amsterdamer Akademie,
1894, Letterkunde*, I, 3.

[2] 1923, 3. 27, 12 ; *cf.* too, 1890, 7.

points upon which the different trends of the
pious opposition could be agreed. This was the
protest for the theocracy against the existing
tyranny, for holy law against injustice and force.
In Khurasan the Qaisite stattholders had stripped
the Umaiyid rule of all credit both in the eyes
of friend and foe, and their conduct towards
the Soghd in particular had conjured up not
only a grave external danger but had also left
in its wake a deep moral indignation which
spread over the circles most nearly concerned.
Now this was the point at which Hârith came
in. He incited the Mawâlî by declaring he
would bring to realisation the freedom from the
subject-tax and the participation in the military
pension which were their due and which had
been promised them, and the Dihqâns and the
people of the villages gathered under his black
standard. He thus followed in the footsteps of
Abû Saidâ, and those of his opinion, as many
as were still alive, were to be found in his
company, e.g. Abu Fâtima al Iyâdî (of Azd)
and Bishr b. Jurmûz adDabbî (of Tamîm).
The leaders of the movement for the bestowing
of equal rights upon the Iranians who had
embraced Islam in the theocracy were again
Arabs, but besides these, numerous Arabs of
Tamîm and Azd also took part in the rising
against the ruling body, and not merely Murjiites.
Hârith accepted any help he could get.

59

The ground he started upon was the "Two
Marches."   At first he unfurled the black
standard in Transoxiana, no doubt in the latter
years of Junaid, from which nothing is reported,
and upon 'Âsim's arrival he spread out his forces
over Tukharistan also.   From Nakhudh *viâ*
Firiâb he went to Balkh after forcing by a
victorious fight a crossing over the Oxus.   The
stattholders of Balkh, Marwrûdh and Herât
could not hold out against him ; all Tukharistan
fell into his hands and even the Arabs themselves, who mostly consisted of Azdites and
Bakrites.   Jabghûia, the Turkish Viceroy in
upper Tukharistan, and the prince of the Khuttal
made common cause with him.

Marw and Abarshahr (Naisabur), the two
westerly districts of Khurasan, were the only
parts still in the undisputed possession of the
Umaiyid rule (1582).   After his successes in
Tukharistan, Hârith's army swelled tremendously ; Arab horsemen and Iranian infantry
were united in it.   With a great force he
now advanced against Marw, where he had
connections with the Tamîm, for he came from
there originally (1890).   'Âsim was going to
retire before him to Abarshahr into the
Qaisite district, and was only with difficulty
prevailed upon to stand his ground.   He beat
back a first attack of Hârith, but when he
learned that he was to be deposed he wanted to

go over to his side. Yahyâ b. Hudain al Bakrî
kept him from doing so, and under the leadership of this sensible man, the Bakr, who till
then had stood with the Azd in the opposition,
wheeled round, because they perceived that the
whole national interest of the Arabs was at stake.
They beyond all others distinguished themselves
in the struggle against Hârith. The latter was
beaten once more, and now re-crossed the Oxus
and there besieged the important town of
Tirmidh.

According to the reports, Khurasan at that
time was directly under the Khalifa in Syria.
'Âsim is made out to have brought upon himself
his deposition, which took place in the beginning
of 117 (735), by asking to be again placed under
the stattholder of Iraq as he had need of his
support, and Khâlid alQasrî is said to have used
this opportunity to get his brother into office.
But it was high time that the Qaisite administration in Khurasan should cease. Another
account has it that Hishâm himself ordered
Khâlid to put his brother in 'Âsim's place. Asad
might well count it an honour to be sent for
the second time to Khurasan under such
difficult circumstances, and he justified the trust
reposed in him. As his assistant he appointed
an Azdite, Judai' alKarmânî, but without selling
himself to the party interest of the Yemenites,
and he liberated Junaid's officials who had been

imprisoned by 'Âsim, notwithstanding that, as Qaisites, they were his foes (1581, 15).

He began activities against Hârith in Transoxiana and there either with clemency or severity subdued several towns which had sided with Hârith, including, perhaps, even Samarqand.[1] Against Hârith himself, who was encamped before Tirmidh, he actually effected nothing, but the citizens of the town, although Iranians, defended themselves so bravely that the latter found it advisable to retire to Tukharistan, and his allies and adherents melted away.

Thereupon Asad also faced about to Tukharistan. To be sure, this district was subdued by Qutaiba, but with the exception of Marwrûdh, only the capital, Balkh, was to any extent a firm seat of the Arab power. Asad retired into Balkh and removed his residence from Marw thither, which proved how important he thought Tukharistan. He also quartered there the Arab garrison, which till then had been settled in the neighbouring place, Bârûqân, and did not

---

[1] It is not actually said that Samarqand had defected to Hârith, nor that Asad won it back again, but onl, that he marched thither and cut off the water from the town, but the latter action can hardly be understood otherwise than as a hostile measure. The water came from Waraghsar; the centre of the canal-system was there. Waragh means "sluice" (*Schott*, for which I know n) High German equivalent, corresponds better to it), and "*Sar*" (like the Semitic "*Râs*") means the outlet of the division of water through the sluices.

mix with the Iranian citizens. But he did not
make the members of the different tribes live
separate, but all together, so as to prevent their
"'Aṣabîya," i.e. their parties and petty jealousies.
To every fighting man he allotted as much
landed property in Balkh as he had possessed in
Baruqan, and he kept up a warm friendship
with the Dihqans, with whom he was popular
before, in order, through them, to have an
influence upon their humbler compatriots. The
rebuilding of Balkh undertaken by him had to
be completed by the Iranian subjects, but in
such a way that the value of the work was
credited in their tax. The survey was entrusted
to the Dihqan Barmak of Naw Bahâr, the
ancestor of the Barmakid family, who later
became so famous, and within reasonable limits he
did all he could to effect a general reconciliation
and blending together of the hostile elements.

Hârith b. Suraij had fled to upper Tukharistan to his relatives in the fortress of Tabûshkân,
but they were not willing to be sacrificed for him,
drove him and his following away, and entered
into negotiations with Asad. But as the latter
learned from the mediators that the fortress was
badly provided with arms and scarcely capable of
defending itself, he sent the Karmânî to attack it.
Thirst compelled the garrison to surrender, and
the captive warriors had to suffer death (1928),
while their wives and children, although of

Arab blood, were sold by auction in the market-place of Balkh.

In A.H. 118 (736) Asad undertook an expedition against the still unsubdued Khuttal, to the north of the Oxus, opposite Balkh, who had been allies of Hârith. Their prince, who resided in Nawâkith, turned to the Khaqan of the Turks for help, but when the latter came advancing from Sûyât *via* Khushwarâgh he sent word to Asad to warn him, for (he said) he did not wish the victory of the Turks but a balance between them and the Arabs. After some delay Asad took it as a hint to turn back, and just when he had got across the Oxus the enemies appeared on the other bank. Amidst the beating of drums and neighing of steeds they plunged into the stream and crossed it, but they did not attack the chief body under Asad himself, but a division which he had sent on in advance with the baggage and captured animals, further down the Oxus. The baggage fell into their hands; the men Asad was just able to save. This was on the last day of Ramadan, 118.[1] He had to be content with getting back to Balkh with a whole skin, and the children sang sarcastic ditties about him.

---

[1] 11th Oct., 736. The dates here vary about a year. For the " day of the baggage " the year 119 is given. Reckoning backwards, however, shows that the correct date is 118.

But the Khaqan gave him no peace. He made for Jabghûia alKharlukhî [1] in eastern Tukharistan, nominally summoned by Hârith b. Suraij who lived there, and from there in the middle of winter he departed with his vassals and allies towards the west. On the 10th Dhulhijja, 118 (19th Dec., 736) Asad got news of this. He gave warning to the country people by beacons to escape to Balkh, left his assistant alKarmânî behind in the town, and himself marched at once against the Khaqan with the garrison troops, which were all he had at his disposal, for he had let the rest go away to their homes at the beginning of winter. The Khaqan was encamped not far from the capital of Jûzjân. He had sent out expeditions on all sides and had only 4,000 men with him when Asad attacked him.[2] By means of a division led by the prince of Jûzjân along by-paths, he at the same time caught him in the

[1] Kharlukh is a Turkish tribe (Ibn Khordâdhbeh, 31). Jabghûia is, even in Qutaiba's time, named as overlord of the Shadh and of the Tarkhan Naizak appointed with or under him. *Cf.* the report on the Khalifa Hishâm in Tab., 1615.

[2] Asad's right wing consisted of Azdites, Tamimites, Juzjanites and the Syrians of Filistîn and Qinnesrîn ; the left of Rabîites and the Syrians of Hims and Urdunn; the vanguard (the centre ?) of the Syrians of Damascus and of the Shurta, the bodyguards and the vassals of Asad. The Syrian troops evidently remained constantly with the stattholder, and did not, like the Arabs of Khurasan, go home in winter. With the Khâqân were Hârith b. Suraij with his following (Soghdians and Babîya), also the king of Soghd, the prince of Shâsh, Kharâbughra of Ushrûsana (the great-grand father of the

rear, and so forced him to a hasty flight, abandoning his wife, whose eunuch saved her from shame by killing her. In the conquered camp where the kettles were still boiling, the Muslim prisoners who were found were set free. Many Turkish women, as well as a huge amount of booty in the shape of cattle, fell into the victor's hand, and Asad made presents of them to the Dihqans of Khurasan [1] who were well-disposed to him. The Turkish expeditionary bands, one of which had pressed on to the church of Marwrudh, were captured.

Any further pursuit of the Khaqan was rendered impossible by the winter. He remained for a while longer in Tukharistan, near Jabghûia, and then made his way back *via* Ushrusana into his own land, accompanied by Hârith b. Suraij. Soon after he was slain by one of his chief men, the frequently mentioned Kûrsûl alTurqashî,[2] and as a result the Turks fell into discord with each other and left the Arabs for a time in peace.

Asad ordered a fast in Balkh to give thanks to God for the victory. When tidings of the

famous Afshîn b. Kâwus), and Jabghûia. The king of Soghd is perhaps the lord of Ishtîkhan who with the Ashkand of Nasaf followed the Khâqân's army to Khuttalân, while the Saghânkhudâh fought for Asad. Iranians fought on both sides. According to 1613, 2f, it seems, moreover, as if Kharâbughra had stayed at home in Ushrusana ; he was at heart hostile to the Khâqân.

[1] Van Vloten misinterprets this simple note (Tab., 1611), O., p. 25, n. 2.   [2] *Cf.* Ibn Khordâdhbeh, 31.

astonishing event reached Syria, Hishâm, backed up by the Qaisites at his court, would not
believe it. Hitherto he had received nothing
but bad news from Khurasan, but Asad's messenger, Muqâtil b. Haiyân an-Nabatî, dispelled
all doubt by his authentic report.

In summer 119 (737) Asad again resumed
the war against the Khuttal. The Turks could
help them no longer, and apparently there
was dissension amongst themselves. A usurper
from Bâmiân, Badartarkhân, had seized the
power (*cf.* 1694). By a shameful breach of
faith Asad got the latter into his power and
delivered him up for execution to an Azdite
who had revenge for bloodshed to carry out
against him.[1] In spite of this he did not effect
much, but contented himself with raids into
the valley of the Khuttal. The following winter,
at the beginning of the year 120, sudden death
overtook him and saved him from being involved
in the fall of his brother Khâlid.[2] The Arab and

[1] Asad had promised him the protection of God, the Prophet, the
Khalifa and the Muslims, but now when he did not keep his word,
Badartarkhân threw a stone into the air saying,—"That is God's
protection!" Then he threw three more stones with the words,—
"There is the protection of Muhammad, the prince of the Believers,
the Muslims!"

[2] Khâlid was deposed in Jumada I, 120 (May, 738), but was still
in office when he heard of his brother's death (1650, 12). In Rajab,
120 Nasr succeeded Asad after an interval of four months (1638).
Asad thus died in Safar, 120 (February, 738). The account that it
happened on the feast of Mihrigan is untenable, for that fell in autumn,
and neither autumn, 119 nor autumn, 120 is a possible date.

Iranian chiefs were in the act of waiting upon him to bring him costly gifts, and Khurâsân, the Dihqân of Herât, made a speech exalting him to the seventh heaven. Asad graciously threw him an apple which he held in his hand, when an internal abscess burst and he died. This is the narrative, but the occasion specified, namely, the feast of Mihrigan, is incorrect, and throws doubt upon the matter, which has a somewhat legendary savour at any rate.

6.   The fall of Khâlid alQasrî, who had been for many years stattholder in Iraq, ushered in the last fatal period of the Umaiyid rule. His successor was a thorough-going Qaisite partisan from the family of Hajjâj, Yûsuf b. Umar. He would have brought a Qaisite into Khurasan as well if Hishâm had not interfered and appointed as Asad's successor old Nasr b. Saiyâr, one of the very few old men who appeared in the history of that time. His age did not affect the freshness of the mind, as is testified not merely by his deeds, but also by the songs in which he gave expression to his feelings to the very end of his life. He had been bred in the district itself and grown grey in the service, and was also recommended to the Khalifa by the fact that he had no family influence at his back and was bound to rely on him for support. For he did not belong to any of the great tribes in Khurasan, but to the Kinâna,

which was there but weakly represented. As
a Kinânite indeed he had leanings towards the
Tamîm, who together with the Kinâna, were
descended from Khindif. He changed the
officials of his ousted predecessor, without, however, ill-treating them and replaced them by
Khindifites, *i. e.*, Tamimites mostly. The seats
of Government were then, with the exception
of the four old ones in Khurasan, still Balkh,
Khwarizm and Samarqand (1664). He moved
the residence from Balkh back to Marw, from
the periphery to the centre of the Arab rule.

At the beginning of his term of office he
carried on war against the Turks and really
weakened them. He marched through the Iron
Gate *viâ* Waraghsar to Samarqand. There
two captive Dihqans were brought before him,
who had opposed the Arab and the native rule
in Bukhara because they thought themselves
unjustly treated. When he condemned them
they tore themselves free, the one wounding the
Arab prefect of Bukhara, who in return cleft
his skull, while the other stabbed the Bukhârâ-
khudâh and was himself slain by the prince of
Juzjan. It is probable that the injustice of
which both had to complain consisted in their inclusion in the subject-tax, for they were Muslims.
Nasr marched from Samarqand, reinforced by
Iranian auxiliary troops, to Ushrûsana and on to
Shâsh, where at that time was the murderer of

the Khaqan, Kûrsûl, the prince of a horde of 4,000
tents. In a fight he fell into the Arabs' hands and
was crucified. Hârith b. Suraij also fought with
the Turks against the Arabs, but was unwilling
to fire the two catapults which he brought with
him against his own particular tribal brethren,
the Tamîm. The upshot was that Nasr granted
peace to the Shâsh on condition that they
turned out Hârith. He then marched to
Farghana but there also contented himself with
a peace treaty and then, without pressing on
over the Jaxartes, turned back. The undertaking may have taken more than one year, but
Madâinî breaks it up in a senseless manner [1]
and differentiates mere variants, gathering
together all the chaff he can get hold of, and
making episodes and anecdotes the main interest.
Balâdhurî mentions only one expedition of Nasr
to Ushrusana, which came to grief.[2] The
brilliant feats ascribed to him by A. Müller,
1, 412, freely following Weil 1, 632, Nasr
certainly never performed, but nevertheless he
made the Turks in Shash renounce the sedition-
ist Hârith b. Suraij, even if they did not deliver
him up, and he withdrew to Fârâb and kept
the peace till the civil war broke out after the

---

[1] According to him Nasr marched (a) to the Iron Gate and turned,
(b) to Samarqand and turned, (c) to the Jaxartes. But (a) and (b) are
only stages for (c).

[2] The date "at the time of Marwân II" is more than unlikely.

death of Walîd II. Nasr also allowed the
emigrant Soghdians, who in the turmoil after
the murder of the Khaqan no longer felt secure
in Shash and Farghana, to return to their old
home, and to this the Arabs of Khurasan
compelled the Khalifa Hishâm to give his
consent.

Some light is thrown upon Nasr's internal
policy by his tax-reform, about which Madâinî
gives a report in Tab., 1688f. He is said to have
declared his programme for this in a speech in
the mosque of Marw; "Bahrâmsîs favoured the
Magians, relieved them of their burdens and
imposed them upon the Muslims. Ishudâd
the son of Gregor [1] in like manner favoured the
Christians, and Aqîba the Jews; I will stand
up for the Muslims, remove their burdens and
impose them upon the unbelievers, only the
Kharâj must be paid fully in accordance with
the written tenet which is fixed for once and
all.[2] As overseer of taxes I appoint Mansûr
b. Umar; to him complaints are to be brought
if a Muslim has to pay the poll-tax or excessive
land-tax, and if an unbeliever has failed to
assume the corresponding burdens." Thereupon, before the end of the week, it is said,

---

[1] This Christian name, hardly recognisable in the Arab writing, is
to be understood.

[2] The proper reading is to be found in the note (r) to Tab., 1688
(taufîr).

30,000 Muslims came forward who had had to pay the poll-tax, and 80,000 unbelievers appeared who had not paid it, and the incongruity was put right. The land-tax was then re-adjusted and there was a re-allotment of the shares which those assessed had to furnish towards the total sum already stipulated. From Marw, at the time of the Umaiyids, 100,000 dirhems were raised, not taking into consideration the land-tax.

The religious communities and the tax-paying communities were thus identical. The chief rabbi collected the tax from the Jews, the bishop from the Christians, the Marzbân [1] from the Magians or Zoroastrians. Naturally the last were by far in the majority, though the number of the Christians must have been pretty considerable. [2] But how could the heads of communities roll the tax off the Magians, Christians and Jews, and on to the Muslims under the very eyes of the Arab powers? The reports, such as they are, in

---

[1] In this case not the chief Magian. *Cf.* 1462, 13.

[2] The Syrian Nestorians, as is well known, had spread far towards the east. The Metropolitan of Marw interred the body of Yazdejard, the last Sasanid, in a sarcophagus (nâûs) (Tab. 1, 2874f. 2881, 2883; *cf.* 2, 1448, 5; 1543, 1). Monks' dwellings and a place St. Sergius near Marw are mentioned 2, 1572, 2, 1925, 13, 1957, 14; a church there 1569, 14, and a church near Marwrûdh, 1612, 11. In the village of Nasrânîya (=Christian village) Nasr left behind his wife Marzbâna upon his flight from Marw (1995, 10, *cf.* 1889, 6). An important place in Tukha-ristan was called Yahûdîya, the town of the Jews.

Madâinî are unintelligible. It is quite incredible that 80,000 men liable to taxation were relieved from it, and 30,000 who were not liable, had to make good in their stead. The state of affairs, probably, by all analogies, amounts to this, that the conversion of the non-Arab subjects to Islam did not free them from their connection with their tax-paying community. The subject-tax was a tribute irrevocably fixed in its amount by the historical act of capitulation, and if the numerous converts had no longer contributed to it, then the rest would have had to pay for them with the result that it would have been no longer possible to raise the amount. The duty of contributing thus descended from fathers to sons as a burden assumed by them at the capitulation even though the latter afterwards embraced Islam. According to this practice the native authorities acted with the approval of the Arab government, for the attempt first made by Umar II to bring about a radical change proved impossible. But still it did not seem right for the new citizens of the theocracy to remain under the same burdens as the non-citizens who were merely there on sufferance. There had to be a difference made between the two classes, but made in such a way that the amount of the fixed sum of tribute-money should not decrease. Nasr solved this problem in the same way as it was solved in former times. Before this the tribute was raised by taxes of various sorts ; the taxes of the landed proprietors as well as those of the colonists went to swell it, and as they all came under the head of the "tribute," so also people spoke of only one tax, which was called the " Kharâj " or "Jizia,"—the names had the same meaning (1507 ff.). But now the contrivance was hit upon that the tribute, in the fixed amount once imposed upon the separate towns and districts, was raised entirely from the landed property. The land-tax was correspondingly re-modelled and collected from all landed proprietors in proportion to their property, no matter whether they were subjects or Muslims,[1] and as it did not affect people but things, it was not considered a disgrace. Side by side with this came the complete separation of the land-tax, now exclusively called " Kharâj," from the poll-tax, which retained the name " Jizia." The poll-tax was unnecessary for the fixed tribute ; its revenue changed, decreasing from year to year in proportion to the increase of the conversions to Islam, for it was removed altogether from the Muslims and continued to be

[1] The pieces of ground came into Muslim ownership not only through the conversion of the old owners but also through purchase and acquisition on the part of the Arabs. Acc. to Tab., 1029, 6 it appears that even before Nasr such Arabs as had acquired the landed property had to pay a tax upon it and that to the Persian magistrate, which they certainly did not do willingly.

exacted only from the non-Muslims, and in fact, from all of these, precisely with the intention of making it a disparaging burden upon their less worthy persons.   In contrast to the procedure considered legitimate in earlier times, whereby the Muslims were relieved from the land-tax also, the judiciousness of the new organisation established by Nasr in Khurasan is apparent. The difference in the treatment of Muslims and non-Muslims persisted.   On the other hand, the Muslims, whether Arabs or Mawâlî, came, in principle, to be upon equal footing,[1] and thus, indeed, a decrease in the fixed state-revenue was avoided, since the variation and gradual decline of the inconsiderable poll-tax did not matter so much.   It is very probable that Nasr's regulations were made not merely for the government district of Marw, but for the whole province on both banks of the Oxus, for there was really nothing peculiar about them, and they extended everywhere in the Islamic kingdom where the conditions were similar.   They represented the binding law which the juridical systematisers since then presupposed to be in existence from the very beginning, while in reality it only evolved itself gradually.   This is

---

[1] In point of fact the Iranians had really to pay far more because the landed property mostly belonged to them, especially to the Dihqâns, who on their part fleeced the peasants. But that was not an injustice.

61

the reason why Madâinî, confused by the later suppositions, does not understand in the slightest what Nasr was faced with, and what he abolished, and gets very astonishing notions of the illegal misusages which prevailed. But he states correctly the positive fact,—that the fixed amount of the Kharâj was re-allotted amongst all the landed proprietors, even the Muslims, but the Jizia, on the other hand, was taken off the Muslims, and imposed only upon the non-Muslims.

Upon this basis of equal rights in Islam there might have been established a permanent balance between Arabs and Iranians, but the time for that was past. The self-destruction of the Arabs in Khurasan began anew. This time it was incited by the revolution in Syria, which set in under Walîd II as a counter-blow of the opposition against the dissolute Qaisite rule. Walîd II succeeded Hishâm at the beginning of Rabî II, 125 (Feb., 743). He at first confirmed Nasr in his office, but, under the influence of the Qaisite leader, the Iraqite stattholder Yûsuf b. Umar,[1] he recalled him some time later and summoned him to the court by the message that he was to bring with him all sorts of musical instruments and other fine things. Nasr intentionally took a good while making

---

[1] He had already in Hishâm's time intrigued with the Qaisites against Nasr (A.H. 123), but to no purpose.

preparations for this and so it fell out that he
was still in Khurasan when the news of the
murder of the Khalifa reached him on New-
year's day, 126.[1] He did not acknowledge the
insurgent, Yazîd III, nor his stattholder in Iraq,
at least not actually, but persuaded the tribes
rather to pay homage to himself as interim Emir
of Khurasan, till the civil war should be over
and there should be again a generally acknowledged Khalifa. Even the Azd and Rabîa, who
hitherto had not been on good terms with him,
fell in with this, and he now no longer neglected
them as formerly at the filling up of posts. His
aim was to make the Arabs of Khurasan act in
concert, so that they should regard the government as their common affair and no longer as a
bone of contention. The neutral and non-party
position which he tried to assume was made
easier for him by the fact that, being a Kinanite
he belonged to none of the large groups. Of
course, the government was his own concern as
well, since he was at the head of it, and a poet
who was devoted to him makes him boastingly
say,—" We balance Qais with Rabîa, and Tamîm

---

[1] Walîd II was murdered about the end of Jumada II, 126 (middle
of April, 744). Nasr received private information of it through a post-
master ten days before the official confirmation, for the *Sikka*, 1845,
21 (1849,10), is doubtless the *Sikkat alBarîd* (1709 5, Lisân 4,53).
But the tidings can hardly have reached him in less than a month's
time, so the New Year at that time did not fall before the middle
May ; *cf.*, p. 461, n. 1.

with Azd, and so the decision lies with Kinana."
He was much annoyed about this absolute
spoiler of all political concord, who fetched
water to his opponents' mills.

But even so it was not long till the Azd and
the Rabîa with them, opposed him again,
recalling the fact that they after all, as
Yemenites, really belonged to the side of Yazîd
III and the Kalbites who were allied with him.
When Nasr was going to pay them the wages
not in ready money but in the gold and silver
vessels which he had collected for Walîd II,
they mutinied openly. The Azdite Judai' al-
Karmânî took the lead and called for vengeance
for the Banû Muhallab (1858, 11) who were
mercilessly persecuted by the Umaiyids, giving
utterance to a saying that found an echo in the
hearts of all the Azdites,—" Under Muhallab
and his son Yazîd they had been allowed to
'devour' Khurasan, but since then they had
never again had their turn, and even under
Asad not so much as they wished." Nasr
certainly seized the person of alKarmânî, arresting him in the Quhandiz of Marw, at the end
of Ramadan, 126 (the middle of July, 744), but
a month after he escaped from prison, and made
for a place in the district of Marw, where an
army of Azd and Rabîa gathered round him.
Nasr marched against him. To be sure, no
battle was fought, for both sides hesitated to

begin, but neither did the peace-negotiations
which they entered upon attain the desired end.
AlKarmânî cherished deep hatred against
Nasr and would not make up his difference
with him.

Most unfortunately, too, Hârith b. Suraij
now emerged from his Turkish exile once more.
It may have been even before the end of 126,
for Yazîd III,[1] who is said to have moved him
to do so, died at the end of 126. As he was an
enemy of alKarmânî, Nasr invited him to come
to Marw from Samarqand, where he had at
first settled, and he made his appearance there
at the end of Ramadan, 127 (beginning of July,
745). But he did not suffer himself to be
attached to Nasr by the honours and gifts with
which the latter loaded him. He upheld against
him the demands of Murjiitism, as practically
understood by him, and was joined by about
3,000 of his Tamimite tribesmen. Nasr went
a good way in compliance with the dangerous
competitor with whom he had saddled himself.
He agreed to grant to the Iranians in the
marches, to whom Hârith had always been
devoted, a written constitution in accordance
with the Murjiite ideas of law and justice, to
appoint there officials well-pleasing to God, and
to bestow the stattholdership upon Hârith

---

[1] Yazîd III was the son of a Soghdian princess (1874) and so may
have had leanings towards the Soghdians.

himself. But this availed him nothing. Hârith
was not sure of him, did not confide to him
the decided enmity to the Umaiyid rule with
which he and the followers of his black flag
were animated, and, probably from egotism,
would not even suffer his presence near him.
Nasr, on his part, would not submit to the sentence of an arbitration court acknowledged by
the other anent his deposition, and so it came to
an open rupture. Hârith encamped before Marw
and from there made an attempt to surprise the
town at the end of Jumada II, 128 (end of March,
746). This attempt, indeed, failed, but Jahm b.
Safwân, the Murjiite recruiting-officer and the
author of a book upon Hârith and his programme,
which he used to read aloud, was taken
prisoner and executed. Then, however, Harith
made an alliance with alKarmânî, of whom
we now hear again for the first time after a
year and a half, and the latter threw himself
into the dispute and gave it a different aspect.
After a battle of several days Nasr thought it
advisable to retire to Naisabur, the chief
position of the Qaisites, and to leave Marw to
the rebels.

The understanding between the insurgents,
however, soon fell through. The Tamîm under
Hârith still grieved that they had helped the
Azd to the victory over their brothers in Marw,
who fought for Nasr, and also they could not

forget that under Asad's stattholdership, after the
taking of the fortress of Tabûshkân, alKarmânî
had caused some hundreds of the relatives and
adherents of Hârith to be executed, and some
of them to be hideously mutilated.   Bishr b.
Jurmûz, Hârith's most important partisan, was
the first to renounce the unnatural alliance,
and several thousands followed him.   In the
struggle which then arose, Harith went over to
him as well and broke with alKarmânî, but the
Azd and their allies conquered the Tamîm and
the Mudar at the end of Rajab, 128 (April, 746),
drove them out of Marw, and demolished their
quarters.   Hârith himself fell, and his body was
nailed to a cross. He received the meet reward
of his deeds, be his sentiments what they might.
In the struggle for Islam against Arabism, for
the oppressed against the oppressors, he allied
himself with death and Satan against the existing power, and moved heaven and earth against
the Umaiyid government.   On his first appearance he led the Turks into the field against the
Arabs, and when that venture failed, he found
a refuge with them for many years.   At his
second appearance he disunited the Tamîm, upon
whose steadfastness at that time the stability
of the Arab rule in Khurasan greatly depended,
and thus he contrived that the Yemen not
merely overthrew the government but also
offered violence to the Mudar.   He was rightly

considered a man of ill omen, the most active precursor of Abû Muslim.[1]

At this critical time Nasr was taken up by the Qaisites in Naisabur, who before this were not friendly to him, and the Mudarites who were driven out of Marw rallied round him. Before this, it is alleged, he had already tried to gain support again for the Khalifate, but so long as Iraq and the Iranian districts belonging to it were in the power of the Khawârij and the Ja'farid Ibn Muâwia, he was cut off from connection with the seat of the Umaiyid rule. It was not till the year 129 that this was changed, when Iraq was subjected to the rule of Marwân by Yazîd b. Umar b. Hubaira. Nasr recognised him as his immediate superior.[2] He never had the intention of renouncing the Umaiyids in general, but only held back till the turmoil of dynasties in Syria had settled, and indeed probably declared for Marwân soon after the latter's succession. Still, the alliance with Ibn Hubaira availed him little. It was upon his own initiative that he set about the task of winning back Marw in the year 129. After

---

[1] His black flags are at 1919, 2f. explained in this sense although formally it is a mistake. In contemporary songs he is strikingly characterised as the disuniter of the Mudar (1935, f.) and as the ally of the heathen against the Arabs (1575f.); "Your Murjiitism has united you with the idolators : your religion is no better than polytheism."

[2] The account that Ibn Hubaira made an alliance with him as early as the beginning of A.H. 127 (Tab., 1917) is a glaring anachronism.

vain attempts of his officers to make the attack,
the man of 80 came advancing in person with
his whole force and alKarmânî came forth to
meet him. Both sides encamped outside of the
town in the "two trenches" which were shewn
long afterwards. From there they were in a
state of conflict for a long time, without getting
to a decisive battle. Urgent appeals for help
sent by Nasr to Marwân and to Ibn Hubaira,[1]
together with a moving description of the
danger, were of no avail, but the fear of a
common foe seemed to bring the Arabs once
again to reason and to a common agreement.
Before their eyes the Abbasid Shiites, mostly
Iranians, had gathered under Abû Muslim's
black standard and erected a strong camp not
far from Marw. The Rabîa, who, though
hitherto allies of the Azd, still naturally took
a middle place, entered the chasm between the
Yemen and the Mudar. Yahyâ b. Hudain, the
most esteemed leader of the Bakr, joined Nasr,
seeing in a combination with the government
the only salvation of the Arab tribes.[2] Matters
got as far as negotiations between Nasr and
Judaiʻ alKarmânî, but they were interrupted
by the fact that a son of Hârith b. Suraij, who
was with Nasr, thought it a good opportunity

---

[1] The famous verses in Tab., 1973 are composed upon this situation.

[2] *Cf.* the poetical appeal of Nasr to the Rabia in Nöldeke's *Delectus*,
p. 88.

to wreak vengeance upon his father's murderer, and assassinated the Karmânî.[1] Still they did not fall through on this account. The defection of the important town of Herat to Abû Muslim made a strong impression upon the Arabs and opened the eyes of the blind as well. AlKarmânî's place was taken by a partisan of his whom we have met with before, the Kharijite Shaibân b. Salama,[2] who on the instigation of Yahyâ b. Hudain concluded with Nasr a year's truce, in consequence of which he was able to enter Marw at the end of 129 (Aug., 747). Not only the Azd acceded to the truce, but also the son of their murdered leader, Alî Ibn alKarmânî. It was a critical turn of affairs for Abû Muslim, but he was wise enough to explain to Ibn alKarmânî that the murder of

---

[1] The tradition certainly shews Nasr too as an accomplice in the murder of alKarmânî, by asserting that he had his dead body nailed to the cross and beside it a fish, the contemptuous emblem of the Azd. But he took a leading part in the negotiations in all seriousness, and not merely with the purpose of compassing an assassination which threatened to be their undoing. The crucifixion of their chief, and especially the episode of the fish, would have put an end for ever to any good feeling from the Azd towards him. And if the son of the murdered man made peace with Nasr immediately after, he was at that time not convinced of the latter's complicity in the murder. Probably Abû Muslim first put the idea into his head. No such objective proof of Nasr's approval of the crime can have been given as a public exhibition by his orders of alKarmânî's body with the fish attached would have been. That would have brought other consequences, and would have been directly opposed to the conciliatory policy of Nasr. The principle *is fecit cui prodest* is wrongly applied here.

[2] *Cf.* note 1 on p. 395.

his father had been caused by Nasr himself,
in order to get him upon his side (beginning of
130, Sepr., 747), and Ibn alKarmânî and the
Azd who followed him now took up arms
against Nasr again. The struggle was carried
on in the suburbs and streets of Marw, apparently lasting a considerable time, and it made Abû
Muslim master of the situation. When he
thought fit, he came into the midst of it and
decided it without striking a blow, in Rabî II,
130, *i.e.* Dec., 748,[1] and the next morning Nasr
fled *viâ* Sarakhs and Tûs to Naisabur. It was
the end of the Arab rule in Khurasan and the
beginning of the end of the Arab rule altogether.

---

[1] The following chapter will enter further into the details and
dates.

CHAPTER IX.

The Fall of the Arab Kingdom.

What has been said in the foregoing chapter about the relationship between Arabs and Iranians refers essentially to the two Marches, and indeed more to Soghdia than to Tukharistan. There the two parties were still in a state of conflict with each other, and while Islam had gained some firm positions, it had not completely prevailed. On the other hand, in Khurasan proper the powers had already formed a balance; a *modus vivendi* had been evolved. The procedure which we see still prevalent in Transoxiana was here by this time played out, and we know nothing about it since we have not sufficient information about the early period after the first conquest. But the result is well worth some degree of review,—the situation, say, in the period from A.H. 100-130.[1]

Arabs and Iranians were not externally separated by different dwelling-places. The old native population still remained in the Arab army towns. Naisabur (Bîward, Sarachs, Nasâ), Marw, Marwrudh and Herat, though the citadels

---

[1] *Cf.* G. van Vloten, *Recherches sur la domination arabe*, Verhandelingen der K. Akademie te Amsterdam, Afd. Letterk. I, 3. Amst., 1894.

were, of course, occupied by the conquerors. Neither did the Arabs keep themselves shut in together at some few points, nor did they confine themselves to the towns which they had selected as military colonies. They had estates, with bondmen, in the country, and some of them even dwelt there, especially in the oasis of Marw where the town formed the centre-point of numerous villages in one irrigation-system. They had Iranian servants and married Iranian wives, and the influence was bound to be noticeable in the children, even in the second generation. But repeated additions from Iraq did not strengthen the Arab element to such a degree that it could ever have measured itself in numbers with the Iranian element, particularly as it was severely decimated by the continual warfare. Incidental accounts make out that there were some 50,000 Arab military in Khurasan, and as the compulsory service was much extended and included quite half of the male sex, the Arab population probably amounted to not much more than 200,000 souls. The Arabs grew accustomed to being Khurasanites ; in the common province they felt at one with the people of the country. They wore trousers like the Iranians (Tab., 2, 1530), drank wine, celebrated the festivals of New Year and Mihrigan, and the prominent ones among them assumed the airs of the Marzbans. Business in general brought with it the necessity of an understanding with the Iranians. Even in Kufa and Basra the speech of the market was, to say the least, just as much Persian as Arabic. It seems to be an exception that Abu Saidâ only spoke Arabic and so was not a suitable apostle of the Soghdians who knew only Persian. In Abû Muslim's army even the Arabs spoke mostly Persian.[1]

Neither did the Iranians in Khurasan on their side, take up a stand compactly hostile and repellent towards the Arabs. The blending process had laid hold of them as well. Their position was in general little changed by the conquest, and that scarcely for the worse. The Arabs managed the defence against outside attacks, *i.e.*, against the Turks, more successfully than had been done under the Sasanid *régime*.[2] They did not interfere much with the internal conditions, but left the government to the Marzbans and Dihqans and only through them came in contact with the subjected population. In the army and government towns, too, the native authorities remained side by side with the Arab, having, in fact, to collect the taxes, and being responsible to the conquerors for their correct payment in the proper amount. But the *misera contribuens plebs* had certainly had to

---

[1] Tab. 3, 51, 4, 64, 18, 65, 14, 16.

[2] It was only during the tribal feud of the Tamîm that the Turks extended their incursions as far as Naisabur (Bal., 415).

pay just as much under the Sasanids. Neither
were the Iranians disturbed in their religion ; in
the tribute-treaties it is everywhere taken for
granted that they retained it. Even in the
towns, where the Arabs lived, they were allowed
to remain heathen, although perhaps the outward signs and tokens of heathendom had there
to be kept somewhat out of sight. But they do
not appear to have had any serious connection
with Zoroastrianism. The most one could say is
that the serene, happy Cult, which had its culminating points in the New Year and Mihrigan
festivals had become endeared to them, and they
could go on observing it even when they embraced Islam, for even the Arabs joined in the
religion of the country, in so far as it was
pleasure. Islam at first attracted the Iranians
not so much for itself as for the advantages it
offered. They employed it as a means to get
closer to the ruling class and participate in its
privileges, and to arabianise themselves, and
then assumed Arab names and were incorporated
with an Arab tribe.[1] Ambitious individuals
ingratiated themselves with the Arabs and

---

[1] *Cf.* Bal. 441 : The princes were converted to Islam and took Arab
names. Muslim Iranians with Iranian names are not generally to be
found at that time. The use of the Kunya is exceedingly frequent
among them : Abu Dâûd, Abu Aun, Abu Muslim, Abu Nasr, etc.
With the Arabs in Khurasan the Kunya is sometimes a *nom de guerre*
(in the strictest sense). Tab. 2, 1289, 15, 1430, 3, 1593, 16, 1627, 4,
1631, 15. Another *nom de guerre*, 1538, 7.

played an ambiguous part as mediators between the nationalities. They were termed the Nusahâ, "the good friends." The best-known of them are Sulaim and Haiyân an Nabatî.

Military service in the events of war of that time and district offered the most favourable opportunity of joining Islam. Following the example of the distinguished Iranians, the Arab gentlemen took with them into the field a personal following of servants (Shâkirîya). These servants also took part in the fighting and sometimes decided the struggle. There were besides special Iranian regiments commanded by Iranian colonels, examples of whom are Huraith b. Qutba and his brother Thâbit in earlier times, and Haiyân an Nabatî and his son Muqâtil later.[1] The Mawali,—here, as elsewhere, this signifies the non-Arabs who had embraced Islam and been received into the Arab tribes,—fought with the Arabs against their old national foes, the Turks. But they also fought for Islam against their Soghdian tribesmen, in so far as the latter were foes of Islam and allies of the Turks. Islam, which they had originally accepted more for external reasons, even took root in their hearts and was taken more

---

[1] There are in addition the contingents of vassal princes who had to render military service, but these were, to a great extent at least, still heathen.

seriously by them than by the Arabs themselves.[1]

But the Mawali were not fully recognised by
the Arabs. If they served in the army they
fought on foot and not on horseback, and if they
distinguished themselves they were regarded
with distrust. True, they certainly received pay
and a share in the spoil, but not a regular
pension ; they did not appear in the Diwan, *i.e.*, the
military pension-list. Although received into
the Arab tribes they were still " People of the
villages " as distinguished from " People of the
tribes," and although Muslims they were nevertheless not relieved of the subject-tax. The tax
to which even the Arab landowners had to contribute, certainly seems not to have been such a
burden for the Khurasanites as for the Transoxianans, who had embraced Islam only with the
view of being freed from it. Still the discontent
of the Soghdians doubtless infected the Khurasanites as well ; Hârith b. Suraij and others saw
to that.

If the Arabs had treated the converted
Iranians as equals, perhaps a blending of the
two nationalities would have been possible, but
as things were, they reared foes for themselves
in their very midst. Instead of smoothing
out the difference, Islam accentuated it. It

---

[1] Tab. 2, 1291, 9 : The Iranians did not join in unless the fighting
was for the religion.

regenerated the Iranians, gave them backbone, and put into their hands a weapon against their masters. For the fall of the Arab power was brought about not by the Transoxianans who had remained Iranian and hostile to the Arabs, but by the Islamised Khurasanites. Islam itself was the ground upon which they began the struggle against the former. It was Islam that united them with those Arabs who, following theocratic principles, opposed the Umaiyid government. It was Arabs who first roused and organised the Mawali.

Conservative Islam placed the Jamâa (Catholicity) above everything, and enjoined agreement with the government and obedience to it. Revolutionary Islam set the idea of the theocracy against the existing organisation, and invited men to fight for God against the Umaiya and their officials, for law and justice against wrong and force. There is little mention of the Khawârij in the far East; but all the same even there they were of more significance than the scanty information about them allows us to suppose. The Harûrite Shaibân b. Salama, with his considerable following, cannot have so suddenly sprung from nowhere as he seems to us to have done. The Murjiites, indeed, are more important, and under the leadership of Hârith b. Suraij had a very considerable effect upon the history. The Khawârij, as well as the Murjiites, in principle, acknowledged no difference in Islam between Arabs and Mawali, but in the end both of them went completely into the background before the Shiites who early spread into Khurasan and became the deciding factor.

The Shia, like the theocratic opposition in general, had their seat in Iraq, but it was from Iraq that the Iranian East was conquered and peopled, and even later the connection was always actively kept up. From Iraq a new influx kept constantly coming into the Oxus districts, not consisting of the most peaceful of men. The Umaiyid stattholders in Iraq, especially Ziâd and Hajjâj, appear to have moved on the dangerous elements from Kufa and Basra to Khurasan, in order to frustrate their desire for action in the holy war. It is significant that Hajjâj kept the Syrians away from it lest they should be infected by the evil spirit. As can be understood, we have no very exact information about the rise of the Shia in Khurasan ; the seed flew through the air and sowed itself. But how wide-spread the Shiite sympathies there were can be perceived from the fact that after the ill-fated attempt at a rebellion by Zaid b. Alî in Kufa, his son Yahyâ received the advice to make for Khurasan, and followed it, too. True he fell in battle against government troops, but his martyrdom evoked

a general uproar, and all the boys who were
born in that year in Khurasan are said to have
been named after him (Mas'ûdî, 6, 3). Abû
Muslim knew what he was about when he
played the avenger of Yahyâ. By so doing, he
struck a note that found an echo everywhere
(Tab., 2, 1985. 3,506f.). Even Ibn Muâwia b.
Ja'far thought he would find a sure abode in
Khurasan. He certainly was mistaken in Abû
Muslim, who had less use for a living Alid than
for a dead one, and had him secretly murdered.
But even Ibn Muâwia was long honoured in
Khurasan as a martyr, and his grave much
visited as a shrine.

If the Arabs in Khurasan had held together
amongst themselves and with the government
the Shia would certainly not have been able to
pierce the joints, but as they would not share
the power with the Mawali, so they did not
bestow it upon each other. The offices and
benefices which the government had to dispose
of were the source and cause of passionate jealousy between the tribes. The so-called 'Asabîya
was a chronic malady of the Arabs, and finally
when the throne of the Umaiyids began to
totter, it became, as we have seen, exceedingly
acute. This state of things was taken advantage of by the special Shia with which the
Abbasids were in league, since they had separated from the Alids and withdrawn from Medina

where they could not compete with them, to Humaima in the mountainous region between Syria and Arabia (ash Sharât).[1]

Among the Shiites there were two main divisions, which, to be sure, were not everywhere distinctly defined: a moderate one, which was distinguished from the ordinary Islam only by the political principle that the Khalifate belonged to the house of the Prophet, and an extreme one with a peculiar dogma which was quite foreign to the original Islam. The extremists went by different names which expressed only insignificant shades of meaning; at first they were called the Sabâ'îya. According to Saif b. Umar these Sabâ'îya were from the beginning the root of all the evil and mischief in the history of the theocracy, the murderers of

---

[1] The ancestor of the Abbasids was the pious manufacturer of tradition Abdullâh Ibn Abbâs, a full cousin of Muhammad and Alî. As after Alî's death he had allowed himself to be bought over by Muâwia, he remained upon good terms with the Umaiyids, only grinding his teeth in secret. His equally pious son Alî b. Abdillâh, nicknamed asSajjâd or Dhul Thafinât, did the same. Under Abdulmalik he went to Damascus to settle, but after the latter's death he was ill-treated by Walîd I and in A. H. 95, under compulsion, it is said, moved his abode to Humaima, near Adhruh, on the Syrian pilgrim-way, where he died in A. H. 118 at a great age. (Tab., 2, 1592.) Even in his life-time his son Muhammad b. Alî was of far more account. He first made his appearance by claiming the Imamate of the Shia and was the instigator of the secret propaganda of the Abbasids, whom he left to do his work in Kufa and Khurasan whilst he himself kept in his refuge in Humaima. He died in Dhulqa'da, 125 (Tab., 2, 1769), and then his son Ibrâhîm b. Muhammad, born in A. H. 82, succeeded him as second Abbasid Imam.

Uthmân and the openers of the Janus-gate of the civil war, the founders of the Kharijite revolutionary party, and the originators of the self-destruction of Islam. They really first attained their historical significance through Mukhtâr, although they were in existence earlier than that.[1] Their home was Kufa and the neighbourhood of Kufa. They consisted not merely of Arabs, but really mostly of Mawali, and they believed in the teaching of Ibn Saba concerning the return of the same spirit in different bodies, especially the spirit of the Prophet in his heirs. These are their three chief characteristics. They were rejected by the distinguished Alids, the descendants of Fâtima, the Prophet's daughter, who held to the basis of the old Islam and Arabism, so they attached themselves to a son of Alî by a second marriage who was called Ibn Hanafîya after his mother, and he allowed them to make him the idol which, according to their doctrine, they required. It did not matter that he remained passive in the background, in fact, for their purpose he was just as good dead as alive. For a while it was said that he had not died but lived in seclusion in the mountain Radwâ, near Medina, ready to appear at the right moment, but afterwards his son Abdullâh Abû Hâshim, who was

---

[1] For Mukhtar *cf.* my treatise upon the Shia (*Göttingen, 1901*), pp. 74 ff.

just as insignificant as himself, was regarded
as his heir in the Imamship. The extremists of
Kufa did not get what they counted upon with
Zaid b. Alî b. Husain. Then Abû Hâshim
moved his residence to Humaima and there got
in league with the Abbasids.[1] When he died in
A. H. 98 he is said to have made over the office
of Imam by express declaration in his will to
the Abbasid Muhammad b. Alî.

Van Vloten has emphatically referred to the
importance of this latter statement.[2] To be sure,
in this form it is probably fictitious [3] but it must
be early, for it has plenty of witnesses,[4] and the
later Abbasids would have been wary about
establishing their claim upon such a basis. It
is also intrinsically true, for Abû Hâshim actually was the predecessor of Muhammad b.
Alî even though he may not formally have
named him as his successor. He had a party
of his own ; his adherents were called the
Hâshimîya,[5] after him, and after his death they
went over to Muhammad b. Alî (Tab., 3,2500).
In Khurasan, according to Tab., 2,1589, there

---

[1] He may have been there earlier than the Abbasids, and they may
have joined him (A. H. 95), but not he them.

[2] *Opkomst der Abbasiden* (*Leiden, 1890*), pp. 18 f. 148.

[3] Acc. to Shahrastânî, 112, 19, Abû Hâshim made a will in favour
of the Kindite Abdullâh b. Amr b. Harb.

[4] Madâinî in Tab. 3, 24. Ibn Sa'd in Wüstenfeld's Register, p. 19,
310 and in Vloten's Opkomst, p. 148.

[5] Shahrastânî, 112 f. In Tab. the name Hâshimîya appears
plainly as the designation of the sect only, in 2, 1589. 1987. 89. It is

was at their head Khidâsh, one of the most successful Shiite recruiting officers, with whom
Muhammad b. Alî originally had an understanding. There is thus some degree of correctness in the account of that will. The Abbasids
joined Abû Hâshim so as to win over the
Hashimiya to themselves.

But this also shows their connection with the
Sabâ'îya of Mukhtâr, for from these worshippers
of Ibn Hanafîya are descended the worshippers
of his son, the Hashimiya. The Sabâ'îya in
Kufa had not become extinct with Mukhtâr;
they still existed in the lower circles. The
esoteric doctrine of the Hashimiya, as it is
represented in Shahrastânî, is in no way different
from that of Ibn Saba. The Abbasid conspiracy
is exactly similar to the Sabaite, as Saif describes
it.[1] Its headquarters were likewise Kufa;
from there the propaganda was spread into
Khurasan. In short, the movement in both
cases was supported by the Iranian Mawali,
and was directed against the Arabism in Islam.
The conformity thus extends to all the points
of importance, to the doctrine and to the
manner of recruiting, to the locality, and to the

generally used in another sense, as a derivative from Hâshim, not from
Abû Hâshim ; just the same as Hâshimîyûn. The ambiguity may have
been acceptable rather than otherwise to the Abbasids. The Hâshi-
mîyât of Kumait are poems upon the Fatimids.

[1] *Skizzen* 6, 124. The originally Jewish Malâhim-books play a part
both cases.

composition of the party. Two more details may be added. The wooden club was the national weapon of the lower Iranian population, and it was already called the " club of the heretics" [1] from the Khashabiya of Mukhtâr, and did not first get the name from those of Abû Muslim. The Mawali of his estate in Khutarnia near Kufa formed Mukhtâr's oldest adherents, and according to Tab., 2,1. 60 (Mas'ûdî, 6, 59) it was from Khutarnia that Abû Muslim also originally came. Should the correctness of these two statements be doubted, they still do not lose their significance, for invention must have its motive and the motive is all that we require. That the Abbasids later on denied the Shiites, by means of whom they had risen, and shook them off, is not surprising (Tab. 3, 39,1). They were inconvenient to them and might go after they had served their purpose.

All this would seem to show that there exists a close connection between the unsuccessful revolution of Mukhtâr and the successful one of Abû Muslim. Notwithstanding that the fire in the year 67 seemed to be extinguished by blood, it still glowed on under its ashes and spread from Kufa to Khurasan. This place offered more favourable conditions, because the Mawali there were more compact, and the Arabs

---

[1] Tab., 2, 694.

opposed to them were much weaker than in Kufa. Mukhtâr was one of the greatest men of Islamic history; he anticipated the future. If the doctrine of *Raj'a* is correct, then the Arab of Khutarnia came to life again in the Maula of Khutarnia.

2. In the year 100 Muhammad b. Alî sent Maisara to Kufa, and he [1] sent the Kufaites Muhammad b. Khunais and Abû 'Ikrima the saddler, also called Abû Muhammad asSâdiq, and Haiyân the grocer, the uncle of Ibrâhîm b. Salima, to Khurasan, with the commission to recruit for him and his house. They returned to Maisara with letters from Khurasanites whom they had won over, and he sent these letters to Muhammad b. Alî. Abû Muhammad asSâdiq selected in Khurasan twelve chiefs (Nuqabâ) and 70 other men, and Muhammad b. Alî gave them directions in writing. So runs Tab., 2,1358. The completion of the hundred years (Tab., 3,24), the 12 apostles and the 70 followers excite suspicion[2]; the reports from later years concur to prove that the affair was not set agoing so designedly. These records are mostly anonymous, only in three of them is Madâinî named as a guarantor. I herewith append their contents.

---

[1] The subject, acc. to Tab., 2, 1358, should have been Muhammad, but is actually, acc. to 2, 1434, Maisara.

[2] Acc. to Tab., 2, 1988, Muhammad b. Alî, in the year 102 or 103, sent his messenger (singular) to Khurasan; after 70 men were won

Tab., 2, 1434. In the year 102 Maisara sent his messengers from Iraq to Khurasan, and there the Abbasid recruiting began. A distinguished Tamîmite drew the attention of the statt-holder of Yazîd II to the doings of these unknown men, who gave themselves out to be merchants. They were arrested, but soon re-leased again as some Khurasanites, mostly of the Rabîa and Yemen, became security for them.

Tab. 2, 1467. In the year 105 Bukair b. Mâhân, till then Junaid's interpreter [1] in Sind, came to Kufa and brought with him four bars of silver and one of gold. He fell into the hands of the Abbasid recruiting-officers, Abû 'Ikrima as-Sâdiq, Maisara, Muhammad b. Khunais, Sâlim alA'yan, and Abû Yahyâ, was won over by them, and gave up his money for Muhammad b. Alî, with whom he also entered into personal relations. After Maisara's death he was put in his place as leader of the recruiting.

Tab., 2, 1488. In the year 107 recruiters were sent to Khurasan by Ibn Mâhân, *viz.* Abû 'Ikrima, Abû Muhammad as-Sâdiq,[2] Muham-mad b. Khunais, Ammâr alIbâdî and others.

---

over, he chose 12 chiefs from amongst them. The names of the twelve are given somewhat differently than in Tab. 2, 1358, and in isolated cases variants are cited. Even the order in the list is not sure. In the Malâhim-books the number 100 may have played a part.

[1] Acc. to 1726, 10 "scribe."

[2] Acc. to 1358, 4 (1467, 7) Abû Ikrima is identical with Abû Muhammad.

A Kindite complained of them to the stattholder Asad, and he had them crucified after
their hands and feet had been sawn off. Ammâr
alone escaped to Kufa. When Muhammad b.
Alî heard the news, he said, "There will be
more of you killed yet."

In Tab., 2, 1492 the same story is repeated
under A. H. 108, with the variation that Ammâr
alone is executed and the others escape.

Tab., 2, 1501, under A. H. 109, acccrding to
Madâinî. During the first stattholdership of
Asad there came to Khurasan in the company
of other Kufaites the first Abbasid recruiter,
Abû Muhammad Ziâd, Maula of the Hamdân,
who before that had stayed for a while in
Damascus. Muhammad b. Alî had directed
him to take up his abode among the Yemen, to
treat the Mudar with consideration, and to
keep clear of a certain Ghâlib in Abarshahr
(Naisabur), who was devoted to the Fatimids.
Others, however, mention Harb b. Uthmân of
Balkh, Maula of the Qais b. Tha'laba, as the
first Abbasid recruiter in Khurasan authorised
by a letter of Muhammad b. Alî. Abû Muhammad Ziâd stayed for a time in Marw (1501, 17),
entertained the people, and recruited for the
Banû Abbâs by means of invectives against the
Umaiyids. Yahyâ b. Uqail alKhuzâî and
Ibrâhîm b. Khattâb alAdawî visited him frequently ; Ghâlib, who came from Abarshahr to

Marw, separated from him after a quarrel. Upon the accusation of the tax-official of Marw, Abû Muhammad Ziâd was banished from Khurasan by Asad, although he gave himself out to be a harmless merchant, but as he still remained there he was executed four days before the festival (1503,6), and his Kufaite companions with him, with the exception of two who were spared because they were too young, or because they renounced the Abbasids. After that another Kufaite came to Marw, Kathîr, who took a lodging with ꞏbû Najm and recruited for the Abbasids. He carried on his work for a year or two, but was uneducated and was replaced by Khaddâsh, so-named because he tore to shreds the Abbasid religion; but his real name was Umâra.[1]

Tab., 2, 1560. In the year 113, under the stattholdership of Junaid several Abbasid recruiters made their appearance. He executed one of them and outlawed the rest.

Tab., 2, 1586 f. In the year 117 Asad, during his second stattholdership, took prisoner several Abbasid recruiters, among them the Khuzâites Sulaimân b. Kathîr, Mâlik b. Haitham, Talha b. Ruzaiq, the Bakrite Khâlid b. Ibrâhîm, the Tamimites Mûsâ b. Ka'b and Lâhiz b. Quraiz. Sulaimân b. Kathîr said they

---

[1] Acc. to 1588, 9 Ammâr b. Yazîd. He is generally called not Khaddâsh but Khidâsh ; Khaddâsh should have the article.

were slandered as belonging to the Azd-Rabîa by the Mudarites, who could not forgive them for their determined stand against Qutaiba. He reminded them that the Mudarites also were opponents of the stattholder. This was effective, and Asad liberated the Khuzâites and the Bakrite, but punished the two Tamimites. He had Mûsâ b. Ka'b's teeth broken out with the bridle of an ass, and 300 stripes given to Lâhiz.[1]

Tab., 2, 1588. In the year 118 Ibn Mâhân sent Ammâr b. Yazîd to Khurasan as leader of the Abbasid propaganda. He changed his name to Khidâsh, took a lodging in Marw, and was very successful. But he turned aside to falsehood, preached libertinism (Dîn al-Khurramîya) and permitted community of wives. Asad arrested him and, as he used very contumacious speech towards him, had one of his hands cut off, his tongue torn out and one eye blinded.

In addition to this Mâdainî in Tab., 2, 1589, has,—When Asad in the year 118 was in Amul, Khidâsh, the head (of the sect) of the Hâshimîya was brought before him. He made his doctor Qur'a cut off his tongue and blind him of an eye, and then handed him over to the justiciary of Amul, who executed him and nailed him to a cross.

---

[1] He dared not execute the Khurasanite Arabs as he did the Kufaite Mawali.

Tab., 2, 1639f. In the year 120 Sulaimân b. Kathîr went from Khurasan to Muhammad b. Alî, no doubt for the following reason. Muhammad was angry with his adherents in Khurasan because they had believed Khidâsh and his lies in preference to him, and broke off correspondence with them. In order to get into communication with him again they sent to him Sulaimân b. Kathîr. Muhammad explained to him the reason of his displeasure and gave him a letter in which, however, there was nothing. But following this, he sent Ibn Mâhân from Kufa as the bearer of a second letter, in which he gave vent to his plain sentiments regarding Khidâsh. But the Khurasanites distrusted Ibn Mâhân and had him sent off. Muhammad then sent sticks tipped, some with iron and some with brass, and Ibn Mâhân distributed them amongst the party-chiefs (Nuqabâ). They then perceived that they had acted contrary to his principles and mended their ways.[1]

Tab., 2, 1726, under A. H. 124, according to Mâdainî. It leaked out that the Abbasid Shiites in Kufa held meetings in a particular house. Consequently their head, Ibn Mâhân, was arrested. In prison he won over to his cause Yûnas Abû 'Âsim and the Ijlite Isâ b. Ma'qil. From the latter, when they were soon after released,

---

[1] They must have understood the meaning of the sticks better than I. They could not have been mere credentials for Ibn Mâhân.

he bought his servant Abû Muslim for 400 dirhems, and presented him to the son of Muhammad b. Alî, Ibrâhîm, who handed him over to the saddler Mûsâ. Initiated by him into the Abbasid doctrine, he made frequent journeys to Khurasan.[1]

In addition there are the anonymous variants, Tab., 2, 1726f. 1769. In the year 124 the Khurasanite party-leaders Sulaimân b. Kathîr, Mâlik b. Haitham, Lâhiz b. Quraiz and Qahtaba b. Shabîb came, whilst on the pilgrimage, to Kufa. There they visited in prison 'Âsim b. Yûnas alIjlî, who was suspected to be a recruiter for the Abbasids, and Îsâ and Idrîs, the two sons of the Ijlite Ma'qil, who as officials of Khâlid alQasrî were imprisoned by Yûsuf b. Umar. Îsa and Idrîs had with them Abû Muslim, who always wept when his masters expressed their political opinions. The Khurasa-nites won him over. They then went on to Mecca,[2] there met in with Muhammad b. Alî, and told him about Abû Muslim. He asked,— " Is he a freeman, or a bondman ? " They replied, " He himself asserts he is free, but Îsâ says he is a bondman." Thereupon he ordered him to be bought and freed. They handed over

---

[1] With the somewhat obscure sentence 1726, 17, *cf.* the continuation in 1949, 14.

[2] The end of 124. Tabari's putting the account not till A. H. 125 makes no difference ; the Hajj is between the two years.

to him 200,000 dirhems and material to the value of 30,000 dirhems, and he disclosed to them that this was probably the last time they would see him, and enjoined them to recognise his son Ibrâhîm after his death. He died on the 1st Dhulqada, 125, aged 63, seven years after the death of his father.

Tab., 2, 1869. In the year 126 the new Imam sent Ibn Mâhân to Khurasan with a letter. He assembled the party-chiefs and recruiters in Marw, informed them of the death of Muhammad, declared Ibrâhîm as his successor, and gave them his letter. They recognised him and paid to him the moneys of the Shia, which he delivered to Ibrâhîm.

Tab., 2, 1916 f. In the year 127 Ibrâhîm appointed in place of the deceased Ibn Mâhân, on the latter's recommendation, the vinegarseller Abû Salama Hafs b. Sulaimân, Maula of the Sabî, as his general-plenipotentiary, and wrote to inform the Khurasanites of it. Abû Salama also presented himself in person to the Khurasanites and received from them the fifth and voluntary gifts. He bore the title " Wizier of the Family of Muhammad " (Tab., 3, 20, 60).

In all these accounts Kufa appears as the Abbasid breeding-ground and centre. Here dwell the representatives and plenipotentiaries of the invisible Imam,—Maisara, Ibn Mâhân, Abû Salama, and likewise their underlings and

65

co-operators. They are all Mawali, of Iranian
nationality and shopkeepers and artisans to
trade. Arabs indeed may also have belonged
to the party but they did not occupy any leading
position. Khurasan, *i.e.*, Marw, is worked from
Kufa; long after the year 100 the recruiters
there are still only Kufaites, stranger merchants.
The beginnings of the propaganda are obscure,
and smothered in bloodshed. Khidâsh was the
first to have any success. He is first mentioned
under A. H. 109; it is questionable whether he
really began his activity then, but it is just as
improbable that he did not come from Kufa till
A. H. 118, the year in which he was killed. The
people of Marw flocked to him, accepted his
word and followed him. He appears as the real
founder of the Abbasid party in Marw, and he
must also have been its organiser. It is no
wonder, then, that it is in A. H. 117 that we for
the first time find some traces of the native
chiefs who were supposed to be appointed as
early as the year 100 by Muhammad b. Alî himself, and that they adhered more to Khidâsh
than to Muhammad. While the mass of the
Shia in Marw consisted of Mawali, the first
chiefs,—there are six of them named in Tab., 2,
1586f.—were Arabs. The most distinguished
among them, who after Khidâsh's death was his
successor, was Sulaimân b. Kathîr. He belonged
to the tribe Khuzâa, who owned certain villages

in the oasis of Marw, and with their Iranian peasants furnished a disproportionately large contingent to the Abbasid Shia. The Khuzâa had an old alliance with the house of the Prophet, and besides they belonged to the Azd, and the latter almost always were in the opposition since the fall of the Muhallabids, so that they were more easily accessible to revolts against the government than the Mudar. Amongst the six party-chiefs called to account by Asad on A. H. 117, there were, moreover, along with three Khuzaites and one Bakrite two Tamîmites as well, so we must not lay too much stress upon the difference of tribe. These Shiites, even the Arabs among them, protested against the Arab nationalism. It was Islam, and not Arabdom, according to their principles which conferred the right of citizenship in the theocracy. Neither were the Mawali in the party excluded from leading positions. Among the twelve chiefs given in Tab., 2, 1358, four Mawali appear side by side with eight Arabs.

After his death, but not till then, Khidâsh was denounced by Muhammad b. Alî. He is said to have been the evil enemy who sowed tares in the wheat, the corrupter as well as the chief of the people, as if he had lighted upon the party and its organisation all ready-made. The bait thrown out by him is said to have been Khurramitism. In reality the sect which he headed and extended was the Hashimiya. The Khurramites were not a sect, but a general libertine tendency. They protested against the Jewry of Islam, as they called it, *i.e.*, against its melancholy Puritanism; they wanted to preserve their right in the religion of nature and gladness, so they joined the native Iranian heathendom. They may have been influenced by socialist ideas as well, which indeed suited excellently with the aims of the Mawali. The communism of wives which Mazdaq had formerly preached is said to have been revived by the Khurramites and Râwandites. Now it is quite credible that Khidâsh did not oppose this tendency, but encouraged it and profited by it, but we are bound to think it improbable that this was a stumbling-block for the Abbasids. At that time they gathered around them the heretics; it was not till later, when they had reached their goal, that they dropped them and became orthodox. At the beginning they tried to divert all the streams of the Shiite opposition to their mill, let them be of any dye they chose. Their first aim was the negative one of overthrowing the Umaiyids. They kept back the positive one of seizing the Khalifate for themselves. They generally showed themselves to their followers not so much in the guise of pretenders as of instruments of the revolution desired by God. They did not put forward their own persons, but the cause, the struggle for right against wrong. They had homage paid, not to themselves and in their name, but for an anonymous person of the family of Muhammad to be agreed upon later. Some even of their founders, who must be regarded as initiated, only later began to have a clear vision of their true aim. As far as they could they did not let it be obvious that they wanted to dislodge the Fatimids, but created the impression that they were working for them, posing in Khurasan and elsewhere as the avengers of the Fatimid martyrs; and still less could they reject and deny the other branch of the Shia, whose support against the latter they must have. The Shia might believe what they liked and live as they pleased; that was to them a secondary consideration. Their first care was that they should adhere to them. The libertinism of the Hashimiya left them cold, but what to them was critical was the independent organisation of the party in Khurasan, which was a sequel to their great rising under the leadership of Khidâsh. In Marw a local committee was formed, which, as we can easily understand, would not suffer itself to be kept in leading-strings by Kufa, without, of course, detracting from fidelity to Muhammad b. Alî himself. But for him there also arose the danger that the reins in Khurasan might slip from his hands, for he held them only through Kufa. So he used the personal authority which he still possessed over the Khurasanite chiefs to induce them to give up their independence and be subordinate to the Wizier in Kufa, and at last he succeeded with difficulty in winning over their leader Sulaimân b. Kathîr. Whilst in A. H. 120 the Khurasanites in Marw rejected the Abbasid Wizier in Kufa, they gave him a friendly reception in A. H. 126 and 127, and also handed over to him the moneys which they had collected. In other cases they delivered them directly to the Imam, and in fact visited him, not in Humaima but in Mecca. The pilgrimage offered the revolutionaries convenient and unobtrusive opportunities of meeting each other. The personal relations with the Imam assumed a more active and, because of the money transaction, a more realistic appearance.

3. Ibrâhîm, the son and successor of Muhammad b. Alî, took a decisive step to get the reins in Khurasan completely into his hands by despatching thither Abû Muslim. The latter's origin is obscure and the accounts of it are uncertain. It is certain that he was not an Arab, but an Iranian, a slave or a client in Kufa. While still a mere youth he there attracted the notice of the Abbasid party, and Ibrâhîm was moved to draw him to himself. He received him into his family, took him into

his interest and made him his confidant. In the year 128 Abû Muslim was given a permanent position as representative of the holy family in Khurasan, where through having frequently visited it before he was well-known, and appointed leader of the cause. The time had come. The mutinous Arab tribes had expelled Nasr from Marw and by risings of every kind and in every quarter the hands of the Umaiyid government were tied.[1]

The adopted Maula offered the Abbasid better guarantees in Khurasan than the free Arab who till then had been at the head of the Hâshimîya there. To be sure Sulaimân b. Kathîr was not to be supplanted straightaway by Abû Muslim, who on the contrary had orders to respect him and to go by his advice. But all the same he found in him a rival who threatened his position. From his antecedents it is understandable that he did not receive him with open arms, and consequently Abû Muslim's position in Marw was a difficult one. It was no asset to him that he married into the family

---

[1] " As the sons of Umaiya since the murder of Walîd were at feud among themselves, and so were fully occupied, the sons of Hâshim and the sons of Alî, likewise relations of the Prophet, dwelling, however, in secure seclusion in Little Arabia, turned this fact to account. They gathered together under the leadership of Ibrâhîm and sent Abû Muslim, their freedman, to Khurasan, to some influential men there to invite them to take part in the struggle against Marwân." Such is the account of Theoph., A.M. 6240.

of one of the chiefs, Abû Najm ; he was regarded as an interloper, could make no headway beside Sulaimân, and thought it advisable
to quit the field in his favour.

He left Marw and made for Kufa again,
but when he was in Qûmis, with one foot already
out of Khurasan, he was induced to turn back.
In Marw a change had come about ; people
now showed themselves ready to render obedience to him as the all-powerful representative
of the heirs of the Prophet, and he now very
successfully took in hand the preparations for
the rising. He seems to have been compelled
to give up this activity because of a journey
to Mecca, which he with a number of his party-
confederates made in Jumada II, 129, in order
to hand over to the Imam there the collected
moneys.[1] But when he reached the western boundary of Khurasan, he made the Taite Qahtaba
b. Shabîb go on to Mecca and himself set out on
the way back to Marw. The pilgrimage was
for him only a pretext. The truth was, he
wished to visit the scattered Shiites of all
shades of opinion, win them over, and prepare
them for the coming revolt. With the aim of
getting into communication with their leaders,
he went through the whole of western
Khurasan as far as the boundaries of Jurjân

---

[1]   The date given (Tab., 2, 1962) is rather early for the pilgrimage.

and back, making a considerable stay at several places which were important for the Shiites. Having got back to Marw, he began to act openly.

I follow the anonymous account in Tab., 2, 1960ff. in distinguishing between the two journeys of Abû Muslim. The first time he left Marw because he could not keep his position there. The second time he journeyed through western Khurasan with the purpose of inciting to agitation under pretence of making the pilgrimage. Madâinî (Tab., 1949ff.) only mentions one journey, the second. He says nothing about the dangerous variance between Abû Muslim and Sulaimân. But, as Van Vloten rightly emphasises,[1] this variance has every ground of probability in its favour. Still, we might, of course, be content with one journey. We might take it that Abû Muslim, as he could not gain a footing in Marw, had attempted to make on his own account a position for himself in western Khurasan. But the pilgrimage which he undertook in common with the Marwites does not fit in with this assumption. Above all, chronological difficulties arise, for the celebration to which they journeyed was the one which was held at the end of 129; Qahtaba only returned from Mecca in A.H. 130. But at

---

[1] *Cf.* the passage cited by him from Maqrîzî for the Ahl alKafiya, Recherches, p. 80.

this time the revolt under Abû Muslim in Marw
was already completely in train, for it broke
out immediately after his return from the insurrection expedition. His breach with Sulaimân
and his consequent compulsory departure from
Marw must have taken place earlier, soon after
his first arrival in the year 128. Possibly the
circumstance that Abû Muslim on both journeys
reached the western boundary of Khurasan and
there turned back, tends to confuse them.

Of the revolt in the villages of the Khuzâa
near Marw in the second half of the year 129
(summer, 747), Tabarî gives the account of
Madâinî (1949ff., 1965ff., 1989ff.), that of Abu'l-
Khattâb (1953ff., 1967ff., 1984ff.), and still
another one which is anonymous (1960ff., 1970ff.,
1992ff.). These agree in certain characteristics
and also in some striking details, but they
present many differences as well. Neither are
they at one in themselves, and taken all
together are extremely unsatisfactory.

First of all we are most prepossessed in
favour of the account of Abu'lKhattâb, which
at the first glance appears the most conclusive.
On Tuesday, 9th Sha'bân, 129 (Tuesday, 25th
April, 747), having again reached the oasis of
Marw from Khurasan, Abû Muslim first took
a lodging in Fanîn, the village of Abû Dâûd
Khâlid b. Ibrâhîm al-Bakrî.[1]) On the 2nd

---

[1] *Cf.* 1960. 14 f.

Ramadan (17th May) he removed from there to
Sîkadanj, the village of Sulaimân b. Kathîr
al Khuzâî. The 25th Ramadan was kept in
view as the date for open action, and notice of
this given to the members of the party in
Marwrudh, Tukharistan and Khwarizm. On this
day, then, the two black standards sent by the
Imam were actually unfurled in Sikadanj, and
beacon-signals were also made to the inhabitants of the neighbouring villages. Within the
next few days they arrived; those from Suqâdim
first, on the 27th Ramadan. The camp numbered
2,200 infantry and 56 horsemen. On the festival of the breaking of the fast, Friday, 1st
Shauwâl, 129 (15th June, 747), the first service
according to the Abbasid ritual was held in
Sikadanj, conducted by Sulaimân b. Kathîr,
following which Abû Muslim held a great ban-
quet. Eighteen days after [1] his public act of
revolt a troop of horse sent by the stattholder
Nasr advanced against him, but it was repulsed
by Abû Nasr Mâlik b. Haitham alKhuzâî near
Âlîn, the wounded and captive leader being
well cared for and then liberated, so that he
might go home and publish the praise of
Abû Muslim. At the beginning of Dhulqaʻda,
Khâzim b. Khuzaima at Tamîmî seized the town
of Marwrudh and killed the Government official
there. Abû Muslim remained 42 days in Sikadanj

---

[1] *Months* in 1957, 17 is a slip.

altogether. On Wednesday, 9th Dhulqa'da (Saturday, 22nd July,) he moved his camp to Mâkhuân, the residence of several Shiites famous later on, and here he settled down for a considerable stay. He appointed officials and fortified the camp. If he had been like another man hitherto, he now assumed the airs of a prince. His army rose to 7,000 men and he had every one registered in a roll according to his father's name and that of his village. The pay amounted to from 3 to 4 dirhems (per month). The people of Suqâdim, 800 strong, he sent to Jîranj to break off Nasr's communications with Marwrudh and Tukharistan. He relegated the servants to a separate camp, and later on sent them to Bîward to Mûsâ b. Ka'b at Tamîmî. Four months after he moved from Makhuan to Alin, as the water there could not be cut off from him ; for he was apprehensive of an attack by the Arabs of Marw, who for this end had made a truce with each other. In Alin he celebrated the feast on the 10th Dhulhijja, 129 (22nd August, 747). Government troops did actually advance from Marw to attack him, and committed all sorts of mischief in the villages, until he put a stop to their doings. Then some wounded prisoners fell into his hands, and he cared for them, and when well, set them free. But the unity of the enemy did not last long, as Alî b. Judai

alKarmânî was induced by Sulaimân b. Kathîr
to break the truce, and they now actually made
Abû Muslim arbitrator in their dispute.   Deputations from both parties, the Mudar and the
Azd-Rabîa, appeared before him and sued for
his favour.   In a solemn conclave he, along
with his 70 fellow-judges, decided for the Azd
against the Mudar, for Alî b. Judai against
Nasr; the Mudar sorrowfully   departed.   After
29 days he again left Alin and returned to
Makhuan, ordering his men to provide themselves with supplies there for the winter, since
God had removed the danger of enemies.   This
took place on Thursday, 15th Safar, 130 (25th
October, 747).   He now stayed 90 days more in
Makhuan, till Thursday, 9th Jumâdâ, when he
marched into Marw.[1] The town proper was in
the hands of Nasr, whom Alî b. Judai, supported by an officer of Abû Muslim, now attacked with energy.   While the   struggle was
raging Abû Muslim made his entrance.   Nasr
surrendered to him, but the next morning he
and his faithful followers fled.   Twenty-four
distinguished Arabs, among them Salm b.
Ahwaz at Tamîmî, Abû Muslim had executed.

[1] Acc. to 1986, 18. 1987, 14 it was the first, acc. to 1984, 14, the
second Jumâdâ. For the 90 days from the middle of Safar onwards,
the first suits better, but for Thursday; the second is better; for the
9th Jumâdâ I fell upon a Monday, the 9th Jumâdâ II upon a
Wednesday. The difference of one day does not matter, as the
beginning of the month frequently varies by a day.

The exactness and completeness of the account does not count for much. This is apparent, for instance, in the duplicate regarding the repulse of an enemy attack in Âlîn and the good treatment of the wounded captives by Abû Muslim, but particularly so in the chronological statements. These contain the clumsiest discrepancies; the longer periods in particular do not fit in at all with the fixed calendar dates. On the 2nd Ramadan 129 (May 17th, 747) Abû Muslim comes to Sîkadanj and stays there 42 days, *i.e.*, till the middle of Shauwal (end of June); but he does not go away to Makhuan till the 9th Dhulqada (22nd July). The duration of the first sojourn in Makhuan is given as 4 months, but as early as the beginning of Dhulhijja (the middle of August), after barely one month, he is in Alin. He stays in Alin 29 days, *i.e.*, till the beginning of Muharram, 130 (middle of September), but he does not return to Makhuan till the middle of Safar (end of October). The second stay in Makhuan lasts 90 days, *i.e.*, till the middle of Jumada I. With this the date of the entry into Marw almost coincides, if we take the 9th of the first and not of the second Jumada.

Abu'l Khattâb, according to Madâinî, requires correction; the Anonymous Version keeps a middle course. According to Madâinî, Abû Muslim was not in Makhuan twice, but

only once. The four months which Abu'l
Khattâb takes for the first sojourn are really
the extent of the whole stay there. The 8
months (4 months + 29 days + 90 days) which
he reckons from the first coming of Abû Muslim
to Makhuan until his definite departure thence,
are curtailed to the half. Certainly Abû Muslim's stay in Makhuan was, even according to
Madâinî, interrupted, but only by a journey
which he personally made to Marw. On his
return from this journey, he stayed, according
to Madâinî, 3 months more in Makhuan ; these
correspond to the 90 days in Abu'l Khattâb.
According to Madâinî and the one account of
Abu'l Khattâb, the return took place at the
beginning of the year 130, and if we reckon
3 months or 90 days from then, then Abû
Muslim struck camp in Makhuan at the beginning of Rabî II, and marched into Marw.
Mâdainî indeed gives the 9th Rabî II for the
entry into Marw, and the anonymous account
agrees with him.[1] This date is further confirmed by the statement that the days then
were very short (1990, 20) ; the 9th Rabiî II,
130 was the 17th Decr., 747 ; the 9th Jumâdâ
I or II mentioned instead by Abu'l Khattâb
(15th January or 14th February, 748) fell more
or less considerably beyond the winter solstice.

---

[1] It is also called the 7th Rabî II, the confusion between 7 and
9 is constantly occurring in Arabic.

Working backwards we get to the beginning of
Dhulhijja, 129 as the commencement of the
sojourn in Makhuan that covered in all four
months. The encampment in Alin did not inter-
rupt it, but preceded it ; according to Madâinî,
Abû Muslim was there [1] in Dhulqa'da, 129.
Unanimous tradition says he was in Sikadanj in
Shauwal and Ramadan. The 42 days which Abu'l
Khattâb puts down to Sikadanj, Madâinî
reckons to Alin, but here Abu'l Khattâb is
certainly right. We must also follow his account in making Fanîn precede Sikadanj.[2]

If this scheme holds, we then gather something like the following idea of the course of
events. The villages of the Khuzâa [3] in which
Abû Muslim shifted his quarters about, lay
near each other in the district of the Kharqân
Canal. The original centre of the conspiracy
was Sikadanj where the chief head of the
Hâshimîya, Sulaimân b. Kathîr, had his seat.
There the black standards which Ibrâhîm b.
Muhammad had sent, were unfurled, and the
beacon-signals kindled. Thither assembled the
members of the party from the nearer and more
remote surrounding districts. There on the 1st
Shauwal, 129 the first Abbasid service was held

---

[1] Bâlîn (1952, 10) is identical with Allin and Alin ; it may have
arisen from bi-Alin (in Alin).

[2] Cf. Van Vloten, Opkomst der Abbasiden, p. 79.

[3] They are so called a potiori, for Fanîn and Mâkhuân were not
specifically Khuzaite.

at which Sulaimân b. Kathîr acted as Imam.
That he only did so upon the command of Abû
Muslim is incredible. At that time in Sikadanj
he was not exactly the person to be dislodged
from the first place ; he kept up the appearance, at least, of the primacy, even though the
leadership of the movement had already slipped
from his hands. Abû Muslim felt hampered by
him, so after 42 days he left Sikadanj, went first
to Alin, and from there about the end of the
year 129, to Makhuan. He made his appearance in Makhuan as lord and ruler, his army
increased, and through it, his power and consequence as well. It was then, too, that he first
aroused the apprehension of the Arabs, who
were beating each other's brains out in Marw,
and this was increased by the successes gained
by the Shiite movement simultaneously at other
points, in Biward, in Marwrudh, and especially
in Herat (Tab., 2, 1966). Moved by the Bakrites who served under him, Shaibân al Harûrî
first of all made his peace with Nasr, and Alî
b. Judai alKarmânî seems to have followed his
example. It looked as if the Arabs had at
last comprehended the danger that threatened
them, and wanted to meet it together. But,
full of distrust of one another, they did nothing
serious against Abû Muslim. The most they
did was to undertake one raid into the district
under his power, which was repulsed byhim

67

without trouble,[1] and after a short time he managed to break up the alliance of the hostile brethren. He betook himself in person from Makhuan to Marw and contrived to make Alî b. Judai withdraw from the truce with the Azd and again enter into hostile relations with Nasr and the Mudar. At the beginning of 130 he returned to Makhuan. He was now absolutely secure from the Arabs and could quietly leave them to themselves till it seemed to him about time to bring home the fruits of their suicidal work. His relationship with the Mudar by no means suffered by his having won over the Azd. On the contrary, they are said to have attempted to attract him from the latter to their side, so that he was courted by both. In any case, they no longer dared to treat him as an enemy, and so it could come about that he entered Marw as judge, and by his intervention put an end to the fierce dispute in which the Arab tribes were dissipating their strength. He decided,—so at least it seemed at first,—to side with the Azd against the Mudar. Of this actual event, the scene reported by Abu 'l Khattâb, how the delegates of the Azd and the Mudar appear in the camp of Makhuan before

---

[1] It has been already pointed out that Abu ' l Khattâb gives two versions (1958f. 1970) of the same affair (at Alin). Both end in Abû Muslim treating the wounded prisoners well so as to gain credit to himself. Both are very much padded ; acc. to Tab. 1970 the hostilities amounted to the theft and slaughter of the peasants' cattle and poultry.

Abû Muslim to submit their quarrel to him for decision, and how he with his 70 assessors gives sentence, is an anticipation. Neither did he as yet make negotiations with Judai al Karmânî, but only with his son Alî, at the end of 129 or beginning of 130, in which he took the initiative. He was the suer, not the sued, as Van Vloten rightly remarks. From a later point of view he did not show to advantage in this situation. He contradicted the ideas people had formed of him by lowering himself in this way. People were inclined to put at an earlier time the peculiarly authoritative position which he finally attained, but this makes it incomprehensible why he waited so long before finally laying hold of it. At the beginning he was not so strong all at once that he could openly oppose the Arabs, so he acted with diplomacy, keeping them in suspense and throwing dust in their eyes. Even with the Mudar he did not spoil things so completely that they counted him their declared enemy. His incitation of a rising against the Umaiyid Government was at that time in the order of things and disturbed nobody, and beyond that he did not show his hand. According to Madâinî (Tab., 2, 1965), the pious scholars of Marw came to him to find out who he was and what he wanted, but he did not have anything to do with them, saying he had more urgent business on hand.

The majority of his adherents consisted of
Iranian peasants and of the Mawali of the
villages of Marw, but there were Arabs among
them also who mostly occupied leading positions. The connecting element was the religion,
the sect. The nucleus of the Khurasanian army,
the "Jund" of the Abbasids, consisted of the
Hashimiya, as is expressly stated in Tab., 2,
1987. It was at the head of the Hashimiya
that Abû Muslim entered Marw, and after the
entry homage was received from them, Abû
Mansûr Talha b. Ruzaiq alKhuzâî administer-
ing the oath. The formula of the oath ran:
"I hold you bound to the Book of God and the
Sunna of the Prophet, and to obedience to him
of the family of the Messenger of God who
may be agreed upon, and not to demand from
your officers either maintenance or money, but
to wait till they give you something of their
own accord;[1] and no one is to do any hurt to his
personal enemy when he has him in his power,
except upon the command of a superior." It is
remarkable that Abû Mansûr, who, as it is
reported, was thoroughly initiated into the
principles and arguments of the sect, lets nothing of these be known as far as the troops
were concerned, but confines himself to genera-
lities. Nor does he yet let the person of the

[2]   Cf. also the Ahl alKafîya (or alKifâya?) in Vloten, *Recherches*,
pp. 66, 80.

Abbasid Imam get outside of the circle of ˌthe Prophet's family. The troops were, before everything, bound to absolute obedience to their officers ; even with these revolutionaries a military turn was given to the religion. The common people were not obliged to ˙know the secrets of their superiors; the black standard was sufficient as their creed. There had long been standards of all colours[1] among the Islamic parties, but nowhere does the standard, its colour and significance, stand out so strikingly as with the Shiites of Khurasan. They even wore the black flag on their bodies. Theophanes calls them the Χουρασανιοι [2] μαυροφόροι "the wearers of black," and in the Continuator Isidori Hispan. (ed. Mommsen, par. 134), they are called *Persarum pullata demonia,* " the black devils." The standard of the Prophet is said to have been black, and hence to have been also that of the Abbasids. In the Apocalyptic books there was

---

[1] *Red* with the Khawârij, Agh., 20, 112, 31. *Black, ibid.* and 99, 9 ; cf. Tab., 2, 1981. 2007. Lisân 11, 329. The opponents of the Abbasids chose *white,* not only the Syrians of Umaiyid tendency, but the Alids as well (Tab., 3, 223. 271. 295. 298. 361. 508.) Certain rebels (Khurramites ?) in Media carried *red* flags and were therefore called the Muhammira (Tab. 3, 493 f. 645f. 1235). One of the Hasanids carried a *yellow* flag with the picture of a serpent (Tab., **3**, 237). Prominent persons had their private colour, which their clients assumed also (Tab., 3, 516). In Arab olden times *black* was the colour of revenge, Agh., 8, 75, 20.

[2] χορασαν or χουρασαν is the correct writing (for Theophanes, like the Syrians, uses the ου short) ; χωρασαν again, is wrong. Both α are long.

mention of the man of the black standards who
would bring in the new era, but Hârith b.
Suraij, who for the first time set the Mawali
in the saddle in the name of Islam, had also
black standards, and Abû Muslim may then
have borrowed them from him because they
were popular among the Mawali.

In verses preserved in Dînawarî, 360, Nasr
b. Saiyâr, the Umaiyid stattholder of Marw,
addresses the Arabs as follows,—" Why do ye
always rekindle the feud between yourselves,
acting as if there were no sensible men among
you, and letting the foe who stand at the door
work their will! They are a mob of men without religion and without consequence, no Arabs
of ours, for us to know, and no Mawali of any
standing. They have a religion which comes
not from the Messenger of God nor is it to be
found in the holy books; it amounts, in truth,
to this, that the Arabs are to be killed." According to Tab., 2, 1937, 1974. 3,25 the Imam
Ibrâhîm b. Muhammad himself is said to have
expressly directed Abû Muslim to leave no Arab
alive in Khurasan. According to Theophanes,
A. M. 6240 the slaves in Khurasan, set on by
Abû Muslim, slew their masters in one night
and equipped themselves with their weapons,
horses and money. In the historical account of
Tabarî of the taking of Marw nothing is
said about this; only Abû Muslim had 24

THE FALL OF THE ARAB KINGDOM 535

distinguished followers of Nasr executed, after the
latter's flight, but he enjoined upon his soldiers
the strictest discipline and forbade any arbitrary
killing. Now it is possible that here, as in
other cases, there exists a moderation in the
Abbasid interest. The Mawali may quite likely
have indulged their fury more bitterly than
appears to be the case according to Tabarî, but
still their national feeling of hostility to the
Arabs must not be too much accentuated. The
movement did not originate with the Iranian
nation, but with a sect of a fairly circumscribed
locality from which the Arabs were not excluded. It had religious motives of a political
and social sort which were to be found in Islam.
It threatened, in principle, not the aliens but
the heretics, —hence the name heretic-clubs for
the weapons of the Mawali.[1] Abû Muslim's
most intimate confidants, Abû Nasr, Abû
Dâûd and others, were Arabs, and it was not
the Arabs *per se*, but the *ruling* Arabs that
were to be fought against, and that by virtue
of Islam, because they rule unjustly and un-
lawfully, supported the godless Umaiyid *régime*
and did not recognise the equal rights of the other
Muslims in the theocracy. The Arab opposition-
party, on the other hand, *e.g.*, the Iraqites and
the Yemen in Khurasan, were first recognised
as confederates. Actually, indeed, the struggle

[1] Agh., 4, 93 ; Dînaw., 360. Tabarî mentions only the Kâfirkûbât
among the Khashabîya of Mukhtâr, 2,694.

against Arabism in Islam amounted to this, that now Iranianism got the upper hand, and the Arabs, even as a nation, were subdued, since their rule had ceased with the Umaiyid rule. Nasr b. Saiyâr foresaw this. It lay in the nature of things, but not in the original purpose. The nationality of the conquerors asserted its ascendancy over Islam, in the swadding-clothes of which it had grown up. Still, originally it was Islam, and not the idea of nationality that was the moving force in the revolt of the Khurasanites,—just as formerly it had been the moving force in the revolt of the Arabs themselves. A new Islam united with a new nation.

4. Abû Muslim sent to Tukharistan his devoted Abû Dâûd alBakrî who had already been active there before (1960, 14f.). After he had succeeded in driving out of Balkh the Umaiyid official Ziâd b. Abdirrahmân al-Qushairî, he was recalled, and Yahyâ b. Nuʻaim alBakrî put in his place. But the latter entered upon negotiations with Ziâd, who was securely established in Tirmidh not very far from Balkh. The result was an alliance of all the Arab tribes of that district, the Mudar, Yemen and Rabîa against the Shia of Khurasan. Even the Iranians of that quarter joined in, their leader Muqâtil b. Haiyân receiving the chief command so that the Arabs should not quarrel over it. The coalition of Arabs and

Iranians against the Shia may serve to correct wrong ideas. This too, deserves notice, that part of the allies carried black standards,— no doubt those of Hârith b. Suraij. Abû Dâûd was now again sent into the field against this alliance. The enemy, after a battle on the Sarjanân, evacuated Balkh again and went back to Tirmidh, and for the second time Abû Dâûd was recalled and the Azdite Uthmân b. Judai alKarmânî, Ali's brother, set over Balkh. But he was unable to keep his position there, for the Mudar of Tirmidh under Muslim b. Abdirrahmân alBâhilî, a nephew of the celebrated Qutaiba expelled him from Balkh. Then Abû Dâûd had to come for the third time ; he was indispensable there. So runs the account in Tabarî 2, 1997 ff., and there is nothing better to substitute for it. [1]

In Khurasan proper Abû Muslim was master of the three easterly regions of the government, Marw, Marwrudh and Herat, but of the western district, Naisabur, only the towns of Nasâ and Biward. In the town of Naisabur the stattholder Nasr b. Saiyâr was established. In Sarakhs there was Shaibân alHarûrî, who soon after Nasr's flight had likewise evacuated Marw, as he could not accommodate himself to the new

---

[1] For later risings in Soghd against Abû Muslim, cf. Tab., 3, 74. 79f.; the Abbasids had a hand in the game too. It was only through Abû Muslim and the Abbasids that Transoxiana was completely subjected to the rule of Islam.

circumstances. Abû Muslim had him attacked there, and he was overcome and slain. His troops, mostly Bakrites, fled to Naisabur and joined Nasr. Now began the fight against Nasr, and from that arose the great war in which the kingdom of the Umaiyids fell to pieces before the black devils of Khurasan. Abû Muslim did not himself take the lead in this, but the leader was Qahtaba b. Shabîb, an Arab of the Taiyi tribe.[1] Qahtaba had been absent during the revolt ; it was only after the taking of Marw that he returned from Mecca, whither he had gone to meet with the Imam Ibrâhîm b. Muhammad at the Hajj. Ibrâhîm had appointed him as his field-marshal by presenting him with a standard, and Abû Muslim confirmed this and gave him the supreme command. Under or alongside of him were Abû Aun Abdulmalik b. Yazîd alAzdî, Khâzim b. Khuzaima at Tamîmî, the Iranian Khâlid b. Barmak of Balkh, and others. [2] Nasr sent his son Tamîm against the advancing army of the Shia, and after the latter was beaten and slain near Tûs, he quitted Naisabur at the end of Shauwal, 130, *i.e.*, the end of June, 748 (Tab., 2, 2016). Some time after Abû Muslim transferred his residence from Marw thither. [3] He took with him his

---

[1]   *Cf.* Hamasa, p. 303ff.

[2]   In Theoph. A.M. 6240 Qahtaba is placed beside Abû Muslim as pretty much of equal account.

[3]   Tab., 3, 3. *Cf.*, however, 3, 59.

ally Alî b. Judai alKarmânî, but on the way
managed to get rid of him for good. At the
same time also his brother Uthmân b. Judai in
Tukharistan was got out of the way by Abû
Dâûd (Tab., 2, 1999f.). The alliance of the Azd
with the Shia, by which the taking of Marw
was effected, had served its purpose, and by the
assassination of the Azdite leader an inconvenient
competition was avoided, for he seems to have
continued to hold an independent and equally
legitimate position side by side with Abû Muslim.

Nasr had gone from Naisabur to Qumis on
the boundary of Jurjan, and with him the
Arabs of Tamîm, Bakr and Qais, who had fled
out of Khurasan. On the order of the Khalifa
the Iraqite stattholder Ibn Hubaira sent Nubâta
b. Hanzala alKilâbî to Jurjan, but the latter
did not co-operate with Nasr, and weakened
him further by enticing to himself the Qaisites
in Nasr's army. Qahtaba first turned against
Nubâta. After advancing into Jurjan in
Dhulqada, 130, he fought a battle with him on
Friday, 1st Dhulhijja (Thursday, 1st August,
748) in which he was defeated and slain.
Meanwhile Nasr seems to have successfully held
out against Hasan, the son of Qahtaba, who was
sent to attack him, and one of the Shiite officers,
Abû Kâmil, went over to him. But after
Nubâta's fall Qumis was no longer a place for
him, and he fled across Media to Hamadan,

without anywhere finding support from the Umaiyid officials. [1] In one of the first months of the year 131, Qahtaba joined his son in Qumis, and thence made for the west, sending his son on in advance. Rai and Hamadan capitulated, but the Syrian troops of the statt-holder there which had fled from Hamadan, and the Khurasanite ones of Nasr b. Saiyâr rallied again in Nihawand and offered a determined resistance to Hasan b. Qahtaba when he besieged them there. 'Âmir b. Dubâra alMurrî was commanded to relieve the town, and with a great and well-equipped Syrian army he took the field in Karman after compelling the Ja'farid Ibn Muâwia to flee. But on the march to Nihawand he was himself attacked by Qah-taba, overcome and slain. [2] The severe and bloody encounter took place near Jâbalq in the district of Ispahan, on Saturday, 23rd Rajab, 131 (Tuesday, 18th March, 749-*sic*). Qahtaba then joined forces with his son before Nihawand. After several months, apparently, according to Tab., 37, 18, in Dhulqada, 131 (June-July, 749), the Syrians in the besieged town decided upon a surrender on their own account, without the knowledge of, or reference to their Khurasanite

---

[1] He died in Sâwa near Hamadân on 12th Rabi I, 131 (9th Nov., 748), aged 85.

[2] For Ιβινδαρα in Theophanes A.M. 6240 there must be read Ιβινδαβαρα acc. to Anastasius, for it is Ibn Dubâra that is meant, and not Nubâta, as Reiske (*Abulfeda I, adn.* 238) wrongly conjectures.

comrades. The latter were put to death without mercy.

The road to Iraq was now clear for Qahtaba. He again sent his son Hasan on in front, and himself followed him from Nihawand *via* Qarmâsîn to Hulwân and Khâniqîn. Cleverly circumventing the stattholder Ibn Hubaira, who had advanced against him across the Tigris with a strong army, and was encamped in Jalûlâ, he crossed the Tigris and marched upon Kufa. In the neighbourhood of Anbâr on the Euphrates he made a preliminary halt. Ibn Hubaira hastened after him and encamped some distance aside, on the left bank of the Euphrates, near Fam Furât Bâdaqlâ, in the upper Fallûja, where the canal to Kufa branched off ; he sent a division in advance to Kufa, under Hauthara b. Suhail alBâhilî. Qahtaba, however, crossed the Euphrates near Dimimmâ, and marched along the right bank to Hâira, a place which lay opposite the camping-ground of Ibn Hubaira. During the night of Wednesday, 8th Muharram, 132 (Wed., 27th Aug., 749) he passed the ford with a little band and surprised the enemy camp. [1] Ibn Hubaira was taken unawares, and retired first to Fam an-Nîl, but did not make a stand there, but withdrew along the Canal an-Nîl into the strong government town of Wasit.

---

[1] Everything is exactly the same as in the activities of Maslama b. Abdilmalik against Yazîd b. Muhallab in A.H. 101 or 102.

When he heard this, Hauthara, who had reached Qasr Ibn Hubaira, now did not venture to advance into Kufa, but united with the stattholder in Wasit. Qahtaba's success was complete, but it cost him his life, for he met his death mysteriously in the confusion by night. From a military stand-point there is no doubt that he accomplished the most for the Abbasids. He brought victory to the black standards, and founded the reputation of their invincibility. Hasan, who had remained stationary on the right bank, took command in his stead, and was able to enter Kufa without striking a blow. There Muhammad, the son of Khâlid alQasrî, martyred by the Umaiyid government, had with the Yemenites attempted a rising in favour of the Abbasids and taken possession of the citadel ; after Hauthara's departure no one troubled him any longer. Upon his advice Hasan made his entrance into the town on Tuesday, 14th Muharram (2nd Sept., 749). On the other hand, in Basra the attempt of the Muhallabid Sufyân b. Muâwia to overthrow the Umaiyid government with the help of the Azd and Rabia, fell through. The Mudar and the Syrians who backed up the stattholder Salm b. Qutaiba alBâhilî, defeated the Azd. Everywhere the Yemen (and Rabîa) joined the revolution, while the Mudar fought for the ruling Arabism. [1]

[1] I have followed the report of old Abû Mikhnaf, whose words appear here for the last time in Tab. 3, 10. 14. 18-20. So he was

The Abbasid authority, hitherto hidden, now came into the open. Abû Salama, the Wezîr of the Prophet's family, emerged from his retirement and took the government in hand ; he resided in Hammâm A'yan, where the Khurasanites were encamped. But the time had come for the Abbasids themselves to leave their lurking-place and come out into the fore-ground. Ibrâhîm b. Muhammad, hitherto their head, had been arrested upon the command of the Khalifa Marwân and taken away from Humaima to Harrân, upon which he is said to have commanded them to go to Kufa and to acknowledge his brother Abu 'lAbbâs as his successor. His imprisonment must therefore have taken place not long before the Khurasanites entered Kufa, for the Abbasids only reached there one month after this event in Safar, 132. There were fourteen of them, of different generations. First, sons of Alî b. Abdillâh b. Abbâs : Dâûd, Îsâ, Sâlih, Ismâîl, Abdullâh and Abdussamad, besides Mûsâ, the son of Dâûd ; then sons of Muhammad b. Alî b. Abdillâh b. Abbâs : Abu'l-Abbâs, Abû Ja'far and Yahyâ ; then grandsons of Muhammad b. Alî : Abdulwahhâb b. Ibrâhîm b. Muhammad and his brother Muhammad, along with Îsa b. Mûsâ b. Muhammad ;

still living after the catastrophe, but must then have been a very old man. Madâinî, the chief narrator in Tabarî, differs in one or two unessential points, and gives some more exact definitions. *Cf.* Masûd², 6, 73. Yaqûbî, 2, 412. Hamasa, 403f.

and finally, from a collateral line, Yahyâ b. Ja'far b. Tammâm b. Abbâs. [1]

The Abbasids were not received in Kufa with open arms. The wezir, Abû Salama, did not consider as a matter of course their claim to the succession of Ibrâhîm b. Muhammad, whom he had personally acknowledged as Imam. Their presence was inconvenient to him, and for some time he tried to conceal the fact of their residence from the Khurasanites, saying that their time was not yet come because Wasit had not yet been conquered. But a confidant of Abû Muslim, Abû Jahm, came secretly and informed them. Then there rode into Kufa twelve Khurasanite chiefs from the camp of Hammâm A'yan, made for the quarter of the Abbasids and did homage to Abu 'lAbbâs, and consequently Abû Salama also was obliged to comply. [2] On Friday, 12th Rabi II, 132 (Friday, 28th Nov., 749) public homage to Abu 'lAbbâs and the new dynasty was paid in the chief

---

[1] Dâûd b. Alî and his son Mûsâ had not come from Humaima but had only joined those taking the field on the way in Dûma, and at the beginning advised them against going on to Kufa. The family did not always unanimously gather round the Imam, Ibrâhîm b. Muhammad. Îsâ and Abdullâh, Ali's sons, and also Ibrâhîm's brother, Abû Ja'far, had for a time attached themselves to the Ja'farid Ibn Muâwia (Tab., 2, 1977). Not only Dâûd b. Alî but Sulaimân b. Alî also, who is not mentioned amongst the 14, appear not to have lived in Humaima, but in Iraq. Cf. Yaqûbî, 2, 419.

[2] Thus Madâinî in Tab., 3, 28ff. diverging somewhat from the parallel report, 34ff. Cf. Masûdî, 6, 92f. Yaqûbî 2, 413.

mosque of Kufa. Abu 'lAbbâs mounted the pulpit and spoke till the fever from which he was suffering compelled him to sit down, and then his uncle, Dâûd b. Alî, who stood three steps below him, got up and continued. The speeches are not authentically handed down to us, but their contents in general suit the situation. The right of the Abbasids to the ruling power is proved from the Word of God, and there is also a polemical aside directed at those Shiites [1] who assert that the Alids have the prior claim, but special emphasis is laid upon the community of the interest of the Abbasids and the Iraqites. [2]   While the Abbasids by their Khurasanite body-guard overthrew the Umaiyids, they at the same time also freed the Iraqites from the Syrian yoke. The 100 years' struggle, up till then a vain one, between Iraq and Syria, now ended with the victory of Iraq ; the seat of government again came to Kufa, where it was in former days under Alî. " Every dynasty has its centre-point ; you are our centre-point." This was, of course, to entice the Kufaites. But the centre of gravity of the kingdom was now really transferred from Damascus to Kufa and Iraq, and that was an event of deep significance. [3]

---

[1] The contemptuous term "Sabaites" included them, 29, 17.

[2] Cf. already Tab., 2, 1816, 7 : عرا قى الهوى

[3] Theoph. A.M. 6241.

Moreover, Abu 'lAbbâs was not so very sure of the Kufaites. He did not set up his residence in their town of Kufa, but among the Khurasanites in Hammâm A'yan. Some time after he transferred it to Hîra and then to Hâshimîya, we may suppose in order to separate himself from Abû Salama, who also lived in Hammâm A'yan. Relations between the two continued strained; Abû Salama sympathised with the Alids and expressed his sympathies so openly as to give grounds for the suspicion that he was not alone in his sentiments, particularly as up till then the reins of the party-leadership had been in his hands. The Khalifa dared not proceed against him; being himself without power and the creature of his alleged instruments, the king-makers, who in addition were well aware of his dubious legitimacy, he was absolutely given over to the good pleasure of others far more influential than himself. He sent his brother Abû Ja'far to Khurasan to ascertain the sentiments of Abû Muslim whose influence over the Khurasanite army was very great. Abû Muslim fortunately had nothing in common with Abû Salama and did the Abbasids the good turn of having him murdered, at the same time causing his old rival in Khurasan, Sulaimân b. Kathîr, the leader of the Nuqabâ, to be put to death, using the pretext that the latter acted in concert with Abû Salama as a ground for

venting upon him his personal hatred. His
confidant, Abû Jahm, controlled and directed
the Khalifa Abu 'lAbbâs.[1]

While these things were being enacted in
the east, the west was simultaneously the scene
of convulsing events.[2] After the fall of Nihawand, in Dhulqada, 131, Qahtaba sent Abû Aun
Abdulmalik b. Yazîd alAzdî to Shahrazur.
After a decisive battle on the 20th Dhulhijja,
131 (10th Aug., 749), he drove out thence the
Syrian troops and established himself in the
district belonging to Mosul, to the north of the
Tigris. After the taking of Kufa, he got reinforcements from there but had to give up the
chief command to the Abbasid Abdullâh b. Alî.
The Khalifa, with the Mesopotamian and Syrian
Arabs, advanced from Harrân across the Tigris
against the Khurasanites, and the battle was
joined on the left bank of the Great Zâb. It
began on the 2nd Jumada II, 132 and ended on
Saturday, 11th Jumada (Sunday, 25th Jany.),
with the complete defeat of Marwân. Theophanes gives his army at 300,000 men; he says
that thousands fled from one thousand, and tens
of thousands from two. This unequal proportion also appears at other times, and can be
understood from the axiom that the victory
depends upon God, who scatters the infidel

---

[1] Yaqûbî, 2, 433. Tab., 3, 67, 88.
[2] Tab., 3, 9f. 38ff., mainly acc. to Madâinî.

horde before the faithful few.   According to an account in Madâinî (Tab., 3, 47) Marwan had at his disposal only 12,000 men.   At first he had the advantage.   The bad ending was partly caused by the Qais not being willing to do any more than the Qudâa.   Besides, there is of course no doubt that the will to win and the confidence of victory were with the Khurasanites.   The Arabs had lost confidence and did not want to be sacrificed.   Marwân produced money with the promise that they should share it if they fought bravely, but they fell at once upon the money and made off with it.   Many of the fugitives were drowned in the Zâb for the bridge was cut down.

Marwân retired across the Tigris to Harran and there remained some time.   It redounds to his credit that he now set free the political prisoners whom he found still in the prison, while those who had attempted to break out before his arrival were slain by his devoted Harranites.   From Harran he went *via* Qinnesrin and Hims to Damascus, and on to the stronghold Abû Futrus near Jaffa, where he sought protection with a man of the Judhamite royal family of the Banû Rauh b. Zinbâ', since the power in that district was no longer in the hand of the Umaiyid government.   From Abû Futrus he fled to the Egyptian sea-port Farmâ, when his pursuers came threateningly close. Abdullâh b. Alî with the Khurasanites followed him, reinforced on the way by his brothers Abdussamad and Sâlih, and marched *via* Mosul, Harran, Mambij, Qinnesrin, Baalbekk and Ain alJarr to Mizza near Damascus, where he pitched his camp. The Syrian towns surrendered to him without a struggle, having, as can be understood, no attachment to Marwân (Masûdî, 6, 84f.). Only the capital of the kingdom, Damascus, had to be besieged. Marwân's son-in-law, Walîd b. Muâwia b. Marwân I was in command there, but the citizens did not back him up with their united strength, and in the end murdered him and opened the gates of the town to Abdullâh b. Alî on the 14th Ramadan, 132 (26th April, 750). A fortnight later he marched on to Abû Futrus, whence he sent his brother Sâlih with Abû Aun to Egypt, in pursuit of Marwân, and he departed thither in Dhulqada, 132 (June, 750). Marwân fled from him from place to place till he got to Bûsîr (Busiris) near Raudâ in the Upper Egyptian province of Ushmûnain. There he took his stand; after a fierce struggle his faithful followers scattered (Theoph.) and he himself fell. A Khurasanite Arab of the Yemenite Balhârith attacked him with his men, calling to them in Persian: "Strike hard, boys!" and killed him. This was at the end of 132, the

beginning of August, 750.[1] His head, and
according to Masûdî, also the insignia of the
Khalifate were sent to Abu 'lAbbâs. His tongue,
according to a verse quoted by BAthir, is said to
have been devoured by a cat. Abû Aun remained in Egypt. He was, of course, the actual
leader of the campaign.

Wasit, the fortified citadel of Iraq founded
by Hajjâj in the marshy district of the Tigris,
was still unsubdued. After the unfortunate
encounter with Qahtaba at Babylon Ibn Hubaira had betaken himself thither with the Syrians,
and some Khurasanite Arabs also gathered about
him, chiefly Bakrites under Yahyâ b. Nuaim.[2]
Hasan b. Qahtaba pursued and besieged him,
and after some time Abû Ja'far, the brother of
the Khalifa Abu 'lAbbâs joined him as his subordinate, but in reality he held the command.
As a matter of fact he was dependent not on
the Khalifa but on Abû Muslim, and the latter
sent Abû Nasr Mâlik b. Haitham alKhuzâî with
a division of Khurasanites to his support. There
was no unity among the besieged; the Yemen
quarrelled with the Nizâr (*i.e.*, Mudar and
Rabîa). Still the town held out eleven months,
and it was not till the news of Marwân's death,
—*i.e.*, in one of the first months of the year 133

---

[1] *Cf.* Agh., 4, 92. Masûdî, 6, 76f. Tanbîh 328. BAthîr 5, 326ff.
Yaqûbî, 2, 414. Yâqût, 4, 760. The day of the month (27th Dhulhijja)
does not suit the given day of the week, Sunday or Monday.

[2] To be distinguished from Yahyâ b. Hudain.

(Autumn, 750), that Ibn Hubaira commenced negotiations. It took 40 days before the jurists had arranged the capitulation so that both sides were satisfied. Abu 'lAbbâs confirmed it, but in spite of that it was not kept. The captive officers, who as token of their office wore a ring, were executed if they belonged to Nizâr and not to Yemen, and finally Ibn Hubaira himself suffered the same fate, after he had given up his body-guard and handed over the state-moneys which he had in his keeping.[1]

This instance of treacherous cruelty is also related by Tabarî. For the rest he chooses to be silent regarding the bloody orgies with which the Abbasids celebrated their victory.[2] They had been treated by the Umaiyids with inconceivable forbearance and they requited this by outlawing them and seizing their estates. They had no human consideration, but carried to its utmost limit the divine wrath and their legitimate revenge. As they had not much to take revenge for, they borrowed from the Alids and acted as their avengers. This gave them at the same time a handle to suppress the latter

---

[1] Laments over the death of Ibn Hubaira in Tab., 3, 70. Hamasa, 372f. Agh., 16, 83ff.

[2] The accounts of it are to be found in Yaqûbî, Masûdî, Ibn Athîr and in Aghânî. The contemporaneous poem of an Ablite or a Maula of the Abalât is also very important, large fragments of which are preserved in Yâqût, 4, 239. 336. 831, and Agh., 4, 91. 10, 105. The Abalât were a lateral branch of the Umaiya.

themselves, as it was not the right of revenge but
its fulfilment that paved the way to the ruling
power, and even procured a legal title to it.
Their precise motive was, of course, a political
one. They wished to render the fallen dynasty
absolutely harmless. The whole affair reminds
us of the extermination of the house of Omri
effected by the prophets.

The chief scene of the outrages committed
upon the Umaiyids was Syria, where Abdullâh
b. Alî had the supreme command. They are
not chargeable to the Khurasanites, as Agh., 4,
94. 96 asserts, for they were strictly disciplin-
ed and did nothing without orders. The outrages were rather committed by command of the
Abbasids (Yaqûbî, 2,427), and it is to be noted
that even the dead did not escape chastisement.
The graves of the Khalifas and other Umaiyids
in Damascus, in Dâbiq and Rusâfa, in Qinnesrin and other places were broken open and their
contents violated, when any remains were to be
found. Umar II, however, and, which is remarkable, even Muâwia were spared. Very
vehemently was the hatred expressed against
Hishâm, who had given some reason for it and
whose death was but recent. His body, only
the nose of which was no longer intact, was
scourged and crucified, and then burned and
the ashes scattered to the winds (Masûdî, 5,
471f.). Upon the living Abdullâh b. Alî's

worst acts were committed in Abû Futrus, where he stayed for a while after driving away Marwân. The story goes that he enticed thither more than 80 Umaiyids with fair promises, inviting them to a meal, exactly as if he had taken Jehu for this pattern. Then, apparently aroused suddenly to revenge by verses which were repeated to him, he had them all felled with clubs, leathern covers spread over them, and on these covers the dinner set, at which the death-rattle of the dying men supplied the music.[1] These touches, the rendering of a song as a signal for a sudden outburst of rage, the duping of the victims by an invitation to dinner, to be sure crop up again on other occasions also, when Abu 'lAbbâs or Dâûd b. Alî are mentioned in place of Abdullâh b. Alî,[2] and may be doubted, but the fact of the great slaughter itself is quite authentic. To the Syrian Arabs it was just as memorable as was the sea of blood in which the dynasty of Omri perished to the ancient Israelites, and the day of Abû Futrus laid its seal upon the Abbasids' foreheads just as did the day of Jezreel upon the house of Jehu. Masûdî, 6, 76 dates the dreadful event the 15th Dhulqada, 132 (25th June, 750). Theophanes wrongly puts it two years later, but his

[1] Kâmil, 707. BAthîr, 5. 32f. Otherwise Yaqûbî, 2, 425f. Agh., 4, 160f.

[2] Agh., 4, 94. The murder of the enemy at the feast is everywhere a common *motif*.

brief and hitherto overlooked account is important because it clearly shows that Abû Futrus
is the old Antipatris.[1]

In Medina and Mecca the executioner of
the Umaiyids[2] was Dâûd b. Alî; in Basra it
was Sulaimân b. Alî. In Hira Abû 'lAbbâs
himself had those put to death who were brought
before him or besought his mercy, amongst
them even Sulaimân b. Hishâm, who, as Muâwia's fiercest foe, deemed himself secure. Even
when the persecution was at last discontinued,
the survivors did not trust themselves abroad.
They kept in hiding, dragging out their existence in mean positions and ever in terror of
becoming outlaws if they were recognised. Only
one grandson of the Khalifa Hishâm escaped
to Spain and there attained to sovereignty.

Now, however, the Syrians, who so far had
adopted a fairly passive course, were at last
enraged by the terrible extirpation of their old
dynasty, the Qaisites no less than the Kalbities.
The Qaisites rose chiefly in Qinnesrin; at their

---

[1]   " In A. M. 6243 the new rulers killed most of the (Christians as)
kindred of the previous dynasty, treacherously massacring them at
Antipatris in Palestine." The identity of Abû Fatrus and Antipatris
is established by the name (Futrus = Patris) and by the fact; Antipatris or Kapharsaba (*Josephus Ant.*, 16, 142, 13, 309) lay just at the
spot In Wâdi'l ' Aujû ' where the fertress of Abû Futrus, acc. to the
description ef the Arabs, is to be lookedf or. Only we do not understand how the Umaiyids can be described as Christians; there is evidently an error or an interpolation.

[2]   Murder scenes in Kufa, Agh., 4, 91f. Yâqût, 4, 244.

head was their most distinguished man, Abu'l
Ward Majzaa b. Kauthar, a grandson of Zufar
b. Hârith, and the Kalbites of Tadmor and the
Arabs of Hims joined them. They had adopted
Abû Muhammad, the Sufyanid freed by Mar-
wân, and he was also acknowledged by Abu'l
Ward as the lawful heir to the Khalifate. But
the insurgents were defeated near Marj al-
Akhram in the neighbourhood of Qinnesrin by
Abdullâh b. Alî and dispersed at the end of the
year 133,[1] i.e., the end of July, 751, and Abu'l
Ward fell along with 500 men of his house.
The Sufyanid fled with his Kalbites first to
Tadmor, then wandered about a fugitive in the
Hijaz, and at last, under the second Abbasid,
Abû Ja'far Mansûr, was seized and put to death.
It is remarkable how the Syrians turned from
the reigning Marwanids to the fallen Sufyanids;
for it was not his personal qualities that Abû
Muhammad had to thank for the position he
attained to immediately after the murder of
Walîd II, but rather the circumstance that he
was descended, not from Marwân I and Abdulmalik, but from Muâwia and Yazîd I. Neither
was he known under his own name but under
that of his house, being called merely as-Sufyânî.
His significance did not fade away at his death;

---

[1] Acc. to Tab., 3, 55 on the last day of the year; but that was not
a Tuesday, as is stated, but a Thursday. Theoph. A.M. 6242 makes the
scene not Quinnesrin but Hims; there may have been fighting there
also.

it even increased. He became first the Messias of the Syrians, to whose second coming they attached their political hopes, and finally, as their opponents kept the field, the precursor of the Antichrist. As a spectre in Islamic eschatology, the house of Umaiya outlived his fall.[1]

5. The Abbasids called their government the " Daula," i.e., the new era.[2] The revolution effected at this time was indeed prodigious.

With the Umaiyids the Syrians made their exit also. They had abandoned to his fate the hated Marwân II, and had not taken action at the right time against the Abbasids, after which they were no longer able to alter the position of things : black had won and white lost the king. To be sure, they retained their sympathy for their old dynasty,[3] and also manifested it in a practical way, but their efforts were in vain since they lacked organisation. Too late their eyes were opened to the fact that it was really a question of their own cause and that it was

---

[1] Snouck Hurgronje, Mahdi, p. 11, and DMZ, 1901, p. 690f.

[2] Tab., 3, 85, 16. 96, 19. 115, 9. Abnâ adDaula are the Khurasanites in the service of the Abbasids ; Kitab adDaula (497, 1) is the name of a prophetic book about the future of the Abbasids. Later Daula means dynasty or kingdom in general. A similar transition is found in Nauba and Uqba (Hudh., 74, 38). But the original meaning has also been preserved, e.g., in the phrase Sâra 'l mâlu daulatan " the estate passed into other hands."

[3] The information in Tab., 3, 2163ff. is interesting. Their recollections centred chiefly around Muâwia We have seen that his grave was a shrine visited for centuries after his death.

themselves who were the sufferers. The seat of government was transferred from Damascus to Kufa and later to Baghdad. Syria lost by the hegemony. Iraq was freed from the yoke of foreign rule which it had strained at in vain for a hundred years, and seemed again to attain to the hegemony which it had once possessed at the time of Alí. The Abbasids showed their political tendency to be positively Iraqite and anti-Syrian.

But at the same time it was decidedly all over with the rule of the Arabs, whose supporters the Umaiyids and the Syrians had been. The old home of the Arabs became so thoroughly savage that the pilgrimage could no longer be made with safety. The Arab tribes were no longer the setting of the theocracy; they lost their privilege entirely. The Mawali were emancipated; the distinction between Arab and non-Arab Muslims vanished. Dislodged from its exclusive position which rested originally upon martial law, Arabism now withdrew into a peaceable and civil sphere and became an international cult in which all Muslims participated. The fundamental part of the cult was the religion, and the Arab religion did not fall to pieces with the Arab nation, but went on gaining strength. The Arab tongue remained the speech of Islam and absorbed the languages of the most important Christian nations in further

Asia and Africa. In use by writers and scholars it seemed even to penetrate to the Iranians, but the poetry preserved the native idiom and restored it to the place of honour.

The Mawali did not actually preponderate over the Arabs as a general thing, but only at one point. The Khurasanites had helped the Abbasids to the victory and with them got a share in the spoil, becoming, in a certain sense, the heirs of the Syrians, though they stood in a different relation to the government from the latter. They were called the Shia (party), the Ansâr (helpers), or the Abnâ (sons) of the Daula.[1] With them lay the external power: they were organised in a military fashion. They held the chief commands, their officers (Quwâd) were allowed to play the part of great lords. They formed the standing army of the Khalifa, and he lived among this his guard. Baghdad was really established not as the capital of an empire, but as the camp of the Khurasanites in which the Khalifa wished to reside, far from Kufa. But in the camp they kept up communication with their home, and the party and army preponderance which they had won in the service of the Abbasids was passed on to their people and province, to the Iranian East. Under the guise of the international Islam, Iranianism triumphed over the Arabs.

[1] Matth. 17, 25.

With the change of dynasty, the internal
mode of government also changed. Whether
Persian influence had a particular effect upon it
may or may not be the case, but it certainly
became quite un-Arab. By the conquest the
Arabs had become a ruling nobility as distinguished from the vanquished. The genealogical
net of their tribal system extended superficially
over the provinces of their kingdom. Under the
Umaiyids this primitive system still persisted in
its fundamentals, though it soon showed itself
to be no longer tenable, but under the Abbasids
it disappeared along with the difference of the
conditions which it presupposed. The Abbasids
were not elevated, like the Umaiyids, over
a wide-spread aristocracy, to which they themselves belonged : the Khurasanites, by whom
they were supported, were not their blood, but
only their instrument. The whole body of the
Muslims stood in the same relation to them,
without natural gradations of political right ;
they alone had the divine right to rule as heirs of
the Prophet. From a technical point of view,
no obstacles stood in the way of their fashioning
the government as seemed in conformity with
the interest of the cause and their own interest.
They brought greater order into the government,
especially into the taxation-system and the
administration of justice, and they showed themselves zealous in opposing and redressing the

grievances of those who applied to them as the supreme court of appeal. But they suppressed the general living interest in politics which in earlier times was part of the religion to a far greater extent than the Umaiyids had contrived to do. The Muslims, Arabs and non-Arabs, were simply subjects and were no longer allowed to take part in public affairs. They were relegated to the realm of trade or agriculture, and at the most might conspire in secret. The state shrank into the court. The Khalifa was surrounded first by a vast, gay company of both sexes, and next by his likewise very numerous family connections, the Hâshimids. But the army, too, belonged to the court, the nucleus of it being always concentrated in the Khalifa's residence. In that way Baghdad was far different not only from Medina but also from Damascus. To the court there further belonged a crowd of civil officials who no longer coincided with the officers, but were mostly creatures and favourites of the ruler. Freedmen were in the majority among them. In earlier times they had indeed enjoyed an influential intimacy, but now they attained to the highest public posts. Raised from the dust, they were again overthrown into the dust. Catastrophes and intrigues leading to such things were at the court the order of the day, and distinguished men who even without office were of consideration, were unwillingly

drawn into them.   Not even in their wives did
the Abbasids any longer set value upon descent;
it was not birth that made people, but the
Khalifa. He clothed them with rank and honour
by means of uniforms and marks of distinction
(tirâz) ; the tailor and the lace-maker had plenty
to do. In place of the aristocracy there came
into being a fawning hierarchy of officials,
openly divided into ranks and controlled through
one another. At the head stood the Wezîr,
who had control of the exchequer, and in later
times became the visible *alter ego* of the invisible Khalifa, so that the latter then only appeared
occasionally as an actor upon the stage, or burst
like a thunderstorm out of his pall of clouds.
The custom also spread more and more of the
stattholders having the provinces in their
charge administered by representatives, and
themselves staying at the court, especially when
they had the prerogative of being princes of the
blood. The under-officials of the government
office were for the most part Christians and Jews,
who easily drew down upon themselves the heat
and envy of the Muslim crowd. Excepting the
Wezîr, the executioner was perhaps the most
outstanding figure among the official personnel.
The Arabs knew no executioner, and the Umaiyids kept none; with the Abbasids he was
indispensable. The leathern carpet beside the
throne which served as a scaffold was part of

71

the insignia of the Khalifate; sudden executions
as well as deliberate barbarities enhanced the
awe of majesty. The pattern was taken from
the Iranians whose Shah exercised the right of
life and death over his subjects. From the Iranians also was taken the office of court-astrologer,
who was consulted on all important undertakings, and actually accompanied the army upon
expeditions. Finally the postmasters are to be
remarked as characteristic of the Abbasid
régime. They were the feelers of the court of
Baghdad stretched out into the provinces, chosen
persons of trust who had to keep secret watch
even over the stattholders. The post was useful
for espionage; the information-service in the
wide kingdom was organised to the highest
degree. Tabarî latterly dates not only the
events, but also the arrival at the court of the
information about them.

The new era was essentially distinguishable
from the old by its relation to the religion. The
Abbasids prided themselves upon the fact that
they brought into power Islam, which had been
suppressed by the Umaiyids. They wanted to
resuscitate the vanished tradition of the Prophet,
as they put it. They encouraged those versed
in the divine law to come to them at Baghdad
from Medina, their former seat, and always
gained their approbation by getting them
to deal even with the political questions

designedly in legal form, and decide them according to the Qoran and Sunna. But in reality they were only making Islam serve their own ends. They cowed the scholars at their court and got even their most objectionable measures justified by them. They rendered the pious opposition harmless by placing it in power; with the fall of the Umaiyids it had reached its goal and was content. Political affairs were in good hands; the Muslims needed to trouble about them no longer. The theocracy was realised and was bound to cease to be the principle of revolution against the existing power. In this direction the Abbasids guided public opinion fairly successfully, and in that epoch the need of peace after such a series of revolutions and struggles was in their favour. The Arabs had spent their rage and bled to death.

One would think that the Abbasids would have favoured the Shia, with which they had originally been allied, but they changed when they had attained to the chief power, turning rather as enemies against the Alids with whom they had formerly been identified, in order to put aside their claims. Even their special adherents, that is to say the extreme Shiites (Rawandites) represented in Iran, were renounced by them. In religion they turned towards the Arabs and away from the Persians.

They denied their origin from the perimeter after they had reached the centre and had the power of the whole in their hands. They conformed to the current Islam of the Jamâa, which formed no special ideas for itself, took religion as a custom, and was content with the tradition which through the worship of God and the law uniformly ruled everyone's practical life. In spite of apparently being opposite, they in this respect took the same course as the Umaiyids, only they stood far more emphatically than the latter for Catholicism, and followed far more decidedly the deviating ways which endangered religious and political unity. As heirs of the Prophet they made better use of the fact that they had not merely the wielding of the temporal power but of the spiritual as well, namely, the Imamate. While the Umaiyids had essentially rested upon a nationality, they supported their government upon a guard and upon the religion. Their Khaliphate may be described as a Caesareopapy. They appointed an inquisitor and set up an inquisition, first against the so-called Zendîqs, who seem to have been shoots of the extreme Persian Shiites.

Even the Khurasanites afterwards became inconvenient to the Abbasids. Mansûr shook off the tutelage of Abû Muslim when he did not need him any longer. In his great qualities

he was far from being a match for him,
but could outdo him in devilry, and compassed
his assassination. But more than anything
else the Khurasanites were still indispensable
in military affairs, and even later were not to
be simply abolished or set aside. An attempt
in this direction set on foot after Hârûn's death
only made for the establishing and strengthening
of their power. No more did the Abbasid
Khalifas succeed in making themselves independent by buying up in great numbers Berbers,
Slavs, Soghdians and Turks, and equipping
them and organising them, in order to play them
off against the Khurasanites. The only result
was that they now came also under the tyranny
of these Mamlûks, especially the Turkish ones,
and in the end were absolutely powerless, and
their kingdom was in pieces.

For one or two centuries the Iranians maintained their dominating position, but they
could not count upon its continuing in their
own house. In Transoxiana, Tukharistan and
Khurasan they were unable to check the advance
of the Turks, which for a while was fended off
by the Arabs. And thus in the end the Turks
fell heirs to the Islamic kingdom into which
they had earlier insinuated themselves as Mam-
luks. In a broader sense we may even reckon
among them the Mongols, who, however, did

not actually become properly at home in Islam but rather passed over it like a devastating storm, without really leaving any but negative traces behind.

———

G.ENERAL INDEX

A

73

R

S

588 ARAB KINGDOM AND ITS FALL

Emendanda

25^{27} : Hijra.
28^{17} : Dihkâns.
31^{20} 33^{28} 79^{6} 80^{9} 111^{13}—delete §
31^{29} : Kharâj-land.
$40^{2\overline{v}}$: willingly.
78^{28} : 3327.
84^{30} : Nahrawân Bridge.
111^{17} : after D. add a note : only
     Ya'qûbî, 2, 256 differs.
116^{13} : Yâsir.
132^{18} : Qorân.
151^{25} : Walîd b. 'Utba.
154^{28} : Tâif.
180^{6} : Παλαιστινης; Δαμασκον
185^{25} : Mikhnaf.
213^{26} : Pococke.
216^{30} : ib. for Yahyâ.

220^{28} : official for pulpit.
222^{13} : great-grandson.
244^{23} : Culturgeschichtliche Streif-
     züge.
270^{19} : 'Âmir.
300^{27} : praetendentes.
310^{23} : continuer of I.
328^{26} : former for latter.
335^{24} : ashes[1]
408^{15} : Iyâs.
420^{3} : castle.
428^{25} : Muhallab for Muh.
432^{28} : Ispahbadh.
447^{31} : Mukhallad for Muh.
554^{26} : Fûtrus.
554^{29} : 'Anjâ '; fortress.
555^{31} : Qinnesrîn.